CORTINA DICTIONARY SERIES

TRAVELER'S FRENCH DICTIONARY

ENGLISH-FRENCH / FRENCH-ENGLISH

by
Teresa Nutting
Licenciée ès Lettres
Aix-en-Provence
and
Michel Marcy
Certifié de Lettres Classiques
Asst. Professor of French
St. Mary's College, Notre Dame, Indiana
•

SERIES GENERAL EDITORS
Dilaver Berberi, Ph.D.
Edel A. Winje, Ed.D.

CORTINA LEARNING INTERNATIONAL, INC.
Publishers • WESTPORT, CT 06880

Library of Congress Cataloging-in-Publication Data

Nutting, Teresa.
   Cortina traveler's French dictionary: English-French, French-
   English / by Teresa Nutting and Michel Marcy.
      p.   cm.
   Rev. ed. of: Cortina/Grosset basic French dictionary. 1975.
   ISBN 0-8327-0722-8 (paper): $6.95
   1. English language—Dictionaries—French. 2. French language
—Dictionaries—English. I. Marcy, Michel. II. Nutting, Teresa.
Cortina/Grosset basic French dictionary. III. Title IV. Title:
Traveler's French dictionary.
PC2640.N85   1993   93-3672
443'.21—dc20   CIP

© Copyright 1993 by Cortina Learning International, Inc.

Printed in the United States of America

HH Editions 9 8 7 6 5 4 3 2 1   9307-16

Contents

Contents

How to Use This Dictionary

Here is a handy, pocket-sized Dictionary that will put French at your fingertips. Whether you are a beginner or already have a working knowledge of French, whether you are a student, a businessperson, or a tourist—this Dictionary will give you what you need to get along in French.

The entries are the heart of the Dictionary; they number almost 11,000 (5000-plus in the English-French section, 5000-plus in the French-English section). On the English side, entries were chosen for their usefulness and applicability to common everyday situations. French entries were selected from words that occur most frequently in the course of everyday life in French-speaking countries. Thus, you will find here the words you will actually hear and speak when using French, whether at home or abroad. In addition, this Dictionary is unique in providing the pronunciation of the French words *on both sides,* so that whenever you encounter them you can immediately pronounce them.

Additional Special Features

In addition to the entries themselves, this Dictionary includes the following extra features to enable you to actually use the French language in a variety of different situations.

Guide to Pronunciation. The pronunciation of each French entry is given in simple English alphabet transcriptions. Thus, the user can pronounce a new word immediately, just by following the simple guide which appears with each entry. The "Key to French Pronunciation," found on page viii, explains French sounds and gives examples of each one, and shows how they compare with English.

Phrases for Use Abroad (page 311). Everyday expressions, requests, statements, questions and answers for specific situations—each with its pronunciation—let you communicate easily.

Menu Reader (page 328). A comprehensive list of food and drink, complete with pronunciation, takes the mystery out of French menus.

Concise French Grammar (page 336). For the user who wishes a quick overview of French grammar, or who wants an explanation of how verbs are conjugated or noun plurals formed, this grammar section is an invaluable aid. It is divided into sections treating nouns, verbs, adjectives, adverbs, sentence formation, etc., for easy reference and use.

Helpful Notes for the Reader

1. *All verbs* are marked *v.*, and irregular verbs are marked *irreg*. There are tables of irregular verbs showing their conjugation at the end of the Dictionary, and the "Concise Grammar" explains the conjugation of regular forms.

2. *Reflexive verbs* are those preceded by *se* or *s'*. These are always used with the reflexive pronoun. See the "Concise Grammar" for an explanation of the use of these verbs.

3. *All French nouns* have a designated gender, and adjectives must agree in gender with the nouns they modify.

4. *Parts of speech* of entries (except verbs) are not marked unless the translation does not indicate the part

of speech or if the word appears more than once as different parts of speech.

5. *Many common or idiomatic expressions* are included in the Dictionary, along with their pronunciation, so that the reader can use them correctly.

Using this Dictionary is sure to make your contact with French-speaking people and their language much more pleasurable and satisfying, whether at home or abroad.

Key to French Pronunciation

Vowels

Note that English vowels are often diphthongs (c*a*ke, for example, is k*a-ee*k), whereas French vowels are not. When an English diphthong is the closest equivalent to a French vowel, be careful to pronounce only the first half of the diphthong.

French spelling	Phonetic symbol	Sound description & Examples
a, â	ah	pronounced like *a* in f*a*ther. *Ex.*: **bal** [*bahl*] dance
e, eu, oeu	uh	pronounced like *a* in *a*bout or like *e* in unstressed th*e*. *Ex.*: **le** [*luh*] the; **feu** [*fuh*] fire; **soeur** [*suhr*] sister
è, ê	e	pronounced like *e* in l*e*t. *Ex.*: **père** [*per*] father; **tête** [*tet*] head
é, er	eh	pronounced like *e* in th*e*y or like *a* in c*a*ke, but not diphthongized. *Ex.*: **parler** [*pahr-leh*] speak; **été** [*eh-teh*] summer
i, y	ee	pronounced like *i* in mach*i*ne or like *ee* in f*ee*t. *Ex.*: **pipe** [*peep*] pipe; **Yves** [*eev*] Yves
i	y	before a vowel, pronounced like *y* in *y*es. *Ex.*: **vieux** [*vyuh*] old
o, au eau	oh	pronounced like *o* in s*o*, but not diphthongized. *Ex.*: **chose** [*shohz*] thing; **bateau** [*bah-toh*] boat
o	o	pronounced like *o* in f*o*r or b*o*y. *Ex.*: **col** [*kol*] collar
ou	oo	pronounced like *oo* in s*oo*n. *Ex.*: **vous** [*voo*] you

| u | ü | no equivalent in English. Pronounce *ee*, then round your lips. *Ex.*: **vu** [*vu*] seen |
| oi | wah | pronounced like *wa* in w*a*ter. *Ex.*: **loi** [*lwah*] law |

Certain vowels in French are nasalized before an *n* or an *m*. Do not pronounce the *n* (or *m*), but pronounce the vowel in your nose:

on	ō	pronounced like *o* in d*o*n't. *Ex.*: **bon** [*bō*] good
un, in	ē̃	pronounced like *a* in gr*a*nt. *Ex.*: **un** [*ē̃*] one; **vin** [*vē̃*] wine
an, en	ã	pronounced like *a* in British c*a*n't. *Ex.*: **blanc** [*blã*] white; **en** [*ã*] in

Glides—combinations of vowels resulting in *w* — are:

| oui, ui | wee | pronounced like *wee* in w*ee*k. *Ex.*: **Louis** [*lwee*] Louis; **lui** [*lwee*] him |

Consonants

French consonants are basically similar to English ones. Final consonants are very often silent (not pronounced), and in such cases won't be marked at all in the transcription. The final consonants most commonly pronounced are *c*, *r*, *f*, and *l*.

H is never pronounced. *R* is pronounced in the back of the mouth, as in gargling. *L* is always pronounced as the first *l* in *l*ittle, never as the second one. The combination *il* is often pronounced *y* (**travail** [*trah-vahy*] work).

Some consonants will be transcribed by others to show how they are always pronounced in French, or how they are pronounced in certain combinations:

ch is always pronounced *sh*, as in *sh*irt: **chat** [*shah*] cat

j is always pronounced *zh*, as in vi*s*ion: **jardin** [*zhahr-dē̃*] garden

gn is always pronounced *ny*, as in ca*ny*on: **ignorant** [*ee-nyo-rã*] ignorant. When this combination occurs at the end of a word, it is marked *ñ* to avoid confusion: **campagne** [*kã-pahñ*] country *qu* is generally pronounced *k*: **quand** [*kã*] when

c is pronounced as *s* before vowels *e* and *i*: **ceci** [*suh-see*] this. When written ç, it is also pronounced *s*: **ça** [*sah*] that. Otherwise it is pronounced *k*: **car** [*kahr*] for; **sac** [*sahk*] purse

g is pronounced *zh*, as in vi*s*ion, before *e* and *i*: **géologie** [*zheh-oh-loh-zhee*] geology. Elsewhere it is *g* as in *g*o: **glace** [*glahs*] ice cream. When a "hard" g is followed by *e* or *i*, the transcription is *gh*: **guerre** [*gher*] war

s is generally pronounced like English *s*: **six** [*sees*] six. But between vowels it is pronounced *z*: **magasin** [*mah-gah-zē*] store. When linking words (see below), it is also *z*: **les amis** [*leh-zah-mee*] the friends

y in the transcription is always pronounced as in *y*ellow, never as in happ*y*. Be careful at the end of words: **travail** [*trah-vahy*] work; **reveil** [*reh-vey*] alarm clock

Parentheses around a symbol mean that the sound is sometimes pronounced and sometimes not. This can occur for two reasons. If the symbol is *uh* it represents an *e* which frequently disappears in normal speech. *Fenêtre* is often pronounced *fnetre*, and so the transcription reads: [*f*(*uh*)-*netr*]. Some *e*'s disappear so often that they haven't been indicated in the transcription at all: *devenir* is transcribed [*duhv-neer*].

If the symbol in parentheses is a consonant, it means that the final consonant is pronounced in the feminine form of the adjective. Final consonants are normally not pronounced, but when you add an *e* to make the adjective feminine, the consonant is no longer final and is pronounced: *vert* (masculine) is pronounced [*ver*]; *verte* (feminine) is pronounced [*vert*], and so the transcription reads [*ver*(*t*)].

Linking

In French, words that go together (noun and article or adjective, or subject and verb) are usually linked in speech if the second word begins with a vowel sound. This frequently means that a final consonant, normally not pronounced, *will* be pronounced in order to link with the following word. Examples:

les autos [*leh-zoh-otoh*] the cars
ils ont [*eel-zō*] they have
de beaux habits [*duh-boh-zah-bee*] beautiful clothes
un petit éléphant [*ē-ptee-teh-leh-fā*] a little elephant
parlent-ils [*pahrl-teel*] are they speaking
répond-il [*reh-po-teel*] does he answer

When linking, *s* and *x* are pronounced as *z*, and *d* is pronounced as *t*.

The letter *h* is never pronounced, but in some words its presence is "felt" enough so that the word beginning with *h* cannot be linked to the word preceding it. For example, *les haches* (the axes) must be pronounced [*leh-ahsh*], not [*leh-zahsh*]. But *les hotels* (the hotels) must be pronounced [*leh-zoh-tel*]. *H*'s that make linking impossible are marked with an asterisk.

General Considerations

In this Dictionary no accents are marked in the pronunciations because all syllables receive more or less equal stress. Some vowels are dropped at times in spoken French, as shown in the transcriptions. Since the natural tendency in English is to stress the beginning of the word, you may want to give slightly stronger emphasis to the last syllable in French. If you do this, and try to speak in the front, rather than the back of your mouth, moving your lips more than you would in English, you will be well on your way to speaking good French.

Abbreviations Used
in This Dictionary

adj.	adjective	*irreg.*	irregular
adv.	adverb	*m.*	masc.
anat.	anatomy	*naut.*	nautical
arch.	architecture	*n.*	noun
art.	article	*obj.*	object
Aux.	auxiliary verb	*pers.*	person, personal
conj.	conjunction	*pl.*	plural
dem.	demonstrative	*prep.*	preposition
eccl.	ecclesiastic	*pron.*	pronoun
f.	feminine	*rel.*	relative
interj.	interjection	*sing.*	singular
interr.	interrogative	*subj.*	subject
invar.	invariable	*v.*	verb

English/French

A

a, un, une [$\bar{e}$, *ün*]
abandon *v.*, abandonner [*ah-bã-do-neh*]
ability, capacité (f) [*kah-pah-see-teh*]
able *adj.*, capable (de) [*kah-pahbl (duh)*]
  be able *v.*, pouvoir (irreg) [*poo-vwahr*]
aboard, à bord (de) [*ah bor (duh)*]
  All aboard [train], En voiture [$\tilde{a}$ *vwah-tür*]
abolish *v.*, abolir [*ah-bo-leer*]
about *adv.*, environ [*ã-vee-rõ*]
about *prep.*, au sujet de [*oh sü-zheh duh*]
above, au-dessus (de) [*oh-tsü (duh)*]
abroad, à l'étranger [*ah leh-trã-zheh*]
absence, absence (f) [*ahp-sãs*]
absent *adj.*, absent [*ahp-sã(t)*]
absent-minded, distrait [*dees-tre(t)*]
absolutely, absolument [*ahp-so-lü-mã*]
absorb *v.*, absorber [*ahp-sor-beh*]
abstract *adj.*, abstrait [*ahp-stre(t)*]
absurd, absurde [*ahp-sürd*]
academy, académie (f) [*ah-kah-deh-mee*]
accelerator, accélérateur (m) [*ahk-seh-leh-rah-tuhr*]
accent *n.*, accent (m) [*ahk-sã*]
accent *v.*, accentuer [*ahk-sã-tweh*]
accept *v.*, accepter [*ahk-sep-teh*]
accessible, accessible [*ahk-se-seebl*]
accident, accident (m) [*ahk-see-dã*]
accidental, accidentel, -elle [*ahk-see-dã-tel*]
accommodations *pl.*, logement (m) [*lozh-mã*]
accompany *v.*, accompagner [*ah-kõ-pah-nyeh*]
accomplish *v.*, accomplir [*ah-kõ-pleer*]
according to, selon [*suh-lõ*]
accordingly, donc, en conséquence [*dõk, ã kõ-seh-kãs*]

1

account *n.*, compte (m) [*kõt*]
  bank account, compte (m) en banque [*kõt-ã-bãk*]
  accounts [of a business], comptabilité (f) [*kõ-tah-bee-lee-teh*]
  on account of, à cause de [*ah kohz duh*]
account for *v.*, rendre compte de [*rãdr kõt duh*]
accountant, comptable (m) [*kõ-tahbl*]
accurate, exact, juste [*ehg-zah(kt), zhüst*]
accusation, accusation (f) [*ah-kü-zah-syõ*]
accuse *v.*, accuser [*ah-kü-seh*]
accustomed to, habitué à [*ah-bee-tweh ah*]
ace, as (m) [*ahs*]
ache *v.*, faire mal [*fer mahl*]
ache *n.*, douleur (f), mal (m) [*doo-luhr, mahl*]
  I have a . . . ache, J'ai mal à . . . . [*zheh mahl ah*]
  headache, mal à la tête [*mahl ah lah tet*]
  My head aches! Ma tête me fait mal! [*mah tet muh feh mahl*]
achieve *v.*, accomplir [*ah-kõ-pleer*]
acid, acide (f) [*ah-seed*]
acknowledge *v.*, admettre (irreg) [*ahd-metr*]
  acknowledge receipt of, accuser réception de [*ah-kü-zeh reh-sep-syõ duh*]
acquaintance, connaissance (f) [*ko-ne-sãs*]
acquit *v.*, acquitter [*ah-kee-teh*]
acre, demi-hectare (m) [*duh-mee ehk-tahr*]
across, à travers [*ah trah-ver*]
  across the street, en face (de) [*ã fahs (duh)*]
act *n.*, acte (m) [*ahkt*]
act [do] *v.*, agir [*ah-zheer*]
act [represent] *v.*, jouer [*zhoo-eh*]
action, action (f) [*ahk-syõ*]
active, actif, -ive [*ahk-teef, ahk-teev*]
activity, activité (f) [*ahk-tee-vee-teh*]
actor, acteur (m) [*ahk-tuhr*]
actress, actrice (f) [*ahk-trees*]
actual, réel, -elle [*reh-el*]
actually, réellement, effectivement [*reh-el-mã, eh-fek-teev-mã*]

adapt v., adapter [ah-dahp-teh]

add v., ajouter, additionner [ah-zhoo-teh, ah-dee-syo-neh]

addition, addition (f) [ah-dee-syõ]

additional, additionnel, -elle; supplémentaire [ah-dee-syo-nel, sü-pleh-mã-ter]

address n., adresse (f) [ah-dres]

address v., adresser [ah-dre-seh]

addressee, destinataire (m) [des-tee-nah-ter]

adequate, adéquat [ah-deh-kwah(t)]

adhesive tape, sparadrap (m) [spah-rah-drah]

adjective, adjectif (m) [ahd-zhek-teef]

adjust v., ajuster [ah-zhüs-teh]

adjustment, ajustement (m) [ah-zhüs-tuh-mã]

administer v., administrer [ahd-mee-nees-treh]

administration, administration (f) [ahd-mee-nees-trah-syõ]

admirable, admirable [ahd-mee-rahbl]

admiral, amiral (m), -aux (pl) [ah-mee-rahl, ah-mee-roh]

admiration, admiration (f) [ahd-mee-rah-syõ]

admire v., admirer [ahd-mee-reh]

admirer n., admirateur, -trice [ahd-mee-rah-tuhr, ahd-mee-rah-trees]

admission [entry], entrée (f) [ã-treh]

admit [let in] v., admettre (irreg), laisser entrer [ahd-metr, leh-seh ã-treh]

admittance, entrée (f), accès (m) [ã-treh, ahk-se]
   no admittance, défense d'entrer [deh-fãs dã-treh]

adopt v., adopter [ah-dop-teh]

adore v., adorer [ah-do-reh]

adult, adulte [ah-dült]

advance n., avance (f) [ah-vãs]
   in advance, en avance [ã-nah-vãs]

advance v., avancer [ah-vã-seh]

advantage, avantage (m) [ah-vã-tahzh]

adventure, aventure (f) [ah-vã-tür]

adverb, adverbe (m) [ahd-verb]

advertise v., annoncer, faire de la réclame [ah-nõ-seh, fer dlah reh-klahm]

advertisement, annonce (f), publicité (f), réclame (f) [ahnŏs, püb-lee-see-teh, reh-klahm]

advice, conseil(s) (m) [kŏ-sey]

  Take my advice, Suivez mes conseils [swee-veh meh kŏ-sey]

  a piece of advice, un conseil [ē kŏ-sey]

advise v., conseiller [kŏ-seh-yeh]

affair, affaire (f) [ah-fer]

affect v., affecter [ah-fek-teh]

affection, affection (f) [ah-fek-syŏ]

affectionate, affectueux, -tueuse [ah-fek-twuh, ah-fek-twuhz]

affirmative, affirmatif, -tive [ah-feer-mah-teef, ah-feer-mah-teev]

afraid: be afraid, avoir peur [ah-vwahr puhr]

Africa, Afrique (f) [ah-freek]

African, africain [ah-freek-ē, ah-freek-en]

after prep. & adv., après [ah-pre]

afternoon, après-midi (m, f) [ah-pre-mee-dee]

afterwards, ensuite, après [ā-sweet, ah-pre]

again, encore [ā-kor]

against, contre [kŏtr]

age, âge (m) [ahzh]

agency, agence (f) [ah-zhās]

  travel agency, agence de voyages [ah-zās duh vwah-yahzh]

agent, agent (m) [ah-zhā]

aggravate v., aggraver [ah-grah-veh]

aggression, agression (f) [ah-gre-syŏ]

aggressive, agressif, -sive [ah-gre-seef, ah-gre-seev]

ago, il y a [eel yah]

  three weeks ago, il y a trois semaines [eel yah trwah smen]

  How long ago . . . ? Il y a combien de temps (que)? [eel yah kŏ-byē duh tā (kuh)]

agree v., être d'accord [etr dah-kor]

agreed, entendu, d'accord [ā-tā-dii, dah-kor]

agreement, accord (m) [ah-kor]

agriculture, agriculture (f) [ah-gree-kül-tür]

ahead, en avant [ā-nah-vā]

  Go ahead! Allez-y! [ah-leh-zee]

aid n., aide [ed]

first aid, premiers soins (m) [*pruh-myeh swē*]
aid *v.,* aider [*eh-deh*]
aim *v.,* viser [*vee-zeh*]
air, air (m) [*er*]
airline, compagnie (f) aérienne [*kŏ-pah-nee ah-ehr-yen*]
airmail, par avion [*pahr ah-vyŏ*]
airplane, avion (m) [*ah-vyŏ*]
airport, aéroport (m) [*ah-eh-roh-por*]
aisle, allée (f) [*ah-leh*]
alarm *n.,* alarme (f), alerte (f) [*ah-lahrm, ah-lert*]
alarm clock, réveil (m) [*reh-vey*]
alcohol, alcool (m) [*ahl-kol*]
alert *adj.,* alerte [*ah-lert*]
alike *adj.,* pareil, -eille; semblable [*pah-rey, sā-blahbl*]
alive, vivant [*vee-vã(t)*]
all *adj.,* tout le, toute la, tous les, toutes les [*too(t)*]
   all right, d'accord [*dah-kor*]
   not at all, pas du tout [*pah dü too*]
   That's all, C'est tout [*seh-too*]
allow *v.,* permettre (irreg) [*per-metr*]
   Allow me! Permettez-moi! [*per-meh-teh-mwah*]
ally *n.,* allié, -ée [*ahl-yeh*]
almond, amande (f) [*ah-mãd*]
almost, presque [*presk*]
alone, seul [*suhl*]
   Leave me alone! Laissez-moi tranquille! [*leh-seh-mwah
    trã-keel*]
along, le long de [*luh lŏ duh*]
aloud, à haute voix [*ah oht vwah*]
Alps, Alpes (f, pl) [*ahlp*]
already, déjà [*deh-zhah*]
Alsace, Alsace (f) [*ahl-zahs*]
also, aussi [*oh-see*]
altar, autel (m) [*oh-tel*]
alteration, retouche (f) [*ruh-toosh*]
although, bien que [*byē kuh*]
altitude, altitude (f) [*ahl-tee-tüd*]
altogether, tout à fait, entièrement [*too-tah fe, ã-tyer-mã*]

always, toujours [*too-zhoor*]
am: I am, je suis [*zhuh-swee*]
ambassador, ambassadeur, -drice [*ã-bah-sah-duhr, ã-bah-sah-drees*]
ambition, ambition (f) [*ã-bee-syõ*]
ambitious, ambitieux, -euse [*ã-bee-syuh, ã-bee-syuhz*]
ambulance, ambulance (f) [*ã-bü-lãs*]
America, Amérique (f) [*ah-meh-reek*]
   North America, Amérique du Nord [*ah-meh-reek dü nor*]
   South America, Amérique du Sud [*ah-meh-reek dü süd*]
American, américain, -caine [*ah-meh-ree-kẽ, ah-meh-ree-ken*]
among, parmi, entre [*pahr-mee, ãtr*]
amount *n.,* quantité (f) [*kã-tee-teh*]
amount to [total] *v.,* s'élever (à) [*sehl-veh (ah)*]
   It amounts to the same thing, Cela revient au même [*suh-lah ruh-vyẽ-toh mem*]
amuse *v.,* amuser [*ah-mü-zeh*]
an, un, une [*ẽ, ün*]
analysis, analyse (f) [*ah-nah-leez*]
ancestor, ancêtre (m, f) [*ã-setr*]
anchor, ancre (f) [*ãkr*]
anchovy, anchois (m) [*ã-shwah*]
ancient, ancien, -ne; antique [*ã-syẽ, ã-syen; ã-teek*]
and, et [*eh*]
angel, ange (m) [*ãzh*]
anger, colère (f) [*ko-ler*]
angle, angle (m) [*ãgl*]
angry, en colère, fâché [*ã ko-ler, fah-sheh*]
   get angry *v.,* se fâcher [*suh fah-sheh*]
animal, animal (m), -aux (pl) [*ah-nee-mahl, ah-nee-moh*]
ankle, cheville (f) [*shuh-veey*]
anniversary, anniversaire (m) [*ah-nee-ver-ser*]
announce *v.,* annoncer [*ah-nõ-seh*]
announcement, annonce (f) [*ah-nõs*]
annoy *v.,* ennuyer, gêner [*ã-nwee-yeh, zheh-neh*]
annoying, ennuyeux, -euse [*ã-nwee-yuh, ã-nwee-yuhz*]
annual, annuel, -elle [*ah-nwel*]

anonymous, anonyme [*ah-no-neem*]

another, un autre, une autre [*ē-nohtr, ü-nohtr*]

answer *n.*, réponse (f) [*reh-pōs*]

answer *v.*, répondre [*reh-pōdr*]

ant, fourmi (f) [*foor-mee*]

antique *n.*, objet (m) ancien [*ob-zheh ã-syē*]

antique dealer, antiquaire (m, f) [*ã-tee-ker*]

anxious, inquiet, -ète [*ē-kyeh, ē-kyet*]

any *adj.*, du, de la, des [*dü, duh lah, deh*]

    No, I don't want any, Non, je n'en veux pas [*nõ, zhnã-vuh pah*]

any [no matter which], n'importe quel [*nē-port-kel*]

anybody, quelqu'un [*kel-kē*]

anyhow, en tout cas [*ã too kah*]

anything, quelque chose, n'importe quoi [*kel-kuh shoz, nē-port kwah*]

anyway, de toute façon [*duh toot fah-sõ*]

anywhere, n'importe où [*nē-port oo*]

apartment, appartement (m) [*ah-pahr-tuh-mã*]

apartment house, immeuble (m) [*ee-muhbl*]

apiece, chacun, chacune [*shah-kē, shah-kün*]

apologize, s'excuser [*sek-skü-zeh*]

appear [seem] *v.*, paraître (irreg), sembler [*pah-retr, sã-bleh*]

appearance, apparance (f) [*ah-pah-rãs*]

appendicitis, appendicite (f) [*ah-pē-dee-seet*]

appetite, appétit (m) [*ah-peh-tee*]

appetizer, apéritif (m) [*ah-peh-ree-teef*]

applaud *v.*, applaudir [*ah-ploh-deer*]

applause, applaudissements (m, pl) [*ah-ploh-dees-mã*]

apple, pomme (f) [*pom*]

application, demande (f) [*duh-mãd*]

apply *v.*, appliquer [*ah-plee-keh*]

appoint *v.*, nommer [*no-meh*]

appointment [date], rendez-vous (m) [*rã-deh-voo*]

appreciate *v.*, apprécier [*ah-preh-syeh*]

apprentice, apprenti, -e [*ah-prã-tee*]

approach *v.*, approcher [*ah-pro-sheh*]

appropriate *adj.*, approprié [*ah-pro-pree-yeh*]

approval, approbation (f) [*ah-pro-bah-syõ*]
approve *v.,* approuver [*ah-proo-veh*]
approximately, environ [*ã-vee-rõ*]
apricot, abricot (m) [*ah-bree-koh*]
April, avril (m) [*ah-vreel*]
apron, tablier (m) [*tah-blee-yeh*]
Arab *n. & adj.,* Arabe (m, f) [*ah-rahb*]
Arabia, Arabie (f) [*ah-rah-bee*]
arbitrary, arbitraire [*ahr-bee-trer*]
arch, voûte (f), arc (m) [*voot, ahrk*]
architect, architecte (m) [*ahr-shee-tekt*]
architecture, architecture (f) [*ahr-shee-tek-tür*]
are: there are, il y a [*eel yah*]
argue *v.,* se disputer [*suh dees-pü-teh*]
argument, argument (m) [*ahr-gü-mã*]
arise *v.,* s'élever [*sehl-veh*]
aristocrat, aristocrate (m, f) [*ah-rees-toh-kraht*]
aristocratic, aristocratique [*ah-rees-toh-krah-teek*]
arm *n.,* bras (m) [*brah*]
armchair, fauteuil (m) [*foh-tuhy*]
army, armée (f) [*ahr-meh*]
around *prep.,* autour de [*oh-toor duh*]
around *adv.,* autour [*oh-toor*]
arrange *v.,* arranger [*ah-rã-zheh*]
arrest *v.,* arrêter [*ah-re-teh*]
arrival, arrivée (f) [*ah-ree-veh*]
arrive *v.,* arriver (*Aux:* ÊTRE) [*ah-ree-veh*]
art, art (m) [*ahr*]
artery, artère (f) [*ahr-ter*]
artichoke, artichaut (m) [*ahr-tee-shoh*]
article, article (m) [*ahr-teekl*]
artificial, artificiel, -elle [*ahr-tee-fee-syel*]
artist, artiste (m, f) [*ahr-teest*]
as, comme [*kom*]
    as . . . as, aussi . . . que [*oh-see . . . kuh*]
    not so . . . as, pas si . . . que [*pah see . . . kuh*]
    as for, quant à [*kã-tah*]
    as much as, autant que [*oh-tã kuh*]

as soon as, aussitôt que [*oh-see-toh kuh*]
ash, cendre (f) [*sãdr*]
ashamed: to be ashamed, avoir honte (f) [*ah-vwahr õt*]
ashore, à terre [*ah ter*]
ashtray, cendrier (m) [*sã-dree-yeh*]
Asia, Asie (f) [*ah-zee*]
aside, de côté, à part [*duh koh-teh, ah pahr*]
ask (for) v., demander [*duh-mã-deh*]
  ask a question, poser une question [*poh-zeh ün kes-tyõ*]
asleep, endormi [*ã-dor-mee*]
  fall asleep v., s'endormir (irreg) [*sã-dor-meer*]
asparagus, asperge (f) [*ah-sperzh*]
aspirin, aspirine (f) [*ah-spee-reen*]
assembly, assemblée (f) [*ah-sã-bleh*]
assistance, aide (f) [*ed*]
assistant n., assistant, -e [*ah-sees-tã, ah-sees-tãt*]
associate n., associé [*ah-so-syeh*]
associate v., s'associer [*sah-so-syeh*]
assume [think] v., supposer [*sü-poh-zeh*]
assumption, supposition (f), hypothèse (f) [*sü-poh-zee-syõ, ee-po-tez*]
assurance, assurance (f) [*ah-sü-rãs*]
assure v., assurer [*ah-sü-reh*]
astonish v., étonner [*eh-to-neh*]
  be astonished, s'étonner [*seh-to-neh*]
astonishing, étonnant [*eh-to-nã(t)*]
at, à [*ah*]
  at first, d'abord [*dah-bor*]
  at last, enfin [*ã-fẽ*]
  at once, tout de suite [*toot sweet*]
  at six o'clock, à six heures [*ah-see-zuhr*]
  at the same time, en même temps [*ã mem tã*]
athletic, athlétique; sportif, -ive [*aht-leh-teek; spor-teef, spor-teev*]
Atlantic, Atlantique (m) [*aht-lã-teek*]
atmosphere [air], atmosphère (f) [*aht-mos-fer*]
atmosphere [surroundings], ambiance (f) [*ã-byãs*]
atomic, atomique [*ah-to-meek*]

attach *v.*, attacher [*ah-tah-sheh*]
attack *v.*, attaquer [*ah-tah-keh*]
attempt *v.*, essayer [*eh-se-yeh*]
attend *v.*, assister (à) [*ah-sees-teh (ah)*]
attendant, employé, -ée [*ã-plwah-yeh*]
attention, attention (f) [*ah-tã-syõ*]
attentive, attentif, -ive [*ah-tã-teef, ah-tã-teev*]
attic (m) grenier [*gruh-nyeh*]
attitude, attitude (f) [*ah-tee-tüd*]
attorney, avocat (m) [*ah-vo-kah*]
attract *v.*, attirer [*ah-tee-reh*]
attractive, joli [*zho-lee*]
auction *n.*, vente (f) aux enchères [*vãt oh-zã-sher*]
audience, public (m) [*püb-leek*]
August, août (m) [*oo(t)*]
aunt, tante (f) [*tãt*]
Australia, Australie (f) [*oh-strah-lee*]
Australian, australien, -enne [*oh-strah-lyẽ, oh-strah-lyen*]
Austria, Autriche (f) [*oh-treesh*]
Austrian, autrichien, -enne [*oh-tree-shyẽ, oh-tree-shyen*]
author, auteur (m) [*oh-tuhr*]
authority, autorité (f) [*oh-to-ree-teh*]
authorize *v.*, autoriser [*oh-to-ree-zeh*]
automatic, automatique [*oh-to-mah-teek*]
automobile, automobile (f), voiture (f) [*oh-toh-mo-beel, vwah-tür*]
autumn, automne (m) [*oh-ton*]
available, disponible [*dees-po-neebl*]
avalanche, avalanche (f) [*ah-vah-lãsh*]
avenue, avenue (f) [*ahv-nü*]
average *adj.*, moyen, -enne [*mwah-yẽ, mwah-yen*]
average *n.*, moyenne (f) [*mwah-yen*]
  on the average, en moyenne [*ã mwah-yen*]
avoid *v.*, éviter [*eh-vee-teh*]
awake *adj.*, réveillé [*reh-veh-yeh*]
awaken *v.*, réveiller, se réveiller [*reh-veh-yeh, suh reh-veh-yeh*]
aware, conscient [*kõ-syã(t)*]
away, absent, au loin [*ah-psã(t), oh lwẽ*]

go away v., partir (irreg; *Aux:* ÊTRE), s'en aller (irreg)
    [*pahr-teer, sã-nah-leh*]
  Go away! Allez-vous en! [*ah-leh-voo-zã*]
awful, terrible [*te-reebl*]
awkward, maladroit [*mah-lah-drwah(t)*]
axe, *hache (f) [*ahsh*]
axle, essieu (m) [*eh-syuh*]

B

baby, bébé (m) [*beh-beh*]
bachelor, célibataire (m, f) [*seh-lee-bah-ter*]
back [anat.], n., dos (m) [*doh*]
back [support] v., soutenir (irreg) [*soot-neer*]
back adv., en arrière [*ã-nahr-yer*]
  be back v., être de retour [*etr duh r(uh)-toor*]
  come back v., revenir (irreg; *Aux:* ÊTRE) [*ruh-v(uh)-neer*]
back adj., arrière, de derrière [*ahr-yer, duh der-yer*]
backwards, en arrière [*ã-nahr-yer*]
bacon, lard (m), poitrine fumée (f) [*lahr, pwah-treen fü-meh*]
bad adj., mauvais [*mo-ve(z)*]
  Too bad! Dommage! [*do-mahzh*]
badly adv., mal [*mahl*]
bad-tempered, de mauvais caractère [*duh mo-ve kah-rahk-ter*]
baggage, bagages (m, pl) [*bah-gazh*]
bait n., appât (m) [*ah-pah*]
bake v., faire cuire (irreg) au four [*fer kweer oh foor*]
bakery, boulangerie (f) [*boo-lãzh-ree*]
balance n., équilibre (m) [*eh-kee-leebr*]
balance v., équilibrer, s'équilibrer [*eh-kee-lee-breh, seh-kee-lee-breh*]
balcony, balcon (m) [*bahl-kõ*]
bald, chauve [*shohv*]
ball, balle (f) [*bahl*]

ball [dance], bal (m) [*bahl*]
ballet, ballet (m) [*bah-leh*]
balloon, ballon (m) [*bah-lõ*]
band, orchestre (m) [*or-kestr*]
bandage *n.*, pansement (m) [*pãs-mã*]
bandaid, tricostéril (m) [*tree-ko-steh-reel*]
bank *adj.*, bancaire [*bã-ker*]
bank *n.*, banque (f) [*bãk*]
banknote, billet (m) de banque [*bee-yehd-bãk*]
baptism, baptême (m) [*bah-tem*]
bar [for drinks], bar (m) [*bahr*]
barber, coiffeur (m) [*kwah-fuhr*]
bare *adj.*, nu [*nü*]
barefoot, pieds nus [*pyeh-nü*]
bargain *n.*, occasion (f) [*o-kah-zyõ*]
bargain *v.*, marchander [*mahr-shã-deh*]
bark [of tree] *n.*, écorce (f) [*eh-kors*]
bark *v.*, aboyer [*ah-bwah-yeh*]
barn, grange (f) [*grãzh*]
barracks, caserne (f) [*kah-zern*]
barrel [cask], tonneau (m), -eaux (pl) [*to-noh*]
barricade, barricade (f) [*bah-ree-kahd*]
base *n.*, base (f) [*bahz*]
basement, sous-sol (m) [*soo-sol*]
basic, fondamental, -aux (m, pl) [*fõ-dah-mã-tal, fõ-dah-mã-toh*]
basin, cuvette (f) [*kü-vet*]
basket, panier (m) [*pah-nyeh*]
bath, bain (m) [*bẽ*]
   take a bath *v.*, prendre un bain [*prã-drẽ-bẽ*]
bathe *v.*, baigner, se baigner [*beh-nyeh, suh beh-nyeh*]
bathing suit, maillot (m) de bain [*mah-yohd-bẽ*]
bathroom, salle (f) de bain [*sahl duh bẽ*]
bathtub, baignoire (f) [*behn-wahr*]
battery [car], batterie (f) [*bah-tree*]
battery [flashlight], pile (f) [*peel*]
battle *n.*, bataille (f) [*bah-tahy*]
bay *n.*, baie (f) [*be*]

be v., être (irreg) [etr]
beach, plage (f) [plahzh]
bean, *haricot (m) [ah-ree-koh]
bear, ours (m) [oors]
bear [carry] v., porter [por-teh]
bear [give birth] v., donner naissance [do-neh ne-sãs]
bear [endure] v., supporter [sü-por-teh]
beard, barbe (f) [bahrb]
beast, bête (f) [bet]
beat n., battement (m) [baht-mã]
beat v., battre (irreg) [bahtr]
beautiful, beau (bel), belle; beaux, belles [boh, bel]
beauty, beauté (f) [boh-teh]
beauty parlor, salon (m) de coiffure [sah-lõd kwah-für]
because, parce que [pahrs kuh]
  because of, à cause de [ah kohz duh]
become, devenir (irreg) [duh-v(uh)-neer]
bed, lit (m) [lee]
bedroom, chambre (f) à coucher [shãbr ah koo-sheh]
bee, abeille (f) [ah-bey]
beef, boeuf (m) [buhf]
beer, bière (f) [byer]
before [place], devant [duh-vã]
before [time], avant [ah-vã]
  before leaving, avant de partir [ah-vãd pahr-teer]
beg v., mendier [mã-dyeh]
beggar n., mendiant, -te [mã-dyã, mã-dyãt]
begin v., commencer [ko-mã-seh]
  begin again, recommencer [ruh-ko-mã-seh]
beginning, commencement (m) [ko-mãs-mã]
behave v., se conduire, se comporter [suh kõ-dweer, suh kõ-por-teh]
behavior, comportement (m) [kõ-por-t(uh)-mã]
behind, derrière [der-yer]
Belgian, belge [belzh]
Belgium, Belgique (f) [bel-zheek]
belief, croyance (f) [krwah-yãs]
believe v., croire (irreg) [krwahr]

bell, cloche (f) [*klosh*]
bellboy, chasseur (m) [*shah-suhr*]
belong (to) v., appartenir (à) (irreg) [*ah-pahr-tuh-neer (ah)*]
belongings, affaires (f, pl) [*ah-fer*]
below adv., en-dessous [*ã-tsoo*]
below prep., en dessous de [*ã tsoo duh*]
belt, ceinture (f) [*sẽ-tür*]
bench, banc (m) [*bã*]
bend, plier [*plee-yeh*]
beneath, dessous [*duh-soo*]
benefit, bénéfice (m) [*beh-neh-fees*]
berth, couchette (f) [*koo-shet*]
beside, à côté (de) [*ah koh-teh (duh)*]
besides, de plus, d'ailleurs [*duh plü(s), dah-yuhr*]
best adv., le mieux [*luh myuh*]
best adj., le meilleur, la meilleure [*luh meh-yuhr, lah meh-yuhr*]
bet n., pari (m) [*pah-ree*]
bet v., parier [*pah-ryeh*]
better adj., meilleur [*meh-yuhr*]
better adv., mieux [*myuh*]
between, entre [*ãtr*]
Beware! Attention! [*ah-tã-syõ*]
beyond, au delà (de) [*oh dlah (duh)*]
Bible, Bible (f) [*bee-bl*]
bicycle, bicyclette (f), vélo (m) [*bee-see-klet, veh-loh*]
bid n., offre (f) [*ofr*]
bid v., faire une offre [*fer ün ofr*]
bill n., addition (f) [*ah-dee-syõ*]
billion, milliard (m) [*meel-yahr*]
bird, oiseau (m), -eaux (pl) [*wah-zoh*]
birth, naissance (f) [*ne-sãs*]
birthday, anniversaire (m) [*ah-nee-ver-ser*]
   Happy birthday, Bon anniversaire, [*bo-nah-nee-ver-ser*]
bishop, évêque (m) [*eh-vek*]
bit: a bit, un peu [*ẽ-puh*]
bite v., mordre (irreg) [*mordr*]
bitter, amer, amère [*ah-mer*]

bitterness, amertume (f) [*ah-mer-tüm*]
black, noir [*nwahr*]
blackboard, tableau noir (m) [*tah-bloh nwahr*]
blade, lame (f) [*lahm*]
blame *n.*, blâme (m) [*blahm*]
blame *v.*, blâmer [*blah-meh*]
blanket, couverture (f) [*koo-ver-tür*]
bleach *n.*, eau (f) de javel [*ohd-zhah-vel*]
bleed *v.*, saigner [*seh-nyeh*]
bless *v.*, bénir [*beh-neer*]
blessing, bénédiction (f) [*beh-neh-deek-syõ*]
blind, aveugle [*ah-vuhgl*]
   color-blind, daltonien, -enne [*dahl-to-nyẽ, dahl-to-nyen*]
blister *n.*, ampoule (f) [*ã-pool*]
block *n.*, bloc (m), cube (m) [*blok, küb*]
   two blocks from here, à deux rues d'ici [*ah duh rü dee-see*]
blond, blonde, blond, blonde [*blõ, blõd*]
blood, sang (m) [*sã*]
blossom *n.*, fleur (f) [*fluhr*]
blossom *v.*, fleurir [*fluh-reer*]
blouse, corsage (m), chemisier (m) [*kor-sahzh, shuh-mee-zyeh*]
blow *n.*, coup (m) [*koo*]
blow *v.*, souffler [*soo-fleh*]
blow-out [flat tire], crevaison (f) [*kruh-ve-zõ*]
blue, bleu [*bluh*]
board, planche (f) [*plãsh*]
boarder, pensionnaire (m, f) [*pã-syo-ner*]
boarding house, pension (f) [*pã-syõ*]
boat, bateau (m), -eaux (pl) [*bah-toh*]
body, corps (m) [*kor*]
boil *v.*, bouillir (irreg) [*boo-yeer*]
bold, audacieux, -euse [*oh-dah-syuh, oh-dah-syuhz*]
bomb, bombe (f) [*bõb*]
bond [financial], obligation (f) [*oh-blee-gah-syõ*]
bone, os (m) [*os*]
   fishbone, arête (f) [*ah-ret*]
book, livre (m) [*leevr*]

bookstore, librairie (f) [*lee-bre-ree*]

boot, botte (f) [*bot*]

border [frontier], frontière (f) [*frõ-tyer*]

bore v., ennuyer [*ã-nwee-yeh*]

boring, ennuyeux, -euse [*ã-nwee-yuh, ã-nwee-yuhz*]

born: be born, naître (irreg; *Aux:* ÊTRE) [*netr*]

borne, porté [*por-teh*]

borrow v., emprunter [*ã-prẽ-teh*]

boss n., patron (m) [*pah-trõ*]

both, les deux [*leh duh*]

bother v., ennuyer, gêner, déranger [*ã-nwee-yeh, zhe-neh,
    deh-rã-zheh*]

   Don't bother, Ne vous dérangez pas [*nuh voo deh-rã-zheh
    pah*]

bottle, bouteille (f) [*boo-tey*]

   baby bottle, biberon (m) [*bee-brõ*]

bottom, fond (m) [*fõ*]

bow [ribbon] n., noeud (m) [*nuh*]

bow v., saluer [*sa-lweh*]

box, boîte (f) [*bwaht*]

boxing, boxe (f) [*boks*]

box-office, bureau (m) de location [*bü-rohd lo-kah-syõ*]

boy, garçon (m) [*gahr-sõ*]

bracelet, bracelet (m) [*brahs-leh*]

brag v., se vanter [*suh vã-teh*]

braid, natte (f) [*naht*]

brain, cerveau (m), -eaux (pl) [*ser-voh*]

brake n., frein (m) [*frẽ*]

brake v., freiner [*fre-neh*]

branch, branche (f) [*brãsh*]

brand n., marque (f) [*mahrk*]

brand-new, tout neuf, toute neuve [*too nuhf, toot nuhv*]

brandy, cognac (m) [*ko-nyahk*]

brass, cuivre (m) [*kweevr*]

brassiere, soutien-gorge (m) [*soo-tyẽ-gorzh*]

brave, courageux, -euse [*koo-rah-zhuh, koo-rah-zhuhz*]

bread, pain (m) [*pẽ*]

break v., casser [*kah-seh*]

breakdown, panne (f) [*pahn*]
breakfast, petit déjeuner (m) [*p(uh)-tee deh-zhuh-neh*]
   have breakfast v., déjeuner [*deh-zhuh-neh*]
breast [anat.], poitrine (f) [*pwah-treen*]
breast [bosom], sein (m) [*sẽ*]
breath, souffle (m) [*soofl*]
   out of breath, à bout de souffle [*ah boot soofl*]
breathe v., respirer [*res-pee-reh*]
breeze, brise (f) [*breez*]
Breton, breton, -onne [*bruh-tõ, bruh-ton*]
brick, brique (f) [*breek*]
bride, mariée (f) [*mahr-yeh*]
bridegroom, marié (m) [*mahr-yeh*]
bridesmaid, demoiselle (f) d'honneur [*duh-mwah-zel do-nuhr*]
bridge n., pont (m) [*põ*]
bright, brillant [*bree-yã(t)*]
brilliant, brillant [*bree-yã(t)*]
bring [something] v., apporter [*ah-por-teh*]
bring [persons] v., amener [*ahm-neh*]
   bring about, entraîner [*ã-tre-neh*]
   bring together, réunir [*reh-ü-neer*]
   bring up [rear], élever [*ehl-veh*]
Britain, Grande Bretagne (f) [*grãd bruh-tahñ*]
British, britannique, anglais [*bree-ta-neek, ã-gle(z)*]
Brittany, Bretagne (f) [*bruh-tañ*]
broad, large [*lahrzh*]
broadcast n., émission (f) [*eh-mee-syõ*]
broil v., griller [*gree-yeh*]
broiled, grillé [*gree-yeh*]
bronze, bronze [*brõz*]
brook n., ruisseau (m), -eaux (pl) [*rwee-soh*]
broom, balai (m) [*bah-le*]
broth, bouillon (m) [*boo-yõ*]
brother, frère (m) [*frer*]
brother-in-law, beau-frère (m) [*boh-frer*]
brown, marron; brun, brune [*mah-rõ; brẽ, brün*]
bruise n., bleu (m) [*bluh*]

brunette, brune (f) [*brün*]
brush [hair], brosse (f) [*bros*]
   paint brush, pinceau (m), -eaux (pl) [*pĕ-soh*]
   toothbrush, brosse à dents [*bro-sah dã*]
brush *v.,* brosser [*bro-seh*]
bucket, seau (m), seaux (pl) [*soh*]
buckle, boucle (f) [*bookl*]
budget *n.,* budget (m) [*büd-zheh*]
bug, insecte (m) [*ĕ-sekt*]
build *v.,* construire (irreg) [*kõ-strweer*]
building, bâtiment (m) [*bah-tee-mã*]
bulb [light], ampoule (f) [*ã-pool*]
Bulgaria, Bulgarie (f) [*bül-gah-ree*]
Bulgarian, bulgare [*bül-gahr*]
bulky, volumineux, -euse [*vo-lü-mee-nuh, vo-lü-mee-nuhz*]
bull, taureau (m), -eaux (pl) [*toh-roh*]
bulletin, bulletin (m) [*bül-tĕ*]
bulletin board, tableau (m) d'affichage [*tah-bloh dah-fee-shahzh*]
bumper, pare-choc (m) [*pahr-shok*]
bundle, paquet (m) [*pah-keh*]
burden *n.,* fardeau (m), -eaux (pl) [*fahr-doh*]
burden *v.,* charger [*shahr-zheh*]
burglar, cambrioleur (m) [*kã-bree-yo-luhr*]
Burgundy, Bourgogne (f) [*boor-goñ*]
burial, enterrement (m) [*ã-ter-mã*]
burn *v.,* brûler [*brü-leh*]
bury *v.,* enterrer [*ã-teh-reh*]
bus, autobus (m) [*oh-toh-büs*]
bush, buisson (m) [*bwee-sõ*]
business, les affaires (pl) [*leh-zah-fer*]
businessman, homme (m) d'affaires [*om-dah-fer*]
busy *adj.,* occupé [*o-kü-peh*]
but, mais [*me*]
butcher, boucher (m) [*boo-sheh*]
butcher shop, boucherie (f) [*boo-shree*]
butter, beurre (m) [*buhr*]
button, bouton (m) [*boo-tõ*]

buy v., acheter [*ahsh-teh*]
buyer, acheteur, -teuse [*ahsh-tuhr, ahsh-tuhz*]
by [near] à côté de [*ah koh-teh duh*]
by [means], par [*pahr*]
　by chance, par *hasard [*pahr ah-zahr*]
bypass, bretelle (f), route (f) de déviation [*bruh-tel, root duh deh-vyah-syō*]

C

cab, taxi (m) [*tahk-see*]
cabbage, chou (m), choux (pl) [*shoo*]
cabin, cabane (f) [*kah-bahn*]
cabinet [government], conseil (m) de ministres [*kō-sey duh mee-neestr*]
cable v., envoyer un télégramme international [*ã-vwah-yeh ē teh-leh-gram ē-ter-nah-syo-nahl*]
cable n., cable (m), télégramme (m) international [*kahbl, teh-leh-grahm ē-ter-nah-syo-nahl*]
café, café (m) [*kah-feh*]
cage, cage (f) [*kahzh*]
cake, gâteau (m), -eaux (pl) [*gah-toh*]
calendar, calendrier (m) [*kah-lã-dree-yeh*]
calf, veau (m), -eaux (pl) [*voh*]
call n., appel (m) [*ah-pel*]
　telephone call, coup de téléphone [*koot teh-leh-fon*]
call v., appeler, crier [*ahp-leh, kree-yeh*]
　call off, décommander [*deh-ko-mã-deh*]
calm, calme [*kahlm*]
camera, appareil photographique (m) [*ah-pah-rey foh-toh-grah-feek*]
　movie camera, caméra (m) [*kah-meh-rah*]
camp n., camp (m) [*kã*]
can [container] n., boîte (f) de conserve [*bwaht duh kō-serv*]
can [be able] v., pouvoir (irreg) [*poov-wahr*]

Canada, Canada (m) [*kah-nah-dah*]

Canadian, canadien, -enne [*kah-nah-dyē, kah-nah-dyen*]

cancel *v.,* annuler [*ah-nü-leh*]

candle, bougie (f), chandelle (f) [*boo-zhee, shã-del*]

candlestick, chandelier (m), bougeoir (m) [*shã-duh-lyeh, boo-zhwahr*]

candy, bonbon (m) [*bõ-bõ*]

cane, canne (f) [*kahn*]

can opener, ouvre-boîte (m) [*oov-ruh-bwaht*]

cap [headgear], casquette (f) [*kahs-ket*]

capable, capable [*kah-pahbl*]

capacity, capacité (f) [*kah-pah-see-teh*]

capital [city], capitale (f) [*kah-pee-tahl*]

capital [money], capital (m), -aux [*kah-pee-tahl, kah-pee-toh*]

captain, capitaine (m) [*kah-pee-ten*]

car, voiture (f) [*vwah-tür*]

    streetcar, tramway (m) [*trahm-weh*]

card, carte (f) [*kahrt*]

    calling card, carte de visite [*kahrt duh vee-zeet*]

    playing cards, cartes à jouer [*kahr-tah zhweh*]

cardboard, carton (m) [*kar-tõ*]

cardinal, cardinal (m), -aux (pl) [*kahr-dee-nahl, kahr-dee-noh*]

care [worry] *n.,* souci (m) [*soo-see*]

care [attention] *n.,* soin (m) [*swē*]

care *v.,* se soucier (de), s'intéresser (à) [*suh soo-syeh (duh), sē-teh-re-seh (ah)*]

    care for, soigner, aimer [*swah-nyeh, eh-meh*]

    I don't care, Ça m'est égal [*sah me-teh-gahl*]

career, carrière (f) [*kah-ryer*]

careful, soigneux, -euse [*swah-nyuh, swah-nyuhz*]

    Be careful! Faites attention! [*fe-tah-tã-syõ*]

carefully, soigneusement [*swah-nyuhz-mã*]

careless, négligent [*neh-glee-zhã(t)*]

cargo, chargement (m) d'un bateau [*shahr-zhuh-mã dē-bah-toh*]

carnival, carnaval (m), -als (pl) [*kahr-nah-vahl*]

carpenter, menuisier (m) [*muh-nwee-zyeh*]

carpet, tapis (m) [*tah-pee*]

carry v., porter [*por-teh*]
  carry away, emporter [*ã-por-teh*]
carve v., découper [*deh-koo-peh*]
case [box], caisse (f) [*kes*]
case [situation], cas (m) [*kah*]
  in any case, en tout cas [*ã too-kah*]
  in that case, dans ce cas [*dãs-kah*]
cash n., argent liquide (m) [*ahr-zhã lee-keed*]
  pay cash v., payer comptant [*peh-yeh kõ-tã*]
cash v., toucher [*too-sheh*]
cashier, caissier, -ière [*ke-syeh, ke-syehr*]
  Pay the cashier, Payez à la caisse [*peh-yeh-zah lah kes*]
castle, château (m), -eaux (pl) [*shah-toh*]
casual, simple [*sẽpl*]
cat, chat (m) [*shah*]
catalog, catalogue (m) [*kah-tah-log*]
catch v., attraper [*ah-trah-peh*]
  catch cold, prendre (irreg) froid [*prãdr frwah*]
cathedral, cathédrale (f) [*kah-teh-drahl*]
Catholic, catholique [*kah-to-leek*]
cattle, bétail (m) [*beh-tahy*]
cauliflower, chou-fleur (m) [*shoo-fluhr*]
cause n., cause (f) [*kohz*]
cause v., causer [*koh-zeh*]
caution n., précaution (f) [*preh-koh-syõ*]
cave, grotte (f) [*grot*]
cavity [teeth], carie (f) [*kah-ree*]
cease v., cesser [*seh-seh*]
ceiling, plafond (m) [*plah-fõ*]
celebrate v., fêter [*fe-teh*]
celebration, fête (f) [*fet*]
celery, céleri (m) [*sel-ree*]
cellar, cave (f) [*kahv*]
cement n., ciment (m) [*see-mã*]
cemetery, cimetière (m) [*seem-tyer*]
center, centre (m) [*sãtr*]
central, central, -aux (m, pl) [*sã-trahl, sã-troh*]
central heating, chauffage (m) central [*shoh-fahzh sã-trahl*]

century, siècle (m) [*syekl*]
cereal, céréale (f) [*seh-reh-ahl*]
  baby cereal, bouillie (f) [*boo-yee*]
ceremony, cérémonie (f) [*seh-reh-mo-nee*]
certain, certain [*ser-tẽ, ser-ten*]
certainly, certainement [*ser-ten-mã*]
certificate, certificat (m) [*ser-tee-fee-kah*]
chain, chaîne (f) [*shen*]
chair, chaise (f) [*shez*]
  deck chair, transat (m) [*trã-saht*]
chalk, craie (f) [*kre*]
champagne, champagne (m) [*shã-pañ*]
champion *n.*, champion, -onne, [*shã-pyõ, shã-pyon*]
chance *n.*, chance (f), *hasard (m) [*shãs, ah-zahr*]
  by chance, par hasard [*pahr ah-zahr*]
  game of chance, jeu (m) de hasard [*zhuh duh ah-zahr*]
  take a chance *v.*, risquer [*rees-keh*]
change *n.*, changement (m) [*shãzh-mã*]
change [coins] *n.*, monnaie (f) [*mo-neh*]
change *v.*, changer [*shã-zheh*]
  change clothes, se changer [*suh shã-zheh*]
change purse, porte-monnaie (m) [*port-mo-neh*]
chapel, chapelle (f) [*shah-pel*]
character, caractère (m) [*kah-rahk-ter*]
character [in literature], personnage (m) [*pehr-soh-nahzh*]
charcoal, charbon (m) de bois [*shahr-bõ duh bwah*]
charge [a battery] *v.*, charger [*shahr-zheh*]
charge [a purchase] *v.*, mettre (irreg) sur le compte [*metr sür luh kõt*]
charity, charité (f) [*shah-ree-teh*]
charm, charme (m) [*shahrm*]
charming, charmant [*shahr-mã(t)*]
chase *v.*, chasser [*shah-seh*]
chat *v.*, bavarder [*bah-vahr-deh*]
chauffeur, chauffeur (m) [*shoh-fuhr*]
cheap, bon marché [*bõ mar-sheh*]
cheat *v.*, tricher [*tree-sheh*]
check [verification] *n.*, contrôle (m) [*kõ-trohl*]

bank check, chèque (m) [*shek*]
baggage check, bulletin (m) [*bül-tē*]
restaurant check, addition (f) [*ah-dee-syõ*]
traveler's check, cheque (m) de voyage [*shek duh vwah-yahzh*]
check *v.*, contrôler, vérifier [*kõ-troh-leh, veh-ree-fyeh*]
checking account, compte courant (m) [*kõt-koo-rã*]
checkroom, vestiaire (m) [*ves-tyer*]
cheek, joue (f) [*zhoo*]
cheerful, joyeux, -euse [*zhwah-yuh, zhwah-yuhz*]
cheese, fromage (m) [*fro-mahzh*]
chemical *adj.*, chimique [*shee-meek*]
cherry, cerise (f) [*suh-reez*]
chest [anat.], poitrine (f) [*pwah-treen*]
chest [furniture], coffre (m) [*kofr*]
chest of drawers, commode (f) [*ko-mod*]
chestnut, marron (m) [*mah-rõ*]
chew *v.*, mâcher [*mah-sheh*]
chicken, poulet (m) [*poo-leh*]
chief *n.*, chef (m) [*shef*]
chief *adj.*, principal, -aux (m, pl) [*prē-see-pahl, prē-see-poh*]
child, enfant (m) [*ã-fã*]
childbirth, accouchement (m) [*ah-koosh-mã*]
childhood, enfance (f) [*ã-fãs*]
children, enfants [*ã-fã*]
chilly, frais, fraîche [*fre, fresh*]
chimney, cheminée (f) [*shmee-neh*]
chin, menton (m) [*mã-tõ*]
China, Chine (f) [*sheen*]
china [porcelain], porcelaine (f) [*pors-len*]
Chinese, chinois [*sheen-wah(z)*]
chocolate, chocolat (m) [*shoh-koh-lah*]
choice, choix (m) [*shwah*]
choke [auto], starter (m) [*stahr-tuhr*]
choose *v.*, choisir [*shwah-zeer*]
chop [cut of meat] *n.*, côtelette (f) [*koht-let*]
Christian, chrétien, -enne [*kre-tyē, kre-tyen*]
Christmas, Noël (m) [*noh-el*]

Merry Christmas, Joyeux Noël [*zhwah-yuh noh-el*]
church, église (f) [*eh-gleez*]
cider, cidre (m) [*seedr*]
cigar, cigare (f) [*see-gahr*]
cigarette, cigarette (f) [*see-gah-ret*]
circle *n.,* cercle (m) [*serkl*]
circulation, circulation (f) [*seer-kü-lah-syŏ*]
circumstance, circonstance (f) [*seer-kŏ-stãs*]
circus, cirque (m) [*seerk*]
citizen, citoyen, -enne [*see-twah-yĕ, see-twah-yen*]
citizenship, nationalité (f) [*nah-syo-nah-lee-teh*]
city, ville (f) [*veel*]
city hall, hôtel (m) de ville [*oh-tel duh veel*]
civilian, civil, -le [*see-veel*]
civilization, civilisation (f) [*see-vee-lee-zah-syŏ*]
claim *n.,* réclamation (f) [*reh-klah-mah-syŏ*]
claim *v.,* réclamer [*reh-klah-meh*]
clam, palourde (f) [*pah-loord*]
class *n.,* classe (f) [*klahs*]
classic, classique [*klah-seek*]
classmate, camarade (m, f) de classe [*kah-mah-rad duh klahs*]
classroom, salle (f) de classe [*sahl duh klahs*]
clean *adj.,* propre [*propr*]
clean *v.,* nettoyer [*neh-twah-yeh*]
cleaner's [shop], teinturerie (f) [*tĕ-tür-ree*]
cleaning, nettoyage (m) [*neh-twah-yahzh*]
cleaning woman, femme (f) de ménage [*fahm duh meh-nahzh*]
clear, clair, net [*kler, net*]
clergy, clergé (m) [*kler-zheh*]
clerk, employé, -ée [*ã-plwa-yeh*]
clever, habile [*ah-beel*]
client, client, -te [*klee-yã(t)*]
climate, climat (m) [*klee-mah*]
climb *v.,* monter (*Aux:* ÊTRE) [*mŏ-teh*]
cloak-room, vestiaire (m) [*vest-yer*]
clock, horloge (m) [*or-lozh*]
   It's ten o'clock, Il est dix heures [*ee-le-dee-zuhr*]
close *v.,* fermer [*fer-meh*]

close [near], près (de) [*pre (duh)*]
closed, fermé [*fer-meh*]
closet, armoire (f), placard (m) [*ahr-mwahr, plah-kahr*]
cloth, tissu (m) [*tee-sü*]
   tablecloth, nappe (f) [*nahp*]
clothes, vêtements (m, pl) [*vet-mã*]
cloud *n.*, nuage (m) [*nii-ahzh*]
cloudy, nuageux, -euse [*nii-ah-zhuh, nii-ah-zhuhz*]
club [association], club (m) [*kluhb*]
clutch [auto], embrayage (m) [*ã-bre-yahzh*]
coach [sports], entraîneur (m) [*ã-tre-nuhr*]
coal, charbon (m) [*shahr-bõ*]
coarse, grossier, -ière [*groh-syeh, groh-syer*]
coast, côte (f) [*koht*]
coat [overcoat], manteau (m), -eaux (pl) [*mã-toh*]
coat [suitcoat], veste (f), veston (m) [*vest, ves-tõ*]
cocktail, cocktail (m) [*kok-tel*]
cocoa, cacao (m) [*kah-kah-oh*]
coconut, noix (f) de coco [*nwaht koh-koh*]
coffee, café (m) [*kah-feh*]
coffin, cercueil (m) [*ser-kuhy*]
coin, pièce (f) (de monnaie) [*pyes (duh mo-neh)*]
coincidence, coïncidence (f) [*ko-ē-see-dãs*]
cold *adj.*, froid [*frwah(d)*]
   be cold *v.*, avoir froid [*ahv-wahr frwah*]
cold *n.*, rhume (m) [*rüm*]
   catch a cold *v.*, s'enrhumer [*sã-rü-meh*]
collar, col (m) [*kol*]
collect *v.*, assembler, collectionner [*a-sã-bleh, ko-lek-syo-neh*]
collection, collection (f) [*ko-lek-syõ*]
college, université (f) [*ü-nee-ver-see-teh*]
colonel, colonel (m) [*ko-lo-nel*]
colony, colonie (f) [*ko-lo-nee*]
color *n.*, couleur (f) [*koo-luhr*]
color *v.*, colorer [*ko-lo-reh*]
column, colonne (f) [*ko-lon*]
comb *n.*, peigne (m) [*peñ*]
comb *v.*, peigner [*peh-nyeh*]

combination, combinaison (f) [kõ-bee-neh-zõ]

come v., venir (irreg; *Aux:* ÊTRE), arriver (*Aux:* ÊTRE)
 [v(uh)-neer, ah-ree-veh]

   come back, come again, revenir (irreg; *Aux:* ÊTRE) [ruh-vneer]

   come by, passer (par) (*Aux:* ÊTRE) [pah-seh (pahr)]

   come down, descendre (*Aux:* ÊTRE) [deh-sãdr]

   come forward, s'avancer [sah-vã-seh]

   come in, entrer (dans) (*Aux:* ÊTRE) [ã-treh (dã)]

   come out, sortir (irreg; *Aux:* ÊTRE) [sor-teer]

   Here he comes!, Le voilà! [luh vwah-lah]

comedy, comédie (f) [ko-meh-dee]

comfort n., confort (m) [kõ-for]

comfort v., consoler [kõ-so-leh]

comfortable, confortable [kõ-for-tahbl]

   Are you comfortable?, Etes-vous à l'aise?, Etes-vous bien?
    [et-voo-zah-lez, et-voo-byẽ]

comma, virgule (f) [veer-gül]

command n., ordre (m) [ordr]

command v., commander [ko-mã-deh]

comment n., commentaire (m) [ko-mã-ter]

commercial, commercial, -aux (m, pl) [ko-mer-syahl, ko-mer-syoh]

commission n., commission (f) [ko-mee-syõ]

committee, comité (m) [ko-mee-teh]

common, commun, ordinaire [ko-mẽ, ko-mün; or-dee-ner]

communicate v., communiquer [ko-mü-nee-keh]

communication, communication (f) [ko-mü-nee-kah-syõ]

communist n. & adj., communiste (m, f) [ko-mü-neest]

community, communauté (f) [ko-mü-noh-teh]

companion, compagnon (m) [kõ-pah-nyõ]

company [firm], compagnie (f) [kõ-pah-nee]

company [guest], invité [ẽ-vee-teh]

compare v., comparer [kõ-pah-reh]

comparison, comparaison (f) [kõ-pah-re-zõ]

compartment, compartiment (m) [kõ-pahr-tee-mã]

compensation, compensation (f) [kõ-pã-sah-syõ]

competent, compétent [kõ-peh-tã(t)]

competition [business], concurrence (f) [kõ-kü-rãs]
competition [sports], compétition (f) [kõ-peh-tee-syõ]
complain v., se plaindre (irreg) [suh plẽdr]
complaint, plainte (f) [plẽt]
complete adj., complet, -ète [kõ-pleh, kõ-plet]
complete v., compléter [kõ-pleh-teh]
completely, complètement [kõ-plet-mã]
complexion, teint (m) [tẽ]
complicate v., compliquer [kõ-plee-keh]
complicated, compliqué [kõ-plee-keh]
compliment n., compliment (m) [kõ-plee-mã]
compose v., composer [kõ-poh-zeh]
composer, compositeur (m) [kõ-poh-zee-tuhr]
compound adj., composé [kõ-poh-zeh]
compromise n., compromis (m) [kõ-pro-mee]
conceal v., cacher [kah-sheh]
conceited, vaniteux, -euse [vah-nee-tuh, vah-nee-tuhz]
conceive v., concevoir (irreg) [kõ-suh-vwahr]
concentrate v., concentrer, se concentrer [kõ-sã-treh, skõ-sã-treh]
concept, concept (m) [kõ-sept]
concerning, concernant, au sujet de [kõ-ser-nã, oh sü-zheh duh]
concert, concert (m) [kõ-ser]
conclusion, conclusion (f) [kõ-klü-zyõ]
condemn v., condamner [kõ-dah-neh]
condense v., condenser [kõ-dã-seh]
condition, condition (f), état (m) [kõ-dee-syõ, eh-tah]
conditional, conditionnel, -elle [kõ-dee-syo-nel]
conduct n., conduite (f) [kõ-dweet]
conduct v., mener [muh-neh]
conductor [of train], contrôleur (m) [kõ-troh-luhr]
conductor [of orchestra], chef (m) d'orchestre [shef dor-kestr]
conference, consultation (f), congrès (m) [kõ-sül-tah-syõ, kõ-gre]
confess v., avouer [ahv-weh]
confession, confession (f) [kõ-fe-syõ]
confident, confiant, sûr [kõ-fyã(t), sür]

confidential, confidentiel, -elle [kõ-fee-dã-syel]
confirm v., confirmer [kõ-feer-meh]
conflict n., conflit (m) [kõ-flee]
confusion, confusion (f) [kõ-fü-zyõ]
congratulate v., féliciter [feh-lee-see-teh]
congratulations, félicitations [feh-lee-see-tah-syõ]
congress, congrès (m) [kõ-gre]
connection [link], relation (f) [ruh-lah-syõ]
connection [transfer], correspondance (f) [ko-res-põ-dâs]
conquer v., conquérir (irreg) [kõ-keh-reer]
conscience, conscience (f) [kõ-syãs]
conscientious, consciencieux, -euse [kõ-syã-syuh, kõ-syã-syuhz]
conscious, conscient [kõ-syã(t)]
consent n., consentement (m) [kõ-sãt-mã]
consent v., consentir (irreg) [kõ-sã-teer]
consequence, conséquence (f) [kõ-seh-kãs]
conservative, conservateur, -trice [kõ-ser-vah-tuhr, kõ-ser-vah-trees]
consider v., considérer [kõ-see-deh-reh]
considerable, considérable [kõ-see-deh-rahbl]
consist (of) v., consister (dans, en) [kõ-sees-teh (dã, ã)]
consistent, conséquent, logique [kõ-seh-kã(t), lo-zheek]
conspicuous, évident [eh-vee-dã(t)]
constant, constant [kõ-stã(t)]
constitute v., constituer [kõ-stee-tweh]
constitution, constitution (f) [kõ-stee-tü-syõ]
construct v., construire (irreg) [kõ-strweer]
construction, construction (f) [kõ-strük-syõ]
consul, consul (m) [kõ-sül]
consulate, consulat (m) [kõ-sü-lah]
consult v., consulter [kõ-sül-teh]
consume v., consommer [kõ-so-meh]
consumer, consommateur (m) [kõ-so-mah-tuhr]
contact n., contact (m) [kõ-tahkt]
contagious, contagieux, -euse [kõ-tah-zhyuh, kõ-tah-zhyuhz]
contain v., contenir (irreg) [kõt-neer]
container, récipient (m) [reh-see-pyã]

contemporary, contemporain [kŏ-tã-po-rĕ, kŏ-tã-po-ren]
contempt, mépris (m) [meh-pree]
contents pl., contenu (m) [kŏt-nii]
contest n., concours (m) [kŏ-koor]
continent n., continent (m) [kŏ-tee-nã]
continue v., continuer [kŏ-tee-nweh]
contract, contrat (m) [kŏ-trah]
contractor, entrepreneur (m) [ã-truh-pruh-nuhr]
contradiction, contradiction (f) [kŏ-trah-deek-syŏ]
contrary, contraire [kŏ-trer]
  on the contrary, au contraire [oh kŏ-trer]
contrast n., contraste (m) [kŏ-trahst]
contribute v., contribuer [kŏ-tree-bweh]
control n., autorité (f), maîtrise (f) [o-to-ree-teh, me-treez]
control v., diriger [dee-ree-zheh]
controversy, controverse (f) [kŏ-troh-vers]
convenient, commode [ko-mod]
convent, couvent (m) [koo-vã]
conversation, conversation (f) [kŏ-ver-sah-syŏ]
convert v., convertir [kŏ-ver-teer]
convict n., forçat, (m) [for-sah]
convict v., convaincre (irreg) [kŏ-vĕkr]
convince v., convaincre (irreg) [kŏ-vĕkr]
cook n., cuisinier, -ière [kwee-zee-nyeh, kwee-zee-nyehr]
cook v., faire la cuisine [fer lah kwee-zeen]
cooking, cuisine (f) [kwee-zeen]
cool adj., frais, fraîche [fre, fresh]
cool v., rafraîchir [rah-fre-sheer]
cooperation, coopération (f) [koh-oh-peh-rah-syŏ]
copper, cuivre (m) [kweevr]
copy n., copie (f) [ko-pee]
copy v., copier, reproduire (irreg) [ko-pyeh, ruh-pro-dweer]
cord, corde (f) [kord]
cordial, cordial, -iaux (m, pl) [kor-dyahl, kor-dyoh]
cork, buchon (m) [boo-shŏ]
corkscrew, tire-bouchon (m) [teer-boo-shŏ]
corn, maïs (m) [mah-ees]
corner, coin (m) [kwĕ]

corporation, société anonyme (f) [*so-syeh-teh ah-no-neem*]

correct *adj.*, correct [*ko-rekt*]

correct *v.*, corriger [*ko-ree-zheh*]

correction, correction (f) [*ko-rek-syõ*]

correspondence, correspondance (f) [*ko-res-põ-dãs*]

corridor, couloir (m), corridor (m) [*kool-wahr, ko-ree-dor*]

corruption, corruption (f) [*ko-rüp-syõ*]

cosmetics *pl.*, produits (m, pl) de beauté [*pro-dweed boh-teh*]

cost *n.*, coût (f), frais (m, pl) [*koo, fre*]
  cost of living, coût de la vie [*koo dlah vee*]

cost *v.*, coûter [*koo-teh*]

cot, lit (m) pliant [*lee plee-yã*]

cottage, petite maison de vacances [*p(uh)-teet me-zõd vah-kãs*]

cotton, coton (m) [*ko-tõ*]

couch, canapé (m), divan (m) [*kah-na-peh, dee-vã*]

cough *n.*, toux (f) [*too*]

cough *v.*, tousser [*too-seh*]

council, conseil (m) [*kõ-sey*]

count [title], comte (m) [*kõt*]

count *v.*, compter [*kõ-teh*]

countess, comtesse (f) [*kõ-tes*]

country [nation], pays (m) [*peh-ee*]

country [rural area], campagne (f) [*kã-pañ*]

couple *n.*, couple (m) [*koopl*]

courage, courage (m) [*koo-rahzh*]

courageous, courageux, -euse [*koo-rah-zhuh, koo-rah-zhuhz*]

course [way], cours (m) [*koor*]
  of course, bien entendu [*bye-nã-tã-dü*]

course [of a meal], plat (m) [*plah*]

court *n.*, cour (f) [*koor*]
  tennis court, court (m) [*koor*]

court *v.*, faire la cour [*fer lah koor*]

courteous, courtois, poli [*koor-twah(z), po-lee*]

courtyard, cour (f) [*koor*]

cousin, cousin, -ine [*koo-zẽ, koo-zeen*]
  first cousin, cousin germain [*koo-zẽ zher-mẽ*]

cover *v.*, couvrir (irreg) [*koo-vreer*]

cover n., couverture (f) [*koo-ver-tür*]
cover charge, couvert (m) [*koo-ver*]
cow, vache (f) [*vahsh*]
coward, lâche (m, f) [*lahsh*]
crab, crabe (m) [*krahb*]
crack n., fissure (f) [*fee-sür*]
cracker, biscuit (m) salé [*bees-kwee sah-leh*]
cradle n., berceau (m), -eaux (pl) [*ber-soh*]
craftsman, artisan (m) [*ahr-tee-zã*]
crank n., manivelle (f) [*mah-nee-vel*]
crash n., collision (f) [*ko-lee-zyō*]
crash v., s'écraser [*seh-krah-zeh*]
crawl v., ramper [*rã-peh*]
crayfish, écrevisse (f) [*eh-kruh-vees*]
crazy, fou, folle [*foo, fol*]
cream, crème (f) [*krem*]
create v., créer [*kreh-eh*]
creation, création (f) [*kreh-ah-syō*]
creature, créature (f) [*kreh-ah-tür*]
credit n., crédit (m) [*kreh-dee*]
creditor, créancier (m) [*kreh-ã-syeh*]
crew, équipage (m) [*eh-kee-pahzh*]
crib, lit (m) d'enfant [*lee-dã-fã*]
crime, crime (m) [*kreem*]
criminal adj. & n., criminel, -elle [*kree-mee-nel*]
crisis, crise (f) [*kreez*]
critic n., critique (m) [*kree-teek*]
critical, critique [*kree-teek*]
criticism, critique (f) [*kree-teek*]
criticize v., critiquer [*kree-tee-keh*]
crook [thief], escroc (m) [*es-kroh*]
crooked, tordu [*tor-dü*]
crop n., récolte (f), culture (f) [*reh-kolt, kül-tür*]
cross n., croix (f) [*krwah*]
cross v., traverser [*trah-ver-seh*]
crossing [by sea], traversée (f) [*trah-ver-seh*]
crossroads, carrefour (m) [*kahr-foor*]
crow, corbeau (m), -eaux (pl) [*kor-boh*]

crowd *n.*, foule (f) [*fool*]

crown, couronne (f) [*koo-ron*]

cruel, cruel, cruelle [*krü-el*]

cruelty, cruauté (f) [*krü-oh-teh*]

cruise *n.*, croisière (f) [*krwah-zyer*]

crumb, miette (f) [*myet*]

crush *v.*, écraser [*eh-krah-zeh*]

cry *n.*, cri (m) [*kree*]

cry *v.*, pleurer [*pluh-reh*]

crystal *n.*, cristal (m), -aux (pl) [*krees-tahl, krees-toh*]

Cuba, Cuba (m) [*kü-bah*]

Cuban, cubain [*kü-bẽ, kü-ben*]

cube, cube (m) [*küb*]

cucumber, concombre (m) [*kõ-kõbr*]

cuff, manchette (f) [*mã-shet*]

cuff links, bouton (m) de manchette [*boo-tõd mã-shet*]

culture, culture (f) [*kül-tür*]

cup, tasse (f) [*tahs*]

cupboard, placard (m) [*plah-kahr*]

cure *n.*, guérison (f) [*gheh-ree-zõ*]

cure *v.*, guérir [*gheh-reer*]

curiosity, curiosité (f) [*kür-yo-zee-teh*]

curious, curieux, -euse [*kür-yuh, kür-yuhz*]

curl *n.*, boucle (f) [*bookl*]

curl *v.*, boucler [*book-leh*]

currency, monnaie (f) [*mo-neh*]

current *adj.*, courant, actuel [*koo-rã(t), ahk-twel*]

curse *v.*, jurer [*zhü-reh*]

curtain, rideau (m), -eaux (pl) [*ree-doh*]

curve [arc], courbe (f) [*koorb*]

curve [of road], virage (m) [*vee-rahzh*]
   dangerous curve, virage dangereux [*vee-rahzh dãzh-ruh*]

cushion, coussin (m) [*koo-sẽ*]

custard, flan (m) [*flã*]

custom *n.*, coutume (f) [*koo-tüm*]

custom made, sur mesure [*sür muh-zür*]

customary, habituel, -elle [*ah-bee-twel*]

customer, client, -te [*klee-yã, klee-yãt*]

customs, douane (f) [*dwahn*]
  customs duty, droit (m) de douane [*drwah duh dwahn*]
  customs officer, douanier (m) [*dwah-nyeh*]
cut [wound] *n.*, coupure (f) [*koo-pür*]
cut [pattern] *n.*, coupe (f) [*koop*]
cut *v.*, couper [*koo-peh*]
cylinder, cylindre (m) [*see-lĕdr*]

D

daily *adj.*, quotidien, -enne [*ko-tee-dyē, ko-tee-dyen*]
daily *adv.*, tous les jours [*too leh zhoor*]
dairy, laiterie (f) [*le-tree*]
daisy, marguerite (f) [*mahr-guh-reet*]
dam, barrage (m) [*bah-rahzh*]
damage *n.*, dommage (m) [*do-mahzh*]
damage *v.*, endommager [*ã-doh-mah-zheh*]
damaged, endommagé [*ã-doh-mah-zheh*]
damp, humide [*ü-meed*]
dance *n.*, danse (f) [*dãs*]
dance *v.*, danser [*dã-seh*]
dancer, danseur, -euse [*dã-suhr, dã-suhz*]
danger, danger (m) [*dã-zheh*]
dangerous, dangereux, -euse [*dã-zhruh, dã-zhruhz*]
dare *v.*, oser [*oh-zeh*]
daring [brave], téméraire [*teh-meh-rer*]
daring [manner], osé [*oh-zeh*]
dark *adj.*, sombre [*sõbr*]
dark [color] *adj.*, foncé [*fõ-seh*]
darkness, obscurité (f) [*ops-kü-ree-teh*]
date [day], date (f) [*daht*]
date [fruit], datte (f) [*daht*]
date [appointment], rendez-vous (m) [*rã-deh-voo*]
daughter, fille, (f) [*feey*]
daughter-in-law, belle-fille [*bel-feey*]

dawn, aube (f) [*ohb*]
day, jour (m) [*zhoor*]
  every day, tous les jours [*too leh zhoor*]
  the next day, le lendemain [*luh lãd-mẽ*]
  day after tomorrow, après-demain [*ah-pred-mẽ*]
  day before yesterday, avant-hier [*ah-vã-tyer*]
day [duration], journée [*zhoor-neh*]
  all day long, toute la journée [*toot lah zhoor-neh*]
daydream *n.,* rêverie (f) [*rev-ree*]
dead, mort [*mor(t)*]
deadly, mortel, -elle [*mor-tel*]
deaf, sourd [*soor(d)*]
deal *n.,* affaire (f) [*ah-fer*]
  a good deal, beaucoup [*boh-koo*]
deal [cards] *v.,* donner, distribuer [*do-neh, dees-tree-bweh*]
deal (with) *v.,* traiter (avec) [*tre-teh (ah-vek)*]
dealer, marchand (m), négociant (m) [*mahr-shã, neh-go-syã*]
dear, cher, chère [*sher*]
death, mort (f) [*mor*]
debt, dette (f) [*det*]
decanter, carafe (f) [*kah-rahf*]
deceased, défunt, décédé [*deh-fẽ(t), deh-seh-deh*]
deceive *v.,* tromper [*trõ-peh*]
December, décembre (m) [*deh-sãbr*]
decency, décence (f) [*deh-sãs*]
decent, décent [*deh-sã(t)*]
deception, tromperie (f) [*trõ-pree*]
decide *v.,* décider [*deh-see-deh*]
decision, décision (f) [*deh-see-zyõ*]
deck [ship], pont (m) [*põ*]
deck [of cards], jeu (m) [*zhuh*]
declaration, déclaration (f) [*deh-klah-rah-syõ*]
declare *v.,* déclarer [*deh-klah-reh*]
decline [refuse] *v.,* refuser [*ruh-fü-zeh*]
decorate *v.,* décorer [*deh-ko-reh*]
decoration, décoration (f) [*deh-ko-rah-syõ*]
decrease *v.,* diminuer [*dee-mee-nweh*]
decree *n.,* décret (m) [*deh-kre*]

deed [act], action (f) [*ahk-syõ*]
deed [legal], act notarié (m) [*ahkt no-tar-yeh*]
deep, profond [*pro-fõ(d)*]
defeat *n.,* défaite (f) [*deh-fet*]
defeat *v.,* battre (irreg) [*bahtr*]
defective, défectueux, -euse [*deh-fek-twuh, deh-fek-twuhz*]
defend *v.,* défendre [*deh-fãdr*]
define *v.,* définir [*deh-fee-neer*]
definite, bien déterminé [*byẽ deh-ter-mee-neh*]
definition, définition (f) [*deh-fee-nee-syõ*]
degree, degré (m) [*duh-greh*]
delay, délai (m), retard (m) [*deh-le, r(uh)-tahr*]
deliberate, délibéré [*deh-lee-beh-reh*]
delicate, délicat [*deh-lee-kah(t)*]
delicious, délicieux, -euse [*deh-lee-syuh, deh-lee-syuhz*]
delight *n.,* joie (f) [*zhwah*]
delight *v.,* enchanter [*ã-shã-teh*]
deliver [from] *v.,* délivrer [*deh-lee-vreh*]
deliver [to] *v.,* livrer [*lee-vreh*]
demand *n.,* demande (f) [*d(uh)-mãd*]
demand [labor] *n.,* revendication (f) [*ruh-vã-dee-kah-syõ*]
demand [require] *v.,* exiger [*ehg-zee-zheh*]
demand [request] *v.,* demander [*d(uh)-mã-deh*]
democracy, démocratie (f) [*deh-mok-rah-see*]
demonstrate [show] *v.,* démontrer [*deh-mõ-treh*]
demonstrate [politically] *v.,* manifester [*mah-nee-fes-teh*]
demonstration, démonstration (f) [*deh-mõ-strah-syõ*]
demonstration [political], manifestation (f) [*mah-nee-fes-tah-syõ*]
denial, refus (m) [*r(uh)-fü*]
density, densité (f) [*dã-see-teh*]
dentist, dentiste (m) [*dã-teest*]
deny *v.,* nier, démentir [*nee-yeh, deh-mã-teer*]
depart *v.,* partir (irreg; *Aux:* ÊTRE) [*pahr-teer*]
department, département (m) [*deh-pahr-tuh-mã*]
department [in a store], rayon (m) [*re-yõ*]
departure, départ (m) [*deh-pahr*]
depend (on) *v.,* dépendre (de) [*deh-pãdr (duh)*]

That depends, Ça dépend [*sah deh-pã*]
dependent *n.*, personne (f) à charge [*per-son ah shahrzh*]
deposit *v.*, déposer [*deh-poh-zeh*]
  make a deposit, verser un accompte (m) [*ver-seh ē-nah-kõt*]
deprive *v.*, priver [*pree-veh*]
depth, profondeur (f) [*pro-fõ-duhr*]
deputy, adjoint (m) [*ahd-zhwē*]
descend *v.*, descendre (*Aux:* ÊTRE) [*deh-sãdr*]
descent, descente (f) [*deh-sãt*]
describe *v.*, décrire (irreg) [*deh-kreer*]
description, description (f) [*des-kreep-syõ*]
desert *n.*, désert (m) [*deh-zer*]
desert *v.*, déserter [*deh-zer-teh*]
deserve *v.*, mériter [*meh-ree-teh*]
desirable, désirable [*deh-zee-rahbl*]
desire *n.*, désir (m) [*deh-zeer*]
desire *v.*, désirer [*deh-zee-reh*]
desk, bureau (m), -eaux (pl) [*bü-roh*]
despair *n.*, désespoir (m) [*deh-zeh-spwahr*]
despair *v.*, désespérer [*deh-zehs-peh-reh*]
desperate, désespéré [*deh-zehs-peh-reh*]
despite, malgré [*mahl-greh*]
dessert, dessert (m) [*deh-ser*]
destiny, destin (m) [*des-tē*]
destroy *v.*, détruire (irreg) [*deh-trweer*]
destruction, destruction (f) [*des-trük-syõ*]
detail, détail (m) [*deh-tahy*]
detective, détective (m) [*deh-tek-teev*]
determine *v.*, déterminer [*deh-ter-mee-neh*]
detour, détour (m), déviation (f) [*deh-toor, deh-vyah-syõ*]
develop *v.*, développer [*dehv-lo-peh*]
development, développement (m) [*dehv-lop-mã*]
device, moyen (m), truc (m) [*mwah-yē, trük*]
devil, diable (m) [*dyahbl*]
devoted, dévoué [*deh-vweh*]
devotion, dévotion (f) [*deh-voh-syõ*]
dew, rosée (f) [*roh-zeh*]

diagnosis, diagnostique (m) [*dyahg-nos-teek*]

dial *n.*, cadran (m) [*kah-drã*]

dial [phone number] *v.*, composer (le numéro) [*kõ-poh-zeh (luh nü-meh-roh)*]

dialogue, dialogue (m) [*dyah-log*]

diamond, diamant (m) [*dyah-mã*]

diaper, couche (f) [*koosh*]

diary, journal (m), -aux (pl) [*zhoor-nahl, zhoor-noh*]

dictate *v.*, dicter [*deek-teh*]

dice [gambling] *n. pl.*, dés (m, pl) [*deh*]

dictation, dictée (f) [*deek-teh*]

dictionary, dictionnaire (m) [*deek-syo-ner*]

die *v.*, mourir (irreg; *Aux* ÊTRE) [*moo-reer*]

diet, régime (m) [*reh-zheem*]

   be on a diet *v.*, suivre (irreg) un régime [*swee-vrĕ-reh-zheem*]

difference, différence (f) [*dee-feh-rãs*]

different, différent [*dee-feh-rã(t)*]

difficult, difficile [*dee-fee-seel*]

difficulty, difficulté (f) [*dee-fee-kül-teh*]

dig *v.*, creuser [*kruh-zeh*]

digestion, digestion (f) [*dee-zhes-tyõ*]

dignity, dignité (f) [*dee-nyee-teh*]

dim *adj.*, faible, incertain [*febl; ĕ-ser-tĕ, ĕ-ser-ten*]

dimension, dimension (f) [*dee-mã-syõ*]

diminish *v.*, diminuer [*dee-mee-nweh*]

dine *v.*, dîner [*dee-neh*]

dining car, wagon-restaurant (m) [*vah-gõ-res-to-rã*]

dining room, salle (f) à manger [*sahl ah mã-zheh*]

dinner, dîner (m) [*dee-neh*]

dinner jacket, smoking (m) [*smo-keen*]

diploma, diplôme (m) [*dee-plohm*]

diplomat, diplomate (m) [*dee-ploh-maht*]

diplomatic, diplomate [*dee-ploh-maht*]

direct *adj.*, direct [*dee-rekt*]

direct *v.*, diriger [*dee-ree-zheh*]

directly, directement [*dee-rek-tuh-mã*]

dirt, saleté (f) [*sahl-teh*]

dirty, sale [*sahl*]

disabled, invalide, multilé [*ē-vah-leed, mü-tee-leh*]

disadvantage, désavantage (m) [*deh-zah-vã-tahzh*]

disagree *v.*, n'être pas d'accord [*netr pah dah-kor*]

   I disagree, Je ne suis pas d'accord [*zhuhn swee pah dah-kor*]

disagreeable, désagréable [*deh-zah-greh-ahbl*]

disagreement, différence (f) [*dee-feh-rãs*]

disappear *v.*, disparaître (irreg) [*dee-spah-retr*]

disappoint *v.*, décevoir (irreg) [*deh-suh-vwahr*]

disappointed, déçu [*deh-sü*]

disapprove *v.*, désapprouver [*deh-zah-proo-veh*]

disaster, désastre (m) [*deh-zahstr*]

discharge [an employee] *v.*, renvoyer [*rã-vwah-yeh*]

discipline *n.*, discipline (f) [*dee-see-pleen*]

disclose *v.*, révéler [*reh-veh-leh*]

discomfort, manque (m) de confort [*mãk duh kõ-for*]

discontinue *v.*, discontinuer, cesser [*dees-kõ-tee-nweh, seh-seh*]

discount [bank] *n.*, escompte (m) [*es-kõt*]

discount [store] *n.*, remise [*ruh-meez*]

discourage *v.*, décourager [*deh-koo-rah-zheh*]

discover *v.*, découvrir (irreg) [*deh-koov-reer*]

discovery, découverte (f) [*deh-koo-vert*]

discuss *v.*, discuter [*dees-kü-teh*]

discussion, discussion (f) [*dees-kü-syõ*]

disease, maladie (f) [*mah-lah-dee*]

disembark *v.*, débarquer [*deh-bahr-keh*]

disgrace *n.*, disgrâce (f) [*dees-grahs*]

disguise *n.*, déguisement (m) [*deh-gheez-mã*]

disgusted, dégoûté [*deh-goo-teh*]

dish, plat (m) [*plah*]

dishes, vaisselle (f, sing) [*ve-sel*]

   do the dishes *v.*, faire la vaisselle [*fer lah ve-sel*]

dishonest, malhonnête [*mah-lo-net*]

dislike *v.*, ne pas aimer [*nuh pah-ze-meh*]

   I dislike that, Je n'aime pas cela (ça) [*zhnem pah slah (sah)*]

dismiss v., renvoyer [rã-vwah-yeh]
disobey v., désobéir (à) [deh-zo-beh-eer (ah)]
disorder, désordre (m) [deh-zordr]
display n., étalage (m) [eh-tah-lahzh]
display v., étaler [eh-tah-leh]
dispute n., dispute (f) [dees-püt]
dissolve v., dissoudre (irreg) [dee-soodr]
distance, distance (f) [dees-tãs]
distant, distant [dees-tã(t)]
distinct, distinct [dees-tẽ(kt)]
distinguish v., distinguer [dees-tẽ-gheh]
distinguished, distingué [dees-tẽ-gheh]
distress, détresse (f) [deh-tres]
distribute v., distribuer [dees-tree-bweh]
distribution, distribution (f), répartition (f) [dees-tree-bü-syõ, reh-pahr-tee-syõ]
district, région (f) [reh-zhyõ]
district [for an election], circonscription (f) [seer-kõ-skreep-syõ]
distrust n., méfiance (f) [meh-fyãs]
distrust [someone] v., se méfier [smeh-fyeh]
disturb v., déranger [deh-rã-zheh]
disturbance, trouble (m) [troobl]
ditch, fossé (m) [foh-seh]
dive v., plonger [plõ-zheh]
divide v., diviser [dee-vee-zeh]
divine, divin [dee-vẽ, dee-veen]
division, division (f) [dee-vee-zyõ]
divorce, n., divorce (m) [dee-vors]
divorce v., divorcer [dee-vor-seh]
dizziness, vertige (m) [ver-teezh]
  feel dizzy v., avoir le vertige [ah-vwahr luh ver-teezh]
do v., faire (irreg) [fer]
  How do you do?, Comment allez-vous? [ko-mã-tah-leh-voo]
  What can I do for you?, Que puis-je faire pour vous? [kuh pweezh fer poor voo]
  do without, se passer de [spah-seh duh]
dock n., quai (m) [keh]

dock v., entrer au port (*Aux:* ÊTRE) [ã-treh oh por]
doctor, médecin (m) [met-sẽ]
  Doctor . . . [title], docteur . . . [dok-tuhr]
document n., document (m) [do-kü-mã]
dog, chien (m) [shyẽ]
doll, poupée (f) [poo-peh]
dollar, dollar (m) [do-lahr]
dome, dôme (m) [dohm]
domestic, domestique [do-mes-teek]
done, fait [fe]
  well-done, bien cuit [byẽ kwee(t)]
donkey, âne (m) [ahn]
door, porte (f) [port]
  car door, portière (f) [por-tyer]
dormitory, dortoir (m) [dor-twahr]
  college dormitory, résidence (f) universitaire [reh-zee-dãs
    ü-nee-ver-see-ter]
dose n., dose (f) [dohz]
double, double [doobl]
doubt n., doute (m) [doot]
doubt v., douter (de) [doo-teh (duh)]
  I doubt it, J'en doute [zhã-doot]
doubtful, douteux, -euse [doo-tuh, doo-tuhz]
down, en bas [ã bah]
  Down with . . . , À bas . . . [ah bah]
  go down, come down v., descendre (*Aux:* ÊTRE) [deh-sãdr]
  sit down v., s'asseoir (irreg) [sah-swahr]
  lie down v., se coucher [skoo-sheh]
downstairs, en bas [ã bah]
downtown, au centre de la ville [oh sãtr duh lah veel]
dowry, dot (f) [dot]
doze v., somnoler [som-no-leh]
dozen, douzaine (f) [doo-zen]
draft [bank], traite (f) [tret]
draft [air], courant (m) d'air [koo-rã der]
drag v., traîner [tre-neh]
drain n., tuyau (m) de vidange [twee-yoh dvee-dãzh]
drain v., faire écouler, égoutter [fer eh-koo-leh, eh-goo-teh]

drama, drame (m) [*drahm*]
dramatic, dramatique [*drah-mah-teek*]
draw [sketch] *v.*, dessiner [*deh-see-neh*]
draw (out) *v.*, tirer [*tee-reh*]
drawer, tiroir (m) [*teer-wahr*]
dream *n.*, rêve (m) [*rev*]
dream *v.*, rêver [*re-veh*]
dress *n.*, robe (f) [*rob*]
  evening dress, robe du soir [*rob dü swahr*]
dress *v.*, habiller, s'habiller [*ah-bee-yeh, sah-bee-yeh*]
dresser, commode (f) [*ko-mod*]
dressmaker, couturière (f) [*koo-tür-yer*]
drink *n.*, boisson (f) [*bwah-sõ*]
drink *v.*, boire (irreg) [*bwahr*]
drip *v.*, tomber (*Aux:* ÊTRE) goutte à goutte [*tõ-beh goo-tah goot*]
drive *v.*, conduire (irreg) [*kõ-dweer*]
driver, chauffeur (m) [*shoh-fuhr*]
driver's license, permis (m) de conduire [*per-meet kõ-dweer*]
drop *n.*, goutte (f) [*goot*]
drop *v.*, laisser tomber [*leh-seh tõ-beh*]
drown *v.*, noyer, se noyer [*nwah-yeh, snwah-yeh*]
drug *n.*, drogue (f) [*drog*]
drugstore, pharmacie (f) [*fahr-mah-see*]
drum, tambour (m) [*tã-boor*]
dry *adj.*, sec, sèche [*sek, sesh*]
dry *v.*, sécher [*seh-sheh*]
dry-clean *v.*, nettoyer à sec [*neh-twa-yeh ah sek*]
duchess, duchesse (f) [*dü-shes*]
duck, canard (m) [*kah-nahr*]
due, dû [*dü*]
  due to, à cause de [*ah kohz duh*]
  fall due *v.*, être dû [*etr dü*]
duke, duc (m) [*dük*]
dull [boring], ennuyeux, -euse [*ã-nwee-yuh, ã-nwee-yuhz*]
dumb [mute], muet, muette [*mü-eh, mü-et*]
dungeon, cachot (m) [*kah-shoh*]

durable, durable [*dü-rahbl*]
during, pendant [*pã-dã*]
dusk, crépuscule (m) [*kreh-püs-kül*]
dust, poussière (f) [*poo-syer*]
dusty, poussiéreux, -euse [*poo-sye-ruh, poo-sye-ruhz*]
Dutch, hollandais [*oh-lã-de(z)*]
duty, devoir (m) [*duh-vwahr*]
  be on duty *v.,* être de service [*etr duh ser-vees*]
duty-free, en franchise [*ã frã-sheez*]
dye *n.,* teinture (f) [*tẽ-tür*]
dye *v.,* teindre (irreg) [*tẽdr*]
dynamite, dynamite (f) [*dee-nah-meet*]

E

each, chaque [*shahk*]
  each one, chacun, -une [*shah-kẽ, shah-kün*]
  each other, l'un l'autre, les uns les autres [*lẽ lohtr, leh-zẽ
  leh-zohtr*]
eager, impatient [*ẽ-pah-syã(t)*]
ear, oreille (f) [*o-rey*]
early *adv.,* tôt, de bonne heure [*toh, duh bo-nuhr*]
earn *v.,* gagner [*gah-nyeh*]
earring, boucle (f) d'oreille [*bookl do-rey*]
earth, terre (f) [*ter*]
earthquake, tremblement (m) de terre [*trã-bluh-mãt ter*]
ease [comfort], aise (f) [*ez*]
ease [competence], facilité (f) [*fah-see-lee-teh*]
easily, facilement [*fah-seel-mã*]
east, est (m) [*est*]
  Near East, Proche Orient (m) [*pro-shor-yã*]
  Middle East, Moyen Orient (m) [*mwah-ye-nor-yã*]
  Far East, Extrême Orient [*ehk-stre-mor-yã*]
Easter, Pâques (m, pl) [*pahk*]
eastern, oriental, -aux (m, pl) [*or-yã-tahl, or-yã-toh*]

easy, facile [*fah-seel*]
   Take it easy! Ne vous en faites pas! [*nuh voo-zã fet pah*]
eat *v.*, manger [*mã-zheh*]
echo *n.*, écho (m) [*eh-koh*]
economical, économique [*eh-ko-no-meek*]
edge *n.*, bord (m) [*bor*]
edible, mangeable [*mã-zhahbl*]
edition, édition (f) [*eh-dee-syõ*]
editor, éditeur, -trice [*eh-dee-tuhr, eh-dee-trees*]
education, instruction (f), enseignement (m) [*ẽ-strük-syõ, ã-se-nyuh-mã*]
effect *n.*, effet (m) [*e-fe*]
effective, efficace [*e-fee-kahs*]
efficient, efficace [*e-fee-kahs*]
effort, effort (m) [*e-for*]
egg, oeuf (m) [*uhf*]
   fried egg, oeuf au plat [*uhf oh plah*]
   hard-boiled egg, oeuf dur [*uhf dür*]
   scrambled eggs, oeufs brouillés [*uh broo-yeh*]
   soft-boiled egg, oeuf à la coque [*uh-fah lah kok*]
Egypt, Egypte (f) [*eh-zheept*]
Egyptian, égyptien, -enne [*eh-zheep-syẽ, eh-zheep-syen*]
eight, huit [*weet*]
eighteen, dix-huit [*dee-zweet*]
eighth, huitième [*wee-tyem*]
eighty, quatre-vingts [*kah-truh-vẽ*]
either . . . or, ou . . . ou [*oo . . . oo*]
elastic, élastique [*eh-lahs-teek*]
elated, ravi [*rah-vee*]
elbow, coude (m) [*kood*]
elderly, agé [*ah-zheh*]
elect *v.*, élire (irreg) [*eh-leer*]
election, élection (f) [*eh-lek-syõ*]
electric, électrique [*eh-lek-treek*]
electricity, électricité (f) [*eh-lek-tree-see-teh*]
elegance, élégance (f) [*eh-leh-gãs*]
elegant, élégant [*eh-leh-gã(t)*]
element, élément (m) [*eh-leh-mã*]

elementary, élémentaire [*eh-leh-mã-ter*]
elephant, éléphant (m) [*eh-leh-fã*]
elevator, ascenseur (m) [*ah-sã-suhr*]
eleven, onze [*õz*]
eliminate v., éliminer [*eh-lee-mee-neh*]
else, autre, d'autre [*ohtr, dohtr*]
  nothing else, rien d'autre [*ryẽ dohtr*]
  someone else, quelqu'un d'autre [*kel-kẽ dohtr*]
  What else? Quoi d'autre? [*kwah dohtr*]
embargo n., embargo (m) [*ã-bahr-go*]
embark v., s'embarquer [*sã-bahr-keh*]
embarrass v., embarrasser [*ã-bah-rah-seh*]
embarrassed, confus, gêné [*kõ-fü(z), zhe-neh*]
embassy, ambassade (f) [*ã-bah-sahd*]
embroidery, broderie (f) [*brod-ree*]
emerald, émeraude (f) [*em-rohd*]
emergency, cas (m) urgent [*kah ür-zhã*]
  in case of emergency, en cas d'urgence [*ã kah dür-zhãs*]
emigrant, émigrant, -e [*eh-mee-grã(t)*]
emigration, émigration (f) [*eh-mee-grah-syõ*]
emotion, émotion (f) [*eh-moh-syõ*]
emphasis, insistance (f) [*ẽ-sees-tãs*]
emphasize v., accentuer [*ah-ksã-tweh*]
employee, employé, -ée [*ã-plwah-yeh*]
employer, employeur (m) [*ã-plwah-yuhr*]
employment, emploi (m) [*ã-plwah*]
employment agency, bureau (m) de placement [*bü-roht-plahs-mã*]
empty, vide [*veed*]
enclose [surround] v., clôturer [*kloh-tü-reh*]
enclose [in letter] v., joindre (irreg) [*zhwẽdr*]
encourage v., encourager [*ã-koo-rah-zheh*]
encouragement, encouragement (m) [*ã-koo-rahzh-mã*]
end [ending] n., fin (f), bout (m) [*fẽ, boo*]
  at the end of the road, au bout du chemin [*oh boo dü shmẽ*]
end [aim] n., but (m) [*bü(t)*]
end v., finir [*fee-neer*]

endless, sans fin [*sã-fẽ*]
endorse *v.*, endosser [*ã-doh-seh*]
endure *v.*, supporter [*sü-por-teh*]
enemy, ennemi (m) [*en-mee*]
energetic, énergique [*eh-ner-zheek*]
energy, énergie (f) [*eh-ner-zhee*]
engaged, fiancé [*fyã-seh*]
engagement [betrothal], fiançailles (f, pl) [*fyã-sahy*]
engagement [appointment], engagement (m) [*ã-gahzh-mã*]
engine, moteur (m) [*moh-tuhr*]
engine [train], locomotive (f) [*lo-koh-moh-teev*]
engineer, ingénieur (m) [*ẽ-zheh-nyuhr*]
engineer [train], mécanicien (m) [*meh-kah-nee-syẽ*]
England, Angleterre (f) [*ã-gluh-ter*]
English, anglais [*ã-gle(z)*]
enjoy *v.*, aimer [*eh-meh*]
   enjoy oneself, s'amuser [*sah-mü-zeh*]
   Enjoy yourself! Amusez-vous bien! [*ah-mü-zeh-voo byẽ*]
enormous, énorme [*eh-norm*]
enough, assez [*ah-seh*]
enroll *v.*, s'inscrire (irreg) [*sẽ-skreer*]
enter *v.*, entrer (*Aux:* ÊTRE) [*ã-treh*]
   Do not enter! N'entrez pas! [*nã-treh pah*]
enterprise, entreprise (f) [*ã-truh-preez*]
entertain [guests] *v.*, recevoir (irreg) [*ruh-suh-vwahr*]
entertain [amuse] *v.*, amuser [*ah-mü-zeh*]
entertaining, amusant [*ah-mü-zã(t)*]
entertainment, divertissement (m) [*dee-ver-tees-mã*]
enthusiasm, enthousiasme (m) [*ã-too-zyahzm*]
entire, entier, -tière [*ã-tyeh, ã-tyer*]
entirely, entièrement [*ã-tyer-mã*]
entrance, entrée (f) [*ã-treh*]
envelope, *n.*, enveloppe (f) [*ã-vlop*]
environment, milieu (m), environnement (m) [*meel-yuh, ã-vee-ron-mã*]
envy *v.*, envier [*ã-vyeh*]
equal, égal, -aux (m, pl) [*eh-gahl, eh-goh*]
equality, égalité (f) [*eh-gah-lee-teh*]

EQ_____46

equipment, équipement (m) [*eh-keep-mã*]
erase *v.*, effacer [*eh-fah-seh*]
eraser, gomme (f) [*gom*]
errand, course (f) [*koors*]
error, erreur (f) [*eh-ruhr*]
escape *v.*, s'échapper [*seh-shah-peh*]
especially, spécialement [*speh-syahl-mã*]
essential, essentiel, -elle [*eh-sã-syel*]
establish *v.*, établir [*eh-tah-bleer*]
establishment, établissement (m) [*eh-tah-blees-mã*]
estate [land], propriété (f) [*pro-pree-yeh-teh*]
estate [inheritance], succession (f) [*sük-ses-syõ*]
esteem *v.*, estimer [*es-tee-meh*]
estimate *n.*, devis (m) [*duh-vee*]
estimate *v.*, estimer [*es-tee-meh*]
eternal, éternel, -elle [*eh-ter-nel*]
Europe, Europe (f) [*uh-rop*]
European, européen, -enne [*uh-ro-peh-ẽ, uh-ro-peh-en*]
eve, veille (f) [*vey*]
   Christmas Eve, la veille de Noël [*lah vey duh noh-el*]
even *adv.*, même [*mem*]
   even so, quand même [*kã mem*]
   even then, même à cette époque [*mem ah se-teh-pok*]
   even though, bien que, même si [*byẽ k(uh), mem see*]
even [number], nombre (m) pair [*nõ-bruh per*]
evening, soir (m), soirée (f) [*swahr, swah-reh*]
   Good evening! Bonsoir! [*bõ-swahr*]
   in the evening, le soir [*luh swahr*]
event, événement (m) [*eh-ven-mã*]
   in the event of, au cas où [*oh kah oo*]
eventually, finalement [*fee-nahl-mã*]
ever, jamais [*zhah-meh*]
   as ever, comme toujours [*kom too-zhoor*]
every, chaque [*shahk*]
   every day, tous les jours [*too leh zhoor*]
everybody, tout le monde [*tool mõd*]
everything, tout [*too*]
everywhere, partout [*pahr-too*]

evidence, preuves (f, pl) [*pruhv*]
evident, évident [*eh-vee-dā(t)*]
evidently, évidemment [*eh-vee-dah-mā*]
evil *adj.*, mauvais [*mo-ve(z)*]
exact, exact [*eg-zah, eg-zahkt*]
exactly, exactement [*eg-zahk-tuh-mā*]
exaggerate *v.*, exagérer [*eg-zah-zheh-reh*]
examination, examen (m) [*eg-zah-mē*]
examine *v.*, examiner [*eg-zah-mee-neh*]
example, exemple (m) [*eg-zāpl*]
exceed *v.*, dépasser [*deh-pah-seh*]
excellent, excellent [*ek-se-lā(t)*]
except, excepté, sauf [*ek-sep-teh, sohf*]
exception, exception (f) [*ek-sep-syō*]
excess, excédent (m) [*ek-seh-dā*]
exchange *n.*, échange (m) [*eh-shāzh*]
exchange [money] *n.*, change (m) [*shāzh*]
   rate of exchange, taux (m) de change, cours (m) [*toht shāzh, koor*]
exchange *v.*, échanger [*eh-shā-zheh*]
excited, agité [*ah-zhee-teh*]
excursion, excursion (f) [*eks-kür-syō*]
excuse *v.*, excuser [*ek-skü-zeh*]
   Excuse me! Excusez-moi!, Pardon! [*ek-skü-zeh-mwah, pahr-dō*]
exercise *n.*, exercice (m) [*eg-zer-sees*]
exhausted, épuisé [*eh-pwee-zeh*]
exhibit *v.*, exposer [*ek-spoh-zeh*]
exhibition, exposition (f) [*eks-poh-zee-syō*]
exile, exil (m) [*eg-zeel*]
exist *v.*, exister [*eg-zees-teh*]
existence, existence (f) [*eg-zees-tās*]
exit *n.*, sortie (f) [*sor-tee*]
expect *v.*, s'attendre (à) [*sah-tā-dr(ah)*]
expedition, expédition (f) [*ek-speh-dee-syō*]
expense, dépense (f) [*deh-pās*]
expensive, cher, chère [*sher*]
experience *n.*, expérience (f) [*eks-per-yās*]

experiment *n.*, expérience (f) [*eks-per-yãs*]
expert, expert [*eks-per(t)*]
explain *v.*, expliquer [*eks-plee-keh*]
explanation, explication (f) [*eks-plee-kah-syõ*]
explore *v.*, explorer [*eks-plo-reh*]
explosion, explosion (f) [*eks-ploh-zyõ*]
export *v.*, exporter [*eks-por-teh*]
express [train], express (m); rapide (m) [*eks-pres, rah-peed*]
express *v.*, exprimer [*eks-pree-meh*]
expression, expression (f) [*eks-pre-syõ*]
extent, étendue (f) [*eh-tã-dü*]
  to a certain extent, jusqu'à un certain point [*zhüs-kah ẽ ser-tẽ pwẽ*]
exterior, extérieur (m) [*eks-ter-yuhr*]
external, extérieur [*eks-ter-yuhr*]
extinguish *v.*, éteindre (irreg) [*eh-tẽdr*]
extra, supplémentaire [*sii-pleh-mã-ter*]
extract *v.*, extraire (irreg) [*ek-strer*]
extraction, extraction (f) [*ek-strahk-syõ*]
extraordinary, extraordinaire [*ek-strah-or-dee-ner*]
extreme, extrême [*ek-strem*]
extremely, extrêmement [*ek-strem-mã*]
eye, oeil (m), yeux (pl) [*uhy, yuh*]
eyebrow, sourcil (m) [*soor-see*]
eye doctor, oculiste (m) [*o-kü-leest*]
eyelash, cil (m) [*seel*]
eyelid, paupière (f) [*poh-pyer*]
eyesight, vue (f) [*vü*]

F

face *n.*, visage (m) [*vee-zahzh*]
face *v.*, faire face à [*fer fahs ah*]
fact, fait (m) [*fe*]
  in fact, en fait [*ã fe(t)*]

factory, usine (f) [*ü-zeen*]

faculty [ability], faculté [*fah-kül-teh*]

faculty [of college], corps professoral (m) [*kor pro-feh-so-rahl*]

fade *v.*, déteindre (irreg) [*deh-tēdr*]

fail *v.*, échouer [*eh-shweh*]

failure, échec (m) [*eh-shek*]

faint *v.*, s'évanouir [*seh-vah-nweer*]

fair [just] *adj.*, juste [*zhüst*]

fair [light] *adj.*, clair [*kler*]

fair [pretty] *adj.*, joli [*zho-lee*]

fair *n.*, foire (f) [*fwahr*]

faith, foi (f) [*fwah*]

faithful, fidèle [*fee-del*]

fall [descent] *n.*, chute (f) [*shüt*]

fall [season] *n.*, automne (m) [*oh-ton*]

fall *v.*, tomber (*Aux:* ÊTRE) [*tō-beh*]

   fall in love (with), tomber amoureux (de) [*tō-beh ah-moo-ruh (duh)*]

false, faux, fausse [*foh, fohs*]

fame, renommée (f) [*ruh-no-meh*]

familiar, bien connu; familier, -ière [*byē ko-nü; fah-meel-yeh, fah-meel-yer*]

family, famille (f) [*fah-meey*]

famous, célèbre [*seh-lebr*]

fan [hand], éventail (m) [*eh-vā-tahy*]

fan [electric], ventilateur (m) [*vā-tee-lah-tuhr*]

far, loin [*lwē*]

   How far? À quelle distance? [*ah kel dees-tās*]

fare [transportation], prix (m) [*pree*]

farewell, adieu (m), -ieux (pl) [*ah-dyuh*]

farm *n.*, ferme (f) [*ferm*]

farmer, agriculteur (m) [*ah-gree-kül-tuhr*]

farmyard, basse-cour (f) [*bahs-koor*]

farther, plus loin [*plü lwē*]

farthest, le plus loin [*luh plü lwē*]

fascinating, fascinant [*fah-see-nā(t)*]

fashion *n.*, mode (f) [*mod*]

fashionable, à la mode [*ah lah mod*]
fast *adj.*, rapide [*rah-peed*]
fast *adv.*, vite [*veet*]
fasten *v.*, attacher [*ah-tah-sheh*]
fat [person] *adj.*, gros, grosse [*groh, grohs*]
fat [animal] *adj.*, gras, grasse [*grah, grahs*]
fat [cooking] *n.*, graisse (f) [*gres*]
fate, destin (m) [*des-tē*]
father, père (m) [*per*]
father-in-law, beau-père (m) [*boh-per*]
fatigue, fatigue (f) [*fah-teeg*]
faucet, robinet (m) [*ro-bee-neh*]
fault *n.*, faute (f) [*foht*]
favor *n.*, faveur (f) [*fah-vuhr*]
  Will you do me a favor? Voulez-vous me faire plaisir?
    [*voo-leh-voom fer ple-zeer*]
favorite, préféré [*preh-feh-reh*]
fear *n.*, peur (f), crainte (f) [*puhr, krēt*]
fear *v.*, craindre (irreg) [*krēdr*]
fearful [afraid], peureux, -euse [*puh-ruh, puh-ruhz*]
fearless, sans crainte [*sã krēt*]
feast *n.*, fête (f) [*fet*]
feather, plume (f) [*plüm*]
feature [of face] *n.*, trait (m) [*tre*]
February, février (m) [*feh-vree-yeh*]
federal, fédéral, -aux (m, pl) [*feh-deh-rahl, feh-deh-roh*]
fee, honoraires (m, pl) [*o-no-rer*]
feed *v.*, nourrir [*noo-reer*]
feel *v.*, sentir (irreg), se sentir (irreg) [*sã-teer, suh sã-teer*]
feeling, sentiment (m) [*sã-tee-mã*]
feet, pieds (m, pl) [*pyeh*]
fellow, collègue (m) [*ko-leg*]
  He's a good fellow! C'est un brave type! [*se-tē brahv teep*]
female, femelle (f) [*fuh-mel*]
feminine, féminin [*feh-mee-nē, feh-mee-neen*]
fence, barrière (f) [*bah-ryer*]
fencing, escrime (f) [*es-kreem*]
fender, aile (f) [*el*]

ferryboat, bac (m) [*bahk*]

festival, festival (m), -aux (pl) [*fes-tee-vahl, fes-tee-voh*]

fever, fièvre (f) [*fyevr*]

few, peu (de) [*puh (duh)*]
  a few, quelques [*kelk*]

fewer, moins (de) [*mwĕ (duh)*]

fiancé, fiancé [*fyã-seh*]

fiancée, fiancée [*fyã-seh*]

field, champ (m) [*shã*]

field glasses, jumelles (f, pl) [*zhü-mel*]

fierce, féroce [*feh-ros*]

fifteen, quinze [*kĕz*]

fifth, cinquième [*sĕ-kyem*]

fifty, cinquante [*sĕ-kãt*]

fig, figue (f) [*feeg*]

fight *n.,* combat (m) [*kõ-bah*]

fight *v.,* se battre (irreg) [*s(uh) bahtr*]

figure [number], chiffre (m) [*sheefr*]

figure [form], silhouette (f) [*seel-wet*]

file [tool] *n.,* lime (f) [*leem*]

file [record] *n.,* dossier (m) [*doh-syeh*]

fill *v.,* remplir [*rã-pleer*]
  Fill up with regular (super), Le plein normal (super) [*luh plĕ nor-mahl (sü-per)*]

filling [tooth], plombage (m) [*plõ-bahzh*]

film, pellicule (f) [*peh-lee-kül*]

filter, filtre (m) [*feeltr*]

filthy, très sale [*tre sahl*]

final, final, -aux (m, pl) [*fee-nahl, fee-noh*]

finally, finalement [*fee-nahl-mã*]

financial, financier, -ière [*fee-nã-syeh, fee-nã-syer*]

find *v.,* trouver [*troo-veh*]

fine [small] *adj.,* fin [*fĕ, feen*]

fine [good] *adj.,* excellent [*ek-se-lã(t)*]

fine *n.,* amende (f) [*ah-mãd*]

finger, doigt (m) [*dwah*]

finish *v.,* finir [*fee-neer*]

fire, feu (m), incendie (m) [*fuh, ĕ-sã-dee*]

Fire! Au feu! [*oh fuh*]
fireman, pompier (m) [*pŏ-pyeh*]
fireplace, cheminée (f) [*shmee-neh*]
firm *n.*, firme (f), entreprise (f) [*feerm, ã-truh-preez*]
firm *adj.*, ferme [*ferm*]
first, premier, -ière [*pruh-myeh, pruh-myer*]
   at first, d'abord [*dah-bor*]
first aid, premiers secours (m) [*pruh-myeh skoor*]
first name, prénom (m) [*preh-nŏ*]
fish *n.*, poisson (m) [*pwah-sŏ*]
fish *v.*, pêcher [*pe-sheh*]
fisherman, pêcheur (m) [*pe-shuhr*]
fishing, pêche (f) [*pesh*]
fist, poing (m) [*pwẽ*]
fit *v.*, aller (irreg) bien [*ah-leh byẽ*]
fitting *n.*, essayage (m) [*eh-se-yazh*]
five, cinq [*sẽ(k)*]
fix [attach] *v.*, attacher [*ah-tah-sheh*]
fix [repair] *v.*, réparer, arranger [*reh-pah-reh, ah-rã-zheh*]
fixed price, prix fixe (m) [*pree feeks*]
flag, drapeau (m), -eaux (pl) [*drah-poh*]
flame, flamme (f) [*flahm*]
flat, plat [*plah(t)*]
flatter *v.*, flatter [*flah-teh*]
flatterer, flatteur, -euse [*flah-tuhr, flah-tuhz*]
flavor [taste] *n.*, saveur (f) [*sah-vuhr*]
flavor *v.*, assaisonner [*ah-se-zo-neh*]
flea, puce (f) [*püs*]
flea market, marché (m) aux puces [*mahr-sheh oh püs*]
flee, fuir (irreg) [*fweer*]
fleet [ships] *n.*, flotte (f) [*flot*]
flesh, chair (f) [*sher*]
flexible, souple [*soopl*]
flight, vol (m) [*vol*]
flirt *v.*, flirter [*fluhr-teh*]
float *v.*, flotter [*flo-teh*]
flood, inondation (f) [*ee-nŏ-dah-syŏ*]
floor, plancher (m) [*plã-sheh*]

flour, farine (f) [*fah-reen*]
flow v., couler [*koo-leh*]
flower, fleur (f) [*fluhr*]
florist, fleuriste (m) [*fluh-reest*]
fluently, couramment [*koo-rah-mã*]
flush [the toilet] v., tirer la chasse [*tee-reh lah shahs*]
flute, flute (f) [*flüt*]
fly n., mouche (f) [*moosh*]
fly v., voler [*vo-leh*]
foam [waves] n., écume (f) [*eh-küm*]
foam [of beverage] n., mousse (f) [*moos*]
foe, adversaire (m) [*ahd-ver-ser*]
fog n., brouillard (m) [*broo-yahr*]
  It's foggy, Il fait du brouillard [*eel fe dü broo-yahr*]
fold v., plier [*plee-yeh*]
follow v., suivre (irreg) [*sweevr*]
fond: to be fond of, aimer [*e-meh*]
food, nourriture (f) [*noo-ree-tür*]
fool n., imbécile (m) [*ẽ-beh-seel*]
foolish, fou, folle; sot, sotte [*foo, fol; soh, sot*]
foot [anat.], pied (m) [*pyeh*]
foot [measure], trente centimètres [*trãt sã-tee-metr*]
football [game], rugby (m) [*rüg-bee*]
football [ball], ballon (m) de rugby [*bah-lõ duh rüg-bee*]
for prep., pour [*poor*]
  for example, par exemple [*pahr eg-zãpl*]
for [time], depuis, pendant [*duh-pwee, pã-dã*]
  I have been here for three hours, Je suis ici depuis trois
    heures [*shswee-zee-see duh-pwee trwah-zuhr*]
  I was there for three days, J'étais là pendant trois jours
    [*zheh-te lah pã-dã trwah zhoor*]
for [because] conj., car [*kahr*]
forbid v., interdire (irreg) [*ẽ-ter-deer*]
force n., force (f) [*fors*]
force v., forcer [*for-seh*]
forehead, front (m) [*frõ*]
foreign, étranger, -ère [*eh-trã-zheh, eh-trã-zher*]
foreign minister, ministre des affaires étrangères [*mee-*

neestr deh-zah-fer eh-trã-zher]

foreign office, ministère des affaires étrangères [*mee-nees-ter deh-zah-fer eh-trã-zher*]

foreign policy, politique internationale (f) [*po-lee-teek ẽ-ter-nah-syo-nahl*]

foreigner, étranger, -ère [*eh-trã-zheh, eh-trã-zher*]

forest, forêt (f) [*fo-re*]

forever, pour toujours [*poor too-zhoor*]

forget *v.,* oublier [*oo-blee-yeh*]

forgive *v.,* pardonner [*pahr-do-neh*]

forgotten, oublié [*oo-blee-yeh*]

fork, fourchette (f) [*foor-shet*]

form [shape] *n.,* forme, (f) [*form*]

form [questionnaire] *n.,* imprimé (m) [*ẽ-pree-meh*]

form *v.,* former [*for-meh*]

formal, formel, -elle [*for-mel*]

formality, formalité (f) [*for-mah-lee-teh*]

former, ancien, -enne [*ã-syẽ, ã-syen*]

formerly, avant, précédemment [*ah-vã, preh-seh-dah-mã*]

formula, formule (f) [*for-mül*]

fort, fort (m), forteresse (f) [*for, for-tuh-res*]

fortunate, heureux, -euse; fortuné [*uh-ruh, uh-ruhz; for-tü-neh*]

  be fortunate *v.,* avoir de la chance [*ah-vwahr dlah shãs*]

fortunately, heureusement [*uh-ruhz-mã*]

fortune, fortune (f) [*for-tün*)

forty, quarante [*kah-rãt*]

forward, en avant [*ã-nah-vã*]

foundation, fondation (f) [*fõ-dah-syõ*]

fountain, fontaine (f) [*fõ-ten*]

fountain pen, stylo (m) [*stee-loh*]

four, quatre [*kahtr*]

fourteen, quatorze [*kah-torz*]

fourth, quatrième [*kah-tree-yem*]

fracture *n.,* fracture (f) [*frahk-tür*]

fragile, fragile [*frah-zheel*]

fragrance, parfum (m) [*pahr-fẽ*]

frame *n.,* cadre (m) [*kahdr*]

France, France (f) [*frãs*]

frank, franc, franche [*frã, frãsh*]

fraud, fraude [*frohd*]

free [not bound] *adj.*, libre [*leebr*]

free [at no cost] *adj.*, gratuit [*grah-twee(t)*]

free *v.*, libérer [*lee-beh-reh*]

freedom, liberté (f) [*lee-ber-teh*]

freeze *v.*, geler [*zhuh-leh*]

freight, frêt (m) [*fre*]

French, français [*frã-se(z)*]

Frenchman, -woman, Français, -se [*frã-se(z)*]

frequent, fréquent [*freh-kã(t)*]

frequently, souvent [*soo-vã*]

fresh, frais, fraiche [*fre, fresh*]

Friday, vendredi (m) [*vã-druh-dee*]

fried, frit [*free(t)*]

friend, ami, amie [*ah-mee*]

friendship, amitié (f) [*ah-mee-tyeh*]

frighten *v.*, faire peur à [*fer puhr ah*]

frog, grenouille (f) [*gruh-nooy*]

from, de [*duh*]

   from now on, désormais [*deh-zor-me*]

front, devant (m) [*duh-vã*]

frost, gelée (f) [*zhuh-leh*]

frown *v.*, froncer les sourcils [*frõ-seh leh soor-see*]

fruit, fruit (m) [*frwee*]

fry *v.*, faire frire (irreg) [*fer freer*]

frying pan, poêle (f) [*pwahl*]

full, plein [*plẽ, plen*]

fun, amusement (m) [*ah-müz-mã*]

   Have fun! Amusez-vous bien! [*ah-mü-zeh-voo byẽ*]

function, fonction (f) [*fõk-syõ*]

funds *pl.*, fonds (m, pl) [*fõ*]

funeral, enterrement (m) [*ã-ter-mã*]

funnel *n.*, entonnoir (m) [*ã-ton-wahr*]

funny, drôle [*drohl*]

fur, fourrure (f) [*foo-rür*]

furious, furieux, -euse [*für-yuh, für-yuhz*]

furnish [provide] *v.*, fournir [*foor-neer*]
furnish [put furniture into] *v.*, meubler [*muh-bleh*]
furnished room, chambre (f) meublée [*shãbr muh-bleh*]
furniture, meubles (m, pl) [*muhbl*]
further *adj.*, ultérieur [*iil-tehr-yuhr*]
furthermore, de plus [*duh plü*]
future, futur (m) [*fü-tür*]
   in the future, à l'avenir [*ah lahv-neer*]

G

gadget, truc (m), appareil (m) [*trük, ah-pah-rey*]
gain *v.*, gagner [*gah-nyeh*]
gallon, gallon (m), quatre litres (m) [*gah-lõ, kahtr leetr*]
gamble *v.*, jouer [*zhweh*]
gambling, jeu (de hasard) (m) [*zhuh (duh ah-zahr)*]
game, jeu (m) [*zhuh*]
gangplank, passerelle (f) [*pahs-rel*]
garage, garage (m) [*gah-rahzh*]
garbage, ordures (f, pl) [*or-dür*]
garden, jardin (m) [*zhahr-dẽ*]
gardener, jardinier (m) [*zhahr-dee-nyeh*]
garlic, ail (m) [*ahy*]
garment, vêtement (m) [*vet-mã*]
garter, jarretière (f) [*zhahr-tyer*]
gas, gaz (m) [*gahz*]
gasoline, essence (f) [*eh-sãs*]
   be out of gas *v.*, être en panne d'essence [*e-trã pahn deh-sãs*]
gasoline station, station service (f), poste à essence (m)
      [*stah-syõ ser-vees, post ah e-sãs*]
gas tank, réservoir à essence (m) [*re-zer-vwahr ah eh-sãs*]
gate, portail (m) [*por-tahy*]
gather *v.*, ramasser [*rah-mah-seh*]
gauge *n.*, jauge (f) [*zhohzh*]
gay, gai [*ghe*]

gear [auto] *n.*, vitesse (f) [*vee-tes*]
  put in gear *v.*, embrayer [*ã-bre-yeh*]
  change gear *v.*, changer de vitesse [*shã-zhehd vee-tes*]
gender, genre (m) [*zhãr*]
general *n.*, général (m), -aux (pl) [*zheh-neh-rahl, zheh-neh-roh*]
general *adj.*, général, -aux (m, pl) [*zhe-neh-rahl, zheh-neh-roh*]
  in general, en général [*ã zheh-neh-rahl*]
general delivery, poste restante (f) [*post res-tãt*]
generation, génération (f)]*zheh-neh-rah-syõ*]
generous, généreux, -euse [*zheh-neh-ruh, zheh-neh-ruhz*]
gentle, doux, douce [*doo, doos*]
gentleman, gentlemen, monsieur, messieurs [*muh-syuh, meh-syuh*]
genuine, véritable [*veh-ree-tahbl*]
geography, géographie (f) [*zheh-oh-grah-fee*]
geometry, géométrie (f) [*zheh-oh-meh-tree*]
germ, microbe (m) [*mee-krob*]
German, allemand [*ahl-mã(d)*]
Germany, Allemagne (f) [*ahl-mañ*]
get [become] *v.*, devenir (irreg; Aux: ÊTRE) [*duh-vneer*]
get [obtain] *v.*, obtenir (irreg) [*op-tuh-neer*]
get [receive] *v.*, recevoir (irreg) [*ruh-suh-vwar*]
  get down, descendre (Aux: ÊTRE) [*deh-sãdr*]
  get in, entrer (Aux: ÊTRE) [*ã-treh*]
  get married, se marier [*smah-ryeh*]
  get off, descendre (irreg; Aux: ÊTRE) [*deh-sãdr*]
  get up, se lever [*sluh-veh*]
ghost, fantôme (m) [*fã-tohm*]
gift, cadeau (m), -eaux (pl) [*kah-doh*]
gifted, doué [*doo-eh*]
gin, gin (m) [*jeen*]
girdle, gaine (f) [*ghen*]
girl, fille (f) [*feey*]
give *v.*, donner [*do-neh*]
  give back, rendre [*rãdr*]
  give in, céder [*seh-deh*]
glad, content [*kõ-tã(t)*]
glance *n.*, coup d'oeil (m) [*koo duhy*]

glance *v.*, jeter un coup d'oeil [*zh(uh)-teh ē koo duhy*]
glass, verre (m) [*ver*]
glasses [eye], lunettes (f, pl) [*lü-net*]
glory, gloire (f) [*glwahr*]
glove, gant (m) [*gã*]
glue, colle (f) [*kol*]
go *v.*, aller (irreg; *Aux:* ÊTRE) [*ah-leh*]
  go across, traverser [*trah-ver-seh*]
  go away, s'en aller (irreg; *Aux:* ÊTRE), partir (irreg; *Aux:* ÊTRE) [*sã-nah-leh, pahr-teer*]
  go back, retourner (*Aux:* ÊTRE) [*ruh-toor-neh*]
  go down, descendre (*Aux:* ÊTRE) [*deh-sãdr*]
  go in, entrer (*Aux:* ÊTRE) [*ã-treh*]
  go on, continuer [*kõ-tee-nweh*]
  go out, sortir (irreg; *Aux:* ÊTRE) [*sor-teer*]
  go to bed, se coucher [*skoo-sheh*]
  go up, monter (*Aux:* ÊTRE) [*mõ-teh*]
  go without, se passer de [*spah-seh duh*]
goal, but (m) [*bü(t)*]
god, dieu (m), -eux (pl) [*dyuh*]
goddaughter, filleule (f) [*fee-yuhl*]
godfather, parrain (m) [*pah-rē*]
godmother, marraine (f) [*mah-ren*]
godson, filleul (m) [*fee-yuhl*]
gold, or (m) [*or*]
golden, d'or [*dor*]
golf, golf (m) [*golf*]
good, bon, bonne [*bõ, bon*]
good afternoon, bonjour [*bõ-zhoor*]
good-bye, au revoir [*ohr-vwahr*]
good evening, bonsoir [*bõ-swahr*]
Good luck, Bonne chance [*bon shãs*]
good morning, bonjour [*bõ-zhoor*]
goodness, bonté (f) [*bõ-teh*]
good night, bonne nuit [*bon nwee*]
goods *pl.*, biens (m, pl), marchandise (f) [*byē, mahr-shã-deez*]
gorgeous, magnifique [*mah-nyee-feek*]
Gothic, gothique [*goh-teek*]

government, gouvernement (m) [goo-ver-nuh-mã]
governor, gouverneur (m) [goo-ver-nuhr]
grace, grâce (f) [grahs]
graceful, grâcieux, -cieuse [grah-syuh, grah-syuhz]
grade [class] n., classe (f) [klahs]
grade [mark] n., note (f) [not]
gradually, peu à peu [puh ah puh]
graduate n., diplômé, -ée [dee-ploh-meh]
graduate v., recevoir (irreg) son diplôme [ruh-suh-vwahr sõ
    dee-plohm]
grain, grain (m) [grẽ]
grammar, grammaire (f) [grah-mer]
grandchildren, petits-enfants (m, pl) [ptee-zã-fã]
granddaughter, petite fille (f) [pteet-feey]
grandfather, grandpère (m) [grã-per]
grandmother, grandmère (f) [grã-mer]
grandparents, grands parents (m, pl) [grã pah-rã]
grandson, petit fils (m) [ptee fees]
grant v., accorder [ah-kor-deh]
grape, raisin (m) [re-zẽ]
grapefruit, pamplemousse (f) [pã-pluh-moos]
grass, herbe (f) [erb]
grateful, reconnaissant [ruh-ko-ne-sã(t)]
gratitude, reconnaissance (f) [ruh-ko-ne-sãs]
grave, n., tombe (f) [tõb]
gravy, sauce (f) [sohs]
gray, gris [gree(z)]
grease n., graisse (f) [gres]
great, grand [grã(d)]
    a great deal, a great many, beaucoup (de) [boh-koo (duh)]
Great Britain, Grande Bretagne (f) [grãd bruh-tahñ]
Greece, Grèce (f) [gres]
Greek, grec, grecque [grek]
green, vert [ver(t)]
greet v., saluer [sahl-weh]
greetings, salutations (f, pl) [sah-lü-tah-syõ]
grief, douleur (f) [doo-luhr]
grind v., moudre (irreg) [moodr]

groan *n.*, gémissement (m) [*zheh-mees-mã*]
groan *v.*, gémir [*zheh-meer*]
grocery, épicerie (f) [*eh-pees-ree*]
ground [earth] *n.*, terre (f) [*ter*]
  on the ground, par terre [*pahr ter*]
ground floor, rez-de-chaussée (m) [*ret-shoh-seh*]
group, groupe (m) [*groop*]
grow [cultivate] *v.*, cultiver [*kül-tee-veh*]
grow [increase] *v.*, croître (irreg) [*krwahtr*]
grow [mature] *v.*, grandir [*grã-deer*]
grudge *n.*, rancune (f) [*rã-kün*]
guarantee *n.*, garantie (f) [*gah-rã-tee*]
guarantee *v.*, garantir [*gah-rã-teer*]
guard *n.*, gardien (m) [*gahr-dyẽ*]
guard [military] *n.*, garde (f) [*gahrd*]
guard *v.*, protéger [*pro-teh-zheh*]
guess *v.*, deviner [*d(uh)-vee-neh*]
guest, invité, -ée [*ẽ-vee-teh*]
guide *n.*, guide (m) [*gheed*]
guilty, coupable [*koo-pahbl*]
guitar, guitare (f) [*ghee-tahr*]
gum [anat.], gencive (f) [*zhã-seev*]
gum [chewing], chewing-gum (m) [*shween-gom*]
gun, fusil (m) [*fü-zee*]
gutter [street], ruisseau (m), -eaux (pl) [*rwee-soh*]
gutter [roof], gouttière (f) [*goo-tyer*]
gymnasium, gymnase (m) [*zheem-nahz*]
gypsy, gitan, gitane [*zhee-tã, zhee-tahn*]

H

habit [custom] *n.*, habitude (f) [*ah-bee-tüd*]
hail *n.*, grêle (f) [*grel*]
hair, cheveux (m, pl) [*shvuh*]
haircut, coupe (f) de cheveux [*koop duh shvuh*]

hairdresser, coiffeur, -euse [*kwah-fuhr, kwah-fuhz*]

half n., moitié (f) [*mwah-tyeh*]

half adj., demi [*dmee*]

  three and a half, trois et demi [*trwah ehd-mee*]

  half past two, deux heures et demie [*duh-zuhr ehd-mee*]

halfway, à mi-chemin [*ah mee-shmē*]

hall [corridor], couloir (m) [*kool-wahr*]

hall [auditorium], salle (f) [*sahl*]

ham, jambon (m) [*zhã-bõ*]

hammer, marteau (m), -eaux (pl) [*mahr-toh*]

hand, main (f) [*mē*]

  on the other hand, d'autre part [*doh-truh pahr*]

handbag, sac (m) à main [*sah-kah mē*]

handkerchief, mouchoir (m) [*moo-shwahr*]

handle n., poignée (f) [*pwah-nyeh*]

handmade, fait main [*fe mē*]

handsome, beau (bel), belle; beaux, belles [*boh, bel*]

hang v., pendre [*pãdr*]

  hang up [telephone], raccrocher [*rah-kro-sheh*]

  Don't hang up, Ne quittez pas [*nuh kee-teh pah*]

happen v., arriver (Aux: ÊTRE) [*ah-ree-veh*]

  What's happening? Qu'est-ce qui se passe? [*kes kees pahs*]

  What happened? Qu'est-ce qui est arrivé? [*kes kye-tah-ree-veh*]

happiness, bonheur (m) [*bo-nuhr*]

happy, heureux, -euse; content [*uh-ruh, uh-ruhz; kõ-tã(t)*]

  Happy Birthday! Bon anniversaire! [*bon-nah-nee-ver-ser*]

  Happy New Year! Bonne Année! [*bo-nah-neh*]

harbor n., port (m) [*por*]

hard [difficult], difficile [*dee-fee-seel*]

hard [solid], dur [*dür*]

hardly, à peine [*ah pen*]

harm v., faire du mal (à) [*fer dü mahl (ah)*]

harmful, nuisible [*nwee-zeebl*]

harp, *harpe (f) [*ahrp*]

harvest, moisson (f) [*mwah-sõ*]

haste, *hâte (f) [*aht*]

hat, chapeau (m), -eaux (pl) [*shah-poh*]

hate *n.*, *haine (f) [*en*]

hate *v.*, *haïr (irreg) [*ah-eer*]

have *v.*, avoir (irreg) [*ah-vwahr*]
  have to [must], devoir [plus infinitive] (irreg) [*duh-vwahr*]

he, il, lui [*eel, lwee*]

head, tête (f) [*tet*]

headache, mal de tête (m) [*mahl duh tet*]

headlight, phare (m) [*fahr*]

headquarters [military], quartier général (m) [*kahr-tyeh
    zheh-neh-rahl*]

headquarters [business], siège (m) [*syezh*]

health, santé (f) [*sã-teh*]
  in good health, en bonne santé [*ã bon sã-teh*]

healthy, sain [*sẽ, sen*]

hear *v.*, entendre [*ã-tãdr*]
  hear of [about], entendre parler de [*ã-tãdr pahr-leh duh*]
  hear that, entendre dire que [*ã-tãdr deer kuh*]

heart, coeur (m) [*kuhr*]
  by heart, par coeur [*pahr kuhr*]

heart attack, crise cardiaque, infarctus [*kreez kahr-dyahk,
    ẽ-fahrk-tüs*]

heat *n.*, chaleur (f) [*shah-luhr*]

heat *v.*, chauffer [*shoh-feh*]

heating, chauffage (m) [*shoh-fahzh*]

heaven, ciel (m), cieux (pl) [*syel, syuh*]

heavy, lourd [*loor(d)*]

Hebrew, hébreu [*eh-bruh*]

heel, talon (m) [*tah-lõ*]

height [of person], taille (f) [*tahy*]

height [elevation], *hauteur (f) [*oh-tuhr*]

heir, héritier (m) [*eh-ree-tyeh*]

heiress, héritière (f) [*eh-ree-tyer*]

hell, enfer (m) [*ã-fer*]

hello, bonjour [*bõ-zhoor*]

hello [telephone], allo! [*ah-loh*]

help *n.*, secours (m) [*skoor*]
  Help! Au secours! [*ohs-koor*]

help v., aider [e-deh]
   I can't help doing it, Je ne peux pas m'empêcher de le
     faire [zhuhn puh pah mã-peh-shehd luh fer]
helpful, utile [ü-teel]
her pron., elle, la, lui [el, lah, lwee]
her poss. adj., son, sa, ses [sõ, sah, seh]
here, ici [ee-see]
   Here it is, Le (la) voilà [luh (lah) vwah-lah]
hers, le sien, la sienne; les siens, les siennes [luh syẽ, lah
     syen; leh syẽ, leh syen]
herself, elle-même [el-mem]
hesitate v., hésiter [eh-zee-teh]
hide v., cacher, se cacher [kah-sheh, skah-sheh]
high, *haut [oh(t)]
high school, école secondaire (f) [eh-kol suh-gõ-der]
hill, colline (f) [ko-leen]
him, le, lui [luh, lwee]
himself, lui-même [lwee-mem]
hinge n., charnière (f) [shahr-nyer]
hip, *hanche (f) [ãsh]
hire v., engager [ã-gah-zheh]
his adj., son, sa, ses [sõ, sah, seh]
his pron., le sien, la sienne; les siens, les siennes [luh syẽ,
     lah syen; leh syẽ, leh syen]
historical, historique [ees-to-reek]
history, histoire (f) [ees-twahr]
hit v., frapper [frah-peh]
hitchhiking, auto-stop (m) [oh-toh-stop]
hold v., tenir (irreg) [t(uh)-neer]
hole, trou (m) [troo]
holiday [religious], fête (f) [fet]
holiday [legal], jour férié (m) [zhoor fehr-yeh]
Holland, *Hollande (f) [oh-lãd]
holy, saint [sẽ(t)]
home, chez-soi (m, invar); maison (f) [sheh-swah, meh-zõ]
   at home, à la maison; chez soi (lui, elle) [ah lah meh-zõ;
     sheh-swah (sheh-lwee, sheh-zel)]
   Make yourself at home, Faites comme chez vous [fet

    kom sheh voo]
honest, honnête [*o-net*]
honey, miel (m) [*myel*]
honeymoon, lune (f) de miel [*lün duh myel*]
honor n., honneur (m) [*o-nuhr*]
honor v., honorer [*o-no-reh*]
hook n., crochet (m) [*kro-sheh*]
hope n., espoir (m) [*es-pwahr*]
hope v., espérer [*es-peh-reh*]
hopeful, plein d'espoir [*plē (plen) des-pwahr*]
hopeless, sans espoir [*sã-zes-pwahr*]
horn [animal or shape], corne (f) [*korn*]
horn [auto], klaxon (m) [*klah-ksō*]
horrible, horrible [*o-reebl*]
horse, cheval (m), -aux (pl) [*shvahl, shvoh*]
hospital, hôpital (m), -aux (pl) [*oh-pee-tahl, oh-pee-toh*]
hospitality, hospitalité (f) [*os-pee-tah-lee-teh*]
host, hôte (m) [*oht*]
hostess, hôtesse (f) [*oh-tes*]
hostile, hostile [*os-teel*]
hot, chaud [*shoh(d)*]
hotel, hôtel (m) [*oh-tel*]
hotel room, chambre d'hôtel (f) [*shãbr doh-tel*]
hour, heure (f) [*uhr*]
hourly, toutes les heures [*toot leh-zuhr*]
house, maison (f) [*me-zõ*]
housekeeper, ménagère (f) [*meh-nah-zher*]
housewife, maîtresse (f) de maison [*me-tres duh meh-zõ*]
how, comment [*ko-mã*]
    How do you do? Comment allez-vous? [*ko-mã-tah-leh-voo*]
    How many?, How much? Combien (de)? [*kõ-byē (duh)*]
however, cependant [*spã-dã*]
human, humain [*ü-mē, ü-men*]
humble, humble [*ēbl*]
humid, humide [*ü-meed*]
humidity, humidité (f) [*ü-mee-dee-teh*]
humorous, humoristique [*ü-mo-rees-teek*]
hundred, cent [*sã*]

Hungarian, *hongrois [õ-grwah(z)]
Hungary, *Hongrie (f) [õ-gree]
hunger, faim (f) [fẽ]
hungry: to be hungry, avoir faim [ah-vwahr fẽ]
hunt v., chasser [shah-seh]
hunter, chasseur (m) [shah-suhr]
hunting, chasse (f) [shahs]
hurry v., se dépêcher [sdeh-pe-sheh]
  be in a hurry v., être pressé [etr pre-seh]
  Hurry up! Dépêchez-vous! [deh-pe-sheh-voo]
hurt v., faire mal [fer mahl]
husband, mari (m) [mah-ree]

I

I, je [zhuh]
ice, glace (f) [glahs]
ice cream, glace (f) [glahs]
idea, idée (f) [ee-deh]
ideal, idéal, -aux (m, pl) [ee-deh-ahl, ee-deh-oh]
identical, identique [ee-dã-teek]
identification card, carte (f) d'identité [kahrt dee-dã-tee-teh]
identify v., identifier [ee-dã-tee-fyeh]
identity, identité (f) [ee-dã-tee-teh]
idiot, idiot [ee-dyoh, e-dyot]
if, si [see]
  even if, même si [mem see]
ignition, allumage (m) [ah-lü-mahzh]
ignorant, ignorant [ee-nyo-rã(t)]
ill, malade [mah-lahd]
illegal, illégal, -aux (m, pl) [ee-leh-gahl, ee-leh-goh]
illness, maladie (f) [mah-lah-dee]
image, image (f) [ee-mahzh]
imagination, imagination (f) [ee-mah-zhee-nah-syõ]
imagine v., imaginer [ee-mah-zhee-neh]

imitate *v.*, imiter [*ee-mee-teh*]
imitation, imitation (f) [*ee-mee-tah-syõ*]
immediate, immédiat [*ee-meh-dyah(t)*]
immediately, immédiatement [*ee-meh-dyaht-mã*]
immense, immense [*ee-mãs*]
immigration, immigration (f) [*ee-mee-grah-syõ*]
immoral, immoral, -aux (m, pl) [*ee-mo-rahl, ee-mo-roh*]
impartial, impartial, -aux (m, pl) [*ẽ-pahr-syahl, ẽ-pahr-syoh*]
impatient, impatient [*ẽ-pah-syã(t)*]
imperfect, imparfait [*ẽ-pahr-fe(t)*]
imperialism, impérialisme (m) [*ẽ-pehr-yah-leesm*]
impolite, impoli [*ẽ-po-lee*]
import *v.*, importer [*ẽ-por-teh*]
importance, importance (f) [*ẽ-por-tãs*]
important, important [*ẽ-por-tã(t)*]
imported, importé [*ẽ-por-teh*]
impossible, impossible [*ẽ-po-seebl*]
impression, impression (f) [*ẽ-pre-syõ*]
impressive, impressionnant [*ẽ-pre-syo-nã(t)*]
improbable, improbable [*ẽ-pro-bahbl*]
improve *v.*, améliorer, s'améliorer [*ah-meh-lyo-reh, sah-meh-lyo-reh*]
improvement, amélioration (f) [*ah-meh-lyo-rah-syõ*]
in, dans, en, à [*dã, ã, ah*]
  in back of, derrière [*der-yer*]
  in front of, devant [*duh-vã*]
  in spite of, malgré [*mahl-greh*]
  Mrs. Smith isn't in, Mme. Smith n'est pas ici [*mah-dahm smith ne pah-zee-see*]
inability, incapacité (f) [*ẽ-kah-pah-see-teh*]
inch, pouce (m) [*poos*]
incident, incident (m) [*ẽ-see-dã*]
inclination, tendance (f) [*tã-dãs*]
include *v.*, inclure (irreg) [*ẽ-klür*]
included, inclus [*ẽ-klü(z)*]
income, revenu (m) [*ruhv-nü*]
income tax, impôt (m) sur le revenu [*ẽ-poh sür luh ruhv-nü*]
incomparable, incomparable [*ẽ-kõ-pah-rahbl*]

incomplete, incomplet, -ète [ẽ-kõ-pleh, ẽ-kõ-plet]
inconvenience, dérangement (m) [deh-rãzh-mã]
incorrect, incorrect [ẽ-ko-rekt]
increase n., augmentation (f) [ohg-mã-tah-syõ]
increase v., augmenter [ohg-mã-teh]
incredible, incroyable [ẽ-krwah-yahbl]
indecent, indécent [ẽ-deh-sã(t)]
indeed, en effet [ã-neh-fe]
indefinite, indéfini [ẽ-deh-fee-nee]
independence, indépendance (f) [ẽ-deh-pã-dãs]
independent, indépendent [ẽ-deh-pã-dã(t)]
India, Inde (f) [ẽd]
Indian, indien, -enne [ẽ-dyẽ, ẽ-dyen]
indicate v., indiquer [ẽ-dee-keh]
indifferent, indifférent [ẽ-dee-feh-rã(t)]
indigestion, indigestion (f) [ẽ-dee-zhes-tyõ]
indignant, indigné [ẽ-dee-nyeh]
indirect, indirect [ẽ-dee-rekt]
indiscreet, indiscret, -ète [ẽ-dees-kreh, ẽ-dees-kret]
individual, individuel, -elle; particulier, -ère [ẽ-dee-vee-dwel; pahr-tee-kü-lyeh, pahr-tee-kü-lyer]
indoors, dans la maison, dedans [dã lah me-zõ, duh-dã]
industrial, industriel, -elle [ẽ-düs-tree-yel]
industry, industrie (f) [ẽ-düs-tree]
inefficient, inefficace [ee-ne-fee-kahs]
inexpensive, bon marché [bõ mahr-sheh]
infant, bébé (m) [beh-beh]
infection, infection (f) [ẽ-fek-syõ]
inferior, inférieur [ẽ-fehr-yuhr]
infinitive, infinitif (m) [ẽ-fee-nee-teef]
influence n., influence (f) [ẽ-flü-ãs]
influence v., influencer [ẽ-flü-ã-seh]
inform v., informer, renseigner [ẽ-for-meh, rã-se-nyeh]
information, information (f), renseignement (m) [ẽ-for-mah-syõ, rã-se-nyuh-mã]
infrequent, infréquent [ẽ-freh-kã(t)]
inherit v., hériter [eh-ree-teh]
inheritance, héritage (m) [eh-ree-tahzh]

initial, initial, -aux (m, pl) [*ee-nee-syahl, ee-nee-syoh*]
injure *v.,* blesser [*ble-seh*]
injury, blessure (f) [*ble-süir*]
injustice, injustice (f) [*ẽ-zhüs-tees*]
ink, encre (f) [*ãkr*]
innkeeper, hôtelier (m) [*oh-tuh-lyeh*]
innocent, innocent [*ee-no-sã(t)*]
innumerable, innombrable [*ee-nõ-brahbl*]
inquire *v.,* demander [*dmã-deh*]
insane, fou, folle [*foo, fol*]
inside *prep. & adv.,* dedans [*duh-dã*]
inside *n.,* intérieur (m) [*ẽ-tehr-yuhr*]
　inside out, à l'envers [*ah lã-ver*]
insist *v.,* insister [*ẽ-sees-teh*]
inspect *v.,* inspecter [*ẽ-spek-teh*]
inspection, inspection (f) [*ẽ-spek-syõ*]
inspector, inspecteur, -trice [*ẽ-spek-tuhr, ẽ-spek-trees*]
inspiration, inspiration (f) [*ẽ-spee-rah-syõ*]
install *v.,* installer [*ẽ-stah-leh*]
instance, exemple (m), cas (m) [*ehg-zãpl, kah*]
　for instance, par exemple [*pah-reg-zãpl*]
instead, à la place [*ah lah plahs*]
　instead of, au lieu de [*oh lyuh duh*]
instinct, instinct (m) [*ẽ-stẽ*]
institution, institution (f), établissement (m) [*ẽ-stee-tü-syõ, eh-tah-blees-mã*]
instruct *v.,* instruire (irreg) [*ẽ-strweer*]
instruction, instruction (f) [*ẽ-strük-syõ*]
instructor, instructeur, -trice [*ẽ-strük-tuhr, ẽ-strük-trees*]
instrument, instrument (m) [*ẽ-strü-mã*]
insufficient, insuffisant [*ẽ-sü-fee-zã(t)*]
insult *n.,* insulte (f) [*ẽ-sült*]
insult *v.,* insulter [*ẽ-sül-teh*]
insurance, assurance (f) [*ah-sü-rãs*]
insurance company, compagnie (f) d'assurances [*kõ-pah-nee dah-sü-rãs*]
insurance policy, police (f) d'assurance [*po-lees dah-sü-rãs*]
insure *v.,* assurer [*ah-sü-reh*]

intact, intact [ē-tah(kt)]
intellectual, intellectuel, -elle [ē-teh-lehk-twel]
intelligent, intelligent [ē-teh-lee-zhã(t)]
intend v., avoir l'intention de [ah-vwahr lē-tã-syõ duh]
intense, intense [ē-tãs]
intention, intention (f) [ē-tã-syõ]
interest [concern] n., intérêt (m) [ē-teh-re]
interest [financial] n., des intérêts [deh-zē-teh-re]
interest v., intéresser [ē-teh-re-seh]
  be interested in v., s'intéresser à [sē-teh-re-seh ah]
interesting, intéressant [ē-teh-re-sã(t)]
interfere v., intervenir (irreg) [ē-ter-vuh-neer]
interior, intérieur (m) [ē-tehr-yuhr]
intermission, entr'acte (m) [ã-trahkt]
internal, interne [ē-tern]
international, international, -aux (m, pl) [ē-ter-nah-syo-nahl, ē-ter-nah-syo-noh]
interpreter, interprète (m) [ē-ter-pret]
intersection, carrefour (m) [kahr-foor]
interval, intervalle (m) [ē-ter-vahl]
interview n., entrevue (f) [ã-truh-vü]
intimate adj., intime [ē-teem]
into, dans, en [dã, ã]
introduce v., présenter [preh-zã-teh]
introduction, introduction (f), présentation (f) [ē-troh-dük-syõ, preh-zã-tah-syõ]
intuition, intuition (f) [ē-twee-syõ]
invalid, invalide (m, f) [ē-vah-leed]
invasion, invasion (f) [ē-vah-zyõ]
invention, invention (f) [ē-vã-syõ]
inventor, inventeur (m) [ē-vã-tuhr]
invest [install] v., investir [ē-ves-teer]
invest [money] v., placer [plah-seh]
invisible, invisible [ē-vee-zeebl]
invitation, invitation (f) [ē-vee-tah-syõ]
invite v., inviter [ē-vee-teh]
invoice, facture (f) [fahk-tür]
involuntary, involontaire [ē-vo-lõ-ter]

Ireland, Irlande (f) [*eer-lãd*]
Irish, irlandais [*eer-lã-de(z)*]
iron [metal] *n.*, fer (m) [*fer*]
iron [for ironing] *n.*, fer à repasser [*fer ahr-pah-seh*]
iron [clothes] *v.*, repasser [*ruh-pah-seh*]
irregular, irrégulier, -ière [*ee-re-gü-lyeh, ee-re-gü-lyer*]
irritate *v.*, irriter [*ee-ree-teh*]
irritation, irritation (f) [*ee-ree-tah-syõ*]
island, île (f) [*eel*]
it, il, elle; le, la [*eel, el; luh, lah*]
Italian, italien, -ienne [*ee-tal-yẽ, ee-tal-yen*]
Italy, Italie (f) [*ee-tah-lee*]
itch *n.*, démangeaison (f) [*deh-mã-zheh-zõ*]
itinerary, itinéraire (m) [*ee-tee-neh-rer*]
its, son, sa, ses [*sõ, sah, seh*]
itself, lui-même, elle-même [*lwee-mem, el-mem*]

J

jack, cric (m) [*kreek*]
jacket, veste (f) [*vest*]
jail, prison (f) [*pree-zõ*]
jam, confiture (f) [*kõ-fee-tür*]
January, janvier (m) [*zhã-vyeh*]
Japan, Japon (m) [*zhah-põ*]
Japanese, japonais [*zhah-po-ne(z)*]
jar [container], bocal (m), -aux (pl) [*bo-kahl, bo-koh*]
jaw, mâchoire (f) [*mah-shwahr*]
jazz *n.*, jazz (m) [*dzhahz*]
jealous, jaloux, -ouse [*zhah-loo, zhah-looz*]
jelly, gelée (f) [*zh(uh)-leh*]
jet plane, avion (m) à réaction [*ah-vyõ ah reh-ahk-syõ*]
Jew, Juif, Juive [*zhweef, zhweev*]
jewel, bijou (m), -oux (pl) [*bee-zhoo*]
jewelry, bijouterie (f) [*bee-zhoo-tree*]

Jewish, juif, juive [*zhweef, zhweev*]
job, travail (m), -aux (pl) [*trah-vahy, trah-voh*]
join v., se joindre à, adhérer à [*suh zhwẽdr ah, ah-deh-reh ah*]
joke n., plaisanterie (f) [*ple-zã-tree*]
joke v., plaisanter [*ple-zã-teh*]
jockey, jockey (m) [*zho-ke*]
journal, journal (m), -aux (pl) [*zhoor-nahl, zhoor-noh*]
journalist, journaliste [*zhoor-nah-leest*]
journey, voyage (m) [*vwah-yahzh*]
joy, joie (f) [*zhwah*]
joyful, joyeux, -euse [*zhwah-yuh, zhwah-yuhz*]
judge n., juge (m) [*zhüzh*]
judge v., juger [*zhü-zheh*]
judgment, jugement (m) [*zhüzh-mã*]
juice, jus (m) [*zhü*]
July, juillet (m) [*zhwee-yeh*]
jump n., saut (m) [*soh*]
jump v., sauter [*soh-teh*]
June, juin (m) [*zhwẽ*]
jungle, jungle (f) [*zhẽgl*]
jury, jury (m) [*zhü-ree*]
just adj. & adv., juste [*zhüst*]
   to have just done v., venir de faire [*vuh-neer duh fer*]
justice, justice (f) [*zhüs-tees*]
justify v., justifier [*zhüs-tee-fyeh*]

K

keep v., garder [*gahr-deh*]
   Keep out! Défense d'entrer! [*deh-fãs dã-treh*]
   Keep quiet! Restez tranquille! [*res-teh trã-keel*]
   keep doing, continuer à faire [*kõ-tee-nweh ah fer*]
   keep from doing, s'empêcher de faire [*sã-peh-sheh tfer*]
kettle, bouilloire (f) [*booy-wahr*]
key n., clef (f) [*kleh*]

KI
KI _____72

kick *n.*, coup de pied (m) [*koot pyeh*]
kid [animal] *n.*, chevreau (m), -eaux (pl) [*shuh-vroh*]
kid [child] *n.*, gosse (m) [*gos*]
kidney [food], rognon (m) [*ro-nyõ*]
kidney [anat.], rein (m) [*rẽ*]
kill *v.*, tuer [*tü-eh*]
kilogram, kilo (m) [*kee-loh*]
kilometer, kilomètre (m) [*kee-lo-metr*]
kind *n.*, sorte (f) [*sort*]
kind *adj.*, bon, bonne [*bõ, bon*]
kindness, bonté (f) [*bõ-teh*]
king, roi (m) [*rwah*]
kingdom, royaume (m) [*rwah-yohm*]
kiss *n.*, baiser (m) [*beh-zeh*]
kiss *v.*, embrasser [*ã-brah-seh*]
kitchen, cuisine (f) [*kwee-zeen*]
kite, cerf-volant [*ser-vo-lã*]
knee, genou (m), -oux (pl) [*zhnoo*]
kneel *v.*, se mettre (irreg) à genoux [*sme-trah zhnoo*]
knife, couteau (m), -eaux (pl) [*koo-toh*]
knock *v.*, frapper [*frah-peh*]
knot *n.*, noeud (m) [*nuh*]
know [something] *v.*, savoir (irreg) [*sah-vwahr*]
know [someone] *v.*, connaître (irreg) [*ko-netr*]
knowledge, connaissance (f) [*ko-ne-sãs*]

L

label, étiquette (f) [*eh-tee-ket*]
labor *n.*, travail (m), -aux (pl) [*trah-vahy, trah-voh*]
laboratory, laboratoire (m) [*lah-bo-rah-twahr*]
lace, dentelle (f) [*dã-tel*]
lack *n.*, manque (m) [*mãk*]
lack [something] *v.*, manquer (de) [*mã-keh (duh)*]
   . . . is lacking, il manque . . . [*eel mãk*]

ladder, échelle (f) [*eh-shel*]
ladies' room, toilette pour dames (f) [*twah-let poor dahm*]
lady, dame (f) [*dahm*]
lake, lac (m) [*lahk*]
lamb, agneau (m), -eaux (pl) [*ah-nyoh*]
lame *adj.*, boîteux, -euse [*bwah-tuh, bwah-tuhz*]
lamp, lampe (f) [*lãp*]
land *n.*, terre (f) [*ter*]
land *v.*, atterir [*ah-te-reer*]
landing, atterissage (m) [*ah-te-ree-sahzh*]
landlord, landlady, propriétaire (m, f) [*pro-pree-yeh-ter*]
landscape, paysage (m) [*peh-ee-zahzh*]
language, language (m), langue (f) [*lã-gahzh, lãg*]
large, grand [*grã(d)*]
last *adj.*, dernier, -ière [*der-nyeh, der-nyer*]
   at last, enfin [*ã-fẽ*]
   last night, hier soir [*yer swahr*]
last *v.*, durer [*dü-reh*]
late, tard [*tahr*]
   It's late, Il est tard [*ee-le tar*]
   I'm late, Je suis en retard [*zhuh swee-zãr-tahr*]
lately, dernièrement [*der-nyer-mã*]
later, latest, tardif, -ive [*tahr-deef, tahr-deev*]
latest, dernier, -ière [*der-nyeh, der-nyer*]
latter, dernier, -ière; celui-ci, celle-ci [*der-nyeh, der-nyer; suh-lwee-see, sel-see*]
laugh, laughter *n.*, rire (m) [*reer*]
laugh *v.*, rire (irreg) [*reer*]
laundry, blanchisserie (f) [*blã-shees-ree*]
law, loi (f) [*lwah*]
law [body of knowledge], droit (m) [*drwah*]
lawful, légal, -aux (m, pl) [*leh-gahl, leh-goh*]
lawn, pelouse (f) [*plooz*]
lawyer, avocat (m) [*ah-vo-kah*]
lay *v.*, poser [*poh-zeh*]
lazy, paresseux, -euse [*pah-re-suh, pah-re-suhz*]
lead [metal] *n.*, plomb (m) [*plõ*]
lead *v.*, conduire (irreg) [*kõ-dweer*]

leader, chef (m) [*shef*]

leaf, feuille (f) [*fuhy*]

leak *n.*, fuite (f) [*fweet*]

lean *v.*, pencher [*pã-sheh*]
  lean on, s'appuyer sur [*sah-pwee-yeh sür*]

learn *v.*, apprendre [*ah-prãdr*]

lease *n.*, bail (m) [*bahy*]

least, moindre, moins [*mwẽdr, mwẽ*]
  at least, au moins [*oh mwẽ*]

leather, cuir (m) [*kweer*]

leave [allow] *v.*, laisser [*le-seh*]

leave [depart] *v.*, sortir de (irreg; *Aux:* ÊTRE), quitter [*sorteer duh, kee-teh*]

lecture *n.*, conférence (f) [*kõ-feh-rãs*]

lecturer, conférencier (m) [*kõ-feh-rã-syeh*]

left [direction], gauche [*gohsh*]
  to the left, à gauche [*ah gohsh*]

leg, jambe (f) [*zhãb*]

legal, légal, -aux (m, pl) [*leh-gahl, leh-goh*]

legible, lisible [*lee-zeebl*]

legitimate, légitime [*leh-zhee-teem*]

leisure, loisir (m) [*lawh-zeer*]

lemon, citron (m) [*see-trõ*]

lemonade, citron pressé (m) [*see-trõ pre-seh*]

lend, prêter [*pre-teh*]

length, longueur (f) [*lõ-guhr*]

lens [of camera], objectif (m) [*ob-zhek-teef*]

lens [of glasses], verre (m) [*ver*]

less, moins [*mwẽ*]
  more or less, plus ou moins [*plü-zoo mwẽ*]

lesson, leçon (f) [*l(uh)-sõ*]

let [permit] *v.*, permettre (irreg), laisser [*per-metr, le-seh*]

letter, lettre (f) [*letr*]

lettuce, laitue (f) [*le-tü*]

level *n.*, niveau (m), -eaux (pl) [*nee-voh*]

level *adj.*, égal, -aux (m, pl) [*eh-gahl, eh-goh*]

liability, responsabilité (f) [*res-põ-sah-bee-lee-teh*]

liar, menteur (m), menteuse (f) [*mã-tuhr, mã-tuhz*]

liberal, libéral, -aux (m, pl) [*lee-beh-rahl, lee-beh-roh*]
liberty, liberté (f) [*lee-ber-teh*]
library, bibliothèque (f) [*bee-blee-yo-tek*]
license *n.,* permis (m) [*per-mee*]
license plate, plaque d'immatriculation [*plahk dee-mah-tree-kü-lah-syõ*]
lid, couvercle (m) [*koo-verkl*]
lie [untruth] *n.,* mensonge (m) [*mã-sõzh*]
lie [tell an untruth] *v.,* mentir (irreg) [*mã-teer*]
lie [rest] *v.,* s'allonger, être couché [*sah-lõ-zheh, etr koo-sheh*]
  lie down, se coucher [*skoo-sheh*]
lieutenant, lieutenant (m) [*lyuht-nã*]
life, vie (f) [*vee*]
lifeboat, canot (m) de sauvetage [*kah-noh tsohv-tahzh*]
life insurance, assurance-vie (f) [*ah-sü-rãs-vee*]
life jacket, gilet de sauvetage (m) [*zhee-leh tsohv-tahzh*]
lift *v.,* soulever [*sool-veh*]
light *n.,* lumière (f) [*lü-myer*]
light *v.,* allumer [*ah-lü-meh*]
light [color] *adj.,* clair [*kler*]
light [weight] *adj.,* léger, -ère [*leh-zheh, leh-zher*]
lighter [cigaret] *n.,* briquet (m) [*bree-keh*]
lighthouse, phare (m) [*fahr*]
lightning, éclairs (m, pl), foudre (f) [*eh-kler, foodr*]
lights [car], phares (m, pl) [*fahr*]
likeable, sympathique [*sẽ-pah-teek*]
like *prep. & adv.,* comme [*kom*]
like *v.,* aimer [*e-meh*]
  Would you like . . . Voudriez-vous . . . [*voo-dree-yeh-voo*]
  I'd like to, Je voudrais bien [*zhvoo-dre byẽ*]
likely, probable [*pro-bahbl*]
likewise, également [*eh-gahl-mã*]
limb [anat.], membre (m) [*mãbr*]
limb [tree], grosse branche [*grohs brãsh*]
limit *n.,* limite (f) [*lee-meet*]
limit *v.,* limiter [*lee-mee-teh*]
line, ligne (f) [*leeñ*]

Hold the line, Ne quittez pas [*nuh kee-teh pah*]
   stand in line *v.*, faire la queue [*fer lah kuh*]
linen [clothing], linge (m) [*lẽzh*]
linen [fabric], toile (f) [*twahl*]
lingerie, lingerie (f) pour femmes [*lẽzh-ree poor fahm*]
lining, doublure (f) [*doo-blür*]
lip, lèvre (f) [*levr*]
lipstick, rouge (m) à lèvres [*roo-zhah levr*]
liquid, liquide [*lee-keed*]
liquor, boisson (f) alcoolique [*bwah-sõ ahl-ko-leek*]
list *n.*, liste (f) [*leest*]
listen (to) *v.*, écouter [*eh-koo-teh*]
literally, littéralement, [*lee-teh-rahl-mã*]
literature, littérature (f) [*lee-teh-rah-tür*]
little *adj.*, petit [*ptee(t)*]
little *adv.*, peu [*puh*]
   a little (bit), un peu [*ẽ puh*]
   little by little, petit à petit [*ptee-tah ptee*]
   very little, très peu [*tre puh*]
live [be alive] *v.*, vivre (irreg) [*veevr*]
live [reside] *v.*, habiter [*ah-bee-teh*]
lively, vivant [*vee-vã(t)*]
liver, foie (m) [*fwah*]
living room, salon (m) [*sah-lõ*]
load (with) *v.*, charger (de) [*shahr-zheh (duh)*]
loaf [of bread], pain (m) [*pẽ*]
loan [to lender] *n.*, prêt (m) [*pre*]
loan [to borrower] *n.*, emprunt (m) [*ã-prẽ*]
lobby [hotel], foyer (m) [*fwah-yeh*]
lobster, *homard (m) [*o-mahr*]
local, local, -aux (m, pl) [*lo-kahl, lo-koh*]
local train, omnibus (m) [*om-nee-büs*]
locate *v.*, trouver [*troo-veh*]
   be located *v.*, se trouver [*stroo-veh*]
location, emplacement (m) [*ã-plas-mã*]
lock *n.*, serrure (f) [*se-rür*]
lock *v.*, fermer à clef [*fer-meh ah kleh*]
locomotive, locomotive (f) [*loh-koh-mo-teev*]

lodging, logement (m) [*lozh-mã*]
logical, logique [*lo-zheek*]
long [distance], long, longue [*lõ, lõg*]
long [time], longtemps [*lõ-tã*]
  How long? Combien de temps? [*kõ-byẽ duh tã*]
  long ago, il y a longtemps [*eel yah lõ-tã*]
long distance [telephone], interurbain [*ẽ-ter-ür-bẽ*]
longer, plus long, plus longtemps [*plü lõ, plü lõ-tã*]
  no longer, ne . . . plus [*nuh . . . plü*]
look at v., regarder [*r(uh)-gahr-deh*]
look for v., chercher [*sher-sheh*]
  Look out! Attention! [*a-tã-syõ*]
look like v., ressembler à [*r(uh)-sã-bleh ah*]
loosen v., desserrer [*deh-seh-reh*]
lord, seigneur (m) [*seh-nyuhr*]
lose v., perdre [*perdr*]
loss, perte (f) [*pert*]
lost, perdu [*per-dü*]
lost and found, bureau des objets trouvés (m) [*bü-roh deh-zob-zheh troo-veh*]
lot [real estate], terrain (m) [*teh-rẽ*]
lot [quantity], lot (m) [*loh*]
  a lot (of), beaucoup (de) [*boh-koo (duh)*]
loud, fort [*for(t)*]
loudspeaker, *haut-parleur (m) [*oh-pahr-luhr*]
love n., amour (m) [*ah-moor*]
love v., aimer [*e-meh*]
  be in love (with) v., être amoureux, -euse (de) [*et-rah-moo-ruh, ah-moo-ruhz (duh)*]
lovely, beau (bel), belle; beaux, belles [*boh, bel*]
lover [sweetheart], amoureux, -euse [*ah-moo-ruh, ah-moo-ruhz*]
lover [paramour], amant, -te [*ah-ma, ah-mãt*]
low adj., bas, basse [*bah, bahs*]
loyal, loyal, -aux (m, pl) [*lwah-yahl, lwah-yoh*]
lubrication [auto], graissage (m) [*gre-sahzh*]
luck, chance (f) [*shãs*]
  good luck, bonne chance [*bon shãs*]

lucky: to be lucky, avoir de la chance [*ah-vwahr duh lah shãs*]

luggage, bagages (m, pl) [*bah-gahzh*]

lunch *n.*, déjeuner (m) [*deh-zhuh-neh*]
   have lunch *v.*, déjeuner [*deh-zhuh-neh*]

lung, poumon (m) [*poo-mõ*]

luxurious, luxueux, -euse [*lük-swuh, lük-swuhz*]

luxury, luxe (m) [*lüks*]

M

machine, machine (f) [*mah-sheen*]

mad [angry], furieux, -euse [*für-yuh, für-yuhz*]

madam, madame (f) [*mah-dahm*]

made, fait [*fe(t)*]

magazine, revue (f) [*r(uh)-vü*]

magic *adj.*, magique [*mah-zheek*]

magnificent, magnifique [*mah-nyee-feek*]

mahogany, acajou (m) [*ah-kah-zhoo*]

maid, bonne (f) [*bon*]

mail *n.*, courrier (m) [*koor-yeh*]

mail *v.*, poster [*po-steh*]

mailbox, boîte (f) aux lettres [*bwaht oh letr*]

mailman, facteur (m) [*fahk-tuhr*]

main, principal, -aux (m, pl) [*prẽ-see-pahl, prẽ-see-poh*]

mainly, surtout [*sür-too*]

maintain *v.*, maintenir (irreg) [*mẽt-neer*]

majority, majorité (f), la plupart (de) [*mah-zho-ree-teh, lah plü-pahr (duh)*]

make *v.*, faire (irreg) [*fer*]

male, mâle (m) [*mahl*]

man, homme (m) [*om*]
   young man, jeune homme (m), jeunes gens (pl) [*zhuh-nom, zhuhn-zhã*]

manage *v.*, diriger, arranger [*dee-ree-zheh, ah-rã-zheh*]

manager, directeur (m), gérant (m) [*dee-rek-tuhr, zheh-rã*]
manicure, manucure (f) [*mah-nü-kür*]
manner, manière (f) [*mah-nyer*]
manufacture *v.,* fabriquer [*fah-bree-keh*]
manufacturer, fabriquant (m) [*fah-bree-kã*]
many, beaucoup (de) [*boh-koo (duh)*]
  How many? Combien (de)? [*kõ-byē (duh)*]
  too many, trop (de) [*troh (duh)*]
map [of city], plan (m) [*plã*]
map [large scale], carte (f) [*kahrt*]
  road map, carte routière [*kahrt roo-tyer*]
marble, marbre (m) [*mahrbr*]
March, mars (m) [*mahrs*]
march *n.,* marche (f) [*mahrsh*]
mark *v.,* marquer [*mahr-keh*]
market, marché (m) [*mahr-sheh*]
marriage, mariage (m) [*mahr-yahzh*]
married, marié [*mah-ryeh*]
marry [someone] *v.,* épouser [*eh-poo-zeh*]
  get married, se marier [*smahr-yeh*]
marvelous, merveilleux, -euse [*mer-ve-yuh, mer-ve-yuhz*]
mass [quantity], masse (f) [*mahs*]
Mass [eccles.], messe (f) [*mes*]
massage *n.,* massage (m) [*mah-sahzh*]
mass production, fabrication (f) en série [*fah-bree-kah-syõ ã seh-ree*]
master *n.,* maître (m) [*metr*]
masterpiece, chef-d'oeuvre (m) [*sheh-duhvr*]
match [for igniting], allumette (f) [*ah-lü-met*]
material, matériel (m) [*mah-ter-yel*]
mathematics, mathématiques (f, pl) [*mah-teh-mah-teek*]
matter *v.,* importer [*ē-por-teh*]
  What's the matter? Qu'est-ce qu'il y a? [*kes keel-yah*]
  It doesn't matter, Ça ne fait rien [*sahn fe ryē*]
mattress, matelas (m) [*maht-lah*]
mature, mûr [*mür*]
May, mai (m) [*meh*]
may *n.,* pouvoir (irreg) [*poo-vwahr*]

It may be, Il se peut . . . [*eel suh puh*]

May I go? Puis-je partir? [*pweezh pahr-teer*]

maybe, peut-être [*puh-tetr*]

mayor, maire (m) [*mer*]

me, me, moi [*muh, mwah*]

meal, repas (m) [*r(uh)-pah*]

mean *v.*, vouloir (irreg) dire [*vool-wahr deer*]

What do you mean? Qu'est-ce que vous voulez dire?
[*kes kuh voo voo-leh deer*]

What does that mean? Qu'est-ce que cela veut dire?
[*kes kuh slah vuh deer*]

means, moyen(s) (m, pl) [*mwah-yē*]

by means of, au moyen de [*oh mwah-yē d(uh)*]

by all means, certainement [*ser-ten-mã*]

by no means, en aucune façon [*ã-noh-kün fah-sõ*]

meanwhile, entretemps, [*ã-truh-tã*]

measles, rougeole (f) [*roo-zhol*]

German measles, rubéole (f) [*rü-beh-ol*]

measure *v.*, mesurer [*muh-zü-reh*]

meat, viande (f) [*vyãd*]

mechanic, mécanicien (m) [*meh-kah-nee-syē*]

mechanical, mécanique [*meh-kah-neek*]

medal, médaille (f) [*meh-dahy*]

medical, médical, -aux (m, pl) [*meh-dee-kahl, meh-dee-koh*]

medicine, médecine (f) [*med-seen*]

Mediterranean, Méditerranée (f) [*meh-dee-te-rah-neh*]

medium *adj.*, moyen, -enne [*mwah-yē, mwah-yen*]

meet [for first time] *v.*, faire la connaissance de [*fer lah ko-ne-sãs d(uh)*]

Glad to meet you, Enchanté [*ã-shã-teh*]

meet [encounter] *v.*, rencontrer [*rã-kõ-treh*]

meeting [group] *n.*, réunion (f) [*re-ü-nyõ*]

meeting [encounter] *n.*, rencontre (f) [*rã-kõtr*]

melon, melon (m) [*m(uh)-lõ*]

melt *v.*, fondre, faire fondre [*fõdr, fer fõdr*]

member, membre (m) [*mãbr*]

memory, mémoire (f) [*meh-mwahr*]

mend *v.*, raccomoder [*rah-ko-mo-deh*]

mental, mental, -aux (m, pl) [*mã-tahl, mã-toh*]

mention *v.,* mentionner [*mã-syo-neh*]

merchandise, marchandise (f) [*mahr-shã-deez*]

merchant, commerçant (m) [*ko-mer-sã*]

merely, simplement [*sē-pluh-mã*]

merit *n.,* mérite (m) [*meh-reet*]

merit *v.,* mériter [*meh-ree-teh*]

merry, joyeux, -euse [*zhwah-yuh, zhwah-yuhz*]

message, message (m) [*meh-sahzh*]

messenger, messager (m) [*meh-sah-zheh*]

metal, métal (m), -aux (pl) [*meh-tahl, meh-toh*]

meter [measure] *n.,* mètre (m) [*metr*]

meter [counter] *n.,* compteur (m) [*kõ-tuhr*]

method, méthode (f) [*meh-tod*]

metric system, système métrique (m) [*sees-tem meh-treek*]

middle, milieu (m), -eux (pl) [*meel-yuh*]

midnight, minuit (m) [*mee-nwee*]

midway, à mi-chemin [*ah mee-shmē*]

mild, doux, douce [*doo, doos*]

mile, mille [*meel*]

military, militaire [*mee-lee-ter*]

milk, lait (m) [*le*]

milliner, modiste (f) [*mo-deest*]

million, million (m) [*mee-lyõ*]

mind *n.,* esprit (m) [*es-pree*]

mind [attend to] *v.,* faire attention à, s'occuper de [*fer ah-tã-syõ ah, so-kü-peh duh*]

   Mind your own business! Occupez-vous de ce qui vous regarde! [*o-kü-peh-voo duh skee voor-gahrd*]

   I don't mind, Cela m'est égal [*sah me-teh-gahl*]

mine *pron.,* le mien, la mienne; les miens, les miennes [*luh myē, lah myen; leh myē, leh myen*]

mine *n.,* mine (f) [*meen*]

miner, mineur (m) [*mee-nuhr*]

mineral, minéral, -aux (m, pl) [*mee-neh-rahl, mee-neh-roh*]

minister [government] *n.,* ministre (m) [*mee-neestr*]

minister [religious] *n.,* pasteur (m) [*pahs-tuhr*]

minor [age], mineur, -eure [*mee-nuhr*]

minority, minorité (f) [*mee-no-ree-teh*]
minus, moins [*mwē*]
minute *n.*, minute (f) [*mee-nüt*]
mirror *n.*, miroir (m) [*meer-wahr*]
miserable, misérable [*mee-zeh-rahbl*]
misfortune, malheur (m) [*mah-luhr*]
Miss, Mademoiselle [*mahd-mwah-zel*]
miss *v.*, manquer [*mã-keh*]
  I miss them, Ils me manquent [*eel muh mãk*]
  I missed the train, J'ai manqué le train [*zheh mã-kehl trē*]
mistake *n.*, erreur (f), faute (f) [*e-ruhr, foht*]
  make a mistake *v.*, se tromper [*strõ-peh*]
mistaken: to be mistaken, se tromper [*strõ-peh*]
mistrust *v.*, se méfier (de) [*smeh-fyeh (duh)*]
misunderstanding, malentendu (m) [*mah-lã-tã-dü*]
mix *v.*, mélanger [*meh-lã-zheh*]
mixture, mélange (m) [*meh-lãzh*]
model *n.*, modèle (m) [*mo-del*]
modern, moderne [*mo-dern*]
modest, modeste [*mo-dest*]
moisture, humidité (f) [*ü-mee-dee-teh*]
moment, moment (m) [*mo-mã*]
monarchy, monarchie (f) [*mo-nahr-shee*]
monastery, monastère (m) [*mo-nahs-ter*]
Monday, lundi (m) [*lē-dee*]
money, argent (m) [*ahr-zhã*]
monotonous, monotone [*mo-no-ton*]
month, mois (m) [*mwah*]
monthly, mensuel, -elle [*mã-swel*]
monument, monument (m) [*mo-nü-mã*]
mood, humeur (f) [*ü-muhr*]
  in a bad mood, de mauvaise humeur [*duh mo-ve-zü-muhr*]
  in a good mood, de bonne humeur [*duh bo-nü-muhr*]
moon, lune (f) [*lün*]
moonlight, clair (m) de lune [*kler duh lün*]
mop, balai (m) à laver par terre [*bah-le ah lah-veh pahr ter*]
moral *adj.*, moral, -aux (m, pl) [*mo-rahl, mo-roh*]
moral *n.*, morale (f) [*mo-rahl*]

morale *n.*, moral (m) [*mo-rahl*]
more, plus [*plü(s)*]
  more and more, de plus en plus [*duh plü-zã plü*]
  more or less, plus ou moins [*plü-zoo mwẽ*]
  no more, ne . . . plus [*nuh . . . plü*]
  once more, encore une fois [*ã-ko-rün fwah*]
  the more . . . the more, plus . . . plus [*plü(z) . . plu(z)*]
moreover, de plus [*duh plü(s)*]
morning, matin (m) [*mah-tẽ*]
  good morning, bonjour [*bõ-zhoor*]
mortgage, hypothèque (f) [*ee-po-tek*]
mosquito, moustique (m) [*moos-teek*]
most, le (la, les) plus [*luh (lah, leh) plü(z)*]
  at the most, au plus [*oh plü(s)*]
  most of, la plupart des [*lah plü-pahr deh*]
  most of the time, la plupart du temps [*lah plü-pahr dü tã*]
mother, mère (f) [*mer*]
mother-in-law, belle-mère (f) [*bel-mer*]
motion, mouvement (m) [*moov-mã*]
motive, motif (m) [*mo-teef*]
motor, moteur (m) [*moh-tuhr*]
motorcycle, motocyclette (f) [*moh-toh-see-klet*]
mountain, montagne (f) [*mõ-tañ*]
mourning *n.*, deuil (m) [*duhy*]
mouth, bouche (f) [*boosh*]
move [change position of] *v.*, bouger [*boo-zheh*]
move [change residence] *v.*, déménager [*deh-meh-nah-zheh*]
movie, film (m) [*feelm*]
  go to the movies *v.*, aller (irreg) au cinéma [*ah-leh oh see-neh-mah*]
movie theater, salle (f) de cinéma (m) [*sahl duh see-neh-mah*]
moving [emotional], émouvant [*eh-moo-vã(t)*]
Mr., Monsieur [*muh-syuh*]
Mrs., Madame [*mah-dahm*]
much, beaucoup (de) [*boh-koo (duh)*]
  as much as, autant que [*oh-tã k(uh)*]
  How much? Combien (de)? [*kõ-byẽ (duh)*]
  too much, trop (de) [*troh (duh)*]

mud, boue (f) [*boo*]
muffler [scarf], cache-col (m) [*kash-kol*]
muffler [auto], pot (m) d'échappement [*poh deh-shahp-mã*]
murder *n.*, meurtre (m) [*muhrtr*]
murderer, meurtrier (m) [*muhr-tree-yeh*]
muscle, muscle (m) [*müskl*]
museum, musée (m) [*mü-zeh*]
mushroom, champignon (m) [*shã-pee-nyõ*]
music, musique (f) [*mü-zeek*]
musical, musical, -aux (m, pl) [*mü-zee-kahl, mü-zee-koh*]
musician, musicien, -enne [*mü-zee-syẽ, mü-see-syen*]
must *v.*, devoir (irreg) [*duh-vwahr*]
   I must go, Je dois partir [*zhdwah pahr-teer*]
   I must have lost my book, J'ai dû perdre mon livre
      [*zheh dü perdr mõ leevr*]
mustache, moustache (f) [*moos-tash*]
mustard, moutarde (f) [*moo-tahrd*]
mutual, mutuel, -elle [*mü-twel*]
   It's mutual, C'est réciproque [*se reh-see-prok*]
my, mon, ma, mes [*mõ, mah, meh*]
myself, moi-même [*mwah-mem*]
mysterious, mystérieux, -euse [*mees-ter-yuh, mees-ter-yuhz*]
mystery, mystère (m) [*mee-ster*]

N

nail [fingernail] *n.*, ongle (m) [*õgl*]
nail [carpentry] *n.*, clou (m) [*kloo*]
nail *v.*, clouer [*kloo-eh*]
naïve, naïf, naïve [*nah-eef, nah-eev*]
naked, nu [*nü*]
name *n.*, nom (m) [*nõ*]
   first name, prénom (m) [*preh-nõ*]
   last name, nom de famille [*nõd fah-meey*]
name *v.*, nommer [*no-meh*]

namely, à savoir [*ah sah-vwahr*]
nap, sieste (f) [*syest*]
napkin, serviette (f) [*ser-vyet*]
  sanitary napkin, serviette hygiénique [*ser-vyet ee-zhyeh-neek*]
narrate v., raconter [*rah-kõ-teh*]
narrow adj., étroit [*eh-trwah(t)*]
nasty, méchant, vilain [*meh-shã(t); vee-lẽ, vee-len*]
nation, nation (f) [*nah-syõ*]
national, national, -aux (m, pl) [*nah-syo-nahl, nah-syo-noh*]
native n., indigène (m, f) [*ẽ-dee-zhen*]
natural, naturel, -elle [*nah-tü-rel*]
naturally, naturellement [*nah-tü-rel-mã*]
nature, nature (f) [*nah-tür*]
naughty, vilain, méchant [*vee-lẽ, vee-len; meh-shã(t)*]
naval, naval, navals (m, pl) [*nah-vahl*]
navy, marine (f) [*mah-reen*]
near, près (de) [*pre (duh)*]
nearly, presque [*presk*]
neat, bien rangé, soigné, ordonné [*byẽ rã-zheh, swah-nyeh, or-do-neh*]
necessary, nécessaire [*neh-seh-ser*]
neck, cou (m) [*koo*]
necklace, collier (m) [*kol-yeh*]
necktie, cravate (f) [*krah-vaht*]
need n., besoin (m) [*buh-zwẽ*]
need v., avoir besoin de [*ah-vwahr buh-zwẽ d(uh)*]
needle, aiguille (f) [*e-gweey*]
negative adj., négatif, -ive [*neh-gah-teef, neh-gah-teev*]
negative n., négatif (m) [*neh-gah-teef*]
neglect v., négliger [*neh-glee-zheh*]
Negro, noir, noire [*nwahr*]
neighbor, voisin, -ine [*vwah-zẽ, vwah-zeen*]
neighborhood, quartier (m) [*kahr-tyeh*]
neither conj., non plus [*nõ plü*]
neither one pron., aucun . . . ne [*oh-kẽ, oh-kün . . . nuh*]
neither . . . nor, ni . . . ni [*nee . . . nee*]
nephew, neveu (m) [*nuh-vuh*]

nerve *n.*, nerf (m) [*ner*]
nervous, nerveux, -euse [*ner-vuh, ner-vuhz*]
net, filet (m) [*fee-leh*]
network, réseau (m), -eaux (pl) [*reh-zoh*]
network [radio, TV] *n.*, chaîne (f) [*shen*]
neutral, neutre [*nuhtr*]
  in neutral [gear], au point mort [*oh pwē mor*]
never, jamais [*zhah-me*]
  Never mind, Ça ne fait rien [*sahn fe ryē*]
nevertheless, néanmoins [*neh-ã-mwē*]
new [not used] *adj.*, neuf, neuve [*nuhf, nuhv*]
new [newly learned] *adj.*, nouveau, -vel (m, sing), -velle
  (f, sing); nouveaux (m, pl) [*noo-voh, noo-vel*]
news, nouvelles (f, pl) [*noo-vel*]
newspaper, journal (m), -aux (pl) [*zhoor-nahl, zhoor-noh*]
newsstand, kiosque (m) [*kyosk*]
next [in order] *adj.*, suivant [*swee-vã(t)*]
next [position or time] *adj.*, prochain [*pro-shē, pro-shen*]
  next month, le mois prochain [*luh mwah pro-shē*]
  next time, la prochaine fois [*lah pro-shen fwah*]
  next to, à côté de [*ah koh-teh d(uh)*]
nice, gentil, -ille [*zhã-tee, zhã-teey*]
nickname, surnom (m) [*sür-nõ*]
niece, nièce (f) [*nyes*]
night, nuit (f) [*nwee*]
  good night, bonne nuit [*bon nwee*]
nightclub, boîte (f) de nuit [*bwaht duh nwee*]
nightgown, chemise (f) de nuit [*shmeez duh nwee*]
nightmare, cauchemar (m) [*kohsh-mahr*]
nine, neuf [*nuhf, nuhv*]
nineteen, dix-neuf [*deez-nuhf*]
ninety, quatre-vingt-dix [*kah-truh-vē-dees*]
ninth, neuvième [*nuh-vyem*]
nipple, tétine (f) [*teh-teen*]
no *adv.*, non [*nõ*]
no *adj.*, aucun, aucune [*oh-kē, oh-kün*]
no longer [no more], ne . . . plus [*nuh . . . plü*]
noble, noble [*nobl*]

nobody, personne [*per-son*]
noise, bruit (m) [*brwee*]
noisy, bruyant [*brwee-yã(t)*]
none, aucun, aucune [*ok-kẽ, oh-kün*]
noodles, nouilles (f, pl) [*nooy*]
noon, midi (m) [*mee-dee*]
nor, ni, non plus [*nee, nõ plu*]
normal, normal, -aux (m, pl) [*nor-mahl, nor-moh*]
north, nord (m) [*nor*]
northeast, nord-est (m) [*nor-est*]
northern, du nord [*dü nor*]
northwest, nord-ouest (m) [*nor-west*]
Norway, Norvège (f) [*nor-vezh*]
Norwegian, norvégien, -ienne [*nor-veh-zhyẽ, nor-veh-zhyen*]
nose, nez (m) [*neh*]
not, ne . . . pas [*nuh . . . pah*]
  not at all, pas du tout [*pah dü too*]
  not even, pas même [*pah mem*]
note *n.*, note (f) [*not*]
note *v.*, noter [*no-teh*]
notebook, carnet (m), cahier (m) [*kahr-ne, kah-yeh*]
nothing, rien [*ryẽ*]
  nothing new, rien de nouveau [*ryẽd noo-voh*]
notice *n.*, avis (m) [*ah-vee*]
notice *v.*, remarquer [*ruh-mahr-keh*]
notify *v.*, avertir [*ah-ver-teer*]
notion, notion (f) [*noh-syõ*]
noun, nom (m) [*nõ*]
novel, roman (m) [*roh-mã*]
novelist, romancier (m) [*ro-mã-syeh*]
novelty, nouveauté (f) [*noo-voh-teh*]
November, novembre (m) [*no-vãbr*]
now, maintenant [*mẽt-nã*]
  from now on, à partir de maintenant [*ah pahr-teer duh mẽt-nã*]
  now and then, de temps en temps [*duh tã-zã tã*]
  until now, jusqu'à maintenant [*zhüs-kah mẽt-nã*]
  by now, à l'heure qu'il est [*ah luhr kee-le*]

three days from now, d'ici trois jours [*dee-see trwah zhoor*]
nowhere, nulle part [*nül pahr*]
number, nombre [*nõbr*]
number [of house], numéro (m) [*nü-meh-roh*]
numerous, nombreux, -euse [*nõ-bruh, nõ-bruhz*]
nun, religieuse (f) [*ruh-lee-zhyuhz*]
nurse *n.*, infirmière (f) [*ẽ-feer-myer*]
nursery, chambre (f) des enfants [*shãbr deh-zã-fã*]
nursery school, école maternelle (f) [*eh-kol mah-ter-nel*]
nut [food], noix (f) [*nwah*]
nut [for a bolt], écrou (m) [*eh-kroo*]
nutmeg, noix (f) de muscade [*nwahd müs-kahd*]
nylon, nylon (m) [*nee-lõ*]

O

oak, chêne (m) [*shen*]
oar, rame (f) [*rahm*]
oath, serment (m) [*ser-mã*]
take an oath *v.*, prêter serment [*pre-teh ser-mã*]
obedient, obéissant [*o-beh-ee-sã(t)*]
obey *v.*, obéir à [*o-beh-eer ah*]
object *n.*, objet (m) [*ob-zhe*]
object to *v.*, faire objection à [*fer ob-zhek-syõ ah*]
objection, objection (f) [*ob-zhek-syõ*]
obligation, obligation (f) [*ob-lee-gah-syõ*]
oblige [compel] *v.*, obliger [*ob-lee-zheh*]
obliged, obligé [*ob-lee-zheh*]
Much obliged, Merci beaucoup [*mer-see boh-koo*]
obscene, obscène [*op-sen*]
observation, observation (f) [*op-ser-va-syõ*]
observe *v.*, observer [*op-ser-veh*]
obstacle, obstacle (m) [*op-stahkl*]
obtain *v.*, obtenir (irreg) [*op-tuh-neer*]
obvious, évident [*eh-vee-dã(t)*]

occasion, occasion (f) [*o-kah-zyō*]
occasionally, de temps en temps [*duh tā-zā tā*]
occupied, occupé [*o-kü-peh*]
occupy *v.*, occuper [*o-kü-peh*]
occur *v.*, avoir lieu [*ah-vwahr lyuh*]
occurrence, événement (m) [*eh-ven-mā*]
ocean, océan (m) [*oh-seh-ā*]
o'clock, heure(s) (f) [*uhr*]
   at three o'clock, à trois heures [*ah trwah-zuhr*]
   It's three o'clock, Il est trois heures [*ee-le trwah-zuhr*]
October, octobre (m) [*ok-tobr*]
odd [unusual], bizarre [*bee-zahr*]
odd [not even], impair [*ē-per*]
odor, odeur (f) [*oh-duhr*]
of, de, d' [*d(uh)*]
   of course, bien entendu [*byē-nā-tā-dü*]
off, enlevé, écarté [*āl-veh, eh-kahr-teh*]
   take off [clothing] *v.*, enlever [*āl-veh*]
   take off [plane] *v.*, décoller [*deh-ko-leh*]
   turn off [light] *v.*, éteindre (irreg) [*eh-tēdr*]
   turn off [water] *v.*, fermer [*fer-meh*]
offend *v.*, offenser [*o-fā-seh*]
offer *n.*, offre (f) [*ofr*]
offer *v.*, offrir (irreg) [*o-freer*]
office, bureau (m), -eaux (pl) [*bü-roh*]
officer [army], officier (m) [*o-fee-syeh*]
officer [organization], responsable (m, f) [*res-pō-sahbl*]
official, officiel, -elle [*o-fee-syel*]
often, souvent [*soo-vā*]
oil [edible] *n.*, huile (f) [*weel*]
oil [petroleum] *n.*, pétrole (m) [*peh-trol*]
oil *v.*, huiler, graisser [*wee-leh, gre-seh*]
oil change, vidange (m) [*vee-dāzh*]
oilcloth, toile (f) cirée [*twahl see-reh*]
oil painting, peinture (f) à l'huile [*pē-tür ah lweel*]
old, vieux (vieil), vieille [*vyuh, vyey*]
   How old are you? Quel âge avez-vous? [*kel ahzh ah-veh-voo*]

older, plus âgé, aîné [*plü-zah-zheh, e-neh*]
old-fashioned, démodé [*deh-mo-deh*]
olive, olive (f) [*o-leev*]
olive oil, huile d'olive [*weel do-leev*]
omelet, omelette (f) [*om-let*]
omission, omission (f) [*o-mee-syõ*]
omit *v.*, omettre (irreg) [*o-metr*]
on, sur, à, en [*sür, ah, ã*]
  turn on [lights] *v.*, allumer [*ah-lü-meh*]
  turn on [water] *v.*, ouvrir (irreg) [*oov-reer*]
  on the contrary, au contraire [*oh kõ-trer*]
  on duty, de service [*d(uh) ser-vees*]
  on foot, à pied [*ah pyeh*]
  on purpose, exprès [*ehk-spre*]
  on the right (left), à droite (gauche) [*ah drwaht (gohsh)*]
  on sale, en vente [*ã vãt*]
  on time, à l'heure [*ah luhr*]
once, une fois (f) [*ün fwah*]
  at once, tout de suite [*toot sweet*]
  once more, encore une fois [*ã-kor ün fwah*]
one, un, une [*ẽ, ün*]
one-way street, rue (f) à sens unique [*rü ah sãs ü-neek*]
one-way ticket, billet aller (m) [*bee-ye ah-leh*]
onion, oignon (m) [*o-nyõ*]
onlooker, spectateur, -trice [*spek-tah-tuhr, spek-tah-trees*]
only *adv.*, seulement [*suhl-mã*]
only *adj.*, seul [*suhl*]
open *adj.*, ouvert [*oo-ver(t)*]
open *v.*, ouvrir (irreg) [*oo-vreer*]
opening, ouverture (f) [*oo-ver-tüir*]
opera, opéra (m) [*o-peh-rah*]
operate *v.*, opérer [*o-peh-reh*]
operation, opération (f) [*o-peh-rah-syõ*]
opinion, opinion (f) [*o-pee-nyõ*]
opportunity, occasion (f) [*o-kah-zyõ*]
oppose [be opposed to] *v.*, s'opposer à [*soh-poh-zeh ah*]
opposite *adj.*, opposé, en face [*oh-poh-zeh, ã fahs*]
optional, facultatif, -tive [*fa-kül-tah-teef, fa-kül-tah-teev*]

or, ou [*oo*]
oral, oral, -aux (m, pl) [*o-rahl, o-roh*]
orange, orange (f) [*o-rãzh*]
orange juice, jus (m) d'orange [*zhü do-rãzh*]
orchard, verger (m) [*ver-zheh*]
orchestra, orchestre (m) [*or-kestr*]
orchid, orchidée (f) [*or-kee-deh*]
order *n.*, ordre (m) [*ordr*]
order *v.*, commander [*ko-mã-deh*]
orderly *adj.*, ordonné [*or-do-neh*]
ordinarily, d'habitude [*dah-bee-tüd*]
ordinary, ordinaire [*or-dee-ner*]
organ [music], orgue (m, sing), orgues (f, pl) [*org*]
organization, organisation (f) [*or-gah-nee-zah-syõ*]
oriental, oriental, -aux (m, pl) [*or-yã-tahl, or-yã-toh*]
original [first], originel, -elle [*o-ree-zhee-nel*]
original [unique], original, -aux (m, pl)[*o-ree-zhee-nahl, o-ree-zhee-noh*]
originally, à l'origine [*ah lo-ree-zheen*]
ornament *n.*, ornement (m) [*or-nuh-mã*]
orphan, orphelin, orpheline [*or-fuh-lẽ, or-fuh-leen*]
other, autre [*ohtr*]
  on the other hand, d'autre part [*doh-truh pahr*]
otherwise, autrement [*oh-truh-mã*]
ought *v.*, devoir (irreg) [*duh-vwahr*]
  You ought to come, Vous devriez venir [*voo duh-vree-yeh vneer*]
our, notre, nos [*notr, noh*]
ours, le nôtre, la nôtre; les nôtres [*luh nohtr, lah nohtr; leh nohtr*]
out, dehors [*duh-or*]
  go out *v.*, sortir (irreg; *Aux:* ÊTRE) [*sor-teer*]
  out of, *hors de [*ord(uh)*]
  The telephone is out of order, Le téléphone est en dérangement [*luh teh-leh-fon e-tã deh-rãzh-mã*]
outdoors, dehors [*duh-or*]
outlet [electrical], prise (f) [*preez*]
outside, dehors [*duh-or*]

outstanding, remarquable [*ruh-mahr-kahbl*]
oven, four (m) [*foor*]
  in the oven, au four [*oh foor*]
over *prep.*, sur, au-dessus, par-dessus [*sür, oht-sü, pahr-duh-sü*]
over [finished], fini [*fee-nee*]
overboard, par-dessus bord [*pahr-duh-sü bor*]
overcoat, pardessus (m) [*pahr-duh-sü*]
overcome *v.*, surmonter [*sür-mõ-teh*]
overdo *v.*, faire trop, forcer [*fer troh, for-seh*]
overflow *v.*, déborder [*deh-bor-deh*]
overhead *n.*, frais généraux (m, pl) [*fre zheh-neh-roh*]
overnight, du soir jusqu'au lendemain [*dü swahr zhüs-koh lãd-mē*]
  stay overnight with *v.*, passer la nuit chez [*pah-seh lah nwee sheh*]
overseas, outre-mer [*oot-ruh-mer*]
overtime, heures (f, pl) supplémentaires [*uhr sü-pleh-mã-ter*]
overturn *v.*, renverser [*rã-ver-seh*]
owe *v.*, devoir (irreg) [*duh-vwahr*]
owing to, à cause de [*ah kohz d(uh)*]
own *adj.*, propre [*propr*]
own *v.*, posséder [*po-seh-deh*]
owner, propriétaire (m) [*pro-pree-yeh-ter*]
ox, boeuf (m), boeufs (pl) [*buhf, buh*]
oxygen, oxygène (m) [*ok-see-zhen*]
oyster, huître (f) [*weetr*]

P

pack *n.*, paquet (m) [*pah-keh*]
pack *v.*, emballer [*ã-bah-leh*]
pack of cards, jeu de cartes (m) [*zhuht kahrt*]
package, paquet (m) [*pah-keh*]
page *n.*, page (f) [*pahzh*]

page *v.*, appeler [*ah-pleh*]
paid, payé [*peh-yeh*]
pail, seau (m), seaux (pl) [*soh*]
pain, douleur (f) [*doo-luhr*]
painful, douloureux, -euse [*doo-loo-ruh, doo-loo-ruhz*]
paint *n.*, peinture (f) [*pĕ-tür*]
paint *v.*, peindre (irreg) [*pĕdr*]
painter, peintre (m) [*pĕtr*]
painting, peinture (f) [*pĕ-tür*]
pair *n.*, paire (f) [*per*]
pajamas, pyjama (m) [*pee-zhah-mah*]
palace, palais (m) [*pah-le*]
pale *adj.*, pâle [*pahl*]
palm tree, palmier (m) [*pahl-myeh*]
pan, casserole (f) [*kahs-rol*]
pancake, crêpe (f) [*krep*]
panic *n.*, panique (f) [*pah-neek*]
pants [trousers] *n.*, pantalon (m) [*pã-tah-lõ*]
pants [underpants] *n.*, caleçon (m), culotte (f) [*kahl-sõ, kü-lot*]
paper, papier (m) [*pah-pyeh*]
   toilet paper, papier hygiénique [*pah-pyeh ee-zhyeh-neek*]
   writing paper, papier à lettres [*pah-pyeh ah letr*]
parade *n.*, défilé (m) [*deh-fee-leh*]
paradise, paradis (m) [*pah-rah-dee*]
paragraph, paragraphe (m) [*pah-rah-grahf*]
parallel, parallèle [*pah-rah-lel*]
paralyze *v.*, paralyser [*pah-rah-lee-zeh*]
parcel, colis (m) [*ko-lee*]
pardon *n.*, pardon (m) [*pahr-dõ*]
pardon *v.*, pardonner [*pahr-do-neh*]
   Pardon me! Pardon! [*pahr-dõ*]
parent, parent (m) [*pa-rã*]
parish, paroisse (f) [*pahr-wahs*]
park *n.*, parc (m) [*pahrk*]
park *v.*, garer [*gah-reh*]
parking, stationnement (m) [*sta-syon-mã*]
   no parking, stationnement inderdit [*sta-syon-mã ĕ-ter-dee*]
parliament, parlement (m) [*pahr-luh-mã*]

parsley, persil (m) [*per-see*]
part [portion] *n.*, partie (f) [*pahr-tee*]
part [role] *n.*, rôle (m) [*rohl*]
part [in hair] *n.*, raie (f) [*re*]
partial [in part], partiel, -elle [*pahr-syel*]
partial [favoring], partial, -aux (m, pl) [*pahr-syahl, pahr-syoh*]
participate *v.*, participer [*pahr-tee-see-peh*]
particular, particulier, -ière [*pahr-tee-kü-lyeh, pahr-tee-kü-lyer*]
particularly, particulièrement [*pahr-tee-kü-lyer-mã*]
partly, en partie [*ã pahr-tee*]
partner [business], associé, -ée [*ah-so-syeh*]
partner [game], partenaire (m, f) [*pahr-tuh-ner*]
party, fête (f), réception (f), soirée (f) [*fet, reh-sep-syõ, swah-reh*]
pass [mountain] *n.*, col (m) [*kol*]
pass *v.*, passer (*Aux:* ÊTRE if intrans) [*pah-seh*]
  pass an examination, réussir à un examen [*reh-ü-seer ah ē-neg-zah-mē*]
passenger, passager, -ère [*pah-sah-zheh, pah-sah-zher*]
passenger train, train (m) de voyageurs [*trē duh vwah-yah-zhuhr*]
passing *adj.*, passager, -ère [*pah-sah-zheh, pah-sah-zher*]
passion, passion (f) [*pah-syõ*]
passionate, passionné [*pah-syo-neh*]
passive, passif, -ive [*pah-seef, pah-seev*]
passport, passeport (m) [*pahs-por*]
past, passé (m) [*pah-seh*]
pastry, pastry shop, pâtisserie (f) [*pah-tees-ree*]
patch [mending] *n.*, pièce (f) [*pyes*]
path, sentier (m) [*sã-tyeh*]
patience, patience (f) [*pah-syãs*]
patient *adj.*, patient [*pah-syã(t)*]
patient [medical] *n.*, client, -te; malade (m, f) [*klee-yã, klee-yãt; mah-lahd*]
pattern *n.*, modèle (m) [*mo-del*]
pattern [for clothes] *n.*, patron (m) [*pah-trõ*]
pause *n.*, pause (f) [*pohz*]

pause *v.*, faire une pause [*fer ün pohz*]
pavement [sidewalk], trottoir (m) [*tro-twahr*]
pavement [street], chaussée (f) [*shoh-seh*]
paw *n.*, patte (f) [*paht*]
pay *v.*, payer [*peh-yeh*]
  pay a compliment, faire un compliment [*fer ē kō-plee-mā*]
  pay attention, faire attention [*fer ah-tā-syō*]
  pay a visit, rendre une visite à [*rē-drün vee-zeet ah*]
  pay cash, payer comptant [*peh-yeh kō-tā*]
payment, paiement (m) [*pe-mā*]
pea, petit pois (m) [*ptee pwah*]
peace, paix (f) [*pe*]
peaceful, paisible [*pe-zeebl*]
peach, pêche (f) [*pesh*]
peak, sommet (m), pic (m) [*so-meh, peek*]
peanut, cacahuète (f) [*kah-kah-wet*]
pear, poire (f) [*pwahr*]
pearl, perle (f) [*perl*]
pebble, caillou (m), -oux (pl) [*ka-yoo*]
pebble [at beach], galet (m) [*gah-leh*]
peculiar, étrange [*eh-trãzh*]
pedal *n.*, pédale (f) [*peh-dahl*]
peddler, colporteur (m) [*kol-por-tuhr*]
pedestrian, piéton [*pyeh-tō*]
pen, stylo (m) [*stee-loh*]
penalty, peine (f) [*pen*]
pencil, crayon (m) [*kre-yō*]
peninsula, presqu'île (f) [*pres-keel*]
people, gens (m, pl) [*zhã*]
pepper, poivre (m) [*pwahvr*]
peppermint, menthe (f) [*mãt*]
percent, pour cent [*poor sã*]
percentage, pourcentage (m) [*poor-sã-tazh*]
perfect *adj.*, parfait [*pahr-fe(t)*]
perfection, perfection (f) [*per-fek-syō*]
performance [theater], représentation (f) [*ruh-pre-zã-ta-syō*]
performance [sports], performance (f) [*per-for-mãs*]
perfume, parfum (m) [*pahr-fē*]

perhaps, peut-être [*puh-tetr*]
period [punctuation], point final (m) [*pwĕ fee-nal*]
period [time], périod (f) [*per-yod*]
  menstrual period, règles (f, pl) [*regl*]
permanent *adj.*, permanent [*per-mah-nã(t)*]
permanent wave, permanente (f) [*per-mah-nãt*]
permission, permission (f) [*per-mee-syõ*]
permit *n.*, permis (m) [*per-mee*]
permit *v.*, permettre (irreg) [*per-metr*]
persist *v.*, persister [*per-sees-teh*]
person, personne (f) [*per-son*]
personal, personnel, -elle [*per-so-nel*]
personality, personalité (f) [*per-so-nah-lee-teh*]
personally, personnellement [*per-so-nel-mã*]
personnel, personnel (m) [*per-so-nel*]
perspiration, transpiration (f) [*trãs-pee-rah-syõ*]
perspire *v.*, transpirer [*trãs-pee-reh*]
persuade *v.*, persuader [*per-swah-deh*]
persuasive, persuasif, -ive [*per-swah-zeef, per-swah-zeev*]
pertaining to, relatif à [*ruh-lah-teef ah*]
petition *n.*, pétition (f) [*peh-tee-syõ*]
petroleum, pétrole (m) [*peh-trol*]
pewter, étain (m) [*eh-tẽ*]
pharmacy, pharmacie (f) [*fahr-mah-see*]
philosopher, philosophe (m) [*fee-lo-zof*]
philosophy, philosophie (f) [*fee-lo-zo-fee*]
phonograph, tourne-disques (m) [*toor-nuh-deesk*]
photograph *n.*, photo (f) [*foh-toh*]
photograph *v.*, photographier [*foh-toh-grah-fyeh*]
photographer, photographe (m) [*foh-toh-grahf*]
physical, physique [*fee-zeek*]
physician, médecin (m) [*med-sẽ*]
pianist, pianiste (m, f) [*pyah-neest*]
piano, piano (m) [*pyah-noh*]
pick *v.*, cueillir (irreg) [*kuh-yeer*]
pick up *v.*, ramasser [*rah-mah-seh*]
pickpocket, pickpocket [*peek-po-ket*]
picture, tableau (m), -eaux (pl) [*tah-bloh*]

picturesque, pittoresque [*pee-to-resk*]
pie, tarte (f) [*tahrt*]
piece, morceau (m), -eaux (pl) [*mor-soh*]
pier, quai (m), jetée (f) [*ke, zh(uh)-teh*]
pig, cochon (m) [*ko-shõ*]
pigeon, pigeon (m) [*pee-zhõ*]
pile *n.,* tas (m) [*tah*]
pill, pillule (f) [*pee-lül*]
pillow, oreiller (m) [*or-eh-yeh*]
pilot *n.,* pilote (m) [*pee-lot*]
pin *n.,* épingle (f) [*eh-pĕgl*]
pin *v.,* épingler [*eh-pĕ-gleh*]
pinch *v.,* pincer [*pĕ-seh*]
pine, pin (m) [*pĕ*]
pineapple, ananas (m) [*ah-nah-nah*]
pink, rose [*rohz*]
pint, demi-litre (m) [*d(uh)mee-leetr*]
pious, pieux, pieuse [*pyuh, pyuhz*]
pipe [plumbing] *n.,* tuyau (m), -aux (pl) [*twee-yoh*]
pipe [smoking] *n.,* pipe [*peep*]
pistol, pistolet (m) [*pees-to-leh*]
pitcher, pichet (m) [*pee-sheh*]
pity *n.,* pitié (f) [*pee-tyeh*]
   What a pity! Quel dommage! [*kel do-mahzh*]
pity *v.,* avoir pitié de [*ah-vwar pee-tyeh d(uh)*]
place *n.,* lieu (m), endroit (m) [*lyuh, ã-drwah*]
   in place of, au lieu de [*oh lyuh d(uh)*]
   take place *v.,* avoir lieu [*ah-vwahr lyuh*]
place *v.,* placer [*plah-seh*]
plain, simple [*sĕpl*]
plan *n.,* plan (m) [*plã*]
plan *v.,* faire un projet [*fer ĕ pro-zheh*]
planet, planète (f) [*plah-net*]
plant *n.,* plante (f) [*plãt*]
plant *v.,* planter [*plã-teh*]
plaster *n.,* plâtre (m) [*plahtr*]
plastic, plastique [*plahs-teek*]
plate, assiette (f) [*ah-syet*]

platform [train], quai (m) [*ke*]

play [drama] *n.*, pièce (f) [*pyes*]

play [a game] *v.*, jouer à [*zhweh ah*]

play [an instrument] *v.*, jouer de [*zhweh d(uh)*]

playground, terrain (m) de jeu [*te-rēd zhuh*]

playmate, camarade (m, f) de jeu [*kah-mah-rahd duh zhuh*]

pleasant, agréable [*ah-greh-ahbl*]

please *v.*, plaire (à) (irreg) [*pler (ah)*]

  please, s'il vous plaît [*seel voo ple*]

  Pleased to meet you, Enchanté de faire votre connaissance [*ã-shã-teh d(uh) fer vot-ruh ko-ne-sãs*]

pleasure, plaisir (m) [*ple-zeer*]

  with pleasure, avec plaisir [*ah-vek ple-zeer*]

pleasure trip, voyage (m) d'agrément [*vwah-yahzh dah-greh-mã*]

plenty (of), beaucoup (de) [*boh-kood(uh)*]

plot *n.*, complot (m) [*kõ-ploh*]

plow *n.*, charrue (f) [*shah-rü*]

plow *v.*, labourer [*lah-boo-reh*]

plug [electric], prise (f) [*preez*]

plum, prune (f) [*prün*]

plumber, plombier (m) [*plõ-byeh*]

plural, pluriel (m) [*plür-yel*]

plus, plus [*plüs*]

pneumonia, pneumonie (f) [*pnuh-mo-nee*]

pocket, poche (f) [*posh*]

pocketbook, sac à main (m) [*sah-kah mē*]

poem, poème (m) [*poh-em*]

poet, poète (m) [*poh-et*]

point [in time or space] *n.*, point (m) [*pwē*]

  point of view, point de vue [*pwēd vü*]

point [tip] *n.*, pointe (f) [*pwēt*]

point out *v.*, indiquer [*ē-dee-keh*]

poison, poison (m) [*pwah-zõ*]

poisonous, vénéneux, -euse [*veh-neh-nuh, veh-neh-nuhz*]

Poland, Pologne (f) [*po-loñ*]

pole [stick], perche (f) [*persh*]

pole [geographical], pôle (m) [*pohl*]

police, police (f) [*po-lees*]
policeman, agent (m) de police [*ah-zhãt po-lees*]
police station, commissariat (m) (de police) [*ko-mee-sahr-yah (duh po-lees)*]
policy, politique (f) [*po-lee-teek*]
Polish, polonais [*po-lo-ne(z)*]
polish *v.,* polir [*po-leer*]
polite, poli [*po-lee*]
political, politique [*po-lee-teek*]
politics, politique (f) [*po-lee-teek*]
pool *n.,* bassin (m) [*bah-sē*]
pool [swimming] *n.,* piscine (f) [*pee-seen*]
poor, pauvre [*pohvr*]
Pope, pape (m) [*pahp*]
poppy, coquelicot (m) [*kok-lee-koh*]
popular, à la mode [*ah lah mod*]
population, population (f) [*po-pü-lah-syõ*]
porch, porche (m) [*porsh*]
pork, porc (m) [*por*]
port [harbor] *n.,* port (m) [*por*]
port [wine] *n.,* porto (m) [*por-toh*]
port [right side] *adj.,* bâbord (m) [*bah-bor*]
portable *adj.,* portatif, -tive [*por-tah-teef, por-tah-teev*]
porter, porteur (m) [*por-tuhr*]
porthole, hublot (m) [*ü-bloh*]
portrait, portrait (m) [*por-tre*]
Portugal, Portugal (m) [*por-tü-gahl*]
Portuguese, portugais [*por-tü-ghe(z)*]
pose *v.,* poser [*poh-zeh*]
position, position (f) [*poh-zee-syõ*]
positive, positif, -tive [*poh-zee-teef, poh-zee-teev*]
possess *v.,* posséder [*po-seh-deh*]
possession, possession (f) [*po-se-syõ*]
possibility, possibilité (f) [*po-see-bee-lee-teh*]
possibly, peut-être [*puh-tetr*]
possible, possible [*po-seebl*]
  as soon as possible, aussitôt que possible [*oh-see-tohk po-seebl*]

post, poteau (m), -eaux (pl) [*poh-toh*]

postage, affranchissement (m) [*ah-frã-shees-mã*]

postage stamp, timbre (m) [*tĕbr*]

post card, carte (f) postale [*kahrt pos-tahl*]

post office, bureau (m) de poste, poste (f) [*bü-rohd post, post*]

postpone *v.,* renvoyer à plus tard [*rã-vwah-yeh ah plü tahr*]

pot, pot (m) [*poh*]

potato, pomme de terre (f) [*pom duh ter*]

  mashed potatoes, purée (f) de pommes de terre [*pü-reht pom duh ter*]

pottery, poterie (f) [*pot-ree*]

pound *n.,* livre (f) [*leevr*]

pour *v.,* verser [*ver-seh*]

poverty, pauvreté (f) [*poh-vruh-teh*]

powder, poudre (f) [*poodr*]

power, pouvoir (m) [*poo-vwahr*]

powerful, puissant [*pwee-sã(t)*]

practical, pratique [*prah-teek*]

practice *v.,* s'exercer [*sehg-zer-seh*]

praise *v.,* louer [*loo-eh*]

pray *v.,* prier [*pree-yeh*]

prayer, prière (f) [*pree-yer*]

precaution, précaution (f) [*pre-koh-syõ*]

precede *v.,* précéder [*pre-seh-deh*]

precious, précieux, -euse [*pre-syuh, pre-syuhz*]

precise, précis [*pre-see(z)*]

precisely, précisément [*pre-see-zeh-mã*]

prefer *v.,* préférer [*pre-feh-reh*]

preferable, préférable [*pre-feh-rahbl*]

preference, préférence (f) [*pre-feh-rãs*]

pregnancy, grossesse (f) [*groh-ses*]

pregnant, enceinte [*ã-sĕt*]

prejudice, préjugé (m) [*pre-zhü-zheh*]

preliminary, préliminaire [*preh-lee-mee-ner*]

preparation, préparation (f) [*pre-pah-rah-syõ*]

prepare *v.,* préparer [*preh-pah-reh*]

prescription, ordonnance (f) [*or-do-nãs*]

presence, présence (f) [*pre-zãs*]
present *adj.*, présent [*pre-zã(t)*]
present [gift] *n.*, cadeau (m), -eaux (pl) [*kah-doh*]
present [time] *n.*, présent (m) [*pre-zã*]
present *v.*, présenter [*pre-zã-teh*]
presentable, présentable [*pre-zã-tahbl*]
preserve *v.*, préserver [*pre-ser-veh*]
president, président (m) [*preh-zee-dã*]
press, presse (f) [*pres*]
press [push, squeeze, urge] *v.*, presser [*pre-seh*]
press [clothes] *v.*, repasser [*r(uh)-pah-seh*]
pressure, pression (f) [*pre-syõ*]
prestige, prestige (m) [*pres-teezh*]
presume *v.*, présumer [*pre-zü-meh*]
pretend [claim] *v.*, prétendre [*pre-tãdr*]
pretend [dissemble] *v.*, faire semblant [*fer sã-blã*]
pretentious, prétentieux, -euse [*pre-tã-syuh, pre-tã-syuhz*]
pretty, joli [*zho-lee*]
prevent *v.*, empêcher [*ã-pe-sheh*]
previous, précédent [*pre-seh-dã(t)*]
previously, auparavant [*oh-pah-rah-vã*]
price *n.*, prix (m) [*pree*]
pride, orgueil (m) [*or-guhy*]
priest, prêtre (m) [*pretr*]
primitive, primitif, -tive [*pree-mee-teef, pree-mee-teev*]
prince, prince (m) [*prẽs*]
princess, princesse (f) [*prẽ-ses*]
principal, principal, -aux (m, pl) [*prẽ-see-pahl, prẽ-see-poh*]
principally, principalement [*prẽ-see-pahl-mã*]
principle, principe (m) [*prẽ-seep*]
print [photo] *n.*, épreuve (f) [*eh-pruhv*]
print *v.*, imprimer [*ẽ-pree-meh*]
printed matter, imprimé (m) [*ẽ-pree-meh*]
printer, imprimeur (m) [*ẽ-pree-muhr*]
prior, antérieur [*ã-tehr-yuhr*]
prison, prison (f) [*pree-zõ*]
prisoner, prisonnier, -ière [*pree-zon-yeh, pree-zon-yer*]
private, privé [*pree-veh*]

privilege, privilège (m) [*pree-vee-lezh*]
prize *n.*, prix (m) [*pree*]
probable, probable [*pro-bahbl*]
probably, probablement [*pro-bahb-luh-mã*]
problem, problème (m) [*pro-blem*]
procedure, procédure (f) [*pro-seh-dür*]
proceed *v.*, procéder [*pro-seh-deh*]
process [method] *n.*, procédé (m) [*pro-seh-deh*]
produce *v.*, produire (irreg) [*pro-dweer*]
product, produit (m) [*pro-dwee*]
production, production (f) [*pro-dük-syõ*]
profession, profession (f) [*pro-fe-syõ*]
professor, professeur (m) [*pro-fe-suhr*]
profit *n.*, profit (m) [*pro-fee*]
profit *v.*, profiter [*pro-fee-teh*]
program *n.*, programme (m) [*pro-grahm*]
progress *n.*, progrès (m) [*pro-gre*]
progressive, progressif, -ive [*pro-gre-seef, pro-gre-seev*]
prohibit *v.*, défendre [*deh-fãdr*]
prohibited, interdit, défendu [*ē-ter-dee(t), deh-fã-dü*]
project *n.*, projet (m) [*pro-zheh*]
prominent, éminent [*eh-mee-nã(t)*]
promise *n.*, promesse (f) [*pro-mes*]
promise *v.*, promettre (irreg) [*pro-metr*]
promotion, promotion (f) [*proh-moh-syõ*]
prompt, prompt [*prõ(t)*]
pronoun, pronom (m) [*pro-nõ*]
pronounce *v.*, prononcer [*pro-nõ-seh*]
pronunciation, prononciation (f) [*pro-nõ-syah-syõ*]
proof, preuve (f) [*pruhv*]
propaganda, propagande (f) [*pro-pah-gãd*]
propeller, hélice (f) [*eh-lees*]
proper, convenable [*kõv-nahbl*]
property, propriété (f) [*pro-pree-yeh-teh*]
proportion, proportion (f) [*pro-por-syõ*]
proposal, proposition (f) [*proh-poh-zee-syõ*]
proposal [marriage], demande (f) en mariage [*duh-mã-dã mahr-yahzh*]

propose v., proposer [*proh-poh-zeh*]
propose [marriage] v., demander en mariage [*dmã-deh ã mahr-yazh*]
proprietor, propriétaire (m) [*pro-pree-yeh-ter*]
prosperity, prospérité (f) [*pros-peh-ree-teh*]
prosperous, prospère [*pros-per*]
protect v., protéger [*pro-teh-zheh*]
protection, protection (f) [*pro-tek-syõ*]
protest v., protester [*pro-tes-teh*]
Protestant, protestant [*pro-tes-tã(t)*]
proud, fier, fière [*fyer*]
prove v., prouver [*proo-veh*]
proverb, proverbe (m) [*pro-verb*]
provide v., fournir [*foor-neer*]
provided that, pourvu que [*poor-vü k(uh)*]
province, province (f) [*pro-vẽs*]
provincial, provincial, -aux (m, pl) [*pro-vẽ-syahl, pro-vẽ-syoh*]
provision [clause], clause (f) [*klohz*]
provisions [supplies], provisions (f, pl) [*pro-vee-zyõ*]
prune, pruneau (m), -eaux (pl) [*prü-noh*]
psychiatrist, psychiatre (m) [*psee-kyahtr*]
psychoanalysis, psychanalyse (f) [*psee-kah-nah-leez*]
psychological, psychologique [*psee-ko-lo-zheek*]
public adj., public, publique [*pü-bleek*]
public n., public (m) [*pü-bleek*]
publication, publication (f) [*pü-blee-kah-syõ*]
publicity, publicité (f) [*pü-blee-see-teh*]
publish v., publier [*pü-blee-yeh*]
pull v., tirer [*tee-reh*]
pulse n., pouls (m) [*poo*]
pump n., pompe (f) [*põp*]
pumpkin, potiron (m), citrouille (f) [*po-tee-rõ, see-trooy*]
punctual, ponctuel, -elle [*põk-twel*]
puncture n., crevaison (f) [*kruh-ve-sõ*]
punish v., punir [*pü-neer*]
punishment, punition (f) [*pü-nee-syõ*]
pupil, élève (m, f) [*eh-lev*]

puppet, marionnette (f) [*mahr-yo-net*]
purchase *n.*, achat (m) [*ah-shah*]
purchase *v.*, acheter [*ahsh-teh*]
pure, pur [*pür*]
purple, violet, -ette [*vyo-leh, vyo-let*]
purpose, but (m) [*bü(t)*]
  on purpose, exprès [*ehk-spre*]
purse, sac (m) [*sahk*]
pursue *v.*, poursuivre (irreg) [*poor-sweevr*]
push *v.*, pousser [*poo-seh*]
put *v.*, mettre (irreg) [*metr*]
  put on [light], allumer [*ah-lü-meh*]
  put on [clothes], mettre (irreg) [*metr*]
  put out [light], éteindre (irreg) [*eh-tēdr*]
pyramid, pyramide (f) [*pee-rah-meed*]

Q

qualification [limitation], réserve (f) [*reh-zerv*]
qualification [ability], titre (m) [*teetr*]
quality, qualité (f) [*kah-lee-teh*]
quantity, quantité (f) [*kã-tee-teh*]
quarrel *n.*, querelle (f) [*kuh-rel*]
quart, environ un litre (m) [*ã-vee-rõ ē leetr*]
quarter, quart (m) [*kahr*]
  quarter hour, quart d'heure [*kahr duhr*]
queen, reine (f) [*ren*]
queer [odd], bizarre [*bee-zahr*]
question *n.*, question (f) [*kes-tyõ*]
question *v.*, questionner [*kes-tyo-neh*]
questionable, contestable [*kõ-tes-tahbl*]
question mark, point (m) d'interrogation [*pwē dē-teh-ro-gah-syõ*]
questionnaire, questionnaire (m) [*kes-tyo-ner*]
quick, rapide [*rah-peed*]

quickly, vite [*veet*]
quiet, tranquille [*trã-keel*]
   Be quiet, Restez tranquille [*res-teh trã-keel*]
quit [stop] *v.*, arrêter [*ah-re-teh*]
quit [doing something] *v.*, cesser (de) [*seh-seh (duh)*]
quite, tout à fait [*too-tah fe*]
quotation [of words], citation (f) [*see-tah-syõ*]
quotation [of price, terms], devis (m) [*duh-vee*]
quotation marks, guillemets (m, pl) [*gheey-meh*]
quote *v.*, citer [*see-teh*]

R

rabbi, rabbin (m) [*rah-bẽ*]
rabbit, lapin (m) [*lah-pẽ*]
rabies, rage (f) [*rahzh*]
race [ethnic group] *n.*, race (f) [*rahs*]
race [contest] *n.*, course (f) [*koors*]
racetrack, champ (m) de courses [*shãt koors*]
racket [in sports], raquette (f) [*rah-ket*]
radiator, radiateur (m) [*rah-dyah-tuhr*]
radical, radical, -aux (m, pl) [*rah-dee-kahl, rah-dee-koh*]
radio, radio (f) [*rah-dyoh*]
radish, radis (m) [*rah-dee*]
rag, chiffon (m) [*shee-fõ*]
railroad, chemin (m) de fer [*shmẽd fer*]
railroad car, wagon (m) [*vah-gõ*]
railroad crossing, passage à niveau [*pah-sah-zhah nee-voh*]
railroad station, gare (f) [*gahr*]
rain *n.*, pluie (f) [*plwee*]
rain *v.*, pleuvoir (irreg) [*pluh-vwahr*]
   It's raining, Il pleut [*eel pluh*]
rainbow, arc (m) en ciel [*ar-kã syel*]
raincoat, imperméable (m) [*ẽ-per-meh-ahbl*]
raise [rear] *v.*, élever [*ehl-veh*]

raise [lift] *v.*, soulever [*sool-veh*]
raisin, raisin sec (m) [*re-zẽ sek*]
random, at random, au *hasard [*oh ah-zahr*]
rape *n.*, viol (m) [*vyol*]
rape *v.*, violer [*vyo-leh*]
rapid, rapide [*rah-peed*]
rapidly, rapidement [*rah-peed-mã*]
rare [unusual], rare [*rahr*]
rare [undercooked], saignant [*se-nyã(t)*]
rarely, rarement [*rahr-mã*]
rash *n.*, éruption (f) [*eh-rüp-syõ*]
rash *adj.*, téméraire [*teh-meh-rɛr*]
rat, rat (m) [*rah*]
rate [price] *n.*, tarif (m) [*tah-reef*]
rate [speed] *n.*, taux (m) [*toh*]
rather (than), plutôt (que) [*plü-toh (kuh)*]
   I would rather . . . , J'aimerais mieux . . . [*zhem-re myuh*]
raw, cru [*krü*]
raw material, matière (f) première [*mah-tyer pruh-myer*]
ray, rayon (m) [*re-yõ*]
razor, rasoir (m) [*rah-zwahr*]
razor blade, lame (f) de rasoir [*lahm duh rah-zwahr*]
reach *v.*, atteindre (irreg) [*ah-tẽdr*]
reaction, réaction (f) [*reh-ahk-syõ*]
read *v.*, lire (irreg) [*leer*]
reading, lecture (f) [*lek-tür*]
ready, prêt [*pre(t)*]
   ready to wear, prêt à porter [*pre-tah por-teh*]
real, réel, réelle [*reh-el*]
real estate, biens immobiliers (m, pl) [*byẽ-zee-mo-beel-yeh*]
realize *v.*, se rendre compte (de) [*srãdr kõt (duh)*]
really, réellement [*reh-el-mã*]
reason *n.*, raison (f) [*re-zõ*]
reasonable, raisonnable [*re-zo-nahbl*]
reassure *v.*, rassurer [*rah-sü-reh*]
rebel *n.*, rebelle (m, f) [*ruh-bel*]
rebel (against) *v.*, se soulever (contre) [*suh sool-veh (kõtr)*]
recall *v.*, rappeler [*rah-pleh*]

receipt, reçu (m) [*ruh-sü*]
receive v., recevoir (irreg) [*ruh-suh-vwahr*]
recent, récent [*reh-sã(t)*]
recently, récemment [*reh-sah-mã*]
reception, réception (f) [*reh-sεp-syõ*]
recession, récession (f) [*reh-se-syõ*]
recipe, recette (f) [*ruh-set*]
recite v., réciter [*reh-see-teh*]
reckless, téméraire [*teh-meh-rer*]
recognize v., reconnaître (irreg) [*ruh-ko-nεtr*]
recommend v., recommander [*r(uh)-ko-mã-deh*]
recommendation, recommendation (f) [*ruh-ko-mã-dah-syõ*]
record [for phonograph] n., disque (m) [*deesk*]
record [in sports] n., record (m) [*ruh-kor*]
   police record, casier (m) judiciaire [*kah-zyeh zhü-dee-syer*]
   school record, livret (m) scolaire [*lee-vre sko-ler*]
recover [something] v., retrouver [*r(uh)-troo-veh*]
recover [from illness] v., se remettre (irreg) [*sruh-metr*]
recovery, guérison (f) [*gheh-ree-zõ*]
recreation, récréation (f) [*reh-kreh-ah-syõ*]
rectangle, rectangle (m) [*rek-tãgl*]
red, rouge [*roozh*]
Red Cross, Croix Rouge (m) [*krwah roozh*]
redeem v., racheter [*rahsh-teh*]
reduce v., réduire (irreg) [*reh-dweer*]
reduction, réduction (f) [*reh-dük-syõ*]
referee, arbitre (m) [*ahr-beetr*]
reference, référence (f) [*reh-feh-rãs*]
refill v., remplir [*rã-pleer*]
refined, raffiné [*rah-fee-neh*]
reflect [light] v., refléter [*r(uh)-fle-teh*]
reflect [think] v., réfléchir [*reh-flεh-sheer*]
reflection, réflexion (f) [*reh-flek-syõ*]
reflex, réflexe (m) [*reh-fleks*]
reform n., réforme (f) [*reh-form*]
reform v., réformer [*reh-for-meh*]
refrain (from) v., s'abstenir (de) (irreg) [*sahp-stuh-neer (duh)*]

refresh v., rafraîchir [rah-fre-sheer]

refreshing, rafraîchissant [rah-fre-shee-sã(t)]

refreshment, rafraîchissement (m) [rah-fre-shees-mã]

refrigerator, frigidaire (m) [free-zhee-der]

refuge, refuge (m) [r(uh)-füzh]

refugee, réfugié, -ée [reh-fü-zhyeh]

refund n., remboursement (m) [rã-boor-suh-mã]

refusal, refus (m) [r(uh)-fü]

refuse v., refuser [r(uh)-fü-zeh]

regain v., regagner [ruh-gah-nyeh]

regard: with regard to, quant à [kã-tah]

regiment, régiment (m) [reh-zhee-mã]

region, région (f) [reh-zhyõ]

register n., registre (m) [ruh-zheestr]

register [at school] v., s'inscrire (irreg) [sẽ-skreer]

register [baggage] v., enregistrer [ãr-zhees-treh]

registered letter, lettre (f) recommandée [letr ruh-ko-mã-deh]

regret n., regret (m) [r(uh)-gre]

regret v., regretter [r(uh)-gre-teh]

regular adj., régulier, -ière [reh-gü-lyeh, re-gü-lyer]

regular gas, normal [nor-mahl]

regulate v., régler [reh-gleh]

regulation, règlement (m) [re-gluh-mã]

rehearsal, répétition (f) [reh-peh-tee-syõ]

reign n., règne (m) [reñ]

reject v., rejeter [ruhsh-teh]

rejoin v., rejoindre (irreg) [r(uh)-zhwẽdr]

relation [connection] n., rapport (m) [ra-por]

relationship [by family] n., parenté (f) [pah-rã-teh]

relative n., parent, -te [pah-rã(t)]

relatively, relativement [ruh-lah-teev-mã]

relax v., détendre (irreg), se détendre (irreg) [deh-tãdr, sdeh-tãdr]

relaxation, détente (f) [deh-tãt]

relevant, pertinent [per-tee-nã(t)]

reliable, sur [sür]

relieve v., soulager [soo-lah-zheh]

religion, religion (f) [r(uh)-lee-zhyõ]

religious, religieux, -euse [*ruh-lee-zhyuh, ruh-lee-zhyuhz*]
reluctant, peu disposé [*puh dees-poh-zeh*]
rely (on) *v.*, compter sur [*kõ-teh sür*]
remain *v.*, rester (*Aux:* ÊTRE) [*res-teh*]
remainder, reste (m) [*rest*]
remark *n.*, remarque (f) [*r(uh)-mahrk*]
remark *v.*, remarquer [*r(uh)-mahr-keh*]
remarkable, remarquable [*r(uh)-mahr-kahbl*]
remedy *n.*, remède (m) [*r(uh)-med*]
remember *v.*, se rappeler, se souvenir (de) [*srah-pleh, suh soov-neer (duh)*]
remind *v.*, rappeler (à) [*rah-pleh (ah)*]
remittance, paiement (m) [*pe-mã*]
remorse, remords (m) [*r(uh)-mor*]
remove *v.*, enlever [*ãl-veh*]
renew *v.*, renouveler [*ruh-noo-vleh*]
rent *n.*, loyer (m) [*lwah-yeh*]
rent *v.*, louer [*loo-eh*]
repair *v.*, réparer [*reh-pah-reh*]
repay *v.*, rembourser [*rã-boor-seh*]
repeat *v.*, répéter [*reh-peh-teh*]
replace *v.*, remplacer [*rã-plah-seh*]
reply *n.*, réponse (f) [*reh-põs*]
reply *v.*, répondre [*reh-põdr*]
report *v.*, rendre compte (de) [*rãdr kõt (duh)*]
report *n.*, rapport (m) [*rah-por*]
reporter, journaliste (m, f) [*zhoor-nah-leest*]
represent *v.*, représenter [*r(uh)-preh-zã-teh*]
representative, représentant (m) [*r(uh)-preh-zã-tã*]
reproduction, reproduction (f) [*r(uh)-pro-dük-syõ*]
republic, république (f) [*reh-pü-bleek*]
reputation, réputation (f) [*reh-pü-tah-syõ*]
request *n.*, demande (f) [*d(uh)-mãd*]
request *v.*, demander [*d(uh)-mã-deh*]
require *v.*, exiger [*ɛg-zee-zheh*]
requirement, exigence (f) [*eg-zee-zhãs*]
rescue *v.*, sauver [*soh-veh*]
research *n.*, recherche (f) [*r(uh)-shersh*]

resemblance, ressemblance (f) [*ruh-sã-blãs*]
resemble *v.,* ressembler (à) [*ruh-sã-bleh (ah)*]
resentment, ressentiment (m) [*ruh-sã-tee-mã*]
reservation, réserve (f) [*reh-serv*]
  We have reservations at . . . Hotel, Nous avons retenu des
    chambres à l'Hotel . . . [*noo-zah-võ ruht-nü deh shã-brah
    loh-tel*]
reserve [a room] *v.,* retenir (irreg) [*ruht-neer*]
reserve [a seat] *v.,* louer [*loo-weh*]
residence, résidence (f) [*reh-zee-dãs*]
resident, résident -te [*re-zee-dã(t)*]
resign *v.,* démissionner [*deh-mee-syo-neh*]
resignation, démission (f) [*deh-mee-syõ*]
resist *v.,* résister [*reh-zees-teh*]
resolution, résolution (f) [*reh-zo-lü-syõ*]
respect *n.,* respect (m) [*re-spe*]
respect *v.,* respecter [*re-spek-teh*]
respectable, respectable [*re-spek-tahbl*]
response, réponse (f) [*reh-põs*]
responsibility, responsabilité (f) [*res-põ-sah-bee-lee-teh*]
responsible, responsable [*res-põ-sahbl*]
rest *v.,* se reposer [*sruh-poh-zeh*]
restaurant, restaurant (m) [*res-to-rã*]
restore *v.,* restaurer [*res-to-reh*]
result *n.,* résultat (m) [*reh-zül-tah*]
resume *v.,* reprendre (irreg) [*ruh-prãdr*]
retail, au détail [*oh deh-tahy*]
retire [be pensioned off] *v.,* prendre (irreg) sa retraite
    [*prãdr sahr-tret*]
retire [withdraw] *v.,* se retirer [*sruh-tee-reh*]
return *n.,* retour (m) [*r(uh)-toor*]
reveal *v.,* révéler [*reh-veh-leh*]
revelation, révélation (f) [*reh-veh-lah-syõ*]
revenge, vengeance (f), revanche (f) [*vã-zhãs, r(uh)-vãsh*]
reverse *n.,* inverse (m) [*ẽ-vers*]
revise *v.,* réviser [*reh-vee-zeh*]
revolution, révolution (f) [*reh-vo-lü-syõ*]
revolver, révolver (m) [*reh-vol-ver*]

reward *n.*, récompense (f) [*reh-kŏ-pãs*]
reward *v.*, récompenser [*reh-kŏ-pã-seh*]
rheumatism, rhumatisme (m) [*rü-mah-teesm*]
rhyme *n.*, rime (f) [*reem*]
rhythm, rythme (m) [*reetm*]
rib, côte (f) [*koht*]
ribbon, ruban (m) [*rü-bã*]
rice, riz (m) [*ree*]
rich, riche [*reesh*]
rid: to get rid of *v.*, se débarasser (de) [*sdeh-bah-rah-seh (duh)*]
ride *n.*, promenade (f) [*prom-nahd*]
ridiculous, ridicule [*ree-dee-kül*]
right [direction], droit [*drwah(t)*]
   on the right, à droite [*ah drwaht*]
right [correct], juste, exact [*zhüst, eg-zah(kt)*]
   all right, très bien [*tre byẽ*]
   be right *v.*, avoir raison [*ah-vwahr re-zõ*]
   right away, tout de suite [*toot sweet*]
right *n.*, droit (m) [*drwah*]
ring [circular band] *n.*, bague (f) [*bahg*]
ring *v.*, sonner [*so-neh*]
ringing, sonnerie (f) [*son-ree*]
rinse *n.*, rinçage (m) [*rẽ-sahzh*]
rinse *v.*, rincer [*rẽ-seh*]
riot *n.*, émeute (f) [*eh-muht*]
rip *v.*, déchirer [*deh-shee-reh*]
ripe, mûr [*mür*]
ripen *v.*, mûrir [*mü-reer*]
rise *v.*, se lever [*s(uh) luh-veh*]
risk *n.*, risque (m) [*reesk*]
ritual *n.*, rites (m, pl) [*reet*]
rival *adj. & n.*, rival, -le (sing); -aux, -ales (pl) [*ree-vahl, ree-voh*]
river, fleuve (m), rivière (f) [*fluhv, reev-yer*]
road, route (f), chemin (m) [*root, shmẽ*]
roar *v.*, rugir [*rü-zheer*]
roast *n.*, rôti (m) [*ro-tee*]
roast *v.*, faire rôtir [*fer ro-teer*]

roasted, rôti [*ro-tee*]
rob *v.,* voler [*vo-leh*]
robber, voleur, -euse [*vo-luhr, vo-luhz*]
robbery, vol (m) [*vol*]
rock *n.,* rocher (m) [*ro-sheh*]
rock *v.,* balancer [*bah-lã-seh*]
rocking chair, chaise (f) à bascule [*shez ah bahs-kül*]
roll [bread] *n.,* petit pain (m) [*ptee pē*]
roll *v.,* rouler [*roo-leh*]
Roman, romain [*ro-mē, ro-men*]
Romanesque, roman [*ro-mã, ro-mahn*]
romantic, romantique [*ro-mã-teek*]
roof, toit (m) [*twah*]
room [apartment] *n.,* pièce (f) [*pyes*]
   double room, chambre à deux lits [*shãbr ah duh lee*]
   single room, chambre à un lit [*shãbr ah ē lee*]
room [space] *n.,* place (f) [*plahs*]
root, racine (f) [*rah-seen*]
rope, corde (f) [*kord*]
rose *n.,* rose (f) [*rohz*]
rotten, pourri [*poo-ree*]
rouge, rouge (m) [*roozh*]
rough, rude [*rüd*]
round [circular], rond [*rõ(d)*]
round trip, aller retour [*ah-leh r(uh)-toor*]
routine, routine (f) [*roo-teen*]
row [line] *n.,* rang (m) [*rã*]
royal, royal, -aux (m, pl) [*rwah-yahl, rwah-yoh*]
rub *v.,* frotter [*fro-teh*]
rubber, caoutchouc (m) [*ka-oot-shoo*]
ruby, rubis (m) [*rü-bee*]
rude, grossier, -ière [*groh-syeh, groh-syer*]
rug, tapis (m) [*tah-pee*]
ruin *n.,* ruine (f) [*rween*]
rule *n.,* règle (f) [*regl*]
rule *v.,* gouverner [*goo-ver-neh*]
ruler [measure], règle (f) [*regl*]
ruler [governor], gouvernant (m) [*goo-ver-nã*]

rum, rhum (m) [*rom*]
rumor, rumeur (f) [*rü-muhr*]
run *v.,* courir (irreg) [*koo-reer*]
   run across, traverser [*trah-ver-seh*]
   run away, partir (irreg; *Aux:* ÊTRE) en courant [*pahr-teer ã koo-rã*]
   run over, écraser [*eh-krah-zeh*]
running, courant [*koo-rã(t)*]
runway, piste (f) d'atterrissage [*peest dah-teh-ree-sahzh*]
rural, rural, -aux (m, pl) [*rü-rahl, rü-roh*]
rush hours, heures d'affluence [*uhr dah-flü-ãs*]
Russian, russe [*rüs*]
rust *n.,* rouille (f) [*rooy*]
rust *v.,* rouiller [*roo-yeh*]
rut *n.,* ornière (f) [*orn-yer*]
rye, seigle (m) [*segl*]

S

sack, sac (m) [*sahk*]
sacred, sacré [*sah-kreh*]
sacrifice *n.,* sacrifice (m) [*sah-kree-fees*]
sad, triste [*treest*]
saddle, selle (f) [*sel*]
sadness, tristesse (f) [*trees-tes*]
safe *adj.,* sûr [*sür*]
   safe and sound, sain et sauf [*sẽ eh sohf*]
safety, sûreté (f) [*sür-teh*]
safety pin, épingle anglaise (f) [*eh-pẽgl ã-glez*]
sail *n.,* voile (f) [*vwahl*]
sail *v.,* aller (irreg; *Aux:* ÊTRE) en bateau [*ah-leh ã bah-toh*]
sailboat, bateau (m) à voile [*bah-toh ah vwahl*]
sailor, matelot (m) [*maht-loh*]
saint *adj. & n.,* saint, -te [*sẽ(t)*]
sake: for the sake of, pour [*poor*]

salad, salade (f) [*sah-lahd*]

salary, traitement (m) [*tret-mã*]

sale, vente (f) [*vãt*]

   for sale, à vendre [*ah vãdr*]

salesclerk, vendeur, -euse [*vã-duhr, vã-duhz*]

salmon, saumon (m) [*soh-mõ*]

salt, sel (m) [*sel*]

salty, salé [*sah-leh*]

same, le même, la même, les mêmes [*luh mem, lah mem, leh mem*]

   all the same, tout de même [*tood mem*]

sample *n.*, échantillon (m) [*eh-shã-tee-yõ*]

sand, sable (m) [*sahbl*]

sandal, sandale (f) [*sã-dahl*]

sandwich, sandwich (m) [*sã-dweetsh*]

sandy, sablonneux, -euse [*sah-blo-nuh, sah-blo-nuhz*]

sane, sain d'esprit [*sẽ des-pree*]

sanitary, sanitaire [*sah-nee-ter*]

sanitary napkins, serviettes (f) hygiéniques [*ser-vyet ee-zhyeh-neek*]

sapphire, saphir (m) [*sah-feer*]

satin, satin (m) [*sah-tẽ*]

satire, satire (f) [*sah-teer*]

satirical, satirique [*sah-tee-reek*]

satisfaction, satisfaction (f) [*sah-tees-fahk-syõ*]

satisfactory, satisfaisant [*sah-tees-fuh-zã(t)*]

satisfied, satisfait [*sah-tees-fe(t)*]

satisfy *v.*, satisfaire (irreg) [*sah-tees-fer*]

Saturday, samedi (m) [*sahm-dee*]

sauce, sauce (f) [*sohs*]

saucer, soucoupe (f) [*soo-koop*]

sausage, saucisse (f) [*soh-sees*]

save [preserve] *v.*, sauver [*soh-veh*]

save [put aside] *v.*, économiser [*eh-ko-no-mee-zeh*]

savings, épargne (f) [*eh-pahrñ*]

savings account, compte (m) à la caisse d'épargne [*kõt ah lah kes deh-pahrñ*]

saw *n.*, scie (f) [*see*]

say *v.*, dire (irreg) [*deer*]
scale [for weighing] *n.*, balance (f) [*bah-lās*]
scale [proportion] *n.*, échelle (f) [*eh-shel*]
scalp, cuir chevelu (m) [*kweer shuh-vlü*]
scandal, scandale (m) [*skā-dahl*]
scar *n.*, cicatrice (f) [*see-kah-trees*]
scarce, rare [*rahr*]
scarcely, à peine [*ah pen*]
scare *v.*, effrayer [*eh-fre-yeh*]
scarf, écharpe (f), foulard (m) [*eh-shahrp, foo-lahr*]
scarlet, écarlate (f) [*eh-kahr-laht*]
scarlet fever, scarlatine (f) [*skahr-lah-teen*]
scatter *v.*, éparpiller [*eh-pahr-pee-yeh*]
scene, scène (f) [*sen*]
scenery, décor (m) [*deh-kor*]
scent *n.*, parfum (m) [*pahr-fē*]
schedule *n.*, horaire (m) [*o-rer*]
scholar, savant (m) [*sah-vā*]
school, école (f) [*eh-kol*]
schoolmate, camarade d'école (m, f) [*kah-mah-rahd deh-kol*]
science, science (f) [*syās*]
scientist, scientifique (m, f) [*syā-tee-feek*]
scissors, ciseaux (m, pl) [*see-zoh*]
scold *v.*, gronder [*grō-deh*]
scorch *v.*, roussir [*roo-seer*]
score *n.*, nombre (m) de points [*nōbr duh pwē*]
scorn *n.*, mépris (m) [*meh-pree*]
scorn *v.*, mépriser [*meh-pree-zeh*]
Scottish, écossais [*eh-ko-se(z)*]
Scotland, Ecosse (f) [*eh-kos*]
scrape *v.*, érafler [*eh-rah-fleh*]
scratch *n.*, égratignure (f) [*eh-grah-tee-nyür*]
scratch *v.*, gratter [*grah-teh*]
scream *n.*, cri (m) [*kree*]
scream *v.*, pousser des cris [*poo-seh deh kree*]
screen [metal] *n.*, grille (f) [*greey*]
screen [motion picture] *n.*, écran (m) [*eh-krā*]
screw *n.*, vis (f) [*vees*]

screwdriver, tournevis (m) [*toor-nuh-vees*]
scrub *v.*, frotter [*fro-teh*]
sculpture, sculpture (f) [*skül-tür*]
sea, mer (f) [*mer*]
seal [animal] *n.*, phoque (m) [*fok*]
seal [stamp] *n.*, sceau (m), sceaux (pl) [*soh*]
seal *v.*, cacheter [*kahsh-teh*]
seam, couture (f) [*koo-tür*]
search for *v.*, chercher [*sher-sheh*]
seaside, bord (m) de la mer [*bor duh lah mer*]
season *n.*, saison (f) [*seh-zõ*]
season *v.*, assaisonner [*ah-seh-zo-neh*]
seat *n.*, siège (m) [*syezh*]
seatbelt, ceinture (f) de sécurité [*sĕ-tür duh seh-kü-ree-teh*]
seated, assis [*ah-see(z)*]
second *adj.*, second, deuxième [*suh-gõ(d), duh-zyεm*]
second *n.*, seconde (f) [*suh-gõd*]
secondary, secondaire [*suh-gõ-der*]
secret *n.*, secret (m) [*suh-kreh*]
secretary, secrétaire (m, f) [*suh-kreh-ter*]
section, section (f) [*sek-syõ*]
securities [financial], valeurs (f, pl) [*vah-luhr*]
security, sécurité (f) [*seh-kü-ree-teh*]
seduce *v.*, séduire (irreg) [*seh-dweer*]
see *v.*, voir (irreg) [*vwahr*]
  Let me see, Faites voir [*fet vwahr*]
  Let's see, Voyons [*vwah-yõ*]
seed, graine (f) [*gren*]
seek *v.*, chercher [*sher-sheh*]
seem *v.*, sembler [*sã-bleh*]
seize *v.*, saisir [*se-zeer*]
seldom, rarement [*rahr-mã*]
select *v.*, choisir [*shwah-zeer*]
self, moi, moi-même [*mwah, mwah-mem*]
self-conscious, gêné [*zhe-neh*]
selfish, égoïste [*ε-go-eest*]
sell *v.*, vendre [*vãdr*]
senate, sénat (m) [*seh-nah*]

senator, sénateur (m) [*seh-nah-tuhr*]
send v., envoyer [*ã-vwah-yeh*]
  send for, envoyer chercher, faire venir [*ã-vwah-yeh sher-sheh, fer vuh-neer*]
sender, expéditeur (m) [*ehk-speh-dee-tuhr*]
sense n., sens (m) [*sãs*]
  common sense, bon sens [*bõ sãs*]
sensible, raisonnable [*re-zo-nahbl*]
sensitive, sensible [*sã-seebl*]
sentence, phrase (f) [*frahz*]
sentimental, sentimental, -aux (m, pl) [*sã-tee-mã-tahl, sã-tee-mã-toh*]
separate adj., séparé [*seh-pah-reh*]
separate v., séparer [*seh-pah-reh*]
separately, séparément [*seh-pah-reh-mã*]
separation, séparation (f) [*seh-pah-rah-syõ*]
September, septembre (m) [*sep-tãbr*]
sergeant, sergent (m) [*ser-zhã*]
series, série (f) [*seh-ree*]
serious, sérieux, -euse [*ser-yuh, ser-yuhz*]
seriously, sérieusement [*ser-yuhz-mã*]
sermon, sermon (m) [*ser-mõ*]
servant, domestique (m, f) [*do-mes-teek*]
serve v., servir (irreg) [*ser-veer*]
service, service (m) [*ser-vees*]
service [church], office (m) [*o-fees*]
set n., ensemble (m) [*ã-sãbl*]
set v., mettre (irreg) [*metr*]
set [clock] v., régler [*reh-gleh*]
settle v., arranger [*ah-rã-zheh*]
seven, sept [*set*]
seventeen, dix-sept [*dee-set*]
seventh, septième [*set-yem*]
seventy, soixante-dix [*swah-sãt-dees*]
sever v., rompre [*rõpr*]
several, plusieurs [*plü-zyuhr*]
severe, sévère [*seh-ver*]
sew v., coudre (irreg) [*koodr*]

sewing machine, machine (f) à coudre [*mah-sheen ah koodr*]
sex, sexe (m) [*seks*]
shade, shadow *n.*, ombre (f) [*õbr*]
shady, ombragé [*õ-brah-zheh*]
shake *v.*, secouer [*suh-kweh*]
  shake hands, serrer la main [*seh-reh lah mē*]
shallow, peu profond [*puh pro-fõ(d)*]
shame, *honte (f) [*õt*]
shameful, *honteux, -euse [*õ-tuh, õ-tuhz*]
shampoo *n.*, shampooing (m) [*shã-pwē*]
shape *n.*, forme (f) [*form*]
share [portion] *n.*, part (f) [*pahr*]
share [stock] *n.*, action (f) [*ahk-syõ*]
share *v.*, partager [*pahr-tah-zheh*]
sharp, aiguisé, pointu [*eh-ghee-zeh, pwē-tü*]
sharpen *v.*, aiguiser [*eh-ghee-zeh*]
shave *v.*, se raser [*srah-zeh*]
shaving brush, blaireau (m), -eaux (pl) [*ble-roh*]
shaving soap, savon à barbe [*sah-võ ah bahrb*]
shawl, châle (m) [*shahl*]
she, elle [*el*]
sheet [bedding], drap (m) [*drah*]
sheet [leaf], feuille (f) [*fuhy*]
shelf, étagère (f), rayon (m) [*eh-tah-zher, re-yõ*]
shell [seashell], coquillage (m) [*ko-kee-yazh*]
shell [eggshell], coquille (f) [*ko-keey*]
shelter *n.*, abri (m) [*ah-bree*]
shift *v.*, changer [*shã-zheh*]
  shift gears, changer de vitesse [*shã-zhehd vee-tes*]
shine *v.*, briller [*bree-yeh*]
shine [shoes] *v.*, cirer [*see-reh*]
ship *n.*, navire (m) [*nah-veer*]
ship *v.*, expédier [*ehks-peh-dyeh*]
shipment, envoi (m) [*ã-vwah*]
shipwreck, naufrage (m) [*noh-frazh*]
shirt, chemise (f) [*shmeez*]
shiver *v.*, trembler de froid [*trã-bleh duh frwah*]
shock *n.*, choc (m) [*shok*]

shock v., choquer [*sho-keh*]
shoe, chaussure (f) [*shoh-sür*]
shoemaker, cordonnier (m) [*kor-do-nyeh*]
shoeshine boy, cireur (m) [*see-ruhr*]
shoot v., tirer [*tee-reh*]
shop n., magasin (m), boutique (f) [*mah-gah-zẽ, boo-teek*]
shop v., faire des achats [*fer deh-zah-shah*]
shop window, vitrine (f) [*vee-treen*]
shore, rivage (m) [*ree-vahzh*]
short, court [*koor(t)*]
  in a short time, dans un petit moment [*dã-zẽ ptee mo-mã*]
shorts, short (m) [*short*]
shortsighted, myope [*myop*]
should :
  We should leave, Nous devrions partir [*noo duh-vree-yõ pahr-teer*]
  We should have left, Nous aurions dû partir [*noo-zor-yõ dü pahr-teer*]
shoulder, épaule (f) [*eh-pohl*]
shout v., crier [*kree-yeh*]
shovel, pelle (f) [*pel*]
show n., spectacle (m) [*spek-tahkl*]
show v., montrer [*mõ-treh*]
shower [bath] n., douche (f) [*doosh*]
shower [rain] n., averse [*ah-vers*]
shrimp, crevette (f) [*kruh-vet*]
shrink v., rétrécir [*reh-treh-seer*]
shudder v., frémir [*freh-meer*]
shut v., fermer [*fer-meh*]
  shut in, enfermer [*ã-fer-meh*]
shutter, volet (m) [*vo-leh*]
shy, timide [*tee-meed*]
sick, malade [*mah-lahd*]
sickness, maladie (f) [*mah-lah-dee*]
side, côté (m) [*koh-teh*]
sideboard, buffet (m) [*bü-feh*]
sidewalk, trottoir (m) [*tro-twahr*]
sidewalk café, terrasse (f) du café [*te-ras dü kah-feh*]

sideways, de côté [*duh koh-teh*]

sigh *n.*, soupir (m) [*soo-peer*]

sight, vue (f) [*vü*]

sightseeing, visite (f) des curiosités [*vee-zeet deh kür-yoh-zee-teh*]

sign [mark] *n.*, signe (m) [*seeñ*]

sign [display] *n.*, enseigne (f) [*ã-señ*]

sign *v.*, signer [*see-nyeh*]

signal *n.*, signal (m), -aux (pl) [*see-nyahl, see-nyoh*]

signal *v.*, signaler [*see-nyah-leh*]

signature, signature (f) [*see-nyah-tür*]

signpost, poteau indicateur (m) [*poh-toh ē-dee-kah-tuhr*]

silence *n.*, silence (m) [*see-lãs*]

silent, silencieux, -euse [*see-lã-syuh, see-lã-syuhz*]

silently, silencieusement [*see-lã-syuhz-mã*]

silk, soie (f) [*swah*]

silly, sot, sotte [*soh, sot*]

silver, argent (m) [*ahr-zhã*]

　　sterling silver, argent massif [*ahr-zhã mah-seef*]

silverware, silver plate, argenterie (f) [*ahr-zhã-tree*]

similar, semblable [*sã-blabl*]

simple, simple [*sēpl*]

simply, simplement [*sē-pluh-mã*]

sin *n.*, péché (m) [*peh-sheh*]

since *conj.*, puisque [*pweesk*]

since *adv.* & *prep.*, depuis [*duh-pwee*]

　　Since when [have you been here], Depuis quand (êtes-vous ici) [*duh-pwee kã (et-voo-zee-see)*]

　　I have been here since Friday, Je suis ici depuis vendredi [*zhuh swee-zee-seed pwee vã-druh-dee*]

sincere, sincère [*sē-ser*]

sincerely yours [close of personal letter], bien amicalement [*byē-nah-mee-kahl-mã*]

sincerely yours [close of business letter], Veuillez agréer, Monsieur (Madame), l'expression de mes sentiments distingués [*not spoken*]

sing *v.*, chanter [*shã-teh*]

singer, chanteur, chanteuse [*shã-tuhr, shã-tuhz*]

single [sole], seul [*suhl*]

single [unmarried], célibataire [*seh-lee-bah-ter*]

sink *n.*, évier (m) [*eh-vyeh*]

sir, Monsieur [*muh-syuh*]

  Dear Sir, Monsieur [*muh-syuh*]

sister, soeur (f) [*suhr*]

sister-in-law, belle-soeur (f) [*bel-suhr*]

sit [be seated] *v.*, être assis [*etr ah-see*]

  sit down *v.*, s'asseoir (irreg) [*sahs-wahr*]

  Sit down, Asseyez-vous [*ah-seh-yeh-voo*]

situation, situation (f) [*see-twah-syō*]

six, six [*sees*]

sixteen, seize [*sez*]

sixth, sixième [*see-zyem*]

sixty, soixante [*swah-sãt*]

size, dimension (f) [*dee-mã-syō*]

size [of clothing], taille (f) [*tahy*]

skate *v.*, patiner [*pah-tee-neh*]

  ice skates, patins à glace [*pah-tē ah glahs*]

  roller skates, patins à roulettes [*pah-tē ah roo-let*]

skating rink, patinoire (f) [*pah-tee-nwahr*]

skeleton, squelette (f) [*skuh-let*]

sketch *n.*, croquis (m) [*kro-kee*]

sketch *v.*, esquisser [*es-kee-seh*]

ski *v.*, faire du ski [*fer dü skee*]

skid *v.*, déraper [*deh-rah-peh*]

skill, habileté (f) [*ah-beel-teh*]

skillful, habile [*ah-beel*]

skin, peau (f), peaux (pl) [*poh*]

skinny, maigre [*megr*]

skirt, jupe (f) [*zhüp*]

skull, crâne (m) [*krahn*]

sky, ciel (m), cieux (pl) [*syel, syuh*]

skyscraper, gratte-ciel (m) [*graht-syel*]

slang, argot (m) [*ahr-goh*]

slap *n.*, gifle (f) [*zheefl*]

slap *v.*, giffler [*zhee-fleh*]

slave, esclave (m, f) [*es-klahv*]

slavery, exclavage (m) [*es-klah-vazh*]
sleep *v.*, dormir (irreg) [*dor-meer*]
sleep *n.*, sommeil (m) [*so-mey*]
sleeping car, wagon-lit (m) [*vah-gõ-lee*]
sleepy: to be sleepy, avoir sommeil [*ah-vwahr so-mey*]
sleeve, manche (f) [*mãsh*]
slender, mince [*mēs*]
slice *n.*, tranche (f) [*trãsh*]
slice *v.*, couper en tranches [*koo-peh ã trãsh*]
slide *v.*, glisser [*glee-seh*]
slip *v.*, glisser [*glee-seh*]
slip [woman's undergarment] *n.*, combinaison (f) [*kõ-bee-ne-zõ*]
slipper, pantoufle (f) [*pã-toofl*]
slippery, glissant [*glee-sã(t)*]
slow, lent [*lã(t)*]
slowly, lentement [*lãt-mã*]
small, petit [*ptee(t)*]
smaller, plus petit [*plü ptee(t)*]
smallpox, variole (f) [*vahr-yol*]
smell *n.*, odeur (f) [*oh-duhr*]
smell *v.*, sentir (irreg) [*sã-teer*]
smile *n.*, sourire (m) [*soo-reer*]
smile *v.*, sourire (irreg) [*soo-reer*]
smoke *n.*, fumée (f) [*fü-meh*]
smoke *v.*, fumer [*fü-meh*]
smoking car, fumeur (m) [*fü-muhr*]
smooth, lisse [*lees*]
snack, goûter (m) [*goo-teh*]
snail, escargot (m) [*es-kahr-goh*]
snake, serpent (m) [*ser-pã*]
sneeze *v.*, éternuer [*eh-ter-nweh*]
snore *v.*, ronfler [*rõ-fleh*]
snow *n.*, neige (f) [*nezh*]
snow *v.*, neiger [*neh-zheh*]
  It's snowing, Il neige [*eel nezh*]
snowflake, flocon (m) de neige [*flo-kõd nezh*]
snowstorm, tempête (f) de neige [*tã-ped duh nezh*]

so [thus], ainsi [*ē-see*]
  and so forth, et ainsi de suite [*eh ē-seet sweet*]
  I don't think so, Je ne le crois pas [*zhuhn luh krwah pah*]
  I think so, Je crois que oui [*shkrwahk wee*]
  so that, afin que (plus subj. clause); afin de (plus infin.)
    [*ah-fē kuh, ah-fē duh*]
so [much], si, tellement [*see, tel-mã*]
  She was so nice, Elle était si gentille [*e-leh-te see zhã-teey*]
  so far, jusqu'ici; jusqu'à un certain point [*zhüs-kee-see;*
    zhüs-kah ē ser-tē pwē]
  so much, so many, tant de [*tã duh*]
  so-so, comme ci comme ça [*kom see kom sah*]
soap, savon (m) [*sah-võ*]
sober [temperate], sobre [*sobr*]
sober [not drunk], pas ivre [*pah-zeevr*]
social, social, -aux (m, pl) [*so-syahl, so-syoh*]
socialist *n. & adj.*, socialiste (m, f) [*so-syah-leest*]
society, société (f) [*so-syeh-teh*]
sock [apparel], chaussette (f) [*shoh-set*]
soda [bicarbonate], bicarbonate (m) (de soude) [*bee-kahr-*
  bo-naht (duh sood)]
soda water, soda (m) [*so-dah*]
sofa, sofa (m) [*soh-fah*]
soft, mou, molle [*moo, mol*]
soiled, sali [*sah-lee*]
soldier, soldat (m) [*sol-dah*]
sole *adj.*, seul, unique [*suhl, ü-neek*]
sole [fish] *n.*, sole (f) [*sol*]
sole [of shoe] *n.*, semelle (f) [*smel*]
solid, solide [*so-leed*]
solitary, solitaire [*so-lee-ter*]
solution, solution (f) [*sol-lü-syõ*]
solve *v.*, résoudre (irreg) [*reh-zoodr*]
some [partitive], de, du, de la, des [*duh, dü, duh lah, deh*]
some [certain], quelque(s) [*kelk*]
someone, quelqu'un [*kel-kē*]
something, quelque chose [*kel-kuh shohz*]
sometimes, quelquefois [*kel-kuh-fwah*]

somewhat, quelque peu [*kel-kuh puh*]

somewhere, quelque part [*kel-kuh pahr*]

somewhere else, quelque part ailleurs [*kel-kuh pahr ah-yuhr*]

son, fils (m) [*fees*]

son-in-law, gendre (m) [*zhãdr*]

song, chanson (f) [*shã-sõ*]

soon, bientôt [*byẽ-toh*]

  as soon as, aussitôt que [*oh-see-toh kuh*]

sooner, plus tôt [*plü toh*]

  sooner or later, tôt ou tard [*toh oo tahr*]

sore *adj.,* douloureux, -euse [*doo-loo-ruh, doo-loo-ruhz*]

sore throat, mal de gorge (m) [*mahl duh gorzh*]

sorrow, chagrin (m) [*shah-grẽ*]

sorrowful, triste [*treest*]

sorry, désolé [*deh-zo-leh*]

  I'm very sorry, Je suis désolé [*zhuh swee deh-zo-leh*]

  be sorry for *v.,* plaindre (irreg) [*plẽdr*]

sort *n.,* sorte (f) [*sort*]

soul, âme (f) [*ahm*]

sound *n.,* son (m) [*sõ*]

sound *v.,* sonner [*so-neh*]

soundproof, insonorisé [*ẽ-so-no-ree-zeh*]

soup, soupe (f) [*soop*]

sour, aigre [*egr*]

south, sud (m) [*süd*]

South America, Amérique du Sud (f) [*ah-me-reek dü siid*]

souvenir, souvenir (m) [*soov-neer*]

space, espace (m) [*es-pahs*]

spacious, spacieux, -euse [*spah-syuh, spah-syuhz*]

Spain, Espagne (f) [*es-pahñ*]

Spaniard, Espagnol, -ole [*es-pah-nyol*]

Spanish, espagnol [*es-pah-nyol*]

spare, de rechange [*duhr-shãzh*]

  spare parts, pièces de rechange [*pyes duhr-shãzh*]

  spare tire, roue (f) de secours [*roo d(uh) suh-koor*]

spark, étincelle (f) [*eh-tẽ-sel*]

sparkplug, bougie (f) [*boo-zhee*]

speak *v.,* parler [*pahr-leh*]

Do you speak English? Parlez-vous anglais? [*par-leh-voo ã-gle*]

special, spécial, -aux (m, pl) [*speh-syahl, speh-syoh*]

special delivery, express [*ek-spres*]

specialist, spécialiste (m, f) [*speh-syah-leest*]

specialty, spécialité (f) [*speh-syah-lee-teh*]

spectacle, spectacle (m) [*spek-tahkl*]

spectacles [glasses], lunettes (f, pl) [*lü-net*]

spectator, spectateur, -trice [*spek-tah-tuhr, spek-tah-trees*]

speech, discours (m) [*dees-koor*]

speed, vitesse (f) [*vee-tes*]

   at full speed, à toute vitesse [*ah toot vee-tes*]

speed limit, limitation de vitesse (f) [*lee-mee-ta-syõd vee-tes*]

speedy, rapide [*rah-peed*]

spell *v.,* épeler [*eh-pleh*]

spelling, orthographe (f) [*or-toh-grahf*]

spend [money] *v.,* dépenser [*deh-pã-seh*]

spend [time] *v.,* passer [*pah-seh*]

spice, épice (f) [*eh-pees*]

spider, araignée (f) [*ah-re-nyeh*]

spill *v.,* renverser [*rã-ver-seh*]

spinach, épinards (m, pl) [*eh-pee-nahr*]

spine, colonne vertébrale (f) [*ko-lon ver-teh-brahl*]

spirit, esprit (m) [*es-pree*]

spiritual, spirituel, -elle [*spee-ree-twel*]

spit *v.,* cracher [*krah-sheh*]

spite: in spite of, malgré [*mahl-greh*]

splendid, splendide [*splã-deed*]

spoil *v.,* gâter [*gah-teh*]

sponge, éponge (f) [*eh-põzh*]

spoon, cuillère (f) [*kwee-yer*]

spoonful, cuillerée (f) [*kweey-reh*]

sport, sport (m) [*spor*]

spot [stain] *n.,* tâche (f) [*tahsh*]

spouse, époux, -ouse [*eh-poo, eh-pooz*]

sprain *n.,* entorse (f) [*ã-tors*]

sprain *v.,* fouler [*foo-leh*]

spray *v.,* asperger [*ahs-per-zheh*]

spread *v.*, étendre [*eh-tãdr*]
spring [season] *n.*, printemps (m) [*prẽ-tã*]
spring [water] *n.*, source (f) [*soors*]
spring [of watch] *n.*, ressort (m) [*ruh-sor*]
spy *n.*, espion (m) [*ehs-pyõ*]
square [public], place (f) [*plahs*]
square [plane figure], carré (m) [*kah-reh*]
squeak *v.*, grincer [*grẽ-seh*]
squeeze *v.*, serrer [*seh-reh*]
stable *n.*, écurie (f) [*eh-kü-ree*]
stadium, stade (m) [*stahd*]
stage [theatre] *n.*, scène (f) [*sen*]
stage [degree] *n.*, stade (m) [*stahd*]
stain *n.*, tâche (f) [*tahsh*]
stain *v.*, tâcher [*tah-sheh*]
stained glass window, vitrail (m), -aux (m, pl) [*vee-trahy, vee-troh*]
stairs, escalier (m) [*es-kah-lyeh*]
stall [auto] *v.*, caler, se caler [*kah-leh, skah-leh*]
stamp *n.*, timbre (m) [*tẽbr*]
stand *v.*, être (se tenir, rester) debout [*etr (stuh-neer, res-teh) duh-boo*]
   stand up, se lever [*sluh-veh*]
standing *adj.*, debout [*duh-boo*]
standing *n.*, position sociale (f) [*poh-zee-syõ so-syahl*]
standpoint, point (m) de vue [*pwẽ d(uh) vü*]
star, étoile (f) [*eh-twahl*]
starboard, tribord (m) [*tree-bor*]
starch, amidon (m) [*ah-mee-dõ*]
start *n.*, départ (m) [*deh-pahr*]
start *v.*, commencer [*ko-mã-seh*]
start [an auto] *v.*, démarrer [*deh-mah-reh*]
starter [auto], démarreur (m) [*deh-mah-ruhr*]
starve *v.*, mourir (irreg) de faim [*moo-reer duh fẽ*]
state *n.*, état (m) [*eh-tah*]
state *v.*, déclarer [*deh-klah-reh*]
statement, déclaration (f) [*deh-klah-rah-syõ*]
stateroom, cabine (f) [*kah-been*]

statesman, homme (m) d'état [*om deh-tah*]
station, gare (f) [*gahr*]
stationary, stationnaire [*stah-syo-ner*]
stationery, papier (m) à lettres [*pah-pyeh ah letr*]
statue, statue (f) [*stah-tü*]
stay v., rester (*Aux:* ÊTRE) [*res-teh*]
    stay at a hotel, descendre (*Aux:* ÊTRE) dans un hôtel
    [*deh-sãdr dã-zẽ-noh-tel*]
steady, ferme [*ferm*]
steak, biftek (m) [*beef-tek*]
steal v., voler [*vo-leh*]
steam, vapeur (f) [*vah-puhr*]
steamship line, compagnie de navigation (f) [*kõ-pa-need(uh)
nah-vee-gah-syõ*]
steel, acier (m) [*ah-syeh*]
steep, raide [*red*]
steering wheel, volant (m) [*vo-lã*]
stenographer, sténo (m, f) [*steh-noh*]
step n., pas (m) [*pah*]
step v., faire un (des) pas [*fer ẽ (deh) pah*]
stepfather, beau-père (m) [*boh-per*]
stepmother, belle-mère (f) [*bel-mer*]
sterilized v., stérilisé [*steh-ree-lee-zeh*]
steward, garçon (m) de cabine [*gar-sõt kah-been*]
stewardess, hôtesse (f) de l'air [*oh-tes duh ler*]
stick n., bâton (m) [*bah-tõ*]
stick [prick] v., piquer [*pee-keh*]
stick [adhere] v., coller [*ko-leh*]
still [yet], encore [*ã-kor*]
stimulant, stimulant (m) [*stee-mü-lã*]
sting n., piqûre (f) [*pee-kür*]
sting v., piquer [*pee-keh*]
stitch n., point (m) [*pwẽ*]
stitch v., piquer [*pee-keh*]
stock [supply] n., provision (f) [*pro-vee zyõ*]
    in stock, en magasin [*ã mah-gah-zẽ*]
stock [financial] n., actions (f, pl) [*ahk-syõ*]
stockbroker, agent (m) de change [*ah-zhãd(uh) shãzh*]

stock exchange, bourse (f) [*boors*]

stocking, bas (m) [*bah*]
  I have a run in my stocking, J'ai filé un bas [*zheh fee-leh ē bah*]

stomach, estomac (m) [*es-to-mah*]

stomachache, mal (m) à l'estomac [*mahl ah les-to-mah*]

stone, pierre (f) [*pyer*]

stop *n.*, arrêt (m) [*ah-re*]

stop *v.*, arrêter, s'arrêter [*ah-re-teh, sah-re-teh*]
  stop (from) *v.*, empêcher (de) [*ã-peh-sheh (duh)*]
  Stop! Arrêtez! [*ah-re-teh*]
  Stop that! Arrêtez de faire cela! [*ah-re-teh duh fer sah*]

store *n.*, magasin (m) [*mah-gah-zē*]
  department store, grand magasin (m) [*grã mah-gah-zē*]

store *v.*, mettre en garde-meuble [*met-rã gahr-duh-muhbl*]

storm, orage (m) [*o-rahzh*]

story [tale], histoire (f) [*ees-twahr*]

story [floor], étage (m) [*eh-tahzh*]

stove, cuisinière (f) [*kwee-zee-nyer*]

straight, droit [*drwah(t)*]
  straight ahead, tout droit [*too drwah*]

strain *n.*, tension (f) [*tã-syō*]

strange, étrange [*eh-trãzh*]

stranger, étranger, -ère [*eh-trã-zheh, eh-trã-zher*]

strap, courroie (f) [*koor-wah*]

straw, paille (f) [*pahy*]

strawberry, fraise (f) [*frez*]

stream, ruisseau (m), -eaux (pl) [*rwee-soh*]

street, rue (f) [*rü*]

streetcar, tramway (m) [*trahm-weh*]

strength, force (f) [*fors*]

strengthen *v.*, renforcer [*rã-for-seh*]

stress *v.*, insister (sur) [*ē-sees-teh (sür)*]

strike [hit] *v.*, frapper [*frah-peh*]

strike [cease working] *v.*, faire grève [*fer grev*]

strike [by labor] *n.*, grève (f) [*grev*]

string, ficelle (f) [*fee-sel*]

strong, fort [*for*]

structure, structure (f) [*strük-tür*]

struggle *n.,* lutte (f) [*lüt*]

struggle *v.,* lutter [*lü-teh*]

stubborn, têtu [*teh-tü*]

student *n. & adj.,* étudiant, -te [*eh-tü-dyã(t)*]

study *n.,* étude (f) [*eh-tüd*]

study *v.,* étudier [*eh-tü-dyeh*]

stumble *v.,* trébucher [*tre-bü-sheh*]

stupid, stupide [*stü-peed*]

style, style (m) [*steel*]

subject *n.,* sujet (m) [*sü-zheh*]

submarine, sous-marin (m) [*soo-mah-rẽ*]

submit *v.,* soumettre (irreg) [*soo-metr*]

subscribe [to magazine] *v.,* s'abonner [*sah-bo-neh*]

subsidize *v.,* subventionner [*süb-vã-syo-neh*]

subsidy, subvention (f) [*süb-vã-syõ*]

substantial, substantiel, -elle [*süb-stã-syel*]

substitute *v.,* substituer [*süb-stee-tweh*]

subtraction, soustraction (f) [*soos-trak-syõ*]

suburb, banlieue (f) [*bã-lyuh*]

subway, métro (m) [*meh-troh*]

succeed *v.,* réussir [*reh-ü-seer*]

success, succès (m) [*sük-se*]

such, tel, telle [*tel*]

  such as, tel (telle) que [*tel kuh*]

sudden, soudain [*soo-dẽ, soo-den*]

suddenly, tout à coup [*too-tah koo*]

suffer *v.,* souffrir (irreg) [*soo-freer*]

sugar, sucre (m) [*sükr*]

sugar bowl, sucrier (m) [*sü-kree-yeh*]

suggest *v.,* suggérer [*süg-zheh-reh*]

suggestion, suggestion (f) [*süg-zhes-tyõ*]

suicide, suicide (m) [*swee-seed*]

  commit suicide *v.,* se suicider [*suh swee-see-deh*]

suit [of clothing] *n.,* costume (m), tailleur (m) [*kos-tüm, tah-yuhr*]

suit v., convenir (irreg) [kōv-neer]
suitable, convenable [kōv-nahbl]
suitcase, valise (f) [vah-leez]
sum n., somme (f) [som]
sum up v., résumer [reh-zü-meh]
summary, résumé (m) [reh-zü-meh]
summer, été (m) [eh-teh]
sun, soleil (m) [so-ley]
sunburn, coup (m) de soleil [koo d(uh) so-ley]
Sunday, dimanche (m) [dee-mãsh]
sunglasses, lunettes (f, pl) de soleil [lü-ned duh so-ley]
sunrise, lever (m) du soleil [luh-veh dü so-ley]
sunset, coucher (m) du soleil [koo-sheh dü so-ley]
sunshine, lumière (f) du soleil [lü-myer dü so-ley]
   in the sunshine, au soleil [oh so-ley]
suntanned, bronzé [brõ-zeh]
superb, superbe [sü-perb]
superficial, superficiel, -elle [sü-per-fee-syel]
superior, supérieur [sü-per-yuhr]
superstitious, superstitieux, -euse [sü-per-stee-syuh, sü-per-stee-syuhz]
supper, souper (m) [soo-peh]
supply n., provision (f) [pro-vee-zyõ]
supply v., fournir [foor-neer]
support n., soutien (m) [soo-tyē]
support v., soutenir (irreg) [soot-neer]
suppose v., supposer [sü-poh-zeh]
supreme, suprême [sü-prem]
sure, sûr [sür]
surely, sûrement [sür-mã]
surface n., surface (f) [sür-fahs]
surgeon, chirurgien, -ienne [shee-rür-zhyē, shee-rür-zhyen, soop-so-nuhz]
surgery, chirurgie (f) [shee-rür-zhee]
surprise n., surprise (f) [sür-preez]
surprise v., surprendre (irreg) [sür-prãdr]
surprising, surprenant [sür-pruh-nã(t)]

surrender *v.*, se rendre [*suh rãdr*]
surround *v.*, entourer [*ã-too-reh*]
surroundings, environs (m, pl) [*ã-vee-rõ*]
survive *v.*, survivre (irreg) [*sür-veevr*]
survivor, survivant, -te [*sür-vee-vã(t)*]
suspect *n.*, suspect, -te [*süs-pe(kt)*]
suspect *v.*, soupçonner [*soop-so-neh*]
suspenders, bretelles (f, pl) [*bruh-tel*]
suspicion, soupçon (m) [*soop-sõ*]
suspicious [distrustful], soupçonneux, -euse [*soop-so-nuh, soop-so-nuhz*]
suspicious [suspected], suspect [*süs-pe(kt)*]
swallow *v.*, avaler [*ah-vah-leh*]
swear *v.*, jurer [*zhü-reh*]
sweater, chandail (m) [*shã-dahy*]
Sweden, Suède (f) [*swed*]
Swedish, suèdois [*sweh-dwah(z)*]
sweep *v.*, balayer [*bah-le-yeh*]
sweet *adj.*, doux, douce; sucré [*doo, doos; sü-kreh*]
sweetheart, chéri, -ie [*sheh-ree*]
swim *v.*, nager [*nah-zheh*]
swimming, nage (f) [*nahzh*]
swimming pool, piscine (f) [*pee-seen*]
swimsuit, maillot (m) de bain [*mah-yoh duh bẽ*]
Swiss, suisse [*swees*]
switch [elec.] *n.*, interrupteur (m) [*ẽ-te-rüp-tuhr*]
Switzerland, Suisse (f) [*swees*]
swollen, enflé [*ã-fleh*]
sword, épée (f) [*eh-peh*]
syllable, syllabe (f) [*see-lahb*]
sympathy, compassion (f) [*kõ-pah-syõ*]
   My deepest sympathy, Mes condoléances sincères [*meh kõ-do-leh-ãs sẽ-ser*]
symphony, symphonie (f) [*sẽ-fo-nee*]
symptom, symptôme (m) [*sẽp-tohm*]
synthetic, synthétique [*sẽ-teh-teek*]
system, système (m) [*sees-tem*]
systematic, systématique [*sees-teh-mah-teek*]

T

table, table (f) [*tahbl*]
  set the table *v.*, mettre (irreg) le couvert [*metr luh koo-ver*]
tablecloth, nappe (f) [*nahp*]
tablespoon, cuillère (f) à soupe [*kwee-yer ah soop*]
tablet [pill], comprimé (m) [*kõ-pree-meh*]
tack [thumb tack] *n.*, punaise (f) [*pü-nez*]
tack [small nail] *n.*, petit clou (m) [*ptee kloo*]
tact, tact (m) [*tahkt*]
tail, queue (f) [*kuh*]
tailor, tailleur (m) [*tah-yuhr*]
take *v.*, prendre (irreg) [*prãdr*]
  take advantage of, profiter de [*pro-fee-teh duh*]
  take after, ressembler à [*ruh-sã-bleh ah*]
  take a walk, se promener [*sprom-neh*]
  take away, emporter [*ã-por-teh*]
  take back, reprendre (irreg) [*ruh-prãdr*]
  take care of, s'occuper de [*so-kü-peh duh*]
  take off, s'envoler [*sã-vo-leh*]
  take place, avoir lieu [*ah-vwahr lyuh*]
  take a seat, s'asseoir (irreg) [*sah-swahr*]
tale, conte (m) [*kõt*]
talent, talent (m) [*tah-lã*]
  be talented *v.*, avoir du talent [*ah-vwahr dü tah-lã*]
talk [conversation] *n.*, conversation (f) [*kõ-ver-sah-syõ*]
talk [speech] *n.*, discours (m) [*dees-koor*]
talk *v.*, parler [*pahr-leh*]
tall, grand [*grã(d)*]
tame *adj.*, domestiqué, dressé [*do-mes-tee-keh, dre-seh*]
tape, ruban (m), bande (f) [*rü-bã, bãd*]
tapestry, tapisserie (f) [*tah-pees-ree*]
tariff, droit (m) de douane [*drwah duh dwahn*]
task, tâche (f) [*tahsh*]

taste *n.*, goût (m) [*goo*]
taste [something] *v.*, goûter [*goo-teh*]
  This tastes like . . . Ceci a le goût de . . . [*suh-see ahl goo duh*]
tax *v.*, imposer [*ē-poh-zeh*]
tax *n.*, impôt (m) [*ē-poh*]
tax-free, exempt d'impôts [*ehg-zā dē-poh*]
taxi, taxi (m) [*tahk-see*]
tea, thé (m) [*teh*]
  iced tea, thé glacé [*teh glah-seh*]
teach *v.*, enseigner [*ā-se-nyeh*]
teacher, enseignant, -te [*ā-se-nyā, ā-se-nyāt*]
teaching, enseignement (m) [*ā-se-nyuh-mā*]
teacup, tasse (f) à thé [*tahs ah teh*]
team, équipe (f) [*eh-keep*]
teapot, théière (f) [*teh-yer*]
tear *v.*, déchirer [*deh-shee-reh*]
teardrop *n.*, larme (f) [*lahrm*]
teaspoon, petite cuillère (f) [*pteet kwee-yer*]
technical, technique [*tek-neek*]
teeth *pl.*, dents (f, pl) [*dā*]
telegram *n.*, télégramme (m) [*teh-leh-grahm*]
telephone *n.*, téléphone (m) [*teh-leh-fon*]
telephone *v.*, téléphoner [*teh-leh-fo-neh*]
telephone book, annuaire (m) du téléphone [*ah-nwer dü teh-leh-fon*]
telephone booth, cabine (f) téléphonique [*kah-been teh-leh-fo-neek*]
telephone call, coup (m) de téléphone [*koot teh-leh-fon*]
telephone number, numéro (m) de téléphone [*nü-meh-roh duh teh-leh-fon*]
telephone operator, téléphoniste [*teh-leh-fo-neest*]
telescope, téléscope (m) [*teh-leh-skop*]
television, télévision (f), télé [*teh-leh-vee-zyō, teh-leh*]
television set, poste (m) de télévision [*pos-tuh duh teh-leh-vee-zyō*]
tell *v.*, dire (irreg) [*deer*]
teller, caissier -ière [*ke-syeh, ke-syer*]

temperature, température (f) [*tã-peh-rah-tür*]
temple [church], temple (m) [*tãpl*]
temporary, temporaire [*tã-po-rer*]
temptation, tentation (f) [*tã-tah-syõ*]
ten, dix [*dees*]
tenant, locataire (m, f) [*lo-kah-ter*]
tendancy, tendance (f) [*tã-dãs*]
tender, tendre [*tãdr*]
tenth, dixième [*dee-zyem*]
term, terme (m) [*term*]
terrace, terrasse (f) [*te-rahs*]
terrible, terrible [*teh-reebl*]
territory, territoire (m) [*teh-ree-twahr*]
terror, terreur (f) [*teh-ruhr*]
test *n.,* examen (m) [*eg-zah-mẽ*]
test *v.,* essayer [*e-se-yeh*]
testify *v.,* témoigner [*teh-mwah-nyeh*]
text, texte (m) [*tekst*]
textile *adj.,* textile [*teks-teel*]
than, que, qu' [*kuh*]
thank *v.,* remercier [*r(uh)-mer-syeh*]
   Thank you, Merci [*mer-see*]
thankful, reconnaissant [*r(uh)-ko-ne-sã(t)*]
that *demons. adj.,* ce (m), cet (m), cette (f) [*suh, set*]
that *demons. pron.,* cela, ça [*suh-lah, sah*]
   Give me that, Donnez-moi cela (ça) [*do-neh-mwah slah (sah)*]
that *rel. pron.,* qui, que [*kee, kuh*]
that *conj.,* que [*kuh*]
   I hope (that) you will come, J'espère que vous viendrez [*zhes-per kuh voo vyẽ-dreh*]
the, le (m, sing), la (f, sing), les (m & f, pl) [*luh, lah, leh*]
theater, théâtre (m) [*teh-ahtr*]
theft, vol (m) [*vol*]
their, leur, leurs [*luhr*]
theirs, le leur, la leur; les leurs [*luh luhr, lah luhr; leh luhr*]
them, les; leur; eux (m), elles (f) [*leh; luhr; uh, el*]
themselves, eux-mêmes (m), elles-mêmes (f) [*uh-mem, el-*

mem]

then [at that time], alors [*ah-lor*]
then [afterwards], ensuite [*ã-sweet*]
  now and then, de temps en temps [*duh tã-zã tã*]
theory, théorie (f) [*teh-o-ree*]
there, là [*lah*]
  there is, there are, il y a [*eel yah*]
therefore, donc [*dõk*]
thermometer, thermomètre (m) [*ter-mo-metr*]
these *adj.,* ces [*seh*]
these *pron.,* ceux-ci, celles-ci [*suh-see, sel-see*]
they, ils, eux (m); elles (f); on (impersonal) [*eel, uh; el; õ*]
thick, épais, épaisse [*eh-pe, eh-pes*]
thief, voleur, -euse [*vo-luhr, vo-luhz*]
thin, mince [*mẽs*]
thing, chose (f) [*shohz*]
think *v.,* penser [*pã-seh*]
  think of [bring to mind], penser à [*pã-seh ah*]
  think of [have an opinion], penser de [*pã-seh duh*]
third [ordinal] *adj.,* troisième [*trwah-zyem*]
third *n.,* tiers [*tyer*]
thirst, soif (f) [*swahf*]
  be thirsty *v.,* avoir soif [*ah-vwahr swahf*]
thirteen, treize [*trez*]
thirty, trente [*trãt*]
this *pron.,* ceci, ce, c' [*suh-see, suh, s'*]
this *adj.,* ce (m), cet (m), cette (f) [*suh, set, set*]
thorn, épine (f) [*eh-peen*]
thoroughly, à fond [*ah fõ*]
those *adj.,* ces [*seh*]
those *pron.,* ceux-ci, celles-ci [*suh-see, sel-see*]
though, bien que [*byẽ kuh*]
thought *n.,* pensée (f) [*pã-seh*]
thoughtful, attentif, -tive [*ah-tã-teef, ah-tã-teev*]
thousand, mille (m, invar) [*meel*]
thread, fil (m) [*feel*]
threat, menace (f) [*muh-nahs*]
threaten *v.,* menacer [*muh-nah-seh*]

three, trois [*trwah*]
thrifty, économe [*eh-ko-nom*]
throat, gorge (f) [*gorzh*]
throne, trône (m) [*trohn*]
through *prep.,* à travers [*ah trah-ver*]
through [finished] *adj.,* fini [*fee-nee*]
   I'm through, J'ai fini [*zheh fee-nee*]
throw *v.,* jeter [*zh(uh)-teh*]
thumb, pouce (m) [*poos*]
thunder, tonnerre (m) [*to-ner*]
Thursday, jeudi (m) [*zhuh-dee*]
thus, ainsi [*ẽ-see*]
ticket, billet (m) [*bee-ye*]
ticket collector, contrôleur (m) [*kõ-troh-luhr*]
ticket window, guichet (m) [*ghee-she*]
tide, marée (f) [*mah-reh*]
tie [apparel] *n.,* cravate (f) [*krah-vaht*]
tie *v.,* lier [*lee-yeh*]
tight, serré [*se-reh*]
tighten *v.,* resserrer [*ruh-se-reh*]
till [until], jusqu'à [*zhüs-kah*]
time [duration], temps (m) [*tã*]
   at the same time, en même temps [*ã mem tã*]
   Have a good time, Amusez-vous bien [*ah-müz-eh voo byẽ*]
   What time is it? Quelle heure est-il? [*ke-luhr e-teel*]
time [instance], fois (f) [*fwah*]
   at times, des fois [*deh fwah*]
timetable, horaire (m) [*o-rer*]
timid, timide [*tee-meed*]
tin, étain (m) [*eh-tẽ*]
tip [gratuity] *n.,* pourboire (m) [*poor-bwahr*]
tip [point] *n.,* bout (m), pointe (f) [*boo, pwẽt*]
tire [of a car] *n.,* pneu (m) [*pnuh*]
   flat tire, pneu crevé (m) [*pnuh kruh-veh*]
tired, fatigué [*fah-tee-gheh*]
tissue paper, papier (m) de soie [*pah-pyeh duh swah*]
title, titre (m) [*teetr*]
to, à, en, vers [*ah, ã, ver*]

toast [bread] *n.*, pain grillé (m) [*pẽ gree-yeh*]

toaster, grille-pain (m) [*greey-pẽ*]

tobacco, tabac (m) [*tah-bah*]

tobacco store, bureau (m) de tabac [*bü-rohd tah-bah*]

today, aujourd'hui [*oh-zhoor-dwee*]

toe, orteil (m) [*or-tey*]

together, ensemble [*ã-sãbl*]

toilet [bath room], cabinet (m) [*kah-bee-neh*]

toilet [grooming], toilette (f) [*twah-let*]

tolerate *v.*, tolérer [*to-leh-reh*]

toll [fee] *n.*, péage (m) [*peh-ahzh*]

tomato, tomate (f) [*to-maht*]

tomato juice, jus (m) de tomate [*zhüt to-maht*]

tomb, tombe (f) [*tõb*]

tomorrow, demain [*d(uh)-mẽ*]

   tomorrow evening, demain soir [*d(uh)-mẽ swahr*]

   tomorrow morning, demain matin [*d(uh)-mẽ mah-tẽ*]

ton, tonne (f) [*ton*]

tone, ton (m) [*tõ*]

tongue, langue (f) [*lãg*]

tonight, ce soir [*suh swahr*]

tonsils, amygdales (f, pl) [*ah-mee-dahl*]

too [also], aussi [*oh-see*]

   too much, too many, trop (de) [*troh (duh)*]

tool, outil (m) [*oo-tee*]

tooth, dent (f) [*dã*]

toothache, mal (m) de dents [*mahl duh dã*]

toothbrush, brosse (f) à dents [*bros ah dã*]

toothpaste, pâte dentifrice (f) [*paht dã-tee-frees*]

toothpick, cure-dents (m, inv) [*kür-dã*]

top [highest point] *n.*, *haut (m), sommet (m) [*oh, so-me*]

top [surface] *n.*, dessus (m) [*duh-sü*]

   on top of, sur [*sür*]

tornado, tornade (f) [*tor-nahd*]

torture *n.*, torture (f) [*tor-tür*]

torture *v.*, torturer [*tor-tü-reh*]

toss *v.*, lancer [*lã-seh*]

total *n.*, total, -aux (m, pl) [*to-tahl, to-toh*]

touch v., toucher [*too-sheh*]
touching, touchant [*too-shã(t)*]
touchy, susceptible [*sü-sep-teebl*]
tough, dur [*dür*]
tour n., tour (m) [*toor*]
tourist, touriste (m, f) [*too-reest*]
tourist office, office (m) du tourisme [*o-fees dü too-reesm*]
tow v., remorquer [*r(uh)-mor-keh*]
tow truck, dépanneuse (f) [*deh-pah-nuhz*]
toward, vers [*ver*]
towel [bath], serviette (f) [*ser-vyet*]
tower, tour (f) [*toor*]
town, ville (f) [*veel*]
townhall, mairie (f) [*me-ree*]
toy, jouet (m) [*zhwe*]
trace n., trace (f) [*trahs*]
track, piste (f) [*peest*]
trade n., commerce (m) [*ko-mers*]
trade [exchange] v., échanger [*eh-shã-zheh*]
trade [do business] v., faire du commerce [*fer dü ko-mers*]
trademark, marque (f) de fabrique [*mahrk duh fah-breek*]
tradition, tradition (f) [*trah-dee-syõ*]
traditional, -elle [*trah-dee-syo-nel*]
traffic, circulation (f) [*seer-kü-lah-syõ*]
tragedy, tragédie (f) [*trah-zheh-dee*]
tragic, tragique [*trah-zheek*]
trail n., piste (f) [*peest*]
train n., train (m) [*trẽ*]
train [educate] v., former [*for-meh*]
train [coach] v., entraîner [*ã-tre-neh*]
training [sports], entraînement (m) [*ã-tren-mã*]
training [school, job], formation (f) [*for-mah-syõ*]
traitor, traître (m) [*tretr*]
transfer [connection] n., correspondance (f) [*ko-res-põ-dãs*]
transform v., transformer [*trãs-for-meh*]
transit, transit (m) [*trã-zeet*]
translate v., traduire (irreg) [*trah-dweer*]
translation, traduction (f) [*trah-dük-syõ*]

translator, traducteur, -trice [*trah-dük-tuhr, trah-dük-trees*]
transmission, transmission (f) [*trãs-mee-syõ*]
transmit *v.,* transmettre (irreg) [*trãs-metr*]
transportation, transport (m) [*trãs-por*]
trap *n.,* piège (m) [*pyezh*]
travel *n.,* voyages (m, pl) [*vwah-yahzh*]
travel *v.,* voyager [*vwah-yah-zheh*]
travel agency, agence (f) de voyages [*ah-zhãs duh vwah-yahzh*]
traveler, voyageur, -euse [*vwah-yah-zhuhr, vwah-yah-zhuhz*]
traveler's check, chèque (m) de voyage [*shek duh vwah-yahzh*]
tray, plateau (m), -eaux (pl) [*plah-toh*]
treason, trahison (f) [*trah-ee-sõ*]
treasure *n.,* trésor (m) [*treh-zor*]
treasurer, trésorier (m) [*tre-zor-yeh*]
treasury, trésorerie (f) [*tre-zor-ree*]
treat *n.,* régal (m), régals (pl) [*reh-gahl*]
   It's my treat, C'est moi qui paie [*se mwah kee pe*]
treat [entertain] *v.,* régaler [*reh-gah-leh*]
treat [deal with] *v.,* traiter [*tre-teh*]
treatment, traitement (m) [*tret-mã*]
treaty, traité (m) [*tre-teh*]
tree, arbre (m) [*ahrbr*]
tremble *v.,* trembler [*trã-bleh*]
trespass [on property] *v.,* entrer (*Aux:* ÊTRE) dans la propriété
   de [*ã-treh dã lah pro-pree-yeh-teh duh*]
   No trespassing, Défense d'entrée [*deh-fãs dã-treh*]
trial [test], essai (m) [*e-se*]
   trial and error, essais (m, pl) et erreurs (f, pl) [*e-se-zeh
   eh-ruhr*]
trial [at law], procès (m) [*pro-se*]
triangle, triangle (m) [*tree-yãgl*]
trick *n.,* tour (m) [*toor*]
   play a trick on *v.,* jouer un tour à [*jweh ẽ toor ah*]
tricycle, tricycle (m) [*tree-seekl*]
trip [journey] *n.,* voyage (m) [*vwah-yahzh*]
trip [stumble] *v.,* trébucher [*treh-bü-sheh*]
triumphant, triomphant [*tree-yõ-fã(t)*]

tropical, tropical, -aux (m, pl) [*tro-pee-kahl, tro-pee-koh*]
trouble *n.*, difficulté (f) [*dee-fee-kül-teh*]
  have car trouble *v.*, être en panne [*e-trã pahn*]
trouble *v.*, déranger [*deh-rã-zheh*]
trousers, pantalon (m) [*pã-tah-lõ*]
truck, camion (m) [*kah-myõ*]
true, vrai [*vre*]
trunk [container], malle (f) [*mahl*]
trunk [of tree], tronc (m) [*trõ*]
trunk [of car], coffre (m) [*kofr*]
trust *n.*, confiance (f) [*kõ-fyãs*]
trust *v.*, faire confiance [*fer kõ-fyãs*]
truth, vérité (f) [*veh-ree-teh*]
try *v.*, essayer [*e-se-yeh*]
  try on, essayer [*e-se-yeh*]
tube, tube (m) [*tüb*]
tuberculosis, tuberculose (f) [*tü-ber-kü-lohz*]
Tuesday, mardi (m) [*mahr-dee*]
tugboat, remorqueur (m) [*ruh-mor-kuhr*]
tune [melody], air (m) [*er*]
tunnel, tunnel (m) [*tü-nel*]
turkey, dinde (f) [*dẽd*]
Turkey, Turquie (f) [*tür-kee*]
Turkish, turc, turque [*türk*]
turn [order] *n.*, tour (m) [*toor*]
turn [curve] *n.*, virage (m) [*vee-rahzh*]
turn *v.*, tourner [*toor-neh*]
  turn around, retourner, se retourner [*r(uh)-toor-neh, sruh-toor-neh*]
  turn away, détourner, se détourner [*deh-toor-neh, sdeh-toor-neh*]
  turn off [light], éteindre (irreg) [*eh-tẽdr*]
  turn off [water], fermer [*fer-meh*]
  turn on [light], allumer [*ah-lümeh*]
  turn on [water], ouvrir [*oov-reer*]
turnip, navet (m) [*nah-ve*]
twelfth, douzième [*doo-zyem*]
twelve, douze [*dooz*]

twenty, vingt [*vẽ*]
twice, deux fois (f) [*duh fwah*]
twin *n.*, jumeau, jumelle [*zhü-moh, zhü-mel*]
twine, ficelle (f) [*fee-sel*]
twist *v.*, tordre [*tordr*]
two, deux [*duh*]
type *n.*, type (m) [*teep*]
typewriter, machine (f) à écrire [*mah-sheen ah eh-kreer*]
typical, typique [*tee-peek*]
typist, dactylographe (m, f), dactylo (m, f) [*dahk-tee-loh-
    graf, dahk-tee-loh*]
tyranny, tyrannie (f) [*tee-rah-nee*]
tyrant, tyran (m) [*tee-rã*]

U

ugly, laid [*le(d)*]
umbrella, parapluie (m) [*pah-rah-plwee*]
unable, incapable [*ẽ-kah-pahbl*]
unanimous, unanime [*ü-nah-neem*]
uncertain, incertain [*ẽ-ser-tẽ, ẽ-ser-ten*]
uncle, oncle (m) [*õkl*]
uncomfortable [of feelings], mal à l'aise [*mahl ah lez*]
uncomfortable [of things], peu confortable [*puh kõ-for-tahbl*]
unconscious, inconscient [*ẽ-kõ-syã(t)*]
uncover *v.*, découvrir (irreg) [*deh-koo-vreer*]
under, sous [*soo*]
underground, souterrain [*soo-te-rẽ, soo-te-ren*]
understand *v.*, comprendre (irreg) [*kõ-prãdr*]
undertake *v.*, entreprendre (irreg) [*ã-truh-prãdr*]
undertaker, entrepreneur (m) de pompes funèbres [*ã-truh-
    pruh-nuhr duh põp fü-nebr*]
underwear, sous-vêtements (m, pl) [*soo-vet-mã*]
undo *v.*, défaire (irreg) [*deh-fer*]
undress *v.*, déshabiller, se déshabiller [*deh-zah-bee-yeh,*

sdeh-zah-bee-yeh]
uneasy, mal à l'aise [*mahl ah lez*]
unemployed, en chômage [*ã shoh-mahzh*]
unemployment, chômage (m) [*shoh-mahzh*]
unequal, inégal, -aux (m, pl) [*ee-neh-gahl, ee-neh-goh*]
unexpected, inattendu [*ee-nah-tã-dü*]
unfair, injuste [*ẽ-zhüst*]
unfaithful, infidèle [*ẽ-fee-del*]
unfavorable, défavorable [*deh-fah-vo-rahbl*]
unforgettable, inoubliable [*ee-noo-blee-yahbl*]
unforeseen, imprévu [*ẽ-preh-vü*]
unforgivable, impardonnable [*ẽ-pahr-do-nahbl*]
unfortunate, malheureux, -euse [*mah-luh-ruh, mah-luh-ruhz*]
unfortunately, malheureusement [*mah-luh-ruhz-mã*]
ungrateful, ingrat [*ẽ-grah(t)*]
unhappy, malheureux, -euse [*mah-luh-ruh, mah-luh-ruhz*]
unhealthy, malsain [*mahl-sẽ, mahl-sen*]
uniform *adj.*, uniforme [*ü-nee-form*]
uniform *n.*, uniforme (m) [*ü-nee-form*]
unimaginable, inimaginable [*ee-nee-mah-zhee-nahbl*]
unimportant, peu important [*puh ẽ-por-tã(t)*]
uninteresting, peu intéressant [*puh ẽ-teh-re-sã(t)*]
union [labor union], syndicat (m) [*sẽ-dee-kah*]
unit, unité (f) [*ü-nee-teh*]
unite *v.*, unir [*ü-neer*]
united, uni [*ü-nee*]
United States, Etats-Unis (m, pl) [*eh-tah-zü-nee*]
unity, unité (f) [*ü-nee-teh*]
universal, universel, -elle [*ü-nee-ver-sel*]
universe, univers (m) [*ü-nee-ver*]
university, université (f) [*ü-nee-ver-see-teh*]
unjust, injuste [*ẽ-zhüst*]
unknown, inconnu [*ẽ-ko-nü*]
unlawful, illégal, -aux (m, pl) [*ee-leh-gahl, ee-leh-goh*]
unless, à moins que [*ah mwẽ kuh*]
unload *v.*, décharger [*deh-shahr-zheh*]
unlock *v.*, ouvrir (irreg) [*oo-vreer*]
unlucky, malheureux, -euse [*mah-luh-ruh, mah-luh-ruhz*]

unoccupied, inoccupé [*ee-no-kü-peh*]
unpack v., défaire (irreg) [*deh-fer*]
unpleasant, désagréable [*deh-zah-greh-ahbl*]
unquestionable, indiscutable [*ē-dees-kü-tahbl*]
unsafe, dangereux, -euse [*dã-zhruh, dã-zhruhz*]
until, jusque [*zhüsk*]
untrue, faux, fausse [*foh, fohs*]
untruthful, menteur, -euse [*mã-tuhr, mã-tuhz*]
unusual, peu commun [*puh ko-mē*]
unwelcome, importun [*ē-por-tē, ē-por-tün*]
unwilling, peu disposé [*puh dees-poh-zeh*]
up, en *haut, vers le *haut [*ã oh, ver luh oh*]
  be up [standing] v., être debout [*e-truh duh-boo*]
  get up v., se lever [*sluh-veh*]
  go up v., monter (*Aux:* ÊTRE) [*mõ-teh*]
  up and down, en *haut et en bas [*ã oh eh ã bah*]
  up to now, jusqu'ici [*zhüs-kee-see*]
upbringing, éducation (f) [*eh-dü-kah-syõ*]
uphill, montant [*mõ-tã(t)*]
upon, sur [*sür*]
upper, supérieur [*sü-pehr-yuhr*]
uproar, vacarme (m) [*vah-kahrm*]
ups and downs, péripéties (f, pl), les *hauts et les bas [*peh-ree-peh-see, leh oh eh leh bah*]
upset adj., bouleversé [*bool-ver-seh*]
upset v., renverser, bouleverser [*rã-ver-seh, bool-ver-seh*]
upside down, à l'envers [*ah lã-ver*]
upstairs, en *haut [*ã oh*]
up-to-date [fashion], â la mode [*ah lah mod*]
up-to-date [report], à jour [*ah zhoor*]
upward, vers le *haut [*ver luh oh*]
urban, urbain [*ür-bē, ür-ben*]
urgent, urgent [*ür-zhã(t)*]
us, nous [*noo*]
  There are three of us Nous sommes trois [*noo som trwah*]
use n., emploi (m), usage (m) [*ã-plwah, ü-zahzh*]
  personal use, usage (m) personnel [*ü-zahzh per-so-nel*]

use v., employer, se servir de (irreg) [*ã-plwah-yeh, suh ser-veer duh*]
  He is using this table, Il se sert de cette table [*eel suh ser duh set tahbl*]
  What is this used for? A quoi cela sert-il? [*ah kwah suh-lah ser-teel*]
  be used to v., être habitué à [*etr ah-bee-tweh ah*]
used, utilisé [*ü-tee-lee-zeh*]
used [car], d'occasion [*do-kah-zyõ*]
useful, utile [*ü-teel*]
useless, inutile [*ee-nü-teel*]
usual, habituel, -elle [*ah-bee-twel*]
usually, d'habitude [*dah-bee-tüd*]

V

vacancy, vide (m) [*veed*]
  no vacancy, complet [*kõ-pleh*]
vacant, libre [*leebr*]
vacation, vacances (f, pl) [*vah-kãs*]
vaccination, vaccination (f) [*vahk-see-nah-syõ*]
vacuum cleaner, aspirateur (m) [*ah-spee-rah-tuhr*]
vague, vague [*vahg*]
vain, vain [*vẽ, ven*]
  in vain, en vain [*ã vẽ*]
valid, valable [*vah-lahbl*]
valley, vallée (f) [*vah-leh*]
valuable, précieux, -euse [*preh-syuh, preh-syuhz*]
value n., valeur (f) [*vah-luhr*]
value v., estimer [*es-tee-meh*]
valve, soupape (f) [*soo-pahp*]
vanilla, vanille (f) [*vah-neey*]
  vanilla flavored, à la vanille [*ah lah vah-neey*]
vanish v., disparaître (irreg) [*dees-pah-retr*]

vanity, vanité (f) [*vah-nee-teh*]
variety, variété (f) [*vah-ryeh-teh*]
various, divers [*dee-ver(s)*]
vary *v.*, varier [*vah-ryeh*]
vast, vaste [*vahst*]
Vatican, Vatican (m) [*vah-tee-kã*]
vault [burial], caveau (m), -eaux (pl) [*ka-voh*]
veal, veau (m), -eaux (pl) [*voh*]
vegetable, légume (m) [*leh-güm*]
vehicle, véhicule (m) [*veh-ee-kül*]
veil *n.*, voile (m) [*vwahl*]
vein, veine (f) [*ven*]
velvet, velours (m) [*vuh-loor*]
verb, verbe (m) [*verb*]
verdict, verdict (m) [*ver-dee(kt)*]
verge, bord (m) [*bor*]
verify *v.*, vérifier [*veh-ree-fyeh*]
verse, vers (m) [*ver*]
vertical, vertical, -aux (m, pl) [*ver-tee-kahl, ver-tee-koh*]
very, très [*tre*]
    very well, très bien [*tre byẽ*]
vest, gilet (m) [*zhee-le*]
veteran, ancien combattant (m) [*ã-syẽ kõ-bah-tã*]
veterinarian, vétérinaire [*veh-teh-ree-ner*]
vex *v.*, vexer [*vek-seh*]
vice, vice (m) [*vees*]
vicinity, environs (m, pl) [*ã-vee-rõ*]
vicious, méchant [*meh-shã(t)*]
victim, victime (f) [*veek-teem*]
victory, victoire (f) [*veek-twahr*]
view *n.*, vue (f) [*vü*]
viewpoint, point (m) de vue [*pwẽ duh vü*]
vigorous, vigoureux, -cuse [*vee-goo-ruh, vee-goo-ruhz*]
village, village (m) [*vee-lahzh*]
villain, scélérat (m) [*seh-leh-rah*]
vine, vigne, (f) [*veeñ*]
vinegar, vinaigre (m) [*vee-negr*]

vineyard, vignoble (m) [*vee-nyobl*]
violate v., violer [*vyo-leh*]
violence, violence (f) [*vyo-lãs*]
violet, violette (f) [*vyo-let*]
violin, violon (m) [*vyo-lõ*]
virgin, vierge (f) [*vyerzh*]
virtue, vertu (f) [*ver-tü*]
virtuous, vertueux, -euse [*ver-twuh, ver-twuhz*]
visa, visa (m) [*vee-zah*]
visible, visible [*vee-zeebl*]
vision, vision (f) [*vee-zyõ*]
visit n., visite (f) [*vee-zeet*]
visit [a person] v., rendre visite à [*rãdr vee-zeet ah*]
visit [a place] v., visiter [*vee-zee-teh*]
visiting card, carte (f) de visite [*kahrt duh vee-zeet*]
visitor, visiteur, -euse [*vee-zee-tuhr, vee-zee-tuhz*]
   She has visitors, Elle a du monde [*el ah dü mõd*]
vital, vital, -aux (m, pl) [*vee-tahl, vee-toh*]
vitamin, vitamine (f) [*vee-tah-meen*]
vocabulary, vocabulaire (m) [*vo-kah-bü-ler*]
vocal, vocal, -aux (m, pl) [*vo-kahl, vo-koh*]
vocalist, chanteur (m), cantatrice (f) [*shã-tuhr, kã-tah-trees*]
vocation, vocation (f) [*vo-kah-syõ*]
vocational, professionnel, -elle [*pro-fe-syo-nel*]
voice n., voix (f) [*vwah*]
volcano, volcan (m) [*vol-kã*]
volume, volume (m) [*vo-lüm*]
voluntary, volontaire [*vo-lõ-ter*]
volunteer n., volontaire (m) [*vo-lõ-ter*]
vomit v., vomir [*voh-meer*]
vote n., vote (m) [*vot*]
vote v., voter [*vo-teh*]
vow n., voeu (m), -eux (pl) [*vuh*]
vowel, voyelle (f) [*vwah-yel*]
voyage n., voyage (m) [*vwah-yahzh*]
vulgar, vulgaire [*vül-gher*]
vulnerable, vulnérable [*vül-neh-rahbl*]

W

wages *pl.*, salaire (m, sing) [*sah-ler*]
waist, taille (f) [*tahy*]
wait *n.*, attente (f) [*ah-tãt*]
wait for *v.*, attendre [*ah-tãdr*]
waiter, garçon (m) [*gahr-sõ*]
waiting room, salle (f) d'attente [*sahl dah-tãt*]
waitress, serveuse (f) [*ser-vuhz*]
   Waitress! Mademoiselle! [*mahd-mwah-zel*]
wake *v.*, réveiller [*reh-ve-yeh*]
   wake up [self], se réveiller [*sreh-ve-yeh*]
walk *n.*, promenade (f) [*prom-nahd*]
   take a walk *v.*, se promener [*sprom-neh*]
walk *v.*, marcher [*mahr-sheh*]
wall, mur (m) [*mür*]
wallpaper, papier (m) peint [*pah-pyeh pẽ*]
wallet, portefeuille (m) [*por-tuh-fuhy*]
walnut, noix (f) [*nwah*]
waltz *n.*, valse (f) [*vahls*]
wander *v.*, errer [*eh-reh*]
want *v.*, vouloir (irreg) [*vool-wahr*]
war, guerre (f) [*gher*]
wardrobe [clothes closet], armoire (f) [*ahrm-wahr*]
wardrobe [clothing], vêtements (m, pl) [*vet-mã*]
warehouse, entrepôt (m) [*ã-truh-poh*]
warm *adj.*, chaud [*shoh(d)*]
warm *v.*, chauffer [*shoh-feh*]
warmth, chaleur (f) [*shah-luhr*]
warn *v.*, avertir [*ah-ver-teer*]
warning, avertissement (m) [*ah-ver-tees-mã*]
warrant, mandat (m) [*mã-dah*]
wash *v.*, laver, se laver [*lah-veh, slah-veh*]
washbasin, lavabo (m) [*lah-vah-boh*]

147

washing machine, machine (f) à laver [*mah-sheen ah lah-veh*]

wasp, guêpe (f) [*ghep*]

waste *v.,* gaspiller [*gahs-pee-yɛh*]

wastebasket, corbeille (f) à papier [*kor-be-yah pah-pyeh*]

watch *n.,* montre (f) [*mõtr*]

   wristwatch, montre-bracelet (f) [*mõtr-brah-sleh*]

watch *v.,* regarder [*r(uh)-gahr-deh*]

   Watch out! Attention! [*ah-tã-syõ*]

watchmaker, horloger [*or-lo-zheh*]

watchman [night], veilleur (m) (de nuit) [*ve-yuhr (duh nwee)*]

water, eau (f), eaux (pl) [*oh*]

   drinking water, eau potable [*oh po-tahbl*]

   fresh water, eau douce [*oh doos*]

   mineral water, eau minérale [*oh mee-neh-rahl*]

   running water, eau courante [*oh koo-rãt*]

   salt water, eau de mer [*ohd mer*]

water closet, cabinet (m) [*kah-bee-ne*]

watercolor, aquarelle (f) [*ah-kwah-rel*]

waterfall, cascade (f) [*kahs-kahd*]

watermelon, pastèque (f) [*pahs-tek*]

waterproof, imperméable [*ẽ-per-meh-ahbl*]

wave *n.,* vague (f) [*vahg*]

wave *v.,* faire signe [*fer seeñ*]

wax *n.,* cire (f) [*seer*]

way [route], chemin (m) [*sh(uh)-mẽ*]

way [manner], façon (f) [*fah-sõ*]

   by the way, à propos [*ah proh-poh*]

   in this way, de cette façon [*duh set fah-sõ*]

we, nous [*noo*]

weak, faible [*febl*]

weakness, faiblesse (f) [*feh-bles*]

wealth, richesse (f) [*ree-shes*]

wealthy, riche [*reesh*]

wean *v.,* sevrer [*suh-vreh*]

weapon, arme (f) [*ahrm*]

wear *v.,* porter [*por-teh*]

   wear out, user [*ü-zeh*]

weather, temps (m) [*tã*]

weave v., tisser [*tee-seh*]

web [spider], toile (f) d'araignée [*twahl dah-re-nyeh*]

wedding, mariage (m) [*mahr-yahzh*]

wedding ring, alliance (f) [*ah-lyās*]

Wednesday, mercredi (m) [*mer-kruh-dee*]

weed n., mauvaise herbe (f) [*moh-ve-zerb*]

week, semaine (f) [*s(uh)-men*]

   last week, la semaine dernière [*lah smen der-nyer*]

   next week, la semaine prochaine [*lah smen pro-shen*]

weekend, fin de semaine (f) [*fē duh suh-men*]

weekly, hebdomadaire [*eb-do-mah-der*]

weep v., pleurer [*pluh-reh*]

weigh v., peser [*puh-zeh*]

weight, poids (m) [*pwah*]

welcome n., bienvenu (m) [*byē-vnü*]

   Welcome! Soyez le bienvenu! [*swo-yeh luh byē-vnü*]

   You're welcome, Je vous en prie; Il n'y a pas de quoi
     [*zhvoo-zā pree; eel nyah paht kwah*]

welfare, bien-être (m) [*byē-netr*]

well [for water] n., puits (m) [*pwee*]

well adv., bien [*byē*]

   very well, très bien [*tre byē*]

   Well! Tiens! [*tyē*]

well-bred, bien élevé [*byē-nehl-yeh*]

well-known, célèbre [*seh-lebr*]

well-off, prospère [*pros-per*]

west, ouest (m) [*west*]

western, occidental, -aux (m, pl) [*ok-see-dā-tahl, ok-see-dā-toh*]

wet, mouillé [*moo-yeh*]

whale, baleine (f) [*bah-len*]

what interr. adj., quel, quelle; quels, quelles [*kel*]

   What road will he take? Quel chemin prendra-t-il? [*kel
     shuh-mē prā-drah-teel*]

   What's the weather like? Quel temps fait-il? [*kel tā fe-teel*]

   What is the date of . . . Quelle est la date de . . . [*ke-le
     lah daht duh . . .*]

what *interr. pron.*, que, qu'est-ce qui, qu'est-ce que, quoi
[*kuh, kes-kee, kes-kuh, kwah*]

  What are you doing here? Que faites-vous ici?, Qu'est-ce
  que vous faites ici? [*kuh fet voo-zee-see, kes-kuh voo
  fet ee-see*]

  What do you think? Que pensez-vous?, Qu'est-ce que
  vous pensez? [*kuh pã-seh-voo, kes-kuh voo pã-seh*]

  What's happening? Qu'est-ce qui se passe?, Que se passe-
  t-il? [*kes-kee spahs, kuh spahs-teel*]

  What are you thinking about? A quoi pensez vous?
  [*ah kwah pã-seh-voo*]

  What else? Quoi d'autre? [*kwah dohtr*]

  What for? Pourquoi? [*poor-kwah*]

what *rel. pron.*, ce qui (subj), ce que (obj) [*skee, skuh*]

  I see what is coming, Je vois ce qui arrive [*zhvwah skyah-
  reev*]

  I don't like what I see, Je n'aime pas ce que je vois
  [*zhnem pah skuhzh vwah*]

whatever, quoi qui, quoi que [*kwah kee, kwah kuh*]

  whatever happens, quoi qu'il arrive [*kwah kee-lah-reev*]

  whatever it may be, quoi que ce soit [*kwahk suh swah*]

  whatever they say, quoi qu'on dise [*kwah kõ deez*]

wheat, blé (m) [*bleh*]

wheel, roue (f) [*roo*]

  steering wheel, volant (m) [*vo-lã*]

wheelbarrow, brouette (f) [*broo-et*]

when, quand [*kã*]

whenever, chaque fois que [*shak fwah kuh*]

where, où [*oo*]

  Where is she? Où est-elle? [*we-tel*]

  Where do you come from? D'où venez-vous? [*doo vneh-
  voo*]

wherever, partout où [*pahr-too oo*]

whether, si [*see*]

  whether or not, si, oui ou non [*see, wee oo nõ*]

which *interr. adj.*, quel, quelle; quels, quelles [*kel*]

which *interr. pron.*, lequel, laquelle; lesquels, lesquelles
[*luh-kel, lah-kel; leh-kel*]

Which have you chosen? Lesquels avez-vous choisis?
[*leh-kel ah-veh-voo shwah-zee*]

which *rel.*, qui, que; lequel [*kee, kuh; luh-kel*]

   the car which is leaving, l'auto qui part [*loh-toh kee pahr*]

   the car which I saw, l'auto que j'ai vue [*loh-tohk zeh vü*]

   the car in which she arrived, l'auto dans laquelle elle est arrivée [*loh-toh dã lah-kel e-le-tah-ree-veh*]

   to which, at which, auquel, à laquelle; auxquels, auxquelles [*oh-kel, ah lah-kel; oh-kel*]

   of which, from which, duquel, de laquelle; desquels, desquelles; dont [*dü-kel, duh lah-kel; deh-kel; dõ*]

   the car of which I speak, l'auto dont je parle [*loh-toh dõsh pahrl*]

while, pendant que [*pã-dã kuh*]

whipped cream, crème Chantilly [*krem shã-tee-yee*]

whisper *v.*, chuchoter [*shü-sho-teh*]

whistle *n.*, sifflet (m) [*see-fleh*]

whistle *v.*, siffler [*see-fleh*]

white, blanc, blanche [*blã, blãsh*]

who, qui [*kee*]

whoever, quiconque (*kee-kõk*]

whole, entier, -ière [*ã-tyeh, ã-tyer*]

wholesale, vente (f) en gros [*vã-tã groh*]

whom *interr.*, qui [*kee*]

whom *rel.*, que; qui [*kuh, kee*]

   The man whom I saw, L'homme que j'ai vu [*lom kuh zeh vü*]

   The man to whom I spoke, L'homme à qui j'ai parlé [*lom ah kee zeh pahr-leh*]

whose *poss. pron.*, de qui, à qui [*duh kee, ah kee*]

   Whose book is this? A qui est ce livre? [*ah kee eh suh leevr*]

whose *rel. pron.*, dont [*dõ*]

   The boy whose book I found, Le garçon dont j'ai trouvé le livre [*luh gar-sõ dõ zheh troo-veh luh leevr*]

why, pourquoi [*poor-kwah*]

   why not, pourquoi pas [*poor-kwah pah*]

wicked, méchant [*meh-shã(t)*]

wide, large [*lahrzh*]

widespread, répandu [*reh-pã-dü*]

widow, veuve (f) [*vuhv*]

widower, veuf (m) [*vuhf*]

width, largeur (f) [*lahr-zhuhr*]

wife, femme (f) [*fam*]

wig, perruque (f) [*pe-rük*]

wild, sauvage [*soh-vahzh*]

will [testament] *n.*, testament (m) [*tes-tah-mã*]

willingly, volontiers [*vo-lõ-tyeh*]

willpower, volonté (f) [*vo-lõ-teh*]

win *v.*, gagner [*gah-nyeh*]

wind *n.*, vent (m) [*vã*]

wind *v.*, remonter [*r(uh)-mõ-teh*]

windmill, moulin (m) à vent [*moo-lẽ ah vã*]

window, fenêtre (f) [*f(uh)-netr*]

   store window, vitrine (f) [*vee-treen*]

windshield, pare-brise (m) [*pahr-breez*]

wine, vin (m) [*vẽ*]

wing, aile (f) [*el*]

winner, gagnant, -ante [*gah-nyã(t)*]

winter, hiver (m) [*ee-ver*]

wipe *v.*, essuyer [*e-swee-yeh*]

wire [filament], fil (m) de fer [*feel duh fer*]

wisdom, sagesse (f) [*sah-zhes*]

wise, sage [*sahzh*]

wish *n.*, souhait (m) [*swe*]

wish *v.*, souhaiter [*swe-teh*]

wit, esprit (m) [*es-pree*]

witch, sorcière (f) [*sor-syer*]

with, avec [*ah-vek*]

withdraw *v.*, retirer, se retirer [*ruh-tee-reh, sruh-tee-reh*]

within, à l'intérieur (de), dedans, dans [*ah lẽ-teh-ryuhr (duh), duh-dã, dã*]

without, sans [*sã*]

witness *n.*, témoin (m) [*teh-mwẽ*]

witness *v.*, être témoin [*etr teh-mwẽ*]

witty, spirituel, -elle [*spee-ree-twel*]
woman, femme (f) [*fahm*]
wonder v., se demander [*s(uh) d(uh)-mã-deh*]
wonderful, merveilleux, -euse [*mer-veh-yuh, mer-veh-yuhz*]
wood, bois (m), [*bwah*]
wooden, en bois [*ã bwah*]
woods, bois (m), forêt (f) [*bwah, fo-re*]
wool, laine (f) [*len*]
woolen, en laine [*ã len*]
word, mot (m) [*moh*]
work [result] n., ouvrage (m) , oeuvre (f) [*oo-vrahzh, uhvr*]
   work of art, oeuvre d'art (f) [*uh-vruh dahr*]
work v., travailler [*trah-vah-yeh*]
  This doesn't work, Ca ne marche pas [*sahn mahrsh pah*]
worker, travailleur, -euse [*trah-vah-yuhr, trah-vah-yuhz*]
  factory worker, ouvrier, -ière [*oo-vree-yeh, oo-vree-yer*]
workshop, atelier (m) [*ah-tuh-lyeh*]
world, monde (m) [*mõd*]
world war, guerre mondiale (f) [*gher mõ-dyahl*]
worm, ver (m) [*ver*]
worn out, usé [*ü-zeh*]
worried, inquiet, -ète [*ẽ-kyeh, ẽ-kyet*]
worry n., inquiétude (f) [*ẽ-kyeh-tüd*]
worry v., s'inquiéter [*sẽ-kyeh-teh*]
worse adj., pire, plus mauvais [*peer, plü mo-ve(z)*]
worse adv., pis, plus mal [*pee, plü mahl*]
worship v., adorer [*ah-do-reh*]
worst, le pire, le plus mauvais [*luh peer, luh plü mo-ve*]
worth: to be worth, valoir (irreg) [*vahl-wahr*]
  It's worth ten francs, Cela vaut dix francs [*sah voh dee frã*]
worthwhile: to be worthwhile v., valoir (irreg) la peine [*vahl-wahr lah pen*]
worthy, digne [*deeñ*]
wound [injury] n., blessure (f) [*ble-sür*]
wounded, blessé [*ble-seh*]
wrap v., envelopper [*ã-vlo-peh*]
wrench [tool] n., clé (f) [*kleh*]

wrestling, catch (m) [*kahtsh*]
wrinkle [face] *n.*, ride (f) [*reed*]
wrinkle [clothes] *n.*, pli (m) [*plee*]
wrinkle *v.*, plisser [*plee-seh*]
wrist, poignet (m) [*pwah-nye*]
wristwatch, montre-bracelet (f) [*mōtr-brah-sleh*]
write *v.*, écrire (irreg) [*eh-kreer*]
writer, écrivain (m), femme écrivain (f) [*eh-kree-vẽ, fahm eh-kree-vẽ*]
writing, écriture (f) [*eh-kree-tür*]
writing paper, papier (m) à lettre [*pah-pyeh ah letr*]
wrong *adj.*, mauvais, incorrect [*mo-vε(z), ẽ-ko-rekt*]
  be wrong *v.*, avoir tort [*ah-vwahr tor*]
wrong *n.*, mal (m), tort (m) [*mahl, tor*]
wrong *v.*, faire tort à [*fer tor ah*]

X, Y, Z

x-ray, radio-(graphie) (f) [*rah-dyoh-(grah-fee)*]
yard [measure], environ un mètre [*ã-vee-rõ ẽ metr*]
yard [around house], jardin (m) [*zhahr-dẽ*]
yarn [filament], fil (m) [*feel*]
yawn *v.*, bâiller [*bah-yeh*]
year, an (m), année, (f) [*ã, ah-neh*]
  last year, l'année dernière [*lah-neh der-nyer*]
  next year, l'année prochaine [*lah-neh pro-shen*]
yearly *adv.*, annuellement [*ah-nwel-mã*]
yearly *adj.*, annuel, -elle [*ah-nwel*]
yell *v.*, *hurler [*ür-leh*]
yellow, jaune [*zhohn*]
yes, oui [*wee*]
yesterday, hier [*yer*]
  the day before yesterday, avant-hier [*ah-vã-tyer*]
yet, encore [*ã-kor*]
you, vous (polite); tu, te, toi (familiar) [*voo; tü, tuh, twah*]

young, jeune [*zhuhn*]

younger, cadet, -ette; plus jeune [*kah-deh, kah-det*; *plü zhuhn*]

your, votre, vos (polite); ton, ta, tes (familiar) [*votr, voh*; *tŏ, tah, teh*]

yours, le vôtre, la vôtre, les vôtres (polite); le tien, la tienne, les tiens, les tiennes (familiar) [*luh vohtr, lah vohtr, leh vohtr*; *luh tyē, lah tyen, leh tyē, leh tyen*]

yourself, vous-même (polite); toi-même (familiar) [*voo-mem*; *twah-mem*]

yours truly, bien amicalement (personal); Veuillez agréer, Monsieur, l'expression de mes sentiments distingués (business) [*not spoken*]

youth, jeunesse (f) [*zhuh-nes*]

zero, zéro (m) [*zeh-roh*]

zipper, fermeture éclair (f) [*fer-muh-tür eh-kler*]

zone, zone (f) [*zohn*]

zoo, zoo (m) [*zoh-oh*]

French/English

A

a *3d pers. sing. present tense of* AVOIR [*ah*] has
à [*ah*] at, in; to, into
  à l'anglaise [*ah lã-glez*] in the English way
abaisser *v.* [*ah-beh-seh*] lower
abandonner *v.* [*ah-bã-do-neh*] abandon
abbé *m.* [*ah-beh*] priest
abeille *f.* [*ah-bey*] bee
abimer *v.* [*ah-bee-meh*] harm
abolir *v.* [*ah-bo-leer*] abolish
abondance *f.* [*ah-bõ-dãs*] abundance
abondant [*ah-bõ-dã(t)*] abundant
abonnement *m.* [*ah-bon-mã*] subscription
s'abonner *v.* [*sah-bo-neh*] subscribe
d'abord [*dah-bor*] at first, first
aboutir (à) *v.* [*ah-boo-teer(ah)*] lead (to); end (in)
aboyer *v.* [*ah-bwah-yeh*] bark
abréviation *f.* [*ah-breh-vyah-syõ*] abbreviation
abri *m.* [*ah-bree*] shelter
abricot *m.* [*ah-bree-koh*] apricot
abriter *v.* [*ah-bree-teh*] shelter
absence *f.* [*ahp-sãs*] absence
absent [*ahp-sã(t)*] absent
absolument [*ahp-so-lü-mã*] absolutely
absorber *v.* [*ahp-sor-beh*] absorb
abstrait [*ahp-stre(t)*] abstract
absurde [*ahp-sürd*] absurd
acajou *m.* [*ah-kah-zhoo*] mahogany
accélérateur *m.* [*ahk-seh-leh-rah-tuhr*] accelerator
accent *m.* [*ahk-sã*] accent
accentuer *v.* [*ahk-sã-tweh*] stress, emphasize
accepter *v.* [*ak-sep-teh*] accept
accès *m.* [*ahk-se*] access

accès interdit [*ahk-se ẽ-ter-dee*] no tresspassing
accident *m.* [*ahk-see-dã*] accident
accidentel, -elle [*ahk-see-dã-tel*] accidental
accommoder *v.* [*ah-ko-mo-deh*] accommodate
accompagner *v.* [*ah-kõ-pah-nyeh*] accompany
accomplir *v.* [*ah-kõ-pleer*] accomplish, achieve
accord *m.* [*ah-kor*] agreement
  être d'accord [*e-truh dah-kor*] agree
  ne pas être d'accord [*nuh pah-ze-truh dah-kor*] disagree
  D'accord [*dah-kor*] All right
accorder *v.* [*ah-kor-deh*] grant
  s'accorder [*sah-kor-deh*] agree
accouchement *m.* [*ah-koosh-mã*] childbirth
accrocher *v.* [*ah-kro-sheh*] hang
accueil *m.* [*ah-kuhy*] reception
accueillir *v. irreg.* [*ah-kuh-yeer*] receive, welcome
accusation *f.* [*ah-kü-zah-syõ*] accusation
accuser *v.* [*ah-kü-zeh*] accuse
  accuser réception de [*ah-kü-zeh reh-sep-syõ duh*]
    acknowledge receipt of
achat *m.* [*ah-shah*] purchase
  faire *v.* des achats [*fer deh-zah-shah*] shop
acheter *v.* [*ahsh-teh*] buy
acheteur, -teuse [*ahsh-tuhr, ahsh-tuhz*] buyer
acide *f.* [*ah-seed*] acid
acier *m.* [*ah-syeh*] steel
acompte *m.* [*ah-kõt*] deposit
acquérir *v. irreg.* [*ah-keh-reer*] acquire
acquisition *f.* [*ah-kee-zee-syõ*] acquisition
acquitter *v.* [*ah-kee-teh*] acquit
acte *m.* [*ahkt*] act
acteur *m.* [*ahk-tuhr*] actor
actif, active [*ahk-teef, ahk-teev*] active
activité *f.* [*ahk-tee-vee-teh*] activity
actrice *f.* [*ahk-trees*] actress
actualité *f.* [*ahk-twah-lee-teh*] current events
  les actualités [*leh-zahk-twah-lee-teh*] newsreel
actuel, -elle [*ahk-twel*] current, present

actuellement [*ahk-twel-mã*] currently
adapter *v.* [*ah-dahp-teh*] adapt
addition *f.* [*ah-dee-syõ*] sum
   l'addition [*lah-dee-syõ*] the check
additionnel, -elle [*ah-dee-syo-nel*] additional
additionner *v.* [*ah-dee-syo-neh*] add up, sum up
adieu *m.* [*ah-dyuh*] farewell
adhérer (à) *v.* [*ah-deh-reh (ah)*] adhere (to), join
adjacent [*ahd-zhah-sã(t)*] adjacent
adjectif *m.* [*ahd-zhek-teef*] adjective
adjoint *m.* [*ahd-zhwē*] deputy, assistant
admettre *v. irreg.* [*ahd-metr*] admit, acknowledge
administration *f.* [*ahd-mee-nees-trah-syõ*] administration
administrer *v.* [*ahd-mee-nees-treh*] administer
admirable [*ahd-mee-rahbl*] admirable
admirateur, -trice [*ahd-mee-rah-tuhr, ahd-mee-rah-trees*]
   admirer
admiration *f.* [*ahd-mee-rah-syõ*] admiration
admirer *v.* [*ahd-mee-reh*] admire
adopter *v.* [*ah-dop-teh*] adopt
adoption *f.* [*ah-dop-syõ*] adoption
adorable [*ah-do-rahbl*] adorable
adorer *v.* [*ah-do-reh*] adore, love
adresse *f.* [*ah-dres*] address
adresser *v.* [*ah-dreh-seh*] address
   s'adresser (à) [*sah-dreh-seh (ah)*] speak, apply (to)
adroit [*ah-drwah(t)*] skillful
adulte [*ah-dült*] adult
adverbe *m.* [*ahd-verb*] adverb
adversaire *m.* [*ahd-ver-ser*] foe
aérer *v.* [*ah-eh-reh*] air
aérien, -enne [*ah-eh-ryē, ah-eh-ryen*] air
aéroport *m.* [*ah-eh-ro-por*] airport
affaires *pl.* [*ah-fer*] belongings, business
affecter *v.* [*ah-fek-teh*] affect
affection *f.* [*ah-fek-syõ*] affection
affectueux, -tueuse [*ah-fek-twuh, ah-fek-twuhz*] affectionate
affiche *f.* [*ah-feesh*] poster

affirmer *v.* [*ah-feer-meh*] affirm

affranchissement *m.* [*ah-frã-shees-mã*] postage

afin que *conj.* [*ah-fẽ kuh*] so that, in order that

afin de *prep.* [*ah-fẽ duh*] so as to, in order to

affreux, -euse [*ah-fruh, ah-fruhz*] horrible

africain [*ah-free-kẽ, ah-free-ken*] African

Afrique *f.* [*ah-freek*] Africa

âge *m.* [*ahzh*] age

    Quel âge avez-vous? [*ke-lahzh ah-veh-voo*] How old are
      you?

    moyen-âge *m.* [*mwah-ye nahzh*] Middle Ages

agé [*ah-zheh*] elderly, old

    agé de trois ans [*ah-zhehd trwah-zã*] three years old

agence *f.* [*ah-zhãs*] agency, branch office

    agence de voyages [*ah-zhãs duh vwah-yahzh*] travel agency

agenda *m.* [*ah-zhẽ-dah*] date book

agent *m.* [*ah-zhã*] agent

    agent de change [*ah-zhãt shãzh*] stockbroker

    agent de police [*ah-zhãt po-lees*] policeman

aggraver *v.* [*ah-grah-veh*] aggravate

agir *v.* [*ah-zheer*] act

    Il s'agit de [*eel sah-zhee duh*] It's a question of

agité [*ah-zhee-teh*] excited

agiter *v.* [*ah-zhee-teh*] agitate, wave

    s'agiter [*sah-zhee-teh*] move around

agneau, -eaux *m.* [*ah-nyoh*] lamb

agrandir *v.* [*ah-grã-deer*] enlarge

agréable [*ah-greh-ahbl*] agreeable, pleasant

agressif, -sive [*ah-gre-seef, ah-gre-seev*] aggressive

agression *f.* [*ah-gre-syõ*] aggression

agricole [*ah-gree-kol*] agricultural

agriculteur *m.* [*ah-gree-kül-tuhr*] farmer

agriculture *f.* [*ah-gree-kül-tür*] agriculture

aide *f.* [*ed*] aid, assistance

aider *v.* [*e-deh*] help

aigre [*egr*] sour

aigu, -uë [*eh-gü*] sharp

aiguille *f.* [*eh-gweey*] needle

aiguiser v. [eh-ghee-zeh] sharpen
ail m. [ahy] garlic
aile f. [el] wing, fender
ailleurs [ah-yuhr] elsewhere
   d'ailleurs [dah-yuhr] besides, moreover
aimable [e-mahbl] kind
aimer v. [e-meh] like, love, enjoy
   J'aimerais mieux . . . [zhem-re myuh] I'd rather . . . ,
      I'd prefer . . .
aîné [eh-neh] older
ainsi [ē-see] thus, so
   ainsi de suite [ē-seet sweet] so forth
ainsi que [ē-see k(uh)] as, well as
air m. [er] air, tune
   courant m. **d'air** m. [koo-rā der] draft
   avoir v. **l'air (de)** [ah-vwahr ler (duh)] look (like)
aise f. [ez] ease
aisé [eh-zeh] well off
ajouter v. [ah-zhoo-teh] add
ajuster v. [ah-zhüs-teh] adjust
alarmer v. [ah-lahr-meh] alarm
alcool m. [ahl-kol] alcohol
alerte adj. [ah-lert] alert
alerte f. [ah-lert] alert
aliment m. [ah-lee-mā] food
alimentaire [ah-lee-mā-ter] nourishing
alimentation f. [ah-lee-mā-tah-syō] nourishment, feeding;
   grocery store
allée f. [ah-leh] path, aisle
allemand [ahl-mā(d)] German
Allemagne f. [ahl-mahñ] Germany
aller v. irreg. [ah-leh] go
   aller à pied [ah-leh ah pyeh] walk
   Comment allez-vous? [ko-mā-tah-leh-voo] How do you
      do?, How are you?
   Allez-vous en! [ah-leh-voo-zā] Go away!
   s'en aller [sā-nah-leh] go away
   aller retour [ah-lehr-toor] round trip

alliance *f.* [*ahl-yãs*] alliance; wedding ring
allié, -ée [*ahl-yeh*] ally, allied
Allô [*ah-loh*] Hello
allonger *v.* [*ah-lõ-zheh*] lengthen
   s'allonger *v.* [*sah-lõ-zheh*] lie down
allumage *m.* [*ah-lü-mahzh*] ignition
allumer *v.* [*ah-lü-meh*] light, turn on [lights]
allumette *f.* [*ah-lü-met*] match
alors [*ah-lor*] then
Alpes *f. pl.* [*ahlp*] Alps
Alsace *f.* [*ahl-zahs*] Alsace
altitude *f.* [*ahl-tee-tüd*] altitude
amande *f.* [*ah-mãd*] almond
amant, -te [*ah-mã(t)*] lover
ambassade *f.* [*ã-bah-sahd*] embassy
ambassadeur, -drice [*ã-bah-sah-duhr, ã-bah-sah-drees*]
   ambassador
ambiance *f.* [*ã-byãs*] spirit, atmosphere
ambitieux, -euse [*ã-bee-syuh, ã-bee-syuhz*] ambitious
ambition *f.* [*ã-bee-syõ*] ambition
ambulance *f.* [*ã-bü-lãs*] ambulance
âme *f.* [*ahm*] soul
amélioration *f.* [*ah-meh-lyo-rah-syõ*] improvement
améliorer, s'améliorer *v.* [*ah-meh-lyo-reh, sah-meh-lyo-reh*]
   improve
amende *f.* [*ah-mãd*] fine
amener *v.* [*ahm-neh*] bring
amer, amère [*ah-mer*] bitter
américain [*ah-meh-ree-kẽ, ah-meh-ree-ken*] American
Amérique *f.* [*ah-meh-reek*] America
   Amérique du Nord (Sud) [*ah-meh-reek dü nor (süd)*]
   North (South) America
amertume *f.* [*ah-mer-tüm*] bitterness
ameublement *m.* [*ah-muh-bluh-mã*] furnishings
ami, amie [*ah-mee*] friend
amical, -aux [*ah-mee-kahl, ah-mee-koh*] friendly
   Bien amicalement [*byẽ-nah-mee-kahl-mã*] Sincerely yours
amidon *m.* [*ah-mee-dõ*] starch

amiral, -aux *m.* [*ah-mee-rahl, ah-mee-roh*] admiral

amitié *f.* [*ah-mee-tyeh*] friendship
   avec les amitiés sincères de [*ah-vek leh-zah-mee-tyeh sē-ser duh*] with best regards from

amour *m.* [*ah-moor*] love

amoureux, -euse [*ah-moo-ruh, ah-moo-ruhz*] in love; lover

ampoule *f.* [*ã-pool*] light-bulb; blister [of skin]

amusant [*ah-mü-zã(t)*] entertaining, amusing

amusement *m.* [*ah-müz-mã*] amusement, fun

amuser *v.* [*ah-mü-zeh*] amuse
   s'amuser [*sah-mü-zeh*] have a good time
   Amusez-vous bien! [*ah-mü-zeh-voo byē*] Have a good time!

amygdales *f. pl.* [*ah-mee-dahl*] tonsils

an *m.* [*ã*] year

analyse *f.* [*ah-nah-leez*] analysis, analyses
   analyses de laboratoire [*ah-nah-leez duh lah-bo-rah-twahr*] laboratory tests, lab work

ananas *m.* [*ah-nah-nah*] pineapple

anarchie *f.* [*ah-nar-shee*] anarchy

ancêtre *m., f.* [*ã-setr*] ancestor

anchois *m.* [*ã-shwah*] anchovy

ancien, -nne [*ã-syē, ã-syen*] former (before noun), ancient (after noun)
   objet *m.* **ancien** [*ob-zhe ã-syē*] antique
   ancien combattant *m.* [*ã-syē kō-bah-tã*] veteran

ancre *f.* [*ãkr*] anchor

âne *m.* [*ahn*] donkey

ange *m.* [*ãzh*] angel

anglais [*ã-gle(z)*] English

angle *m.* [*ãgl*] angle

Angleterre *f.* [*ã-gluh-ter*] England

animal, -aux *m.* [*ah-nee-mahl, ah-nee-moh*] animal

année *f.* [*ah-neh*] year
   l'année prochaine [*lah-neh pro-shen*] next year
   l'année dernière [*lah-neh der-nyer*] last year
   Bonne Année [*bo-nah-neh*] Happy New Year

anniversaire *m.* [*ah-nee-ver-ser*] anniversary, birthday
   Bon anniversaire! [*bon-nah-nee-ver-ser*] Happy Birthday!,

Happy Anniversary!

annonce f. [ah-nõs] announcement, advertisement

annoncer v. [ah-nõ-seh] announce

annuaire m. (**de téléphone**) [ah-nwer (duh teh-leh-fon)] telephone book

annuel, -elle [ah-nwel] annual, yearly

annuellement [ah-nwel-mã] yearly

annuler v. [ah-nü-leh] cancel

anonyme [ah-no-neem] anonymous

antérieur [ã-tehr-yuhr] prior

anticiper v. [ã-tee-see-peh] anticipate

antiquaire m., f. [ã-tee-ker] antique dealer

août m. [oo] August

apercevoir v. irreg. [a-per-suh-vwahr] catch sight of
  s'apercevoir (de) [sah-per-suh-vwahr (duh)] realize

apéritif m. [ah-peh-ree-teef] appetizer

apparence f. [ah-pah-rãs] appearance; looks

appareil m. [ah-pah-rey] appliance, gadget
  appareil ménagers [ah-pah-rey meh-nah-zheh] household appliances
  appareil photographique m. [ah-pah-rey foh-toh-grah-feek] camera

apparaître v. irreg. [ah-pah-retr] appear

appartement m. [ah-pahr-tuh-mã] apartment

appartenir v. irreg. [ah-pahr-tuh-neer] belong

appel m. [ah-pel] call, bid [in bridge]

appeler v. [ah-pleh] call
  s'appeler [sah-pleh] be named

appendicite f. [ah-pẽ-dee-seet] appendicitis

appétit m. [ah-peh-tee] appetite

applaudir v. [ah-ploh-deer] applaud, cheer

applaudissements m. pl. [ah-ploh-dees-mã] applause

appliquer v. [ah-plee-keh] apply

apporter v. [ah-por-teh] bring

apprécier v. [ah-preh-syeh] appreciate

apprendre v. irreg. [ah-prãdr] learn

apprenti, -ie [ah-prã-tee] apprentice

approbation f. [ah-pro-bah-syõ] approval

approcher, s'approcher *v.* [*ah-pro-sheh, sah-pro-sheh*]
  approach
approprié [*ah-pro-pree-yeh*] appropriate
approprier, s'approprier *v.* [*ah-pro-pree-yeh, sah-pro-pree-yeh*] appropriate
approuver *v.* [*ah-proo-veh*] approve
appuyer *v.* [*ah-pwee-yeh*] lean
  s'appuyer (sur) [*sah-pwee-yeh (sür)*] lean (on); stress
après *prep. & adv.* [*ah-pre*] after, afterwards
  d'après [*dah-pre*] according to
  après-midi *m., f.* [*ah-pre-mee-dee*] afternoon
  après demain [*ah-pred-mē*] the day after tomorrow
  après que *conj.* [*ah-pre kuh*] after
aquarelle *f.* [*ah-kwah-rel*] watercolor
Arabe *m., f.* [*ah-rahb*] Arab
Arabie *f.* [*ah-rah-bee*] Arabia
araignée *f.* [*ah-reh-nyeh*] spider
arbitraire [*ahr-bee-trer*] arbitrary
arbitre *m.* [*ahr-beetr*] arbitrator, referee
arbre *m.* [*ahrbr*] tree
arc *m.* [*ahrk*] bow [for arrows], arch
  arc-boutant *m.* [*ahrk-boo-tā*] flying buttress
  arc-en-ciel *m.* [*ahr-kã-syel*] rainbow
  arc en plein cintre [*ahr-kã plē sētr*] semi-circular arch
architecte *m.* [*ahr-shee-tekt*] architect
architecture *f.* [*ahr-shee-tek-tür*] architecture
ardoise *f.* [*ahr-dwahz*] slate
arête *f.* [*ah-ret*] fishbone
argent *m.* [*ahr-zhã*] money, silver
  argent massif [*ahr-zhã mah-seef*] sterling silver
argenterie *f.* [*ahr-zhã-tree*] silverware, silver plate
argot *m.* [*ahr-goh*] slang
argument *m.* [*ahr-gü-mã*] argument
aristocrate *m., f.* [*ah-rees-to-kraht*] aristocrat
aristocratique [*ah-rees-to-krah-teek*] aristocratic
arme *f.* [*ahrm*] weapon
armée *f.* [*ahr-meh*] army
armoire *f.* [*ahr-mwahr*] closet, cupboard

arracher v. [ah-rah-sheh] pull out, pull away
arranger v. [ah-rã-zheh] arrange, fix
arrêt m. [ah-re] stop
arrêter v. [ah-reh-teh] stop, arrest
  s'arrêter [sah-reh-teh] stop (oneself), halt
  Arrêtez! [ah-reh-teh] Stop!
arrhes f. pl. [ahr] deposit
arrière m. [ahr-yer] back, rear
  en arrière [ã-nahr-yer] backwards, behind
  à l'arrière [ah lahr-yer] in the back
  arrière-grand-mère f. [ahr-yer-grã-mer] great-grandmother
  arrière-pensée f. [ahr-yer-pã-seh] ulterior motive
  arrière-plan m. [ahr-yer-plã] background
arrivée f. [ah-ree-veh] arrival
arriver v. [ah-ree-veh] arrive, happen
arrondissement m. [ah-rõ-dees-mã] district
arroser v. [ah-roh-zeh] water
art m. [ahr] art
artère f. [ahr-ter] artery
artichaut m. [ahr-tee-shoh] artichoke
article m. [ahr-teekl] article
artificiel, -elle [ahr-tee-fee-syel] artificial
artisan m. [ahr-tee-zã] craftsman
artiste m., f. [ahr-teest] artist
as m. [ahs] ace
ascenseur m. [ah-sã-suhr] elevator
Asie f. [ah-zee] Asia
asile m. [ah-zeel] asylum
asperge f. [ah-sperzh] asparagus
aspirateur m. [ah-spee-rah-tuhr] vacuum cleaner
aspirine f. [ah-spee-reen] aspirin
assaisonnement m. [ah-se-zon-mã] seasoning
assaisonner v. [ah-se-zo-neh] flavor, season
assemblée f. [ah-sã-bleh] assembly, meeting
asseoir v. irreg. [ah-swahr] seat
  s'asseoir [sah-swahr] sit down
  Asseyez-vous [ah-seh-yeh voo] Sit down, Have a seat,
    Be seated

être assis [*e-trah-see(z)*] be seated
assez [*ah-seh*] enough
assiette *f.* [*ah-syet*] plate
assis [*ah-see(z)*] seated
assistant, -te [*ah-sees-tã(t)*] assistant
assister *v.* [*ah-sees-teh*] assist
   assister à [*ah-sees-teh ah*] attend
associé, -ée [*ah-so-syeh*] associate
associer, s'associer *v.* [*ah-so-syeh, sah-so-syeh*] associate
assurance *f.* [*ah-sü-rãs*] insurance [life, fire]; assurance
   compagnie *f.* d'assurances [*kõ-pah-nyee dah-sü-rãs*]
     insurance company
   police *f.* d'assurance [*po-lees dah-sü-rãs*] insurance policy
assurément [*ah-sü-reh-mã*] certainly
assurer *v.* [*ah-sü-reh*] assure, insure
atelier *m.* [*ah-tuh-lyeh*] workshop
athlétique [*aht-leh-teek*] athletic
Atlantique *m.* [*aht-lã-teek*] Atlantic
atmosphère *f.* [*aht-mos-fer*] atmosphere
atomique [*ah-to-meek*] atomic
attacher *v.* [*ah-tah-sheh*] attach, fasten
attaque *f.* [*ah-tahk*] attack
attaquer *v.* [*ah-tah-keh*] attack
atteindre *v. irreg.* [*ah-tẽdr*] reach
attendre *v.* [*ah-tãdr*] wait (for)
   s'attendre à [*sah-tã-drah*] expect
   en attendant [*ã-nah-tã-dã*] meanwhile
attente *f.* [*ah-tãt*] wait
attentif, -ve [*ah-tã-teef, ah-tã-teev*] attentive
attention *f.* [*ah-tã-syõ*] attention
   Attention! [*ah-tã-syõ*] Look out!
atterrir *v.* [*ah-teh-reer*] land
attérrissage *m.* [*ah-teh-ree-sahzh*] landing
attirer *v.* [*ah-tee-reh*] attract
attitude *f.* [*ah-tee-tüd*] attitude
attraper *v.,* [*ah-trah-peh*] catch
au: à le [*oh*] to the, at the
aube *f.* [*ohb*] dawn

aucun *adj. & pron.* [*oh-kẽ, oh-kün*] no, none
audacieux, -euse [*oh-dah-syuh, oh-dah-syuhz*] bold
au-dessous (de) [*ot-soo (duh)*] below
au-dessus (de) [*oht-sü (duh)*] above
auditeur, -trice [*oh-dee-tuhr, oh-dee-trees*] listener
augmentation *f.* [*og-mã-tah-syõ*] increase
augmenter *v.* [*og-mã-teh*] increase
aujourd'hui [*oh-zhoor-dwee*] today
auparavant [*oh-pah-rah-vã*] previously
auprès (de) [*oh-pre (duh)*] near
auquel [*oh-kel*] to whom, which
au revoir [*ohr-vwahr*] good-bye
aussi [*oh-see*] also, too
   aussi . . . que [*oh-see . . . k(uh)*] as . . . as
aussitôt [*oh-see-toh*] immediately
   aussitôt que [*oh-see-toh k(uh)*] as soon as
Australie *f.* [*os-trah-lee*] Australia
australien, -enne [*os-trah-lyẽ, os-trah-lyen*] Australian
autant de, autant que [*oh-tã d(uh), oh-tã k(uh)*] as much
   (as), so much (as)
autel *m* [*o-tel*] altar
auteur *m.* [*oh-tuhr*] author
auto *f.* [*oh-toh*] car
autobus *m.* [*oh-toh-büs*] bus
autocar *m.* [*oh-toh-kahr*] bus
automatique [*oh-toh-mah-teek*] automatic
automne *m.* [*o-ton*] autumn
automobile *f.* [*o-to-mo-beel*] automobile
autoriser *v.* [*o-to-ree-zeh*] authorize
autorité *f.* [*o-to-ree-teh*] authority, control
auto-stop *m.* [*o-to-stop*] hitch-hiking
autour *adv.* [*oh-toor*] around
autour de *prep.* [*oh-toor duh*] around, about
autre [*ohtr(uh)*] other
   un (une) autre [*ẽ-nohtr, ü-nohtr*] another
   l'un l'autre, les uns les autres [*lẽ lohtr, leh-zẽ leh-zohtr*]
    each other
   d'autre [*dohtr*] else

    quoi d'autre? [*kwah dohtr*] what else?

autrefois [*oh-truh-fwah*] formerly

autrement [*oh-truh-mã*] otherwise

Autriche *f.* [*oh-treesh*] Austria

autrichien, -enne [*oh-tree-shē, oh-tree-shyen*] Austrian

aux: **à les** [*oh*] to the, at the

auxquels, auxquelles [*oh-kel*] to which, to whom

avalanche *f.* [*ah-vah-lãsh*] avalanche

avaler *v.* [*ah-vah-leh*] swallow

avance *f.* [*ah-vãs*] advance

    à l'avance [*ah lah-vãs*] beforehand, ahead of time

    en avance [*ã-nah-vãs*] in advance, early

avancer, s'avancer *v.* [*ah-vã-seh, sah-vã-seh*] advance

avant *prep. & adv.* [*ah-vã*] before

    en avant (de) [*ã-nah-vã (duh)*] ahead (of)

    avant de faire [*ah-vãd fer*] before doing

avant-hier [*ah-vã-tyer*] the day before yesterday

avant que *conj.* [*ah-vã kuh*] before

avantage *m.* [*ah-vã-tahzh*] advantage

avare *m., f.* [*ah-vahr*] miser

avec [*ah-vek*] with

avenir *m.* [*ahv-neer*] future

    à l'avenir [*ah lahv-neer*] in the future

aventure *f.* [*ah-vã-tür*] adventure

avenue *f.* [*ahv-nü*] avenue

averse *f.* [*ah-vers*] shower

avertir *v.* [*ah-ver-teer*] warn, notify

avertissement *m.* [*ah-ver-tees-mã*] warning

aveugle [*ah-vuhgl*] blind

avez *2d pers. pl. pres. tense of* AVOIR [*ah-veh*] you have

avion *m.* [*ah-vyõ*] airplane

    avion à réaction [*ah-vyõ ah reh-ahk-syõ*] jet

    par avion [*pah-rah-vyõ*] airmail

avis *m.* [*ah-vee*] notice, opinion

avocat *m.* [*ah-vo-kah*] attorney, lawyer

avoir *v. irreg.* [*ah-vwahr*] have

    avoir besoin [*ah-vwahr buhz-wē*] need

    avoir chaud [*ah-vwahr shoh*] be hot

avoir faim [*ah-vwahr fẽ*] be hungry
avoir froid [*ah-vwahr frwah*] be cold
avoir l'air (de) [*ah-vwahr ler (duh)*] look (like)
avoir peur [*ah-vwahr puhr*] be afraid
avoir raison [*ah-vwahr re-zõ*] be right
avoir soif [*ah-vwahr swahf*] be thirsty
avoir tort [*ah-vwahr tor*] be wrong
avons *1st pers. pl. present tense of* AVOIR [*ah-võ*] we have
avouer *v.* [*ah-vweh*] confess, admit
avril *m.* [*ah-vreel*] April
ayant [*pres. part. of* AVOIR] [*e-yã*] having

B

bâbord *m.* [*bah-bor*] port
baccalauréat (bac, bachot) *m.* [*bah-kah-lo-reh-ah (bahk,*
    bah-shoh)] baccalaureate examination
bagages *m. pl.* [*bah-gahzh*] baggage, luggage
bague *f.* [*bahg*] ring
baigner *v.* [*beh-nyeh*] bathe, wash
    se baigner [*s(uh) beh-nyeh*] take a bath, go swimming
baignoire *f.* [*behñ-wahr*] bathtub
bail *m.* [*bahy*] lease
bâiller *v.* [*bah-yeh*] yawn
bain *m.* [*bẽ*] bath
    salle *f.* **de bains** [*sahl duh bẽ*] bathroom
    prendre un bain [*prã-drẽ bẽ*] take a bath
baiser *m.* [*beh-zeh*] kiss
baisse *f.* [*bes*] drop
    en baisse [*ã bes*] falling
baisser *v.* [*beh-seh*] lower
bal *m.* [*bahl*] dance, ball
balai *m.* [*bah-le*] broom
balance *f.* [*bah-lãs*] scale
balancer *v.* [*bah-lã-seh*] rock

balayer *v.* [*bah-leh-yeh*] sweep
balcon *m.* [*bahl-kō*] balcony
balle *f.* [*bahl*] ball
ballet *m.* [*bah-le*] ballet
ballon *m.* [*bah-lō*] ball
banane *f.* [*bah-nahn*] banana
banc *m.* [*bã*] bench
banlieue *f.* [*bã-lyuh*] suburbs
banque *f.* [*bãk*] bank
banquier *m.* [*bã-kyeh*] banker
baptême *m.* [*bah-tem*] baptism
bar *m.* [*bahr*] bar
barbe *f.* [*bahrb*] beard
barrage *m.* [*bah-rahzh*] dam
barrer *v.* [*bah-reh*] bar
barrière *f.* [*bahr-yer*] barrier, fence
bas, basse [*bah(s)*] low
   À bas . . . ! [*ah bah*] Down with . . . !
   en bas [*ã bah*] down, downstairs
bas *m.* [*bah*] stocking
   J'ai filé un bas [*zheh fee-leh ē bah*] I have a run in my
      stocking
base *f.* [*bahz*] base
basse-cour *f.* [*bahs-koor*] farmyard
bataille *f.* [*bah-tahy*] battle
bateau, -eaux *m.* [*bah-toh*] boat
   bateau à voile [*bah-toh ah vwahl*] sailboat
bâtiment *m.* [*bah-tee-mã*] building
bâton *m.* [*bah-tō*] stick
battement *m.* [*baht-mã*] beat
batterie *f.* [*bah-tree*] battery
battre *v. irreg.* [*bahtr*] beat, defeat
   se battre [*s(uh) bahtr*] fight
beau (bel), belle; beaux, belles [*boh, bel*] beautiful,
   handsome
beaucoup (de) [*boh-koo (duh)*] much, many; a great deal
   (of), a lot (of)
beau-frère, beaux-frères *m.* [*boh-frer*] brother-in-law,

brothers-in-law

beau-père *m.* [*boh-per*] father-in-law, stepfather

beauté *f.* [*boh-teh*] beauty

   produits *m. pl.* **de beauté** [*pro-dwee d(uh) boh-teh*] cosmetics

bébé *m.* [*beh-beh*] baby, infant

belge [*belzh*] Belgian

Belgique [*bel-zheek*] Belgium

belle-fille *f.* [*bel-feey*] daughter-in-law

belle-mère *f.* [*bel-mer*] mother-in-law, stepmother

belle-soeur *f.* [*bel-suhr*] sister-in-law

bénédicité *m.* [*beh-neh-dee-see-teh*] grace, blessing

bénédiction *f.* [*beh-neh-deek-syõ*] blessing

bénéfice *m.* [*beh-neh-fees*] benefit, profit

bénir *v.* [*beh-neer*] bless

berceau, -eaux *m.* [*ber-soh*] cradle

besoin *m.* [*buh-zwẽ*] need

   avoir besoin de [*ah-vwahr buh-zwẽ d(uh)*] need

bétail *m.* [*beh-tahy*] cattle, livestock

bête *f.* [*bet*] beast

bête *fam.* [*bet*] stupid

beurre *m.* [*buhr*] butter

biberon *m.* [*bee-brõ*] baby bottle

bible *f.* [*beebl*] bible

bibliothèque *f.* [*bee-blee-yo-tek*] library, bookcase

bicarbonate *m.* **de soude** [*bee-kahr-bo-naht duh sood*] sodium bicarbonate

bicyclette *f.* [*bee-see-klet*] bicycle

bien *m.* [*byẽ*] good

bien *adv.* [*byẽ*] well, quite

   très bien [*tre byẽ*] very well

   bien entendu [*byẽ-nã-tã-dü*] of course

bien-être *m.* [*byẽ-netr*] welfare, well-being

bien que *conj.* [*byẽ (k(uh))*] although

bientôt [*byẽ-toh*] soon

bienvenu *m.* [*byẽ-vnü*] welcome

   Soyez le bienvenu! [*swah-yehl byẽ-vnü*] Welcome!

bière *f.* [*byer*] beer

biftek *m.* [*beef-tek*] steak

bijou, -oux *m.* [*bee-zhoo*] jewel
bijouterie *f.* [*bee-zhoo-tree*] jewelry
billet *m.* [*bee-ye*] ticket
  billet de banque [*bee-yed bāk*] banknote
biscuit *m.* [*bees-kwee*] cracker, cookie
blaireau, -eaux *m.* [*ble-roh*] shaving brush; badger
blâme *m.* [*blahm*] blame
blâmer *v.* [*blah-meh*] blame
blanc, blanche [*blā(sh)*] white
blanchir *v.* [*blā-sheer*] bleach, blanch
blanchisserie *f.* [*blā-shees-ree*] laundry
blé *m.* [*bleh*] wheat
blesser *v.* [*ble-seh*] injure, wound
blessure *f.* [*ble-sür*] injury
bleu [*bluh*] blue
bloc *m.* [*blok*] block
blond, blonde [*blŏ(d)*] blond
blouse *f.* [*blooz*] smock, lab coat
bocal, -aux *m.* [*bo-kal, bo-koh*] jar
boeuf, -s *m.* [*buhf, buh*] ox, steer; beef
bois *m.* [*bwah*] wood, woods
  en bois [*ã bwah*] wooden
boire *v. irreg.* [*bwahr*] drink
boisson *f.* [*bwah-sŏ*] drink
boîte *f.* [*bwaht*] box
  boîte de conserve [*bwaht duh kŏ-serv*] can
  boîte aux lettres [*bwah-toh letr*] mail box
bombardements *m. pl.* [*bŏ-bahr-duh-mã*] bombing
bombe *f.* [*bŏb*] bomb
bon, bonne [*bŏ, bon*] good
  bon marché [*bŏ mahr-sheh*] cheap
bonbon *m.* [*bŏ-bŏ*] a piece of candy
  des bonbons [*deh bŏ-bŏ*] candy
bonheur *m.* [*bo-nuhr*] happiness
bonne *f.* [*bon*] maid
Bonjour! [*bŏ-zhoor*] Good morning!, Good afternoon!
Bonsoir! [*bŏ-swahr*] Good evening!
bonté *f.* [*bŏ-teh*] goodness, kindness

bord *m.* [*bor*] edge
  à bord (de) [*ah bor (duh)*] aboard
  le bord de la mer [*luh bor d(uh) lah mer*] sea-shore
botte *f.* [*bot*] boot
bouche *f.* [*boosh*] mouth
boucher *m.* [*boo-sheh*] butcher
boucherie *f.* [*boosh-ree*] butcher shop
bouchon *m.* [*boo-shō*] stopper, cork
  tire-bouchon *m.* [*teer boo-shō*] corkscrew
boucle *f.* [*bookl*] curl [of hair], buckle [of belt]
boucle d'oreille [*bookl do-rey*] earring
boue *f.* [*boo*] mud
bougeoir *m.* [*boozh-wahr*] candlestick
bouger *v.* [*boo-zheh*] move
bougie *f.* [*boo-zhee*] candle, sparkplug
bouillant [*boo-yā(t)*] boiling
bouillie *f.* [*boo-yee*] baby cereal, porridge
bouillir *v. irreg.* [*boo-yeer*] boil
bouilloire *f.* [*booy-wahr*] kettle
bouillon *m.* [*boo-yō*] broth
boulangerie *f.* [*boo-lāzh-ree*] bakery
boule *f.* [*bool*] ball
bouleverser *v.* [*bool-ver-seh*] upset
boulon *m.* [*boo-lō*] bolt
Bourgogne *f.* [*boor-goñ*] Burgundy
Bourse *f.* [*boors*] stock exchange
bout *m.* [*boo*] end
bouteille *f.* [*boo-tey*] bottle
boutique *f.* [*boo-teek*] shop
bouton *m.* [*boo-tō*] button, pimple
boxe *f.* [*boks*] boxing
bracelet *m.* [*brahs-le*] bracelet
branche *f.* [*brāsh*] branch
bras *m.* [*brah*] arm
brasserie *f.* [*brahs-ree*] brewery; saloon, café
bref, brève [*bref, brev*] brief
Bretagne *f.* [*bruh-tahñ*] Brittany
bretelle *f.* [*bruh-tel*] suspender; by-pass

breton, -onne [*bruh-tō, bruh-ton*] Breton
brillant [*bree-yã(t)*] bright, brilliant
briller *v.* [*bree-yeh*] *shine*
brique *f.* [*breek*] brick
briquet *m.* [*bree-ke*] lighter
brise *f.* [*breez*] breeze
briser *v.* [*bree-zeh*] break
britannique [*bree-tah-neek*] British
broderie *f.* [*brod-ree*] embroidery
bronze [*brōz*] bronze
brosse *f.* [*bros*] brush
   brosse à dents [*bro-sah dã*] toothbrush
brosser *v.* [*bro-seh*] brush
brouette *f.* [*broo-et*] wheelbarrow
brouillard *m.* [*broo-yahr*] fog
   Il fait du brouillard [*eel fe dü broo-yahr*] It's foggy
bruit *m.* [*brwee*] noise
brûler *v.* [*brü-leh*] burn
brûlure *f.* [*brü-lür*] burn
brun [*brē, brün*] brown, brunette
bruyant [*brwee-ã(t)*] noisy
budget *m.* [*büd-zhe*] budget
buffet *m.* [*bü-fe*] buffet, sideboard
buisson *m.* [*bwee-sō*] bush
bulgare [*bül-gahr*] Bulgarian
Bulgarie *f.* [*bül-gah-ree*] Bulgaria
bulletin *m.* [*bül-tē*] bulletin, baggage check, ballot
bureau, -eaux *m.* [*bü-roh*] desk, office
   bureau de poste [*bü-rohd post*] post office
   bureau de location [*bü-rohd lo-kah-syō*] box office
   bureau de tabac [*bü-rohd tah-bah*] tobacco store
but *m.* [*bü*] aim, goal, purpose
buvard *m.* [*bü-vahr*] blotter

C

ça (cela) [*sah*] that
cabane *f.* [*kah-bahn*] cabin
cabine *f.* [*kah-been*] cabin, stateroom
   cabine téléphonique [*kah-been teh-leh-fo-neek*]
     téléphone booth
cabinet *m.* [*kah-bee-ne*] cabinet; toilet
cable *m.* [*kahbl*] cable
cacahuète *f.* [*kah-kah-wet*] peanut
cacao *m.* [*kah-kah-oh*] cocoa
cacher *v.* [*kah-sheh*] hide, conceal
   se cacher [*skah-sheh*] hide oneself
cachot *m.* [*kah-shoh*] dungeon
cadeau, -eaux *m.* [*kah-doh*] gift
cadet, -ette [*cah-de(t)*] younger, youngest
cadran *m.* [*kah-drã*] dial
cadre *m.* [*kahdr*] frame [for picture]; framework [theoretical]
café *m.* [*kah-feh*] café, coffee
cafetière *f.* [*kahf-tyer*] coffee pot
cage *f.* [*kahzh*] cage
cahier *m.* [*kah-yeh*] notebook
caillou, -oux *m.* [*kah-yoo*] pebble
caisse *f.* [*kes*] case, crate; cashier
   Payez à la caisse [*peh-yeh ah lah kes*] Pay the cashier
caissier, -ière [*kes-yeh, kes-yer*] cashier, bank teller
calculer *v.* [*kahl-kü-leh*] calculate
caleçon *m.* [*kahl-sõ*] underpants
calendrier *m.* [*kah-lã-dree-yeh*] calender
calme [*kahlm*] calm
caler, se caler *v.* [*kah-leh, s(uh) kah-leh*] stall
camarade *m., f.* [*kah-mah-rahd*] comrade
   camarade de classe [*kah-mah-rahd duh klahs*] classmate
   camarade de jeu [*kah-mah-rahd duh zhuh*] playmate

cambrioleur *m.* [*kã-bree-o-luhr*] burglar

caméra *m.* [*kah-meh-rah*] movie camera

camion *m.* [*kah-myõ*] truck

camp *m.* [*kã*] camp

campagne *f.* [*kã-pahñ*] country
  à la campagne [*ah lah kã-pahñ*] in the country

camper *v.* [*kã-peh*] camp

Canada *m.* [*kah-nah-dah*] Canada

canadien, -enne [*kah-nah-dyẽ, kah-nah-dyen*] Canadian

canal, -aux *m.* [*kah-nal, kah-noh*] canal

canapé *m.* [*kah-nah-peh*] sofa, couch

canard *m.* [*kah-nahr*] duck

candidat [*kã-dee-dah(t)*] candidate

caniche *f.* [*kah-neesh*] poodle

canne *f.* [*kahn*] cane

canon *m.* [*kah-nõ*] cannon

canot *m.* [*kah-noh*] small boat
  canot de sauvetage [*kah-nohd sohv-tahzh*] life-boat

caoutchouc *m.* [*kah-oot-shoo*] rubber

capable [*kah-pahbl*] able, capable

capacité *f.* [*kah-pah-see-teh*] capacity, ability

capitaine *m.* [*kah-pee-ten*] captain

capital, -aux *adj.* [*kah-pee-tahl, kah-pee-toh*] capital

capital, -aux *m.* [*kah-pee-tahl, kah-pee-toh*] capital

car [*kahr*] for

caractère *m.* [*kah-rahk-ter*] character, disposition
  de bon (mauvais) caractère [*duh bõ (mo-ve) kah-rahk-ter*]
  good- (bad-) tempered

carafe *f.* [*kah-rahf*] decanter [for wine], pitcher

carburant *m.* [*kahr-bü-rã*] fuel

cardinal, -aux *m.* [*kahr-dee-nahl, kahr-dee-noh*] cardinal

caresser *v.* [*kah-reh-seh*] caress

cargaison *f.* [*kahr-ghe-zõ*] cargo

carie *f.* [*kah-ree*] cavity [of a tooth]

carnaval, -als *m.* [*kahr-nah-vahl*] carnival

carnet *m.* [*kahr-ne*] notebook
  carnet de chèques [*kahr-ned shek*] checkbook

carotte *f.* [*kah-rot*] carrot

carré *m.* [*kah-reh*] square

carrefour *m.* [*kahr-foor*] crossroads, intersection

carrelage *m.* [*kahr-lahzh*] tile floor

carrément [*kah-reh-mã*] squarely, frankly

carrière *f.* [*kahr-yer*] career

carte *f.* [*kahrt*] card; map, chart

   cartes à jouer [*kahr-tah zhweh*] playing cards

   carte postale [*kahrt pos-tahl*] postcard

   carte de séjour [*kahrt duh seh-zhoor*] resident's card

   carte de visite [*kahrt duh vee-zeet*] calling card

carton *m.* [*kahr-tõ*] carton, cardboard

cas *m.* [*kah*] case, situation

   au cas où [*oh kah oo*] in the event of

   en cas de [*ã kah d(uh)*] in case of

   dans ce cas [*dãs kah*] in that case

   en tout cas [*ã too kah*] anyhow, in any case

   selon le cas [*suh-lõl kah*] as the case may be

caserne *f.* [*kah-zern*] barracks

casier judiciaire *m.* [*kah-zyeh zhü-dee-syer*] police record

casquette *f.* [*kahs-ket*] cap

casser *v.* [*kah-seh*] break

casserole *f.* [*kahs-rol*] pan

catch *m.* [*kahtsh*] wrestling

catégorie *f.* [*kah-teh-go-ree*] category

cathédrale *f.* [*kah-teh-drahl*] cathedral

catholique [*kah-to-leek*] Catholic

cauchemar *m.* [*kosh-mahr*] nightmare

cause *f.* [*kohz*] cause, reason

   à cause de [*ah kohz d(uh)*] because of, on account of

cave *f.* [*kahv*] cellar

caveau, -eaux *m.* [*kah-voh*] tomb, vault

ce *dem. adj. m.* [*s(uh)*] this, that

ce, c' *demons. pron.* [*s(uh)*] it, this, he, she

ceci [*suh-see*] this

céder *v. irreg.* [*seh-deh*] cede, give in

ceinture *f.* [*sẽ-tür*] belt

   ceinture de sécurité [*sẽ-tür d(uh) seh-kü-ree-teh*] safety belt

cela (ça) *pron.* [*s(uh)-lah (sah)*] that

C'est cela [*se slah*] That's it
célèbre [*seh-lebr*] famous
céleri *m.* [*sel-rée*] celery
célibataire *adj.* [*seh-lee-bah-ter*] single
célibataire *m., f.* [*seh-lee-bah-ter*] bachelor, single woman
celle-ci, celle-là; celles-ci, celles-là [*sel-see, sel-lah*]
   this one, that one; these, those
celui-ci, celui-là [*suh-lwee-see, suh-lwee-lah*] this one, that
   one
cendre *f.* [*sãdr*] ash, cinder
cendrier *m.* [*sã-dree-yeh*] ashtray
censé [*sã-seh*] supposed to
cent [*sã*] hundred
centime *m.* [*sã-teem*] centime
centimètre *m.* [*sã-tee-metr*] centimeter [.39 inch]
ce qui, ce que [*skee, skuh*] what, that which
central, -aux [*sã-trahl, sã-troh*] central
centre *m.* [*sãtr*] center
  centre-ville *m.* [*sã-truh-veel*] downtown
cependant [*s(uh)-pã-dã*] however
cercle *m.* [*serkl*] circle
cercueil *m.* [*ser-kuhy*] coffin
céréale *f.* [*seh-reh-ahl*] cereal
cérémonie *f.* [*seh-reh-mo-nee*] ceremony
cerf-volant *m.* [*ser-vo-lã*] kite
cerise *f.* [*s(uh)-reez*] cherry
certain [*ser-tẽ, ser-ten*] certain
certainement [*ser-ten-mã*] certainly
certificat *m.* [*ser-tee-fee-kah*] certificate
cerveau, -eaux *m.* [*ser-voh*] brain [anat.]
cervelle *f.* [*ser-vel*] brains [food]
ces [*seh*] these, those
cesser (de faire) *v.* [*seh-seh (duh fer)*] cease (doing),
   discontinue
c'est-à-dire [*se-tah deer*] that's to say
cet, cette *dem. adj.* [*set*] this, that
ceux [*suh*] the ones, they
ceux-ci, ceux-là [*suh-see, suh-lah*] these, those

chacun, -une [*shah-kẽ, shah-kün*] each, every one

chagrin *m.* [*shah-grẽ*] sorrow

chaîne *f.* [*shen*] chain; network [radio, T.V.]

chair *f.* [*sher*] flesh

chaise *f.* [*shez*] chair

châle *m.* [*shahl*] shawl

chaleur *f.* [*shah-luhr*] heat, warmth

chambre *f.* [*shãbr*] room

  chambre à coucher [*shã-brah koo-sheh*] bedroom

  chambre d'hôtel [*shã-bruh doh-tel*] hotel room

  chambre à un lit [*shã-brah ẽ lee*] single room

  chambre à deux lits [*shã-brah duh lee*] double room

  chambre meublée [*shã-bruh muh-bleh*] furnished room

  chambre forte [*shã-bruh fort*] vault

champ *m.* [*shã*] field

  champ de courses [*shãd koors*] racetrack

champagne *m.* [*shã-pahñ*] champagne

champignon *m.* [*shã-pee-nyõ*] mushroom

champion, -onne [*shã-pyõ, shã-pyon*] champion

chance *f.* [*shãs*] chance, luck

  avoir *v.* **de la chance** [*ah-vwahr dlah shãs*] have good luck, be lucky

  Bonne chance! [*bon shãs*] Good luck!

chandail *m.* [*shã-dahy*] sweater

chandelier *m.* [*shã-duh-lyeh*] candlestick

chandelle *f.* [*shã-del*] candle

change *m.* [*shãzh*] foreign exchange

  taux *m.* **de change** [*tohd shãzh*] rate of exchange

changement *m.* [*shãzh-mã*] change

changer *v.* [*shã-zheh*] change

  se changer [*s(uh) shã-zheh*] change clothes

chanson *f.* [*shã-sõ*] song

chanter *v.* [*shã-teh*] sing

chanteur, chanteuse [*shã-tuhr, shã-tuhz*] singer

chantier *m.* [*shã-tyeh*] construction site

chapeau, -eaux *m.* [*shah-poh*] hat

chapelle *f.* [*shah-pel*] chapel

chapiteau, -eaux *m.* [*shah-pee-toh*] capital

chapitre *m.* [*shah-peetr*] chapter
chaque [*shahk*] each, every
charbon *m.* [*shahr-bõ*] coal
charcuterie *f.* [*shahr-kü-tree*] pork butcher's, delicatessen
charger *v.* [*shahr-zheh*] load, burden entrust
   charger une batterie [*shahr-zheh ün bah-tree*] charge a
      battery
   personne *f.* **à charge** [*per-son ah shahrzh*] dependent
charité *f.* [*shah-ree-teh*] charity
charmant [*shar-mã(t)*] charming
charme *m.* [*shahrm*] charm
charnière *f.* [*shahr-nyer*] hinge
charrue *f.* [*shah-rü*] plow
chasse *f.* [*shahs*] hunting
chasser *v.* [*shah-seh*] chase, hunt
chasseur *m.* [*shah-suhr*] hunter; bellboy
chat *m.* [*shah*] cat
château, -eaux *m.* [*shah-toh*] castle
chaud [*shoh*] hot
   Il fait chaud [*eel fe shoh*] It's hot
   avoir *v.* **chaud** [*ah-vwahr shoh*] be hot
chauffage *m.* [*shoh-fahzh*] heating
chauffer *v.* [*shoh-feh*] heat
chauffeur *m.* [*shoh-fuhr*] driver, chauffeur
chaussée *f.* [*shoh-seh*] street, roadway
chaussette *f.* [*shoh-set*] sock
chaussure *f.* [*shoh-sür*] shoe
chauve [*shohv*] bald
chef *m.* [*shef*] chief, leader
chef-d'oeuvre *m.* [*she-duhvr*] masterpiece
chemin *m.* [*sh(uh)-mẽ*] road, path, way
   chemin de fer [*sh(uh)-mẽd fer*] railroad
   à mi-chemin [*ah meesh-mẽ*] midway
cheminée *f.* [*sh(uh)-mee-neh*] chimney, fireplace, mantel
chemise *f.* [*sh(uh)-meez*] shirt
   chemise de nuit [*sh(uh)-meez duh nweet*] nightgown
chemisier *m.* [*sh(uh)-mee-zyeh*] blouse
chêne *m.* [*shen*] oak

chèque *m.* [*shek*] check
    chèque de voyage [*shek duh vwah-yahzh*] traveler's check
cher, chère [*sher*] dear, expensive
chercher *v.* [*sher-sheh*] look for, search for
chéri, -ie [*sheh-ree*] sweetheart, darling
cheval, -aux *m.* [*sh(uh)-vahl, sh(uh)-voh*] horse
    monter *v.* **à cheval** [*mõ-teh ahsh-vahl*] ride
chevalier *m.* [*sh(uh)-vah-lyeh*] knight
cheveux *m. pl.* [*sh(uh)-vuh*] hair
    se faire *v.* **couper les cheveux** [*sfer koo-peh leh-shvuh*] have
    a haircut
cheville *f.* [*sh(uh)-veey*] ankle
chèvre *f.* [*shevr*] goat
chevreau, -eaux *m.* [*shuh-vroh*] kid
chez [*sheh*] at the home of, at the place of business of
    chez-soi *m. inv.* [*sheh-swah*] home
    Faites comme chez vous [*fet kom sheh voo*] Make yourself
    at home
chic [*sheek*] smart
chien *m.* [*shyẽ*] dog
chiffon *m.* [*shee-fõ*] rag
chiffre *m.* [*sheefr*] figure
chimique *adj.* [*shee-meek*] chemical
Chine *f.* [*sheen*] China
chinois [*shee-nwah(z)*] Chinese
chirurgie *f.* [*shee-rür-zhee*] surgery
chirurgien, -ienne [*shee-rür-zhyẽ, shee-rür-zhyen*] surgeon
choc *m.* [*shok*] shock
chocolat *m.* [*sho-ko-lah*] chocolate
choisir *v.* [*shwah-zeer*] choose
choix *m.* [*shwah*] choice
chômage *m.* [*shoh-mahzh*] unemployment
    en chômage [*ã shoh-mahzh*] unemployed
choquant [*sho-kã(t)*] offensive, shocking
choquer *v.* [*sho-keh*] shock
chose *f.* [*shohz*] thing
chou, choux *m.* [*shoo*] cabbage
chou-fleur, choux-fleurs *m.* [*shoo-fluhr*] cauliflower

chrétien, -enne [*kreh-tyē, kreh-tyen*] Christian
chuchoter *v.* [*shü-sho-teh*] whisper
chute *f.* [*shüt*] fall
cicatrice *f.* [*see-kah-trees*] scar
cidre *m.* [*seedr*] cider
ciel, cieux *m.* [*syel, syuh*] sky, heaven
cierge *f.* [*syerzh*] candle
cigare *f.* [*see-gahr*] cigar
cigarette *f.* [*see-gah-ret*] cigarette
cil *m.* [*seel*] eyelash
ciment *m.* [*see-mã*] cement
cimetière *m.* [*seem-tyer*] cemetery
cinéma *m.* [*see-neh-mah*] movies, movie theater
cinq [*sē(k)*] five
cinquante [*sē-kãt*] fifty
cinquième [*sē-kyem*] fifth
circonscription *f.* [*seer-kõ-skreep-syō*] electoral district
circonstance *f.* [*seer-kõ-stãs*] circumstance
circulation *f.* [*seer-kü-lah-syō*] circulation [of blood], traffic
cire *f.* [*seer*] wax
cirer *v.* [*see-reh*] shine, wax
cireur *m.* [*see-ruhr*] shoeshine boy
cirque *m.* [*seerk*] circus
ciseau *m.* [*see-zoh*] chisel
   ciseaux *pl.* [*see-zoh*] scissors
citation *f.* [*see-tah-syō*] quotation
citer *v.* [*see-teh*] quote
citoyen, -enne [*see-twah-yē, see-twah-yen*] citizen
citron *m.* [*see-trõ*] lemon
citrouille *f.* [*see-trooy*] pumpkin
civil, -le [*see-veel*] civilian
civilisation *f.* [*see-vee-lee-zah-syō*] civilization
civisme *m.* [*see-veezm*] good citizenship
clair [*kler*] light, bright, clear
clair *m.* **de lune** [*kler duh lün*] moonlight
classe *f.* [*klahs*] class
classer *v.* [*klah-seh*] classify
classique [*klah-seek*] classic

clef f. [*kleh*] key; wrench
clergé m. [*kler-zheh*] clergy
client, -te [*klee-ā(t)*] customer, client
clientèle f. [*klee-ã-tel*] clientele
climat m. [*klee-mah*] climate
clinique f. [*klee-neek*] private hospital
cloche f. [*klosh*] bell
clocher m. [*klo-sheh*] steeple
cloître m. [*klwahtr*] cloister
clou m. [*kloo*] nail
clouer v. [*kloo-eh*] nail
cochon m. [*ko-shō*] pig
cocktail m. [*kok-tel*] cocktail
coeur m. [*kuhr*] heart
   par coeur [*pahr kuhr*] by heart
coffre m. [*kofr*] chest; auto trunk
cognac m. [*ko-nyahk*] brandy
coiffer, se coiffer v. [*kwah-feh, s(uh) kwah-feh*] comb [one's]
   hair
coiffeur m. [*kwah-fuhr*] barber, beauty operator
coin m. [*kwĕ*] corner
coincidence f. [*ko-ē-see-dãs*] coincidence
col m. [*kol*] collar; mountain pass
colère f. [*ko-ler*] anger
   en colère [*ã ko-ler*] angry
colis m. [*ko-lee*] parcel
colle f. [*kol*] glue
collection f. [*ko-lek-syō*] collection
collectionner v. [*ko-lek-syo-neh*] collect
collègue m., f. [*ko-leg*] colleague
coller v. [*ko-leh*] stick, glue
collier m. [*kol-yeh*] necklace, beads
colline f. [*ko-leen*] hill
collision f. [*ko-lee-zyō*] collision, crash
colonel m. [*ko-lo-nel*] colonel
colonie f. [*ko-lo-nee*] colony
coloniser v. [*ko-lo-nee-zeh*] colonize, settle
colonne f. [*ko-lon*] column

colonne vertébrale f. [ko-lon ver-teh-brahl] spine
colorer v. [ko-lo-reh] color
combat m. [kõ-bah] fight
Combien (de)? [kõ-byē (duh)] How much? How many?
   Combien de temps? [kõ-byēd tā] How long?
combinaison f. [kõ-bee-ne-zõ] combination, slip
   [undergarment]
combiner v. [kõ-bee-neh] combine
combler v. [kõ-bleh] fill
comédie f. [ko-meh-dee] comedy
comédien, -enne [ko-meh-dyē, ko-meh-dyen] comedian
comité m. [ko-mee-teh] committee
commander v. [ko-mã-deh] command, order
comme [kom] like, as
   comme ci comme ça [kom see kom sah] so-so
commencement m. [ko-mãs-mã] beginning
commencer (à faire) v. [ko-mã-seh (ah fer)] begin (to do)
comment [ko-mã] how
commerçant, -te [ko-mer-sã(t)] merchant, storekeeper
commerce m. [ko-mers] trade
commercial, -aux [ko-mer-syahl, ko-mer-syoh] commercial
commettre v. irreg. [ko-metr] commit
commissaire m. **de police** [ko-mee-ser duh po-lees] police
   superintendent
commissariat m. **de police** [ko-mee-sahr-yah duh po-lees]
   police station
commission f. [ko-mee-syõ] commission
commode [ko-mod] convenient
commode f. [ko-mod] dresser, chest of drawers
commun [ko-mē, ko-mün] common
communauté f. [ko-mü-noh-teh] community
commune f. [ko-mün] municipality
communication f. [ko-mü-nee-kah-syõ] communication,
   telephone call
communiquer v. [ko-mü-nee-keh] communicate
communisme m. [ko-mü-neezm] communism
communiste n. & adj. [ko-mü-neest] communist
compagnie f. [kõ-pah-nyee] company

compagnie aérienne [kõ-pah-nyee ah-eh-ryen] airline
compagnie de navigation [kõ-pah-nyeed nah-vee-gah-syõ]
   steamship line
compagnon m. [kõ-pah-nyõ] companion
comparaison f. [kõ-pah-re-zõ] comparison
comparer v. [kõ-pah-reh] compare
compartiment m. [kõ-pahr-tee-mã] compartment
compatriote m., f. [kõ-pah-tree-ot] compatriot
compensation f. [kõ-pã-sah-syõ] compensation
compétent [kõ-peh-tã(t)] competent
compétition f. [kõ-peh-tee-syõ] competition
complément m. [kõ-pleh-mã] complement
complet, -ète [kõ-ple(t)] complete
   Complet [kõ-ple] Full, No vacancy
complet m. [kõ-ple] suit
complètement [kõ-plet-mã] completely
completer v. [kõ-pleh-teh] complete
compliment m. [kõ-plee-mã] compliment
compliqué [kõ-plee-keh] complicated
compliquer v. [kõ-plee-keh] complicate
complot m. [kõ-ploh] plot
comportement m. [kõ-por-tuh-mã] behavior
comporter v. [kõ-por-teh] comprise
   se comporter [s(uh) kõ-por-teh] behave
composé [kõ-poh-zeh] compound
composer v. [kõ-poh-zeh] compose, dial [a telephone]
compositeur m. [kõ-poh-zee-tuhr] composer
comprendre v. irreg. [kõ-prãdr] understand
comprimé m. [kõ-pree-meh] tablet
comprimer v. [kõ-pree-meh] compress
compromis m. [kõ-pro-mee] compromise
comptable m. [kõ-tahbl] accountant, bookkeeper
comptabilité f. [kõ-tah-bee-lee-teh] bookkeeping, accounts
comptant [kõ-tã] cash
compte m. [kõt] account
   compte courant [kõt koo-rã] checking account
   compte-cheques [kõt-shek] checking account
   compte-rendu [kõt-rã-dü] report, book review

rendre v. **compte de** [*rãdr kõt d(uh)*] account for
se rendre v. **compte de** [*s(uh) rãdr kõt d(uh)*] realize
compter (sur) v. [*kõ-teh (sür)*] count; rely (on)
comptoir m. [*kõ-twahr*] counter
concentrer, se concentrer v. [*kõ-sã-treh, skõ-sã-treh*]
    concentrate
concept m. [*kõ-sept*] concept
concernant [*kõ-ser-nã*] concerning
concert m. [*kõ-ser*] concert
concevoir v. *irreg.* [*kõ-s(uh)-vwahr*] conceive
concierge m., f. [*kõ-syerzh*] housekeeper, doorkeeper
conclure v. *irreg.* [*kõ-klür*] conclude
conclusion f. [*kõ-klü-zyõ*] conclusion
concombre m. [*kõ-kõbr*] cucumber
concours m. [*kõ-koor*] contest, competitive examination
concurrence f. [*kõ-kü-rãs*] competition
condamnation f. [*kõ-dah-nah-syõ*] condemnation
condamner v. [*kõ-dah-neh*] condemn
condenser v. [*kõ-dã-seh*] condense
condition f. [*kõ-dee-syõ*] condition
conditionnel, -elle [*kõ-dee-syo-nel*] conditional
conduire v. *irreg.* [*kõ-dweer*] drive, lead
  se conduire [*s(uh) kõ-dweer*] behave
conduite f. [*kõ-dweet*] conduct
confection f. [*kõ-fek-syõ*] ready-to-wear
conférence f. [*kõ-feh-rãs*] lecture
conférencier m. [*kõ-feh-rã-syeh*] lecturer
confesser v. [*kõ-feh-seh*] confess
  se confesser [*s(uh) kõ-feh-seh*] go to confession
confession f. [*kõ-fe-syõ*] confession
confiance f. [*kõ-fyãs*] confidence, trust
  faire v. **confiance** [*fer kõ-fyãs*] trust
confiant [*kõ-fyã(t)*] trusting, confident
confidentiel, -elle [*kõ-fee-dã-syel*] confidential
confier v. [*kõ-fyeh*] entrust
confirmer v. [*kõ-feer-meh*] confirm
confiture f. [*kõ-fee-tür*] jam
conflit m. [*kõ-flee*] conflict

confondre v. [kõ-fõdr] confuse
confort m. [kõ-for] comfort
confortable [kõ-for-tahbl] comfortable
  peu (pas) confortable [puh (pah) kõ-for-tahbl] uncomfortable
confusion f. [kõ-fü-zyõ] confusion
congé m. [kõ-zheh] holiday
congrès m. [kõ-gre] congress, conference
connaissance f. [ko-ne-sãs] acquaintance, knowledge
  faire v. **la connaissance de** [fer lah ko-ne-sãs duh] meet, make the acquaintance of
connaissement m. [ko-nes-mã] bill of lading
connaître v. irreg. [ko-netr] know
conquérir v. irreg. [kõ-keh-reer] conquer
consacrer v. [kõ-sah-kreh] devote
conscience f. [kõ-syãs] consciousness, conscience
consciencieux, -euse [kõ-syã-syuh, kõ-syã-syuhz] conscientious
conscient [kõ-syã(t)] aware, conscious
conseil m. [kõ-sey] advice, council
  conseil m. **de ministres** [kõ-seyd mee-neestr] cabinet
conseiller v. [kõ-se-yeh] advise, recommend
consentir v. irreg. [kõ-sã-teer] consent
conséquence f. [kõ-seh-kãs] consequence
  en conséquence [ã kõ-seh-kãs] therefore, accordingly
conséquent [kõ-seh-kã(t)] consistent
  par conséquent [pahr kõ-seh-kã] consequently
conservateur, -trice [kõ-ser-vah-tuhr, kõ-ser-vah-trees] conservative
conservatoire m. [kõ-ser-vah-twahr] music school
conserver v. [kõ-ser-veh] preserve
considérable [kõ-see-deh-rahbl] considerable
considérer v. [kõ-see-deh-reh] consider
consigne f. [kõ-seeñ] baggage check
  mettre v. irreg. **à la consigne** [me-trah lah kõ-seeñ] check
consister à v. [kõ-sees-teh (ah)] consist in
  consister en [kõ-sees-teh ã] consist of
consoler f. [kõ-so-leh] console, comfort

consommateur *m.* [*kõ-so-mah-tuhr*] consumer
consommation *f.* [*kõ-so-mah-syõ*] consumption; beverage, drink
consommer *v.* [*kõ-so-meh*] consume, consummate
constamment [*kõ-stah-mã*] constantly
constant [*kõ-stã(t)*] constant
constater *v.* [*kõ-stah-teh*] note
constituer *v.* [*kõ-stee-tweh*] constitute
constitution *f.* [*kõ-stee-tü-syõ*] constitution
construction *f.* [*kõ-strük-syõ*] construction
construire *v. irreg.* [*kõ-sɪrweer*] build
consul *m.* [*kõ-sül*] consul
consulat *m.* [*kõ-sü-lah*] consulate
consultation *f.* [*kõ-sül-tah-syõ*] office call, conference
consulter *v.* [*kõ-sül-teh*] consult
contact *m.* [*kõ-tahkt*] contact
contagieux, -euse [*kõ-tah-zhyuh, kõ-tah-zhyuhz*] contagious
conte *m.* [*kõt*] tale
contemporain [*kõ-tã-po-rē, kõ-tã-po-ren*] contemporary
contenir *v. irreg.* [*kõt-neer*] contain
content [*kõ-tã(t)*] happy, glad
contenu *m.* [*kõt-nü*] contents
contestable [*kõ-tes-tahbl*] questionable
continent *m.* [*kõ-tee-nã*] continent
continuer (à, de) *v.* [*kõ-tee-nweh (ah, duh)*] continue (to)
contraire [*kõ-trer*] contrary
  au contraire [*oh kõ-trer*] on the contrary
contraste *m.* [*kõ-trahst*] contrast
contrat *m.* [*kõ-trah*] contract
contre [*kõtr*] against
contribuer *v.* [*kõ-tree-bweh*] contribute
contrôle *m.* [*kõ-trohl*] check
contrôler *v.* [*kõ-troh-leh*] check, verify
contrôleur *m.* [*kõ-troh-luhr*] inspector; ticket-taker, train conductor
controverse *f.* [*kõ-tro-vers*] controversy
convaincre *v. irreg.* [*kõ-vēkr*] convince, convict
convenable [*kõ-vnahbl*] suitable, proper

convenir *v. irreg.* [kŏ-vneer] suit
conversation *f.* [kŏ-ver-sah-syŏ] conversation
convertir *v.* [kŏ-ver-teer] convert
coopération *f.* [ko-o-peh-rah-syŏ] cooperation
copie *f.* [ko-pee] copy
copier *v.* [ko-pyeh] copy
coquelicot *m.* [kok-lee-koh] poppy
coquillage *m.* [ko-kee-yahzh] seashell
coquille *f.* [ko-keey] shell
corbeau, -eaux *m.* [kor-boh] crow
corbeille *f.* [kor-bey] basket
   corbeille à papier [kor-bey ah pah-pyeh] wastebasket
corde *f.* [kord] cord, rope
cordial, -iaux [kor-dyahl, kor-dyoh] cordial
cordonnier *m.* [kor-do-nyeh] shoemaker
corne *f.* [korn] horn
corps *m.* [kor] body
correct *adj.* [ko-rekt] correct
correction *f.* [ko-rek-syŏ] correction
correspondance *f.* [ko-res-pŏ-dās] correspondence; train
      connection
correspondre *v.* [ko-res-pŏdr] correspond
corriger *v.* [ko-ree-zheh] correct
corrompre *v.* [ko-rŏpr] corrupt, bribe
corrompu [ko-rŏ-pü] corrupt
corruption *f.* [ko-rüp-syŏ] corruption
corsage *m.* [kor-sahzh] blouse, dress bodice
costume *m.* [kos-tüm] suit
côte *f.* [koht] coast; rib
côté *m.* [koh-teh] side
   à côté de [ah koh-teh d(uh)] beside, near, next to
   de côté [d(uh) koh-teh] aside, sideways
côtelette *f.* [koht-let] chop, cutlet
coton *m.* [ko-tŏ] cotton
cou *m.* [koo] neck
couche *f.* [koosh] diaper
coucher *m.* **de soleil** [koo-shehd so-ley] sunset
coucher *v.* [koo-sheh] lay, put to bed

se coucher [*s(uh) koo-sheh*] lie down, go to bed
couchette *f*. [*koo-shet*] berth
coude *m*. [*kood*] elbow
coudre *v*. *irreg*. [*koodr*] sew
   machine *f*. **à coudre** *f*. [*mah-shee-nah koodr*] sewing machine
couler *v*. [*koo-leh*] flow
couleur *f*. [*koo-luhr*] color
couloir *m*. [*kool-wahr*] hall, corridor
coup *m*. [*koo*] blow
   coup de feu [*kood fuh*] shot
   coup d'oeil [*koo duhy*] glance
   coup de pied [*kood pyeh*] kick
   coup de soleil [*kood so-ley*] sunburn
   tout à coup [*too-tah koo*] suddenly
coupable [*koo-pahbl*] guilty
coupe *f*. [*koop*] cut
couper *v*. [*koo-peh*] cut
couple *m*. [*koopl*] couple
coupure *f*. [*koo-pür*] cut
cour *f*. [*koor*] court, courtyard
   faire *v*. **la cour à** [*fer lah koor ah*] court
courage *m*. [*koo-rahzh*] courage
courageux, -euse [*koo-rah-zhuh, koo-rah-zhuhz*] brave
couramment [*koo-rah-mã*] fluently
courant *adj*. [*koo-rã(t)*] running, current
courant *m*. [*koo-rã*] current
   courant d'air [*koo-rã der*] draft
courbe *f*. [*koorb*] curve
courir *v*. *irreg*. [*koo-reer*] run
couronne *f*. [*koo-ron*] crown
courrier *m*. [*koor-yeh*] mail
cours *m*. [*koor*] course
   cours du change [*koor dü shãzh*] rate of exchange
   Quel est le cours du dollar? [*kel el koor dü do-lahr*]
     What is the rate of exchange for dollars?
course *f*. [*koors*] race, errand
court [*koor(t)*] short
courtois [*koor-twah(z)*] courteous

cousin, -ine [*koo-zē, koo-zeen*] cousin
  cousin (-ine) germain (-aine) [*koo-zē zher-mē, koo-zeen zher-men*] first cousin
coussin *m.* [*koo-sē*] cushion
coût *m.* [*koo*] cost
  coût de la vie [*kood lah vee*] cost of living
couteau, -eaux *m.* [*koo-toh*] knife
coûter *v.* [*koo-teh*] cost
couteux, -euse [*koo-tuh, koo-tuhz*] costly
coutume *f.* [*koo-tüm*] custom
couture *f.* [*koo-tür*] sewing, seam
couturière *f.* [*koo-tür-yer*] dressmaker
couvent *m.* [*koo-vā*] convent, monastery
couvercle *m.* [*koo-verkl*] lid
couvert *adj.* [*koo-ver(t)*] covered
  vente *f.* **à couvert** [*vā-tah koo-ver*] sale for delivery
couvert *m.* [*koo-ver*] fork and spoon, place at table, restaurant cover charge
  mettre *v. irreg.* **le couvert** [*metr luh koo-ver*] set the table
couverture *f.* [*koo-ver-tür*] blanket, cover
couvrir *v. irreg.* [*koov-reer*] cover
crabe *m.* [*krahb*] crab
cracher *v.* [*krah-sheh*] spit
craie *f.* [*kre*] chalk
craindre *v. irreg.* [*krēdr*] fear
crainte *f.* [*krēt*] fear
crâne *m.* [*krahn*] skull
cravate *f.* [*krah-vaht*] necktie
crayon *m.* [*kre-yō*] pencil
créancier *m.* [*kreh-ā-syeh*] creditor
création *f.* [*kreh-ah-syō*] creation
créature *f.* [*kreh-ah-tür*] creature
crédit *m.* [*kreh-dee*] credit
créer *v.* [*kreh-eh*] create
crème *f.* [*krem*] cream
  crème Chantilly [*krem shā-tee-yee*] sugared whipped cream
crêpe *f.* [*krep*] crepe, pancake

crépuscule *m.* [*kreh-püs-kül*] dusk
creuser *v.* [*kruh-zeh*] dig
creux, -euse [*kruh, kruhz*] hollow
crevaison *f.* [*kruh-ve-zõ*] blow-out
crever *v.* [*kruh-veh*] burst
  J'ai crevé [*zheh kruh-veh*] I have (had) a flat tire
crevette *f.* [*kruh-vet*] shrimp
cri *m.* [*kree*] cry, scream
  pousser *v.* **des cris** [*poo-seh deh kree*] scream
cric *m.* [*kreek*] jack
crier *v.* [*kree-eh*] call, shout
crime *m.* [*kreem*] crime
criminel, -elle *adj. & n.* [*kree-mee-nel*] criminal
crise *f.* [*kreez*] crisis, heart attack
cristal, -aux *m.* [*krees-tahl, krees-toh*] crystal
critique *adj.* [*kree-teek*] critical
critique *f.* [*kree-teek*] review, criticism
critique *m.* [*kree-teek*] critic
critiquer *v.* [*kree-tee-keh*] criticize
crochet *m.* [*kro-she*] hook, crochet work
croire *v. irreg.* [*krwahr*] believe
  Je crois que oui [*zhuh krwahk wee*] I think so
  Je ne le crois pas [*zhuhn luh krwah pah*] I don't think so
croisement *m.* [*krwahz-mã*] crossing
croiser *v.* [*krwah-zeh*] cross
croisière *f.* [*krwah-zyer*] cruise
croître *v. irreg.* [*krwahtr*] grow
croix *f.* [*krwah*] cross
  Croix Rouge *m.* [*krwah roozh*] Red Cross
croquis *m.* [*kro-kee*] sketch
croûte *f.* [*kroot*] crust
croyance *f.* [*krwah-yãs*] belief
cru [*krü*] raw
cru *past part. of* CROIRE [*krü*] believed
cruauté *f.* [*krü-oh-teh*] cruelty
crudités *f. pl.* [*krü-dee-teh*] raw vegetables
cruel, -elle [*krü-el*] cruel
Cuba *m.* [*kü-bah*] Cuba

cubain [*kü-bē̃, kü-ben*] Cuban
cube *m.* [*küb*] cube, block
cueillir *v. irreg.* [*kuh-yeer*] pick
cuillère *f.* [*kwee-yer*] spoon
   petite cuillère [*p(uh)-teet kwee-yer*] teaspoon
   cuillère à soupe [*kwee-yer ah soop*] tablespoon
  cuillerée *f.* [*kweey-reh*] spoonful
 cuir *m.* [*kweer*] leather
  cuir chevelu [*kweer chuhv-lü*] scalp
cuire *v. irreg.* [*kweer*] cook
  cuire au four [*kweer oh foor*] bake
cuisine *f.* [*kwee-zeen*] kitchen, cooking
  faire *v.* **la cuisine** [*fer lah kwee-zeen*] cook
cuisinier, -ière, *m., f.* [*kwee-zee-nyeh, kwee-zee-nyer*] cook
cuisinière *f.* [*kwee-zee-nyer*] stove
cuisse *f.* [*kwees*] thigh
cuit [*kwee(t)*] cooked
  bien cuit [*byē̃ kwee(t)*] well done
cuivre *m.* [*kweevr*] copper, brass
culotte *f.* [*kü-lot*] pants
culte *m.* [*kült*] worship
cultivateur *m.* [*kül-tee-vah-tuhr*] farmer
cultiver *v.* [*kül-tee-veh*] cultivate, grow
culture *f.* [*kül-tür*] culture; crop
cure *f.* [*kür*] cure
curé *m.* [*kü-reh*] pastor
cure-dents *m. inv.* [*kür-dā̃*] toothpick
curieux, -euse [*kür-yuh, kür-yuhz*] curious
curiosité *f.* [*kür-yoh-zee-teh*] curiosity
cuvette *f.* [*kü-vet*] basin
cycliste *m., f.* [*see-kleest*] cyclist

D

d': de [*duh*] of, from

dame *f.* [*dahm*] lady

danger *m.* [*dā-zheh*] danger

dangereux, -euse [*dāzh-ruh, dāzh-ruhz*] dangerous

dans [*dā*] in

dactylographe, dactylo *m., f.* [*dahk-tee-lo-grahf, dahk-tee-loh*] typist

danse *f.* [*dās*] dance

danser *v.* [*dā-seh*] dance

danseur, -euse [*dā-suhr, dā-suhz*] dancer

date *f.* [*daht*] date

datte *f.* [*daht*] date [fruit]

davantage [*dah-vā-tahzh*] more

de [*d(uh)*] of, from

dé *m.* [*deh*] die [gambling], thimble

déballer *v.* [*deh-bah-leh*] unpack

débarquer *v.* [*deh-bahr-keh*] disembark

débarrasser *v.* [*deh-bah-rah-seh*] rid

  se débarrasser de [*s(uh) deh-bah-rah-seh duh*] get rid of

déborder *v.* [*deh-bor-deh*] overflow

debout *adv.* [*duh-boo*] upright, standing

  être (se tenir, rester) debout [*e-truh (stuh-neer, res-teh) duh-boo*] stand

se débrouiller *v.* [*s(uh) deh-broo-yeh*] get along

début *m.* [*deh-bü*] beginning

décédé [*deh-seh-deh*] deceased

décembre *m.* [*deh-sābr*] December

décence *f.* [*deh-sās*] decency

décent [*deh-sā(t)*] decent

décevoir *v. irreg.* [*dehs-vwahr*] disappoint

décharger *v.* [*deh-shahr-zheh*] unload, relieve

déchirer *v.* [*deh-shee-reh*] tear, rip

197

décider v. [*deh-see-deh*] decide
  se décider [*sdeh-see-deh*] make up one's mind
décision f. [*deh-see-zyõ*] decision
déclaration f. [*deh-klah-rah-syõ*] declaration, statement
déclarer v. [*deh-klah-reh*] declare
décommander v. [*deh-ko-mã-deh*] call off
décor m. [*deh-kor*] decoration, scenery
décoration f. [*deh-ko-rah-syõ*] decoration
décorer v. [*deh-ko-reh*] decorate
découper v. [*deh-koo-peh*] cut up, cut out, carve [meat]
décourager v. [*deh-koo-rah-zheh*] discourage
découvert [*deh-koo-ver(t)*] uncovered, exposed
  compte m. **découvert** [*kõt deh-koo-ver*] overdrawn account
  crédit m. **à découvert** [*kreh-dee ah deh-koo-ver*] unsecured
    credit
  vente f. **à découvert** [*vã-tah deh-koo-ver*] sale for futures
découverte f. [*deh-koo-vert*] discovery
découvrir v. irreg. [*deh-koo-vreer*] discover, uncover
décret m. [*deh-kre*] decree
décrire v. irreg. [*deh-kreer*] describe
décrocher v. [*deh-kro-sheh*] unhook, disconnect
déçu [*deh-sü*] disappointed
dedans [*duh-dã*] inside, indoors
défaire v. irreg. [*deh-fer*] undo, unpack
défaite f. [*deh-fet*] defeat
défaut m. [*deh-foh*] defect
défavorable [*deh-fah-vo-rahbl*] unfavorable
défectueux, -euse [*deh-fek-twuh*, *deh-fek-twuhz*] defective
défendre v. [*deh-fãdr*] defend, prohibit
défendu [*deh-fã-dü*] forbidden
Défense d'entrer [*deh-fãs dã-treh*] Keep out
défi m. [*deh-fee*] challenge, dare
défilé m. [*deh-fee-leh*] parade
définir v. [*deh-fee-neer*] define
définition f. [*deh-fee-nee-syõ*] definition
défunt [*deh-fẽ(t)*] deceased
dégoûté [*deh-goo-teh*] disgusted
degré m. [*duh-greh*] degree

déguisement *m.* [*deh-gheez-mā*] disguise

dehors [*duh-or*] out, outside, outdoors

déjà [*deh-zhah*] already

déjeuner *m.* [*deh-zhuh-neh*] lunch, noon meal
   petit déjeuner [*ptee deh-zhuh-neh*] breakfast

déjeuner *v.* [*deh-zhuh-neh*] have breakfast, have lunch

delà: au dela de [*ohd lahd(uh)*] beyond

délai *m.* [*deh-le*] delay, time-limit

délibéré [*deh-lee-beh-reh*] deliberate

délicat [*deh-lee-kah(t)*] delicate

délicieux, -euse [*deh-lee-syuh, deh-lee-syuhz*] delicious

délivrer *v.* [*deh-lee-vreh*] deliver

demain [*d(uh)-mē*] tomorrow
   demain matin [*d(uh)-mē mah-tē*] tomorrow morning
   après-demain [*ah-pred-mē*] the day after tomorrow

demande *f.* [*d(uh)-mād*] request, application
   demande en mariage [*d(uh)-mā-dā mahr-yahzh*] proposal

demander *v.* [*d(uh)-mā-deh*] ask, ask for
   demander à [someone] **de faire** [something] [*d(uh)-mā-deh*
    ah . . . dfer . . .] ask [someone] to do [something]
   demander [something] **à** [someone] [*d(uh)-mā-deh . . .*
    ah . . .] ask [someone] for [something]
   se demander [*suhd-mā-deh*] wonder

démarrer *v.* [*deh-mah-reh*] start [car]

démarreur *m.* [*deh-mah-ruhr*] starter

déménager *v.* [*deh-meh-nah-zheh*] move [change residence]

démenti *m.* [*deh-mā-tee*] denial

démentir *v.* [*deh-mā-teer*] deny, contradict

demi [*d(uh)-mee*] half
   deux heures et demie [*duh-zuhr ed-mee*] half past two

démission *f.* [*deh-mee-syō*] resignation

démissionner *v.* [*deh-mee-syo-neh*] resign

démocratie *f.* [*deh-mo-krah-see*] democracy

démodé [*deh-mo-deh*] old-fashioned

demoiselle *f.* [*d(uh)-mwah-zel*] young lady
   demoiselle d'honneur [*d(uh)-mwah-zel do-nuhr*] bridesmaid,
    flower girl

démolir *v.* [*deh-mo-leer*] demolish

démonstration f. [*deh-mõ-strah-syõ*] demonstration
démontrer v. [*deh-mõ-treh*] demonstrate, prove
dense [*dãs*] dense
densité f. [*dã-see-teh*] density
dent f. [*dã*] tooth
  mal m. **de dents** [*mahl duh dã*] toothache
  brosse f. **à dents** [*bro-sah dã*] toothbrush
dentelle f. [*dã-tel*] lace
dentifrice f. [*dã-tee-frees*] toothpaste
dentiste m. [*dã-teest*] dentist
dépanneuse f. [*deh-pah-nuhz*] tow truck
départ m. [*deh-pahr*] departure, start
département m. [*deh-pahr-tuh-mã*] department
dépasser v. [*deh-pah-seh*] exceed, pass
se dépêcher v. [*s(uh)-deh-pe-sheh*] hurry
  Dépêchez-vous! [*deh-pe-sheh-voo*] Hurry up!
dépendre (de) v. [*deh-pãdr (duh)*] depend (on)
  Cela dépend [*slah deh-pã*] That depends
dépense f. [*deh-pãs*] expense, cost
dépenser v. [*deh-pã-seh*] spend
déplacement m. [*deh-plahs-mã*] traveling
déplacer v. [*deh-plah-seh*] move
déposer v. [*deh-poh-zeh*] deposit
depuis [*d(uh)-pwee*] since, for [time, duration]
  Depuis quand êtes-vous ici? [*duh-pwee kã et-voo ee-see*]
    Since when have you been here?
  Je suis ici depuis vendredi [*shswee-zee-seed-pwee vã-
    druh-dee*] I have been here since Friday
  Je suis ici depuis trois jours [*shswee-zee-seed-pwee trwah
    zhoor*] I have been here for three days
dérangement m. [*deh-rãzh-mã*] inconvenience
  en dérangement [*ã deh-rãzh-mã*] out of order
déranger v. [*deh-rã-zheh*] bother, disturb
déraper v. [*deh-rah-peh*] skid
dernier, -ière [*der-nyeh, der-nyer*] last, latest; latter
dernièrement [*der-nyer-mã*] lately
derrière m. [*der-yer*] rear, bottom
  de derrière [*duh der-yer*] back, hind

derrière *prep. & adv.* [*der-yer*] behind, in back (of)
des: de les [*deh*] some, any; of the
dès [*de*] from
désagréable [*deh-zah-greh-ahbl*] disagreeable
désapprouver *v.* [*deh-zah-proo-veh*] disapprove
désastre *m.* [*deh-zahstr*] disaster
désavantage *m.* [*deh-zah-vã-tahzh*] disadvantage
descendre *v.* [*deh-sãdr*] descend, come down, go down,
    take down
descente *f.* [*deh-sãt*] descent
description *f.* [*des-kreep-syõ*] description
désert *m.* [*deh-zer*] desert
déserter *v.* [*deh-zer-teh*] desert
désespéré [*deh-zes-peh-reh*] desperate
désespérer *v.* [*deh-zes-peh-reh*] despair
désespoir *m.* [*deh-zes-pwahr*] despair
déshabiller *v.* [*deh-zah-bee-yeh*] undress [someone or
    something]
  se déshabiller [*sdeh-zah-bee-yeh*] undress [oneself], get
    undressed
désigner *v.* [*deh-zee-nyeh*] designate
désintéressé [*deh-zĕ-teh-re-seh*] disinterested
désir *m.* [*deh-zeer*] desire
désirable [*deh-zee-rahbl*] desirable
désirer *v.* [*deh-zee-reh*] desire
désobéir (à) *v.* [*deh-zo-beh-eer (ah)*] disobey
désolé [*deh-zo-leh*] desolate
  Je suis désolé [*shswee deh-zo-leh*] I'm very sorry
désordre *m.* [*deh-zordr*] disorder
désormais [*deh-zor-me*] from now on
desquels, -quelles [*deh-kel*] of whom, of which, from whom,
    from which
dessein *m.* [*deh-sĕ*] plan
desserrer *v.* [*deh-seh-reh*] loosen
dessert *m.* [*deh-ser*] dessert
desservir *v.* [*deh-ser-veer*] clear the table
dessin *m.* [*deh-sĕ*] drawing
dessiner *v.* [*deh-see-neh*] draw

dessous *m.* [*d(uh)-soo*] lower part, bottom
dessus *m.* [*d(uh)-sü*] top
destin *m.* [*des-tē*] destiny, fate
destinataire *m.* [*des-tee-nah-ter*] addressee
destruction *f.* [*des-trük-syō*] destruction
détaché [*deh-tah-sheh*] unfastened, loose
détail *m.* [*deh-tahy*] detail
  au détail [*oh deh-tahy*] retail
détective *m.* [*deh-tek-teev*] detective
déteindre *v. irreg.* [*deh-tēdr*] fade
détendre, se détendre *v.* [*deh-tãdr, sdeh-tãdr*] relax
détente *f.* [*deh-tãt*] relaxation
déterminé [*deh-ter-mee-neh*] determined, definite
déterminer *v.* [*deh-ter-mee-neh*] determine
détester *v.* [*deh-tes-teh*] detest
détour *m.* [*deh-toor*] detour
détourner *v.* [*deh-toor-neh*] turn aside, turn away
  se détourner [*sdeh-toor-neh*] turn away
détresse *f.* [*deh-tres*] distress
détruire *v. irreg.* [*deh-trweer*] destroy
dette *f.* [*det*] debt
deuil *m.* [*duhy*] mourning
deux [*duh*] two
  les deux [*leh duh*] both
deuxième [*duh-zyem*] second
devant [*d(uh)-vã*] before, in front of
devant *m.* [*d(uh)-vã*] front
développement *m.* [*dehv-lop-mã*] development
développer *v.* [*dehv-lo-peh*] develop
devenir *v. irreg.* [*duhv-neer*] become
déviation *f.* [*deh-vyah-syō*] detour
deviner *v.* [*d(uh)-vee-neh*] guess
devis *m.* [*d(uh)-vee*] estimate
devoir *m.* [*d(uh)-vwahr*] duty
devoir *v. irreg.* [*d(uh)-vwahr*] owe
  devoir (plus infin.) [*d(uh)-vwahr*] must, have to
dévotion *f.* [*deh-voh-syō*] devotion
dévoué [*deh-vweh*] devoted

diable *m.* [*dyahbl*] devil
diagnostic *m.* [*dyahg-nos-teek*] diagnosis
dialecte *m.* [*dyah-lekt*] dialect
dialogue *m.* [*dyah-log*] dialogue
diament *m.* [*dyah-mã*] diamond
diarrhée *f.* [*dyah-reh*] diarrhea
dictée *f.* [*deek-teh*] dictation
dicter *v.* [*deek-teh*] dictate
dictionnaire *m.* [*deek-syo-ner*] dictionary
dieu *m.* [*dyuh*] god
   Mon Dieu! [*mõ dyuh*] Good heavens!
différence *f.* [*dee-feh-rãs*] difference
différent [*dee-feh-rã(t)*] different
difficile [*dee-fee-seel*] difficult, hard
difficulté *f.* [*dee-fee-kül-teh*] difficulty, trouble
digérer *v.* [*dee-zheh-reh*] digest
digestion *f.* [*dee-zhes-tyõ*] digestion
digne [*deeñ*] worthy
dignité *f.* [*dee-nyee-teh*] dignity
dimanche *m.* [*dee-mãsh*] Sunday
dimension *f.* [*dee-mã-syõ*] dimension, size
diminuer *v.* [*dee-mee-nweh*] decrease
dinde *f.* [*dẽd*] turkey
dîner *m.* [*dee-neh*] dinner
dîner *v.* [*dee-neh*] dine, have dinner
diplomate *adj.* [*dee-plo-maht*] diplomatic
diplomate *m.* [*dee-plo-maht*] diplomat
diplôme *m.* [*dee-plohm*] diploma
dire *v. irreg.* [*deer*] say, tell
direct [*dee-rekt*] direct
directement [*dee-rek-tuh-mã*] directly
directeur *m.* [*dee-rek-tuhr*] director, manager
direction *f.* [*dee-rek-syõ*] direction, management
diriger *v.* [*dee-ree-zheh*] direct, control
discipline *f.* [*dee-see-pleen*] discipline
discontinuer *v.* [*dees-kõ-tee-nweh*] discontinue
discours *m.* [*dees-koor*] speech, talk
discussion *f.* [*dees-kü-syõ*] discussion

discuter *v.* [*dees-kü-teh*] discuss
disgrâce *f.* [*dees-grahs*] disgrace
disparaître *v. irreg.* [*dees-pah-retr*] disappear
disponible [*dees-po-neebl*] available
dispute *f.* [*dees-püt*] dispute
disputer *v.* [*dees-pü-teh*] dispute, contest
  se disputer [*s(uh) dees-pü-teh*] argue
disque *m.* [*deesk*] record
dissoudre *v. irreg.* [*dee-soodr*] dissolve
distance *f.* [*dees-tãs*] distance
  A quelle distance? [*ah kel dees-tãs*] How far?
distant [*dees-tã(t)*] distant, reserved
distinct [*dees-tẽ(kt)*] distinct
distingué [*dees-tẽ-gheh*] distinguished
distinguer *v.* [*dees-tẽ-gheh*] distinguish
distrait [*dees-tre(t)*] absent-minded
distribuer *v.* [*dees-tree-bweh*] distribute, deal [cards]
distribution *f.* [*dees-tree-bü-syõ*] distribution, cast [theatre]
divan *m.* [*dee-vã*] couch
divers [*dee-ver(s)*] various
divertissement *m.* [*dee-ver-tees-mã*] amusement, entertainment
divin [*dee-vẽ, dee-veen*] divine
diviser *v.* [*dee-vee-zeh*] divide
division *f.* [*dee-vee-syõ*] division
divorce *m.* [*dee-vors*] divorce
divorcer *v.* [*dee-vor-seh*] divorce
dix [*dees*] ten
dix-huit [*deez-weet*] eighteen
dixième [*dee-zyem*] tenth
dix-neuf [*deez-nuhf*] nineteen
dix-sept [*dee-set*] seventeen
dizaine *f.* [*dee-zen*] ten
docteur *m.* [*dok-tuhr*] doctor
document *m.* [*do-kü-mã*] document
doigt *m.* [*dwah*] finger
dollar *m.* [*do-lahr*] dollar
domaine *m.* [*do-men*] estate
dôme *m.* [*dohm*] dome

domestique [*do-mes-teek*] domestic
domestique *m., f.* [*do-mes-teek*] servant
dommage *m.* [*do-mahzh*] damage
  Quel dommage! [*kel do-mahzh*] What a pity!
domicile *m.* [*do-mee-seel*] residence
don *m.* [*dõ*] gift
donc [*dõ(k)*] therefore, so
donne *f.* [*don*] deal [of cards]
donner *v.* [*do-neh*] give, deal [cards]
dont [*dõ*] of whom, of which, from whom, from which, whose
  L'homme dont je parle [*lom dõzh parl*] The man of whom
    I am speaking
dormir *v. irreg.* [*dor-meer*] sleep
dortoir *m.* [*dor-twahr*] dormitory
dos *m.* [*doh*] back
dose *f.* [*dohz*] dose
dossier *m.* [*doh-syeh*] file
dot *f.* [*dot*] dowry
douane *f.* [*dwahn*] customs
  droit *m.* **de douane** [*drwahd dwahn*] customs duty
douanier *m.* [*dwah-nyeh*] customs officer
double [*doobl*] double
doublure *f.* [*doo-blür*] lining
doucement [*doos-mã*] gently
douche *f.* [*doosh*] shower
doué [*dweh*] gifted
douleur *f.* [*doo-luhr*] pain, sorrow, grief
douloureux, -euse [*doo-loo-ruh, doo-loo-ruhz*] painful
doute *m.* [*doot*] doubt
  sans doute [*sã doot*] doubtless
douter *v.* [*doo-teh*] doubt
  J'en doute [*zhã doot*] I doubt it
  se douter [*sdoo-teh*] suspect
  Je m'en doutais [*zhmã doo-te*] I thought as much
douteux, -euse [*doo-tuh, doo-tuhz*] doubtful
doux, douce [*doo(s)*] gentle, soft, mild [weather]
douzaine *f.* [*doo-zen*] dozen
douze [*dooz*] twelve

douzième [*doo-zyem*] twelfth
dramatique [*drah-mah-teek*] dramatic
drame *m.* [*drahm*] drama
drap *m.* [*drah*] sheet
drapeau, -eaux *m.* [*drah-poh*] flag
drogue *f.* [*drog*] drug
droit [*drwah(t)*] straight, right
   à droite [*ah drwaht*] on the right
   tout droit [*too drwah*] straight ahead
droit *m.* [*drwah*] law, right
   droits civiques *m. pl.* [*drwah see-veek*] civil rights
drôle [*drohl*] funny
   une drôle d'histoire [*ün drohl dees-twahr*] a strange story
du: de le [*dü*] of the, from the, some, any
duquel [*dü-kel*] of whom, of which
dur [*dür*] hard, tough
durable [*dü-rahbl*] durable
durée *f.* [*dü-reh*] duration
durer *v.* [*dü-reh*] last
dynamite *f.* [*dee-nah-meet*] dynamite

E

eau, eaux *f.* [*oh*] water
   eau courante [*oh koo-rãt*] running water
   eau douce [*oh doos*] fresh water
   eau de Javel [*ohd zhah-vel*] bleach
   eau de mer [*ohd mer*] salt water
   eau minérale [*oh mee-neh-rahl*] mineral water
   eau potable [*oh po-tahbl*] drinking water
écarter *v.* [*eh-kar-teh*] separate
   s'écarter [*seh-kar-teh*] turn away
échange *m.* [*eh-shãzh*] exchange
échanger *v.* [*eh-shã-zheh*] exchange
échantillon *m.* [*eh-shã-tee-yõ*] sample

prendre v. irreg. **un échantillon** [prã-drē-neh-shã-tee-yō] sample

échapper, s'échapper v. [eh-shah-peh, seh-shah-peh] escape

écharpe f. [eh-sharp] scarf

échec m. [eh-shek] failure

échecs m. pl. [eh-shek] chess

échelle f. [eh-shel] scale, ladder

écho m. [eh-koh] echo

échouer v. [eh-shweh] fail

éclair m. [eh-kler] eclair, flash of lightning

éclaircir v. [eh-kler-seer] clarify

éclairer v. [eh-kleh-reh] light

éclater v. [eh-klah-teh] burst, explode

école f. [eh-kol] school

    école secondaire [eh-kol suh-gõ-der] high school

écolier, -ière [eh-kol-yeh, eh-kol-yer] pupil

économe adj. [eh-ko-nom] thrifty

économie f. [eh-ko-no-mee] economy

économique [eh-ko-no-meek] economical

économiser v. [eh-ko-no-mee-zeh] save, economize

écorce f. [eh-kors] bark

écossais [eh-ko-se(z)] Scottish; plaid [fabric]

Ecosse f. [eh-kos] Scotland

écouter v. [eh-koo-teh] listen to

écran m. [eh-krã] screen

écraser v. [eh-krah-zeh] crush

    s'écraser [seh-krah-zeh] crash

écrevisse f. [eh-kruh-vees] crayfish

s'écrier v. [seh-kree-eh] cry out

écrire v. irreg. [eh-kreer] write

écriture f. [eh-kree-tür] writing

écrivain m., **femme écrivain** f. [eh-kree-vē, fah-meh-kree-vē] writer

écrou m. [eh-kroo] nut

écume f. [eh-küm] foam

écurie f. [eh-kü-ree] stable

édifice m. [eh-dee-fees] building

éditeur, -trice [eh-dee-tuhr, eh-dee-trees] editor

édition *f.* [*eh-dee-syō*] edition
éducation *f.* [*eh-dü-kah-syō*] education, bringing up
effacer *v.* [*eh-fah-seh*] erase
effectivement [*eh-fek-teev-mã*] indeed, really
effet *m.* [*e-fe*] effect; bill [commerce]
  en effet [*ã-ne-fe*] indeed
effets *m. pl.* [*e-fe*] belongings
efficace [*eh-fee-kahs*] efficient, effective
effort *m.* [*e-for*] effort
effrayer *v.* [*eh-freh-yeh*] scare, frighten
égal, -aux [*eh-gahl, eh-goh*] equal, regular
  Ça m'est égal [*sah me-teh-gahl*] I don't care
également [*eh-gahl-mã*] likewise
égalité *f.* [*eh-gah-lee-teh*] equality
égard *m.* [*eh-gahr*] regard
  à cet égard [*ah se-teh-gahr*] in this respect
égarer *v.* [*eh-gah-reh*] mislead
  s'égarer [*seh-gah-reh*] get lost
église *f.* [*eh-gleez*] church
égoiste [*eh-go-eest*] selfish
égout *m.* [*eh-goo*] sewer
égoutter *v.* [*eh-goo-teh*] drain
égratignure *f.* [*eh-grah-tee-nyür*] scratch
Egypte *f.* [*eh-zheept*] Egypt
égyptien, -ienne [*eh-zheep-syē, eh-zheep-syen*] Egyptian
élastique [*eh-lahs-teek*] elastic
élection *f.* [*eh-lek-syō*] election
électricien, -enne [*eh-lek-tree-syē, eh-lek-tree-syen*] electrician
électricité *f.* [*eh-lek-tree-see-teh*] electricity
électrique [*eh-lek-treek*] electric
électrophone *m.* [*eh-lek-tro-fon*] record player
élégance *f.* [*eh-leh-gãs*] elegance
élégant [*eh-leh-gã(t)*] elegant
élément *m.* [*eh-leh-mã*] element
élémentaire [*eh-leh-mã-ter*] elementary
éléphant *m.* [*eh-leh-fã*] elephant
élève *m., f.* [*eh-lev*] pupil
élever *v.* [*el-veh*] raise, lift up; rear, bring up [children]

bien élevé [byē-nel-veh] well bred
s'élever [sel-veh] rise, stand, amount
éliminer v. [eh-lee-mee-neh] eliminate
élire v. irreg. [eh-leer] elect
elle [el] she, her, it
  elle-même [el mem] herself, itself
elles f. [el] they, them
  elles-mêmes [el mem] themselves
éloigner v. [eh-lwah-nyeh] take away
embargo m. [ã-bahr-goh] embargo
emballage m. [ã-bah-lahzh] packing
emballer v. [ã-bah-leh] pack, wrap
embarrasser v. [ã-bah-rah-seh] embarrass
s'embarquer v. [sã-bahr-keh] embark
embrasser v. [ã-brah-seh] kiss
embrayage m. [ã-bre-yahzh] clutch
embrayer v. [ã-bre-yeh] put in gear
émeraude f. [em-rohd] emerald
émettre v. irreg. [eh-metr] emit
émeute f. [eh-muht] riot
émigrant, -te [eh-mee-grã(t)] emigrant
émigration f. [eh-mee-grah-syõ] emigration
éminent [eh-mee-nã(t)] prominent
émission f. [eh-mee-syõ] program, broadcast
emmagasiner v. [ã-mah-gah-zee-neh] store, accumulate
emmener v. [ãm-neh] take away
émotion f. [eh-moh-syõ] emotion
émouvant [eh-moo-vã(t)] moving
empêcher (de) v. [ã-pe-sheh (duh)] stop (from), keep (from)
  s'empêcher (de) [sã-pe-sheh (duh)] refrain (from), keep
    (from)
empereur m. [ã-pruhr] emperor
emplacement m. [ã-plahs-mã] location
emploi m. [ã-plwah] employment, use
  emploi du temps [ã-plwah dü tã] schedule
employé, -ée [a-plwah-yeh] employee, clerk
employer v. [ã-plwah-yeh] employ
employeur m. [ã-plwah-yuhr] employer

emporter *v.* [*ã-por-teh*] carry away
  s'emporter [*sã-por-teh*] become angry
  l'emporter sur [*lã-por-teh sür*] prevail over
emprunt *m.* [*ã-prē*] loan
emprunter *v.* [*ã-prē-teh*] borrow
en [*ã*] in, into, to; as
en *pron.* [*ã*] some, any
  Il en a [*ee-lã nah*] He has some [of them]
  Je n'en ai pas [*zhnã-neh pah*] I don't have any [of them]
enceinte [*ã-sēt*] pregnant
enchanter *v.* [*ã-shã-teh*] delight
  Enchanté! [*ã-shã-teh*] Glad to meet you!
encombré [*ã-kõ-breh*] burdened, crowded
encore [*ã-kor*] again, still, more
  encore une fois [*ã-kor ün fwah*] once more
  pas encore [*pah ã-kor*] not yet
encouragement *m.* [*ã-koo-rahzh-mã*] encouragement
encre *f.* [*ãkr*] ink
encourager *v.* [*ã-koo-rah-zheh*] encourage, cheer
en-dessous (de) [*ãd-soo*] below, beneath
endommagé [*ã-do-mah-zheh*] damaged
endommager *v.* [*ã-do-mah-zheh*] damage
s'endormir *v. irreg.* [*sã-dor-meer*] fall asleep
endosser *v.* [*ã-do-seh*] endorse, assume
endroit *m.* [*ã-drwah*] place
énergie *f.* [*eh-ner-zhee*] energy
énergique [*eh-ner-zheek*] energetic
enfance *f.* [*ã-fãs*] childhood
enfant *m.* [*ã-fã*] child
enfer *m.* [*ã-fer*] hell
enfermer *v.* [*ã-fer-meh*] shut in
enfin [*ã-fē*] at last
enflé [*ã-fleh*] swollen
enfler *v.* [*ã-fleh*] swell
engagement *m.* [*ã-gahzh-mã*] engagement
engager *v.* [*ã-gah-zheh*] engage, hire
enlever *v.* [*ãl-veh*] take off, remove
ennemi *m.* [*en-mee*] enemy

ennui *m.* [*ã-nwee*] boredom
ennuyer *v.* [*ã-nwee-yeh*] bore, bother
ennuyeux, -euse [*ã-nwee-yuh, ã-nwee-yuhz*] annoying, boring
énorme [*eh-norm*] enormous, huge
enquête *f.* [*ã-ket*] inquiry
enregistrer *v.* [*ãr-zhees-treh*] record, check [luggage]
s'enrhumer *v.* [*sã-rü-meh*] catch a cold
enseignant, -te [*ã-se-nyã(t)*] teacher
enseigne *f.* [*ã-señ*] sign
enseignement *m.* [*ã-señ-mã*] teaching, education
enseigner *v.* [*ã-se-nyeh*] teach
ensemble *adv.* [*ã-sãbl*] together
ensemble *m.* [*ã-sãbl*] set, whole
ensuite [*ã-sweet*] afterwards, then
entendre *v.* [*ã-tãdr*] hear
  entendre dire (que) [*ã-tãdr deer (kuh)*] hear (that)
  entendre parler de [*ã-tãdr pahr-leh d(uh)*] hear of (about)
entendu [*ã-tã-dü*] agreed, understood
  bien entendu [*byē-nã-tã-dü*] of course
enterrement *m.* [*ã-ter-mã*] burial, funeral
enterrer *v.* [*ã-teh-reh*] bury
enthousiasme *m.* [*ã-too-zyahsm*] enthusiasm
entier, -tière [*ã-tyeh, ã-tyer*] entire, whole
entièrement [*ã-tyer-mã*] entirely
entorse *f.* [*ã-tors*] sprain
entourer *v.* [*ã-too-reh*] surround
entr'acte *m.* [*ã-trahkt*] intermission
entraîner *v.* [*ã-tre-neh*] bring about, train [sports]
entre [*ãtr*] between, among
entrée *f.* [*ã-treh*] entrance, admission
entrepôt *m.* [*ã-truh-poh*] warehouse
entreprendre *v. irreg.* [*ã-truh-prãdr*] undertake
entrepreneur *m.* [*ã-truh-pruh-nuhr*] contractor, businessman
entreprise *f.* [*ã-truh-preez*] enterprise, firm
entrer (dans) *v.* [*ã-treh (dã)*] enter, go in, come in
entretemps [*ã-truh-tã*] meanwhile
entretien *m.* [*ã-truh-tyē*] upkeep
entrevue *f.* [*ã-truh-vü*] interview

enveloppe *f.* [*ãv-lop*] envelope
envelopper *v.* [*ãv-lo-peh*] wrap
envers *m.* [*ã-ver*] wrong side
  à l'envers [*ah lã-ver*] upside down, inside out
envie *f.* [*ã-vee*] wish, desire
  avoir *v.* **envie de** [*ah-vwahr ã-veed*] want, feel like
envier *v.* [*ã-vyeh*] envy
environ *adv.* [*ã-vee-rõ*] about, approximately
environnement *m.* [*ã-vee-ron-mã*] surroundings, environment
environs *m. pl.* [*ã-vee-rõ*] surroundings, vicinity
envisager *v.* [*ã-vee-zah-zheh*] consider
envoi *m.* [*ã-vwah*] shipment, sending
s'envoler *v.* [*sã-vo-leh*] take off [plane], fly away
envoyer *v.* [*ã-vwah-yeh*] send
  envoyer chercher [*ã-vwah-yeh sher-sheh*] send for
épais, épaisse [*eh-pe, eh-pes*] thick
épargne *f.* [*eh-pahrñ*] savings
  caisse *f.* **d'épargne** [*kes deh-pahrñ*] savings bank
épargner *v.* [*eh-pahr-nyeh*] save
épaule *f.* [*eh-pohl*] shoulder
épée *f.* [*eh-peh*] sword
épeler *v.* [*eh-pleh*] spell
épice *f.* [*eh-pees*] spice
épicerie *f.* [*eh-pees-ree*] grocery store
épinards *m. pl.* [*eh-pee-nar*] spinach
épine *f.* [*eh-peen*] thorn
épingle *f.* [*eh-pẽgl*] pin
  épingle anglaise [*eh-pẽ-glã-glez*] safety pin
épingler *v.* [*eh-pẽ-gleh*] pin
éponge *f.* [*eh-põzh*] sponge
époque *f.* [*eh-pok*] period
épouser *v.* [*eh-poo-zeh*] marry
époux, -ouse [*eh-poo, eh-pooz*] spouse; husband, wife
épreuve *f.* [*eh-pruhv*] trial; photo, print
éprouver *v.* [*eh-proo-veh*] test
épuisé [*eh-pwee-zeh*] exhausted
épuiser *v.* [*eh-pwee-zeh*] exhaust
équilibre *m.* [*eh-kee-leebr*] equilibrium, balance

équilibrer v. [eh-kee-lee-breh] balance
équipage m. [eh-kee-pahzh] crew
équipe f. [eh-keep] team
équipement m. [eh-keep-mã] equipment
équivalent m. [eh-kee-vah-lã] equivalent
érafler v. [eh-rah-fleh] scrape
errer v. [e-reh] wander
erreur f. [e-ruhr] error
éruption f. [eh-rüp-syõ] rash
escalier m. [es-kah-lyeh] staircase, stairs
escargot m. [es-kahr-goh] snail
esclavage m. [es-klah-vahzh] slavery
esclave m., f. [es-klahv] slave
escompte m. [es-kõt] discount
escrime f. [es-kreem] fencing
espace m. [es-pahs] space
Espagne f. [es-pahñ] Spain
espagnol n. & adj. [es-pah-nyol] Spaniard, Spanish
espèce f. [es-pes] kind
espérance f. [es-peh-rãs] hope
espérer v. [es-peh-reh] hope
espion m. [es-pyõ] spy
espoir m. [es-pwahr] hope
  plein d'espoir [plē des-pwahr] hopeful
  sans espoir [sã-zes-pwahr] hopeless
esprit m. [es-pree] mind, spirit, wit
esquisser v. [es-kee-seh] sketch
essai m. [eh-se] trial
  essais m. pl. **et erreurs** f. pl. [eh-se-zeh e-ruhr] trial
    and error
essayage m. [eh-se-yahzh] fitting
essayer v. [eh-seh-yeh] try, try on [clothing]
essence f. [eh-sãs] gasoline
essentiel, -elle [eh-sã-syel] essential
essieu m. [eh-syuh] axle
essuyer v. [eh-swee-yeh] wipe
est m. [est] east
est 3d pers. sing. pres. tense of ÊTRE [e] is

Est-ce que . . . [*es k(uh)*] Is it that . . .

estimer *v.* [*es-tee-meh*] estimate, esteem

estomac *m.* [*es-to-mahk*] stomach

et [*eh*] and

établir *v.* [*eh-tah-bleer*] establish

établissement *m.* [*eh-tah-blees-mã*] institution, extablishment

étage *m.* [*eh-tahzh*] floor, story

étagère *f.* [*eh-tah-zher*] shelf

étain *m.* [*eh-tẽ*] tin, pewter

étalage *m.* [*eh-tah-lahzh*] display

étaler *v.* [*eh-tah-leh*] display

étang *m.* [*eh-tã*] pool

état *m.* [*eh-tah*] state, condition

état-civil *m.* [*eh-tah-see-veel*] civil status

Etats-Unis *m. pl.* [*eh-tah-zü-nee*] United States

été *m.* [*eh-teh*] summer

éteindre *v. irreg.* [*eh-tẽdr*] turn off, turn out [a light]; extinguish [a fire]

étendre *v.* [*eh-tãdr*] hang out, lay out, spread

étendue *f.* [*eh-tã-dü*] extent, range

éternel, -elle [*eh-ter-nel*] eternal

éternuer *v.* [*eh-ter-nweh*] sneeze

êtes *2d pers. pl. pres. tense of* ÊTRE [*et*] you are

étincelle *f.* [*eh-tẽ-sel*] spark

étiquette *f.* [*eh-tee-ket*] label, tag

étoile *f.* [*eh-twahl*] star

étonnant [*eh-to-nã(t)*] astonishing, surprising

étonner *v.* [*eh-to-neh*] surprise

étouffer *v.* [*eh-too-feh*] smother

étrange [*eh-trãzh*] strange

étranger, -ère *n.* [*eh-trã-zheh, eh-trã-zher*] foreigner
　à l'étranger [*ah leh-trã-zheh*] abroad

étranger, -ère *adj.* [*eh-trã-zheh, eh-trã-zher*] foreign

être *m.* [*etr*] being

être *v. irreg.* [*etr*] be

étroit [*eh-trwah(t)*] narrow

étude *f.* [*eh-tüd*] study

étudiant, -te *n. & adj.* [*eh-tü-dyã(t)*] student
étudier *v.* [*eh-tü-dyeh*] study
étui *m.* [*eh-twee*] case
Europe *f.* [*uh-rop*] Europe
européen, -enne [*uh-ro-peh-ē, uh-ro-peh-en*] European
eux *m.* [*uh*] them
eux-mêmes [*uh-mem*] themselves
s'évanouir *v.* [*seh-vahn-weer*] faint
événement *m.* [*eh-ven-mã*] event
évêque *m.* [*eh-vek*] bishop
éventail *m.* [*eh-vã-tahy*] fan
évidemment [*eh-vee-dah-mã*] evidently
évident [*eh-vee-dã(t)*] evident
évier *m.* [*eh-vyeh*] sink
éviter *v.* [*eh-vee-teh*] avoid
évolution *f.* [*eh-vo-lü-syö*] evolution, change
exact [*eg-zah(kt)*] exact
exactement [*eg-zahk-tuh-mã*] exactly
exagérer *v.* [*eg-zah-zheh-reh*] exaggerate
examen *m.* [*eg-zah-mē*] examination
    réussir *v.* **à un examen** [*reh-ü-see-rah ē-neg-zah-mē*] pass
    an examination
examiner *v.* [*eg-zah-mee-neh*] examine
excellent [*ek-se-lã(t)*] excellent
excepté [*ek-sep-teh*] except
exception *f.* [*ek-sep-syö*] exception
excès *m.* [*ek-se*] excess
exclusif, -ive [*eks-klü-zeef, eks-klü-zeev*] exclusive
excursion *f.* [*eks-kür-syö*] excursion, trip
excuse *f.* [*eks-küz*] excuse
excuser *v.* [*eks-kü-zeh*] excuse, pardon
    s'excuser [*seks-kü-zeh*] apologize
exemplaire *m.* [*eg-zã-pler*] copy
exemple *m.* [*eg-zãpl*] example
    par exemple [*pah-reg-zãpl*] for instance, for example
s'exercer *v.* [*seg-zer-seh*] practice
exercise *m.* [*eg-zer-sees*] exercise
exigence *f.* [*eg-zee-zhãs*] requirement

exigeant [*eg-zee-zhã(t)*] demanding
exiger *v.* [*eg-zee-zheh*] demand, require
exil *m.* [*eg-zeel*] exile
existence *f.* [*eg-zees-tãs*] existence
exister *v.* [*eg-zees-teh*] exist
expédier *v.* [*eks-peh-dyeh*] send, ship
expéditeur *m.* [*eks-peh-dee-tuhr*] sender
expédition *f.* [*eks-peh-dee-syõ*] expedition
expérience *f.* [*eks-peh-ryãs*] experience, experiment
expert [*eks-per(t)*] expert
explication *f.* [*eks-plee-kah-syõ*] explanation
expliquer *v.* [*eks-plee-keh*] explain
exploiter *v.* [*eks-plwah-teh*] exploit
explorer *v.* [*eks-plo-reh*] explore
explosion *f.* [*eks-ploh-zyõ*] explosion
exporter *v.* [*eks-por-teh*] export
exposer *v.* [*eks-poh-zeh*] exhibit
exposition *f.* [*eks-poh-zee-syõ*] exhibition
exprès [*eks-pre*] on purpose
express *m.* [*eks-pres*] special delivery, express train
expression *f.* [*eks-pre-syõ*] expression
exprimer *v.* [*eks-pree-meh*] express
extérieur [*eks-teh-ryuhr*] exterior, external
extraction *f.* [*eks-trahk-syõ*] extraction
extraire *v. irreg.* [*eks-trer*] extract
extraordinaire [*eks-trah-or-dee-ner*] extraordinary
extrême [*eks-trem*] extreme
extrêmement [*eks-trem-mã*] extremely

F

fabrication *f.* **en série** [*fah-bree-kah-syõ ã seh-ree*]
    mass production
fabriquant *m.* [*fah-bree-kã*] manufacturer
fabriquer *v.* [*fah-bree-keh*] make, manufacture

face *f.* [*fahs*] side
  en face (de) [*ã fahs (duh)*] across the street, on the other side
fâché [*fah-sheh*] angry
fâcher *v.* [*fah-sheh*] make angry
  se fâcher [*sfah-sheh*] get angry
facile [*fah-seel*] easy
facilement [*fah-seel-mã*] easily
facilité *f.* [*fah-see-lee-teh*] ease
façon *f.* [*fah-sõ*] way, manner
  de toute façon [*duh toot fah-sõ*] anyhow, anyway
  en aucune façon [*ã-noh-kün fah-sõ*] by no means
facteur *m.* [*fahk-tuhr*] mailman
facture *f.* [*fahk-tür*] bill, invoice
facultatif, -tive [*fah-kül-tah-teef, fah-kül-tah-teev*] optional
faculté *f.* [*fah-kül-teh*] faculty
faible [*febl*] weak
faiblesse *f.* [*fe-bles*] weakness
faillite *f.* [*fah-yeet*] bankruptcy
faim *f.* [*fẽ*] hunger
  avoir *v.* **faim** [*ah-vwahr fẽ*] be hungry
faire *v. irreg.* [*fer*] make, do
  faire attention [*fe-rah-tã-syõ*] pay attention
  faire beau (chaud, froid) [*fer boh (shoh, frwah)*] be nice
    (hot, cold) [weather]
  Il fait beau aujourd'hui [*eel fe boh oh-zhoor-dwee*] It's a
    nice day today
  faire du soleil (du vent) [*fer dü so-ley (dü vã)*] be sunny
    (windy)
  faire face à [*fer fahs ah*] face
  faire mal à [*fer mahl ah*] hurt
  faire construire une maison [*fer kõ-strwee-rün me-zõ*]
    have a house built
  faire parler [*fer pahr-leh*] make [someone] talk
  faire peur à [*fer puh-rah*] frighten
  faire plaisir à [*fer pleh-zeer ah*] please
  faire une promenade [*fer ün prom-nahd*] take a walk
  se faire [*s(uh) fer*] become, be done
  s'y faire [*see fer*] get used to

s'en faire [sã fer] worry
  Ne vous en faites pas! [nuh voo-zã fet pah] Don't get
    upset!
faire-part m. [fer-pahr] announcement
fait m. [fe] fact
  en fait [ã fe] in fact
falloir v. irreg. [fahl-wahr] be necessary
fameux, -euse [fah-muh(z)] famous, good
familial, -aux adj. [fah-meel-yahl, fah-meel-yoh] family
familier, -ière [fah-meel-yeh, fah-meel-yer] familiar
famille f. [fah-meey] family
fantôme m. [fã-tohm] ghost
farce f. [fahrs] practical joke
fardeau, -eaux m. [fahr-doh] burden
farine f. [fah-reen] flour
fascinant [fah-see-nã(t)] fascinating
fatigant [fah-tee-gã(t)] tiring
fatigue f. [fah-teeg] fatigue
fatigué [fah-tee-gheh] tired
fatiguer v. [fah-tee-gheh] tire
faut: il faut [eel foh] it is necessary
faute f. [foht] fault, mistake
fauteuil m. [foh-tuhy] armchair
faux, fausse [foh(s)] false
faveur f. [fah-vuhr] favor
favoriser v. [fah-vo-ree-zeh] favor
fédéral, -aux [feh-deh-rahl, feh-deh-roh] federal
félicitations f. pl. [feh-lee-see-tah-syõ] congratulations
féliciter v. [feh-lee-see-teh] congratulate
féminin [feh-mee-nẽ, feh-mee-neen] feminine
femme f. [fahm] woman, wife
  femme de chambre [fahm duh shãbr] chambermaid
  femme de ménage [fahm duh meh-nahzh] cleaning woman
fendre v. [fãdr] split
fenêtre f. [f(uh)-netr] window
fer m. [fer] iron
ferme adj. [ferm] firm
ferme f. [ferm] farm

fermé [*fer-meh*] closed
fermer *v.* [*fer-meh*] close; turn off
  fermer à clef [*fer-meh ah kleh*] lock
fermeture *f.* [*fer-muh-tür*] closing
  fermeture annuelle [*fer-muh-tü-rahn-wel*] closed for vacation
  fermeture éclair [*fer-muh-tü-reh-kler*] zipper
fermier *m.* [*fer-myeh*] farmer
festival, -aux *m.* [*fes-tee-vahl, fes-tee-voh*] festival
fête *f.* [*fet*] feast, celebration, holiday, party
fêter *v.* [*feh-teh*] celebrate
feu *m.* [*fuh*] fire
  Au feu! [*oh fuh*] Fire!
feuille *f.* [*fuhy*] leaf; sheet of paper
février *m.* [*feh-vree-yeh*] February
fiançailles *f. pl.* [*fyã-sahy*] engagement
fiancé [*fyã-seh*] engaged
fiancé, -ée [*fyã-seh*] fiancé, fiancée
  se fiancer *v.* [*s(uh) fyã-seh*] become engaged
ficelle *f.* [*fee-sel*] string
fidèle [*fee-del*] faithful
fier, fière [*fyer*] proud
fièvre *f.* [*fyevr*] fever
figue *f.* [*feeg*] fig
fil *m.* [*feel*] thread, yarn
  fil de fer [*feel duh fer*] wire
filet *m.* [*fee-le*] net
fille *f.* [*feey*] daughter, girl
filleul, -eule [*fee-yuhl*] godson, goddaughter
film *m.* [*feelm*] movie, movie film
fils *m.* [*fees*] son
filtre *m.* [*feeltr*] filter
fin [*fẽ, feen*] fine, thin, small
fin *f.* [*fẽ*] end, ending
  sans fin [*sã fẽ*] endless, interminable
  fin de semaine [*fẽd suh-men*] week-end
final, -aux [*fee-nahl, fee-noh*] final
finalement [*fee-nahl-mã*] eventually, finally
financier, -ière [*fee-nã-syeh, fee-nã-syer*] financial

finir *v.* [*fee-neer*] finish, end
firme *f.* [*feerm*] firm
fissure *f.* [*fee-sür*] crack
flamme *f.* [*flahm*] flame
flan *m.* [*flã*] custard
flatter *v.* [*flah-teh*] flatter
flatteur, -euse [*flah-tuhr, flah-tuhz*] flatterer
flèche *f.* [*flesh*] arrow, church spire
fleur *f.* [*fluhr*] flower, blossom
fleurir *v.* [*fluh-reer*] blossom
fleuriste *m.* [*fluh-reest*] florist
fleuve *m.* [*fluhv*] river
flirter *v.* [*fluhr-teh*] flirt
flotte *f.* [*flot*] fleet
flotter *v.* [*flo-teh*] float
flute *f.* [*flüt*] flute
foi *f.* [*fwah*] faith
foie *m.* [*fwah*] liver
foin *m.* [*fwẽ*] hay
foire *f.* [*fwahr*] fair
fois *f.* [*fwah*] time
   une fois [*ün fwah*] once
   deux fois [*duh fwah*] twice
   encore une fois [*ã-ko-rün fwah*] once more
   des fois [*deh fwah*] at times
   chaque fois que [*shahk fwah k(uh)*] whenever
   Il était une fois [*ee-leh-te-tün fwah*] Once upon a time
      there was (were)
foncé [*fõ-seh*] dark [color]
fonction *f.* [*fõk-syõ*] function
fonctionnaire *m., f.* [*fõk-syo-ner*] civil servant
fonctionnement *m.* [*fõk-syon-mã*] working
fonctionner *v.* [*fõk-syo-neh*] function, work
fond *m.* [*fõ*] bottom
   à fond [*ah fõ*] thoroughly
   au fond [*oh fõ*] after all
fondamental, -aux [*fõ-dah-mã-tahl, fõ-dah-mã-toh*] basic,
   fundamental

fondation *f.* [*fõ-dah-syõ*] foundation
fondre *v.* [*fõdr*] melt
fonds *m. pl.* [*fõ*] funds
fontaine *f.* [*fõ-ten*] fountain
football *m.* [*foot-bohl*] soccer
forçat *m.* [*for-sah*] convict
force *f.* [*fors*] force
forcer *v.* [*for-seh*] compel, force
forêt *f.* [*fo-re*] forest
forgeron *m.* [*for-zhuh-rõ*] blacksmith
formalité *f.* [*for-mah-lee-teh*] formality
formation *f.* [*for-mah-syõ*] formation, training
forme *f.* [*form*] form, shape
formel, -elle [*for-mel*] formal
former *v.* [*for-meh*] form, train
formidable [*for-mee-dahbl*] wonderful
formule *f.* [*for-mül*] formula
fort [*for(t)*] strong, loud
fort *m.* [*for*] fort
forteresse *f.* [*for-tuh-res*] fort
fortune *f.* [*for-tün*] fortune
fossé *m.* [*fo-seh*] ditch
fou, folle [*foo, fol*] crazy, foolish, insane
foudre *f.* [*foodr*] lightning, thunderbolt
fouet *m.* [*fweh*] whip
fouiller *v.* [*foo-yeh*] search
foulard *m.* [*foo-lahr*] scarf
foule *f.* [*fool*] crowd
fouler *v.* [*foo-leh*] sprain
four *m.* [*foor*] oven
  au four [*oh foor*] in the oven
fourchette *f.* [*foor-shet*] fork
fourmi *f.* [*foor-mee*] ant
fournir *v.* [*foor-neer*] furnish, provide
fourrure *f.* [*foo-rür*] fur
foyer *m.* [*fwah-yeh*] hearth; lobby
fracture *f.* [*frahk-tür*] fracture
fragile [*frah-zheel*] fragile

frais, fraîche [*fre(sh)*] chilly, cool; fresh
frais *m. pl.* [*fre*] expenses
    frais généraux [*fre zheh-neh-roh*] overhead
fraise *f.* [*frez*] strawberry
franc, franche [*frã(sh)*] frank
franc *m.* [*frã*] franc
français [*frã-se(z)*] French
France *f.* [*frãs*] France
franchement [*frãsh-mã*] frankly, really
frapper *v.* [*frah-peh*] hit, strike, knock
fraternel, -elle [*frah-ter-nel*] brotherly
fraude *f.* [*frohd*] fraud
frein *m.* [*frẽ*] brake
freiner *v.* [*freh-neh*] brake
frémir *v.* [*freh-meer*] shudder
fréquent [*freh-kã(t)*] frequent
frère *m.* [*frer*] brother
frèt *m.* [*fre*] freight
frigidaire *m.* [*free-zhee-der*] refrigerator
frire *v. irreg.* [*freer*] fry
frit [*free(t)*] fried
froid [*frwah(d)*] cold
    Il fait froid [*eel fe frwah*] It's cold
    avoir *v.* **froid** [*ah-vwahr frwah*] be cold
fromage *m.* [*fro-mahzh*] cheese
froncer *v.* **les sourcils** [*frõ-seh leh soor-see*] frown
front *m.* [*frõ*] forehead
frontière *f.* [*frõ-tyer*] border
frotter *v.* [*fro-teh*] rub, scrub
fruit *m.* [*frwee*] fruit
fuir *v. irreg.* [*fweer*] flee
fuite *f.* [*fweet*] flight, escape; leak
fumée *f.* [*fü-meh*] smoke
fumer *v.* [*fü-meh*] smoke
fumeur *m.* [*fü-muhr*] smoker, smoking car
furieux, -euse [*für-yuh, für-yuhz*] furious
fusil *m.* [*fü-zee*] gun, rifle
futur *m.* [*fü-tür*] future

G

gâcher *v.* [*gah-sheh*] spoil
gagnant, -ante [*gah-nyã(t)*] winner
gagner *v.* [*gah-nyeh*] earn, gain, win
gai [*ghe*] gay
gain *m.* [*ghẽ*] gain
gaine *f.* [*ghen*] girdle
galet *m.* [*gah-le*] pebble
galon *m.* [*gah-lõ*] braid
gant *m.* [*gã*] glove
garage *m.* [*gah-rahzh*] garage
garagiste *m.* [*gah-rah-zheest*] garage man
garantie *f.* [*gah-rã-tee*] guarantee
garantir *v.* [*gah-rã-teer*] guarantee
garçon *m.* [*gahr-sõ*] boy, waiter
   garçon de cabine [*gahr-sõd kah-been*] steward
garde *m., f.* [*gahrd*] guard
garde-meuble *m.* [*gahr-duh-muhbl*] furniture storage
garder *v.* [*gahr-deh*] keep
gardien *m.* [*gahr-dyẽ*] guardian, guard
gare *f.* [*gahr*] station
garer *v.* [*gah-reh*] park
garnir *v.* [*gahr-neer*] decorate
gaspiller *v.* [*gahs-pee-yeh*] waste
gâteau, -eaux *m.* [*gah-toh*] cake
gâter *v.* [*gah-teh*] spoil
gauche, à gauche [*gohsh, ah gohsh*] left
gaz *m.* [*gahz*] gas
gazon *m.* [*gah-zõ*] grass
gelée *f.* [*zh(uh)-leh*] frost; jelly
geler *v.* [*zh(uh)-leh*] freeze
gémir *v.* [*zheh-meer*] groan
gémissement *m.* [*zheh-mees-mã*] groan

gencive *f.* [*zhã-seev*] gum

gendarme *m.* [*zhã-dahrm*] policeman

gendre *m.* [*zhãdr*] son-in-law

gêné [*zheh-neh*] inconvenienced, embarrassed, self-conscious

gêner *v.* [*zheh-neh*] inconvenience, bother

général, -aux *n. & adj.* [*zheh-neh-rahl, zheh-neh-roh*] general
   en général [*ã zheh-neh-rahl*] in general

génération *f.* [*zheh-neh-rah-syõ*] generation

généreux, -euse [*zheh-neh-ruh, zheh-neh-ruhz*] generous

génie *m.* [*zheh-nee*] genius

genou, -oux *m.* [*zh(uh)-noo*] knee
   se mettre *v. irreg.* **a genoux** [*sme-trahzh-noo*] kneel

genre *m.* [*zhãr*] gender, kind

gens *m. pl.* [*zhã*] people

gentil, gentille [*zhã-tee(y)*] nice

géographie *f.* [*zheh-o-grah-fee*] geography

géométrie *f.* [*zheh-o-meh-tree*] geometry

gérant *m.* [*zheh-rã*] manager

gibier *m.* [*zhee-byeh*] game [animals]

gifle *f.* [*zheefl*] slap

gifler *v.* [*zhee-fleh*] slap

gilet *m.* [*zhee-le*] vest
   gilet de sauvetage [*zhee-led sohv-tahzh*] life-jacket

gin *m.* [*dzheen*] gin

gitan [*zhee-tã, zhee-tahn*] gypsy

glace *f.* [*glahs*] ice, ice-cream

glaçon *m.* [*glah-sõ*] ice cube

glissant [*glee-sã(t)*] slippery

glisser *v.* [*glee-seh*] slide; slip

gloire *f.* [*glwahr*] glory

golf *m.* [*golf*] golf

gomme *f.* [*gom*] eraser

gonfler *v.* [*gõ-fleh*] inflate

gorge *f.* [*gorzh*] throat
   avoir *v.* **mal à la gorge** [*ah-vwahr mah-lah lah gorzh*] have a sore throat

gosse *m., f.* [*gos*] kid, youngster

gothique [*go-teek*] gothic
gourmand [*goor-mã(d)*] glutton
goût m. [*goo*] taste
goûter m. [*goo-teh*] snack
goûter v. [*goo-teh*] taste
goutte f. [*goot*] drop
gouttière f. [*goo-tyer*] gutter
gouvernement m. [*goo-ver-nuh-mã*] government
gouverner v. [*goo-ver-neh*] govern, rule
gouverneur m. [*goo-ver-nuhr*] governor
grâce f. [*grahs*] grace
gracieux, -cieuse [*grah-syuh, grah-syuhz*] graceful, gracious
grain m. [*grẽ*] grain, corn; particle, speck
graine f. [*gren*] seed
graissage m. [*gre-sahzh*] lubrication
graisse f. [*gres*] grease, fat
graisser v. [*greh-seh*] grease, oil
gramme m. [*grahm*] gram
grammaire f. [*grah-mer*] grammar
grand [*grã(d)*] big, tall, great, large
Grande Bretagne f. [*grãd bruh-tahñ*] Great Britain
grandeur f. [*grã-duhr*] greatness
grandir v. [*grã-deer*] grow older, taller
grand-mère f. [*grã-mer*] grandmother
grand-père m. [*grã-per*] grandfather
grands-parents m. pl. [*grã-pah-rã*] grandparents
grange f. [*grãzh*] barn
gras, grasse [*grah, grahs*] fat, oily
gratte-ciel m. [*graht-syel*] skyscraper
gratter v. [*grah-teh*] scratch
gratuit [*grah-twee(t)*] free
grave [*grahv*] grave, solemn
gravure f. [*grah-vür*] print, illustration
grec, grecque [*grek*] Greek
Grèce f. [*gres*] Greece
grêle f. [*grel*] hail
grenier m. [*gruh-nyeh*] attic, granary
grenouille f. [*gruh-nooy*] frog

grève *f.* [*grev*] strike
   faire *v.* **grève** [*fer grev*] strike, go on strike
gréviste *m. f.* [*greh-veest*] striker
griffer *v.* [*gree-feh*] scratch
grille *f.* [*greey*] grill, screen
grillé [*gree-yeh*] broiled
grille-pain *m.* [*greey-pē*] toaster
griller *v.* [*gree-yeh*] broil
grimace *f.* [*gree-mahs*] grimace, grin
grimper *v.* [*grē-peh*] climb
grincer *v.* [*grē-seh*] creak
grippe *f.* [*greep*] flu
gris [*gree(z)*] grey
gronder *v.* [*grŏ-deh*] scold
gros, grosse [*groh, grohs*] fat
grossesse *f.* [*groh-ses*] pregnancy
grossier, -ière [*groh-syeh, groh-syer*] coarse, rough, rude
grossièreté *f.* [*groh-syer-teh*] rudeness
grossir *v.* [*groh-seer*] put on weight
grotte *f.* [*grot*] cave
groupe *m.* [*groop*] group
guêpe *f.* [*ghep*] wasp
guère: ne . . . guère [*nuh . . . gher*] hardly, scarcely
guérir *v.* [*gheh-reer*] cure
guérison *f.* [*gheh-ree-zŏ*] recovery, healing
guerre *f.* [*gher*] war
   guerre mondiale [*gher mŏ-dyahl*] world war
guichet *m.* [*ghee-she*] ticket-window, counter
guide *m.* [*gheed*] guide, guide-book
guillemets *m. pl.* [*gheey-me*] quotation marks
guitare *f.* [*ghee-tahr*] guitar
gymnastique *f.* [*zheem-nahs-teek*] gymnastics

H

habile [*ah-beel*] clever
habileté *f.* [*ah-beel-teh*] skill
habiller *v.* [*ah-bee-yeh*] dress
   s'habiller [*sah-bee-yeh*] get dressed
habitant *m.* [*ah-bee-tã*] inhabitant
habiter *v.* [*ah-bee-teh*] live, inhabit
habits *m. pl.* [*ah-bee*] clothes
habitude *f.* [*ah-bee-tüd*] habit
   d'habitude [*dah-bee-tüd*] usually, ordinarily
habituer, s'habituer *v.* [*ah-bee-tweh, sah-bee-tweh*] get used to
habitué, -ée (à) [*ah-bee-tweh (ah)*] accustomed (to), used (to)
habituel, -elle [*ah-bee-twel*] customary, usual
*hache *f.* [*ahsh*] axe
*haine *f.* [*en*] hate
*haïr *v. irreg.* [*ah-eer*] hate
*hâle *m.* [*ahl*] tan
haleine *f.* [*ah-len*] breath
*hanche *f.* [*ãsh*] hip
*hardi [*ahr-dee*] bold
*haricot *m.* [*ah-ree-koh*] bean
*harpe *f.* [*ahrp*] harp
*hasard *m.* [*ah-zahr*] chance, luck
   au hasard [*oh ah-zahr*] at random
   par hasard [*pahr ah-zahr*] by chance
   jeu *m.* **de hasard** [*zhuh duh ah-zahr*] game of chance
*hâte *f.* [*aht*] haste
*hausse *f.* [*ohs*] increase
*haut *m.* [*oh*] top
*haut [*oh(t)*] high
   en haut [*ã oh*] up, at the top, above, upstairs
   vers le haut [*ver luh oh*] upward
*hauteur *f.* [*oh-tuhr*] height

*haut-parleur *m.* [*oh-pahr-luhr*] loudspeaker
hebdomadaire [*eb-do-mah-der*] weekly
hectare *m.* [*ek-tahr*] two and one-half acres
*hélas [*eh-lahs*] alas
hélice *f.* [*eh-lees*] propeller
herbe *f.* [*erb*] grass
   mauvaise herbe [*mo-ve-zerb*] weed
héritage *m.* [*eh-ree-tahzh*] inheritance
hériter *v.* [*eh-ree-teh*] inherit
héritier *m.* [*eh-ree-tyeh*] heir
héritière *f.* [*eh-ree-tyer*] heiress
*héros *m.* [*eh-roh*] hero
hésiter *v.* [*eh-zee-teh*] hesitate
heure *f.* [*uhr*] hour
   Quelle heure est-il? [*kel uhr e-teel*] What time is it?
   Il est trois heures [*ee-le trwah-zuhr*] It's three o'clock
   Il est trois heures cinq [*ee-le trwah-zuhr sĕk*] It is five
     past three
   Il est trois heures et demie [*ee-le trwah-zuhr ehd-mee*]
     It is half past three
   Il est trois heures moins le quart [*ee-le trwah-zuhr mwē*
     luh kahr] It is a quarter to three
   à l'heure [*ah luhr*] on time
   de bonne heure [*d(uh) bo-nuhr*] early
   tout à l'heure [*too-tah luhr*] a while ago, in a little while
   C'est l'heure [*se luhr*] It's time
   A tout à l'heure! [*ah too-tah luhr*] So long! See you soon!
   toutes les heures [*toot leh-zuhr*] hourly
   à l'heure actuelle [*ah luhr ahk-twel*] nowadays
   heures supplémentaires [*uhr sü-pleh-mã-ter*] overtime
   heures d'affluence [*uhr dah-flü-ãs*] rush hours
heureusement [*uh-ruhz-mã*] fortunately
heureux, -euse [*uh-ruh, uh-ruhz*] happy, lucky, fortunate
*heurter *v.* [*uhr-teh*] strike
hier [*yer*] yesterday
   avant-hier [*ah-vã-tyer*] the day before yesterday
   hier soir [*yer swahr*] last night
histoire *f.* [*ees-twahr*] history; story

historique [*ees-to-reek*] historical

hiver *m.* [*ee-ver*] winter

*__hollandais__ [*o-lã-de(z)*] Dutch

*__Hollande__ *f.* [*o-lãd*] Holland

*__homard__ *m.* [*o-mahr*] lobster

homme *m.* [*om*] man

  homme d'affaires [*om dah-fer*] businessman

  homme d'état [*om deh-tah*] statesman

  jeune homme [*zhuh-nom*] young man

  jeunes gens [*zhuhn zhã*] young people

*__Hongrie__ *f.* [*õ-gree*] Hungary

*__hongrois__ [*õ-grwah(z)*] Hungarian

honnête [*o-net*] honest

honneur *m.* [*o-nuhr*] honor

honoraires *m. pl.* [*o-no-rer*] fee

honorer *v.* [*o-no-reh*] honor

*__honte__ *f.* [*õt*] shame

  avoir *v.* **honte** [*ah-vwahr õt*] be ashamed

*__honteux, -euse__ [*õ-tuh, õ-tuhz*] shameful

hôpital, -aux *m.* [*o-pee-tahl, o-pee-toh*] hospital

horaire *adj.* [*o-rer*] hourly

horaire *m.* [*o-rer*] schedule

horloge *f.* [*or-lozh*] clock

horloger *m.* [*or-lo-zheh*] watchmaker

horrible [*o-reebl*] horrible

*__hors de__ [*or d(uh)*] out of

*__hors d'oeuvre__ *m. invar.* [*or duhvr*] relishes, hors d'oeuvre, appetizer

hospitalité *f.* [*os-pee-tah-lee-teh*] hospitality

hostile [*os-teel*] hostile

hôte *m.* [*oht*] host; guest

hôtel *m.* [*oh-tel*] hotel

  hôtel de ville [*oh-tel duh veel*] city hall, town hall

hôtelier *m.* [*oh-tuh-lyeh*] innkeeper, hotel keeper

hôtesse, *f.* [*oh-tes*] hostess

  hôtesse de l'air [*oh-tes duh ler*] stewardess

huile *f.* [*weel*] oil

huiler *v.* [*wee-leh*] oil

*huit [*wee(t)*] eight
*huitième [*wee-tyem*] eighth
huître *f.* [*weetr*] oyster
humain [*ü-mē*, *ü-men*] human
humanité *f.* [*ü-mah-nee-teh*] humanity
humble [*ēbl*] humble
humeur *f.* [*ü-muhr*] mood
   de bonne humeur [*duh bo-nü-muhr*] in a good mood
humide [*ü-meed*] damp, humid
humidité *f.* [*ü-mee-dee-teh*] humidity, moisture
humoristique [*ü-mo-rees-teek*] humorous
hypothèque *f.* [*ee-po-tek*] mortgage
hypothèse *f.* [*ee-po-tez*] hypothesis, assumption

I

ici [*ee-see*] here
   par ici [*pahr ee-see*] this way
   d'ici trois jours [*dee-see trwah zhoor*] three days from now
idéal, -aux *adj. & n.* [*ee-deh-ahl*, *ee-deh-oh*] ideal
idée *f.* [*ee-deh*] idea
identifier *v.* [*ee-dã-tee-fyeh*] identify
identique [*ee-dã-teek*] identical
identité *f.* [*ee-dã-tee-teh*] identity
idiot [*ee-dyoh*, *ee-dyot*] idiot, idiotic
ignorant [*ee-nyo-rã(t)*] ignorant
ignorer *v.* [*ee-nyo-reh*] not know
il [*eel*] he, it
   Il y a [*eel yah*] There is, There are
   il y a trois ans [*eel yah trwah-zã*] three years ago
île *f.* [*eel*] island
illégal, -aux [*ee-leh-gahl*, *ee-leh-goh*] illegal
ils [*eel*] they
image *f.* [*ee-mahzh*] image
imagination *f.* [*ee-mah-zhee-nah-syõ*] imagination

imaginer v. [*ee-mah-zhee-neh*] imagine
imbécile m. [*ē-beh-seel*] fool
imitation f. [*ee-mee-tah-syō*] imitation
imiter v. [*ee-mee-teh*] imitate
immatriculation f. [*ee-mah-tree-kü-lah-syō*] registration
   plaque f. **d'immatriculation** [*plahk dee-mah-tree-kü-lah-syō*] license plate
immédiat [*ee-meh-dyah(t)*] immediate
immédiatement [*ee-meh-dyaht-mā*] immediately
immense [*ee-mās*] immense
immeuble m. [*ee-muhbl*] apartment house
immigration f. [*ee-mee-grah-syō*] immigration
immoral, -aux [*ee-mo-rahl, ee-mo-roh*] immoral
impair [*ē-per*] odd
impardonnable [*ē-pahr-do-nahbl*] unforgivable
imparfait [*ē-pahr-fe(t)*] imperfect
impartial, -aux [*ē-pahr-syahl, ē-pahr-syoh*] impartial
impasse f. [*ē-pahs*] dead-end street
impatient [*ē-pah-syā(t)*] impatient, eager
impérialisme m. [*ē-peh-ryah-leesm*] imperialism
imperméable adj. [*ē-per-meh-ahbl*] waterproof
imperméable m. [*ē-per-meh-ahbl*] raincoat
impoli [*ē-po-lee*] impolite
importance f. [*ē-por-tās*] importance
important [*ē-por-tā(t)*] important
   peu important [*puh ē-por-ta(t)*] unimportant
importé [*ē-por-teh*] imported
importer v. [*ē-por-teh*] import; be important, matter
   n'importe comment [*nē-port ko-mā*] no matter how
   n'importe lequel [*nē-port luh-kel*] either, anyone
   n'importe où [*nē-por-too*] anywhere
   n'importe quand [*nē-port kā*] at any time
   n'importe quel [*nē-port kel*] any
   n'importe qui [*nē-port kee*] just anyone
   n'importe quoi [*nē-port kwah*] anything
   peu importe [*puh ē-port*] no matter; it makes no difference
imposer v. [*ē-po-zeh*] impose; tax
impossible [*ē-po-seebl*] impossible

impôt *m.* [*ē-poh*] tax
   impôt sur le revenu [*ē-poh sür luh ruhv-nü*] income tax
   exempt d'impôts [*eg-zā(t) dē-poh*] tax free
impression *f.* [*ē-preh-syō*] impression
imprévu [*ē-preh-vü*] unforeseen
imprimé *m.* [*ē-pree-meh*] form, printed matter
imprimer *v.* [*ē-pree-meh*] print
imprimeur *m.* [*ē-pree-muhr*] printer
improbable [*ē-pro-bahbl*] improbable
inattendu [*ee-nah-tā-dü*] unexpected
incapable [*ē-kah-pahbl*] incapable
incapacité *f.* [*ē-kah-pah-see-teh*] inability, incompetence
incendie *m.* [*ē-sā-dee*] fire
incertain [*ē-ser-tē, ē-ser-ten*] uncertain
incident *m.* [*ē-see-dā*] incident
incliner *v.* [*ē-klee-neh*] bend, bow
inclure *v. irreg.* [*ē-klür*] include
inclus [*ē-klü(z)*] included
incomparable [*ē-kō-pah-rahbl*] incomparable
incomplet, -ète [*ē-kō-pleh, ē-kō-plet*] incomplete
inconnu [*ē-ko-nü*] unknown
inconscient [*ē-kō-syā(t)*] unconscious
inconvenient *m.* [*ē-kō-veh-nyā*] disadvantage
incorrect [*ē-ko-rekt*] incorrect
incroyable [*ē-krwah-yahbl*] incredible
Inde *f.* [*ēd*] India
indécent [*ē-deh-sā(t)*] indecent
indécis [*ē-deh-see(z)*] undecided
indéfini [*ē-deh-fee-nee*] indefinite
indépendance *f.* [*ē-deh-pā-dās*] independence
independent [*ē-deh-pā-dā(t)*] independent
indicateur *m.* [*ē-dee-kah-tuhr*] timetable
indifférent [*ē-dee-feh-rā(t)*] indifferent
indigène *m., f.* [*ē-dee-zhen*] native
indigestion *f.* [*ē-dee-zhes-tyō*] indigestion
indigné [*ē-dee-nyeh*] indignant
indien, -enne [*ē-dyē, ē-dyen*] Indian
indiquer *v.* [*ē-dee-keh*] point out

indirect [*ē-dee-rekt*] indirect
indiscret, -ète [*ē-dees-kre(t)*] indiscreet
indiscutable [*ē-dees-kü-tahbl*] unquestionable
indispensable [*ē-dees-pã-sahbl*] indispensable
individu *m.* [*ē-dee-vee-dü*] individual
individuel, -elle [*ē-dee-vee-dwel*] individual
industrie *f.* [*ē-düs-tree*] industry
industriel, -elle [*ē-düs-tree-el*] industrial
inefficace [*ee-neh-fee-kahs*] inefficient
inégal, -aux [*ee-neh-gahl, ee-neh-goh*] unequal
inexcusable [*ee-nek-skü-zahbl*] inexcusable
infarctus *m.* [*ē-fahrk-tüs*] heart attack
infection *f.* [*ē-fek-syõ*] infection
inférieur [*ē-feh-ryuhr*] inferior
infidèle [*ē-fee-del*] unfaithful
infiniment [*ē-fee-nee-mã*] infinitely
infinitif *m.* [*ē-fee-nee-teef*] infinitive
infirmière *f.* [*ē-feer-myer*] nurse
infirmité *f.* [*ē-feer-mee-teh*] disease, disability
influence *f.* [*ē-flü-ãs*] influence
influencer *v.* [*ē-flü-ã-seh*] influence
information *f.* [*ē-for-mah-syõ*] information
informer *v.* [*ē-for-meh*] inform
ingénieur *m.* [*ē-zheh-nyuhr*] engineer
initiative *f.* [*ee-nee-syah-teev*] initiative
injection *f.* [*ē-zhek-syõ*] injection
injure *f.* [*ē-zhür*] insult
injuste [*ē-zhüst*] unjust, unfair
injustice *f.* [*ē-zhüs-tees*] injustice
innocent [*ee-no-sã(t)*] innocent
innombrable [*ee-nõ-brahbl*] innumerable
inoccupé [*ee-no-kü-peh*] unoccupied
inondation *f.* [*ee-nõ-dah-syõ*] flood
inoubliable [*ee-noo-blee-ahbl*] unforgettable
inouï [*een-wee*] unheard-of
inquiet, -ète [*ē-kyeh, ē-kyet*] anxious, uneasy
inquiéter *v.* [*ē-kyeh-teh*] bother
   s'inquiéter [*sē-kyeh-teh*] worry

inquiétude *f.* [*ē-kyeh-tüd*] worry
inscription *f.* [*ē-skreep-syõ*] registration, enrollment
s'inscrire *v. irreg.* [*sē-skreer*] enroll, register
insecte *m.* [*ē-sekt*] insect; bug
insistance *f.* [*ē-sees-tãs*] insistance, emphasis
insister (sur) *v.* [*ē-sees-teh*] insist (on), stress
insonorisé [*ē-so-no-ree-zeh*] soundproof
insouciant [*ē-soo-syã(t)*] heedless
inspecter *v.* [*ē-spek-teh*] inspect
inspecteur, -trice [*ē-spek-tuhr, ē-spek-trees*] inspector
inspection *f.* [*ē-spek-syõ*] inspection
inspiration *f.* [*ē-spee-rah-syõ*] inspiration
installation *f.* [*ē-stah-lah-syõ*] moving in, settling
installer *v.* [*ē-stah-leh*] install
  s'installer [*sē-stah-leh*] move in, get settled
instant *m.* [*ē-stã*] instant
  à l'instant [*ah lē-stã*] right now
instinct *m.* [*ē-stē*] instinct
instituteur, -trice [*ē-stee-tü-tuhr, ē-stee-tü-trees*] teacher
institution *f.* [*ē-stee-tü-syõ*] institution
instructeur, -trice [*ē-strük-tuhr, ē-strük-trees*] instructor
instruction *f.* [*ē-strük-syõ*] instruction, education
instruire *v. irreg.* [*ē-strweer*] instruct
instrument *m.* [*ē-strü-mã*] instrument
insuffisant [*ē-sü-fee-zã(t)*] insufficient
insulte *f.* [*ē-sült*] insult
insulter *v.* [*ē-sül-teh*] insult
intellectuel, -elle [*ē-teh-lek-twel*] intellectual
intelligent [*ē-teh-lee-zhã(t)*] intelligent
intense [*ē-tãs*] intense
intention *f.* [*ē-tã-syõ*] intention
  avoir *v.* **l'intention (de)** [*ah-vwahr lē-tã-syõ (duh)*] intend
interdire *v. irreg.* [*ē-ter-deer*] forbid
interdit [*ē-ter-dee(t)*] forbidden, prohibited
intéressant [*ē-teh-re-sã(t)*] interesting
intéresser *v.* [*ē-teh-reh-seh*] interest
  s'intéresser (à) *v.* [*sē-teh-reh-seh (ah)*] care for, be interested (in)

intérêt *m.* [*ē-teh-re*] interest
intérieur *m.* [*ē-tehr-yuhr*] inside, interior
   à l'intérieur [*ah lē-tehr-yuhr*] within
internat *m.* [*ē-ter-nah*] boarding school
international, -aux [*ē-ter-nah-syo-nahl, ē-ter-nah-syo-noh*]
   international
interne [*ē-tern*] internal
interprète *m.* [*ē-ter-pret*] interpreter
interrompre *v.* [*ē-teh-rōpr*] interrupt
interrupteur *m.* [*ē-teh-rüp-tuhr*] switch
interurbain [*ē-ter-ür-bē, ē-ter-ür-ben*] long-distance
intervalle *m.* [*ē-ter-vahl*] interval
intervenir *v. irreg.* [*ē-ter-vuh-neer*] intervene, interfere
intime [*ē-teem*] intimate
introduction *f.* [*ē-tro-dük-syō*] introduction
introduire *v. irreg.* [*ē-tro-dweer*] introduce
intuition *f.* [*ē-twee-syō*] intuition
inutile [*ee-nü-teel*] useless
invalide [*ē-vah-leed*] invalid, disabled
invasion *f.* [*ē-vah-zyō*] invasion
inventeur *m.* [*ē-vã-tuhr*] inventor
invention *f.* [*ē-vã-syō*] invention
inverse *m.* [*ē-vers*] reverse
investir *v.* [*ē-ves-teer*] invest
invisible [*ē-vee-zeebl*] invisible
invitation *f.* [*ē-vee-tah-syō*] invitation
invité, -ée [*ē-vee-teh*] guest, company
inviter *v.* [*ē-vee-teh*] invite
involontaire [*ē-vo-lō-ter*] involuntary
irlandais *n. & adj.* [*eer-lã-de(z)*] Irish
Irlande *f.* [*eer-lãd*] Ireland
irrégulier, -ière [*ee-reh-gü-lyeh, ee-reh-gü-lyer*] irregular
irrésistible [*ee-reh-zees-teebl*] irresistible
irriter *v.* [*ee-ree-teh*] irritate
isolé [*ee-zo-leh*] isolated, lonely
israelien, -enne *n. & adj.* [*eez-rah-eh-lyē, eez-rah-eh-lyen*]
   Israeli
israélite *n. & adj.* [*eez-rah-eh-leet*] Jew, Jewish; Israelite

Italie f. [*ee-tah-lee*] Italy
italien, -enne n. & adj. [*ee-tahl-yĕ, ee-tahl-yen*] Italian
itinéraire m. [*ee-tee-neh-rer*] itinerary
ivoire m. [*ee-vwahr*] ivory

J

jadis [*zhah-dees*] formerly
jalousie f. [*zhah-loo-zee*] jealousy
jaloux, -ouse [*zhah-loo, zhah-looz*] jealous
jamais [*zhah-me*] ever, never
jambe f. [*zhãb*] leg
jambon m. [*zhã-bõ*] ham
janvier m. [*zhã-vyeh*] January
Japon m. [*zhah-põ*] Japan
japonais n. & adj. [*zhah-po-ne(z)*] Japanese
jardin m. [*zhahr-dĕ*] garden
jardinier, -ière [*zhahr-dee-nyeh, zhahr-dee-nyer*] gardener
jarretière f. [*zhahr-tyer*] garter
jauge f. [*zhohzh*] gauge
jaune [*zhohn*] yellow
jazz m. [*dzhahz*] jazz
je [*zhuh*] I
jetée f. [*zh(uh)-teh*] pier
jeter v. [*zh(uh)-teh*] throw
jeu m. [*zhuh*] game
    jeu de cartes [*zhuhd kahrt*] deck of cards
jeudi m. [*zhuh-dee*] Thursday
jeune [*zhuhn*] young
jeunesse f. [*zhuh-nes*] youth
jockey m. [*zho-ke*] jockey
joie f. [*zhwah*] joy, delight
joindre v. irreg. [*zhwĕdr*] join, bring together, meet
    se joindre à [*suh zhwĕ-drah*] join with [someone]
joli [*zho-lee*] pretty, nice

joue *f.* [*zhoo*] cheek
jouer *v.* [*zhweh*] play; gamble
   jouer à un jeu [*zhweh ah ẽ zhuh*] play a game
   jouer d'un instrument [*zhweh dẽ-nẽ-strü-mã*] play an instrument
jouet *m.* [*zhwe*] toy
jouir *v.* [*zhweer*] enjoy
jour *m.* [*zhoor*] day
   tous les jours [*too leh zhoor*] daily, every day
journal, -aux *m.* [*zhoor-nahl, zhoor-noh*] newspaper, journal
journaliste *m., f.* [*zhoor-nah-leest*] journalist, reporter
journée *f.* [*zhoor-neh*] day
   toute la journée [*toot lah zhoor-neh*] all day long
joyeux, -euse [*zhwah-yuh, zhwah-yuhz*] cheerful, joyful
juge *m.* [*zhüzh*] judge
jugement *m.* [*zhüzh-mã*] judgment
juger *v.* [*zhü-zheh*] judge
juif, juive [*zhweef, zhweev*] Jew, Jewish
juillet *m.* [*zhwee-ye*] July
juin *m.* [*zhwẽ*] June
jumeau, -jumelle [*zhü-moh, zhü-mel*] twin brother, twin sister
jumelles *f. pl.* [*zhü-mel*] opera glasses, field glasses
jument *f.* [*zhü-mã*] mare
jungle *f.* [*zhẽgl*] jungle
jupe *f.* [*zhüp*] skirt
jupon *m.* [*zhü-põ*] petticoat
jurer *v.* [*zhü-reh*] swear
jury *m.* [*zhü-ree*] jury
jus *m.* [*zhü*] juice
jusque [*zhüsk*] until, up to
   jusqu'ici [*zhüs-kee-see*] so far
juste *adj. & adv.* [*zhüst*] just, accurate, fair
justement [*zhüs-tuh-mã*] precisely
justice *f.* [*zhüs-tees*] justice
justifier *v.* [*zhüs-tee-fyeh*] justify

K

kilogramme *m.* [*kee-lo-grahm*] kilogram [2.2 pounds]
kilomètre *m.* [*kee-lo-metr*] kilometer [.61 mile]
kiosque *m.* [*kyosk*] newsstand
klaxon *m.* [*klahk-son*] horn

L

l': **le, la** [*l*] the; him, her, it
la *art.* [*lah*] the
la *pron.* [*lah*] her, it
là [*lah*] there
  là-bas [*lah-bah*] over there
  là-haut [*lah-oh*] up there
laboratoire *m.* [*lah-bo-rah-twahr*] laboratory
labourer *v.* [*lah-boo-reh*] plow
lac *m.* [*lahk*] lake
lacet *m.* [*lah-se*] lace
lâche *m. f.; n. & adj.* [*lahsh*] coward, cowardly
lâcher *v.* [*lah-sheh*] let go
laid [*le(d)*] ugly
lainage *m.* [*le-nahzh*] wool garment
laine *f.* [*len*] wool
  en laine [*ã len*] woolen
laisser *v.* [*leh-seh*] leave (behind); let, allow
  laisser entrer [*leh-seh ã-treh*] admit
lait *m.* [*le*] milk
laiterie *f.* [*let-ree*] dairy
laitue *f.* [*leh-tü*] lettuce
lame *f.* [*lahm*] blade

lame de rasoir [*lahm duh rahz-wahr*] razor blade
lampe *f.* [*lãp*] lamp
lancer *v.* [*lã-seh*] toss
langage *m.* [*lã-gahzh*] language
langouste *f.* [*lã-goost*] spiny lobster
langue *f.* [*lãg*] tongue, language
lapin *m.* [*lah-pẽ*] rabbit
laquelle [*lah-kel*] which, who, whom
lard *m.* [*lahr*] bacon
large [*lahrzh*] wide, broad
   large d'esprit [*lahrzh des-pree*] broad-minded
largeur *f.* [*lahr-zhuhr*] width
larme *f.* [*lahrm*] tear
lavabo *m.* [*lah-vah-boh*] washbasin
laver *v.* [*lah-veh*] wash
   se laver [*slah-veh*] wash [oneself]
le *art.* [*luh*] the
le *pron.* [*luh*] him, it
leçon *f.* [*l(uh)-sõ*] lesson
lecteur, -trice [*lek-tuhr, lek-trees*] reader
lecture *f.* [*lek-tür*] reading
légal, -aux [*leh-gahl, leh-goh*] legal, lawful
léger, -ère [*leh-zheh, leh-zher*] light
légitime [*leh-zhee-teem*] legitimate
légume *m.* [*leh-güm*] vegetable
lendemain *m.* [*lãd-mẽ*] the next day
lent [*lã(t)*] slow
lentement [*lãt-mã*] slowly
lequel, laquelle; lesquels, lesquelles [*luh-kel, lah-kel, leh-kel*]
   whom, which
   La chaise sur laquelle j'étais assise [*lah shez sür lah-kel*
    zheh-te ah-seez] The chair on which I was sitting
lequel, laquelle *interr.* [*luh-kel, lah-kel*] which, which one
   Lequel voulez-vous? [*luh-kel voo-leh-voo*] Which [one] do
    you want?
les *art.* [*leh*] the
les *pron.* [*leh*] them
lesquels, -quelles [*leh-kel*] which, whom

lessive *f.* [*leh-seev*] washing
lettre *f.* [*letr*] letter
   lettre recommandée [*letr ruh-ko-mã-deh*] registered letter
leur, leurs *adj.* [*luhr*] their
leur *pron.* [*luhr*] to them
le leur, la leur *pron.* [*luh luhr, lah luhr*] theirs
lever *m.* **de soleil** [*l(uh)-vehd so-ley*] sunrise
se lever *v. irreg.* [*sluh-veh*] get up, stand up, rise
lèvre *f.* [*levr*] lip
libéral, -aux [*lee-beh-rahl, lee-beh-roh*] liberal
libérer *v.* [*lee-beh-reh*] free
liberté *f.* [*lee-ber-teh*] liberty, freedom
librairie *f.* [*lee-bre-ree*] bookstore
libre [*leebr*] free, vacant
libre-service *m.* [*lee-bruh-ser-vees*] cafeteria
licence *f.* [*lee-sãs*] university diploma, masters
lier *v.* [*lee-eh*] bind, tie up
lieu *m.* [*lyuh*] place
   avoir *v.* **lieu** [*ah-vwahr lyuh*] take place
   au lieu de [*oh lyuh duh*] instead of
lièvre *m.* [*lyevr*] hare
ligne *f.* [*leeñ*] line
lime *f.* [*leem*] file
limitation *f.* [*lee-mee-tah-syõ*] limitation
   limitation de vitesse [*lee-mee-tah-syõd vee-tes*] speed limit
limite *f.* [*lee-meet*] limit
limiter *v.* [*lee-mee-teh*] limit
linge *m.* [*lẽzh*] linen, clothes
liquide [*lee-keed*] liquid
lire *v. irreg.* [*leer*] read
lisible [*lee-zeebl*] legible
lisse [*lees*] smooth
liste *f.* [*leest*] list
lit *m.* [*lee*] bed
   lit d'enfant [*lee dã-fã*] crib
litre *m.* [*leetr*] liter [1.1 quarts]
littéralement [*lee-teh-rahl-mã*] literally
littérature *f.* [*lee-teh-rah-tür*] literature

livre *f.* [*leevr*] pound
livre *m.* [*leevr*] book
livrer *v.* [*lee-vreh*] deliver
livret *m.* [*lee-vre*] booklet
local, -aux [*lo-kahl, lo-koh*] local
locataire *m., f.* [*lo-kah-ter*] tenant
locomotive *f.* [*lo-ko-mo-teev*] engine, locomotive
logement *m.* [*lozh-mã*] housing, accommodations
loger *v.* [*lo-zheh*] house
logique [*lo-zheek*] logical, consistent
loi *f.* [*lwah*] law
loin (de) [*lwẽ (duh)*] far (from)
   au loin [*oh lwẽ*] far away
lointain [*lwẽ-tẽ, lwẽ-ten*] far away
loisir *m.* [*lwah-zeer*] leisure
long, longue [*lõ, lõg*] long
   le long de [*luh lõ d(uh)*] along
   à la longue [*ah lah lõg*] in the end
longtemps [*lõ-tã*] long, a long time
   il y a longtemps [*eel yah lõ-tã*] long ago
longueur *f.* [*lõ-guhr*] length
lorsque [*lorsk*] when
louer *v.* [*lweh*] rent; praise; reserve [a place]
lourd [*loor(d)*] heavy
loyal, -aux [*lwah-yahl, lwah-yoh*] loyal
loyer *m.* [*lwah-yeh*] rent
lui [*lwee*] him, her, it
   lui-même [*lwee-mem*] himself; itself
lumière *f.* [*lü-myer*] light
lundi *m.* [*lẽ-dee*] Monday
lune *f.* [*lün*] moon
   lune de miel [*liin duh myel*] honeymoon
lunettes *f. pl.* [*lü-net*] eyeglasses
   lunettes de soleil [*lü-net duh so-ley*] sunglasses
lutte *f.* [*lüt*] struggle
lutter *v.* [*lü-teh*] struggle
luxe *m.* [*lüks*] luxury

luxueux, -euse [*lük-swuh, lük-swuhz*] luxurious
lycée *m.* [*lee-seh*] high school, junior college

M

m':me [*m*] me
M.: Monsieur [*muh-syuh*] Mr.
ma [*mah*] my
mâcher *v.* [*mah-sheh*] chew
machine *f.* [*mah-sheen*] machine
   machine à écrire [*mah-sheen ah eh-kreer*] typewriter
   machine à laver [*mah-sheen ah lah-veh*] washing machine
mâchoire *f.* [*mah-shwahr*] jaw
Madame, Mesdames *f.* [*mah-dahm, meh-dahm*] madam, Mrs.
Mademoiselle, Mesdemoiselles *f.* [*mahd-mwah-zel, med-mwah-zel*] Miss
   Mademoiselle! [*mahd-mwah-zel*] Waitress!
magasin *m.* [*mah-gah-zē*] store, shop
   grand magasin *m.* [*grā mah-gah-zē*] department store
magique [*mah-zheek*] magic
magistrat *m.* [*mah-zhee-strah*] judge
magnifique [*mah-nyee-feek*] magnificent, gorgeous
mai *m.* [*me*] May
maigre [*megr*] thin
maigrir *v.* [*me-greer*] lose weight
maille *f.* [*mahy*] stitch
maillot *m.* **de bain** [*may-yoh duh bē*] swimsuit, bathing suit
main *f.* [*mē*] hand
   fait main [*fe mē*] handmade
main-d'oeuvre *f.* [*mē-duhvr*] labor
maintenant [*mēt-nā*] now
   à partir de maintenant [*ah pahr-teer duh mēt-nā*] from now on
   jusqu'à maintenant [*zhüs-kah mēt-nā*] until now
maintenir *v. irreg.* [*mēt-neer*] maintain

maire *m.* [*mer*] mayor
mairie *f.* [*meh-ree*] town hall
mais [*me*] but
maïs *m.* [*mah-ees*] corn
maison *f.* [*me-zõ*] house, home
  à la maison [*ah lah me-zõ*] at home
maître *m.* [*metr*] master
maîtresse *f.* [*me-tres*] mistress
  maîtresse de maison [*me-tres duh me-zõ*] housewife
maitrise *f.* [*meh-treez*] control, mastery
majeur [*mah-zhuhr*] major
majorité *f.* [*mah-zho-ree-teh*] majority
mal, maux *m.* [*mahl, moh*] pain, evil, difficulty
  mal de gorge [*mahl duh gorzh*] sore throat
  mal de mer [*mahl duh mer*] sea-sickness
  mal à l'aise [*mah-lah lez*] uneasy, uncomfortable
  avoir *v.* **mal à** [*ah-vwahr mah-lah*] have a . . . ache
  avoir *v.* **mal à la tête** [*ah-vwahr mah-lah lah tet*] have a
    headache
  faire *v.* **mal** [*fer mahl*] hurt
  J'ai mal! [*zheh mahl*] It hurts!, I have a pain!
mal *adv.* [*mahl*] badly
  pas mal [*pah mahl*] not bad, pretty good
malade *adj.* [*mah-lahd*] sick, ill
malade *n.* [*mah-lahd*] patient
maladie *f.* [*mah-lah-dee*] disease, sickness, illness
maladroit [*mah-lah-drwah(t)*] awkward
malentendu *m.* [*mah-lã-tã-dü*] misunderstanding
malgré [*mahl-greh*] despite, in spite of
malheur *m.* [*mah-luhr*] bad luck, misfortune
malheureusement [*mah-luh-ruhz-mã*] unfortunately
malheureux, -euse [*mah-luh-ruh, mah-luh-ruhz*] unfortunate,
    unhappy
malhonnête [*mah-lo-net*] dishonest
malle *f.* [*mahl*] trunk
malsain [*mahl-sẽ, mahl-sen*] unhealthy
manche *m.* [*mãsh*] handle
manche *f.* [*mãsh*] sleeve; English Channel

manchette *f.* [*mã-shet*] cuff
  bouton *m.* **de manchette** [*boo-tõd mã-shet*] cuff links
mandat *m.* [*mã-dah*] money order; arrest warrant
mangeable [*mã-zhahbl*] edible
manger *v.* [*mã-zheh*] eat
manière *f.* [*mah-nyer*] manner
manifestation *f.* [*man-nee-fes-tah-syõ*] manifestation,
  demonstration
manifester *v.* [*mah-nee-fes-teh*] show, demonstrate
  [politically]
manivelle *f.* [*mah-nee-vel*] crank
manoeuvre *m.* [*mah-nuhvr*] unskilled worker
manoeuvre *f.* [*mah-nuhvr*] maneuver
manoeuvrer *v.* [*mah-nuh-vreh*] maneuver
manque *m.* [*mãk*] lack
manquer *v.* [*mã-keh*] be lacking, miss
  manquer (de) [*mã-keh (duh)*] lack
  J'ai manqué le train [*zheh mã-kehl trẽ*] I missed the train
  Ils me manquent [*eel muh mãk*] I miss them
manteau, -eaux *m.* [*mã-toh*] coat
manucure *f.* [*mah-nü-kür*] manicurist
maquillage *m.* [*mah-kee-yahzh*] make-up
marais *m.* [*mah-re*] marsh
marbre *m.* [*mahrbr*] marble
marchand *m.* [*mahr-shã*] merchant, dealer
marchander *v.* [*mahr-shã-deh*] bargain
marchandise *f.* [*mahr-shã-deez*] goods, merchandise
marche *f.* [*mahrsh*] step [of stairs], walk, march
  faire *v.* **marche arrière** [*fer mar-shahr-yer*] back up
marché *m.* [*mahr-sheh*] market
  bon marché [*bõ mahr-sheh*] cheap
  marché aux puces [*mahr-sheh oh püs*] flea-market
marcher *v.* [*mahr-sheh*] walk
mardi *m.* [*mahr-dee*] Tuesday
marée *f.* [*mah-reh*] tide
marguerite *f.* [*mahr-guh-reet*] daisy
mari *m.* [*mah-ree*] husband
mariage *m.* [*mahr-yahzh*] marriage, wedding

marié *m.* [*mahr-yeh*] bridegroom, groom
mariée *f.* [*mahr-yeh*] bride
se marier *v.* [*smahr-yeh*] get married
marin *m.* [*mah-rē*] sailor
marine *f.* [*mah-reen*] navy
marionnette *f.* [*mah-ryo-net*] puppet
marmite *f.* [*mahr-meet*] pot
marque *f.* [*mahrk*] mark, brand
  marque de fabrique [*mahrk duh fah-breek*] trademark
marquer *v.* [*mahr-keh*] mark
marraine *f.* [*mah-ren*] godmother
marron *m.* [*mah-rõ*] chestnut; brown [color]
mars *m.* [*mahrs*] March
marteau, -eaux *m.* [*mahr-toh*] hammer
masculin [*mahs-kü-lē, mahs-kü-leen*] masculine
massage *m.* [*mah-sahzh*] massage
masse *f.* [*mahs*] mass
mât *m.* [*mah*] mast
matelas *m.* [*maht-lah*] mattress
matelot *m.* [*maht-loh*] sailor
matériel *m.* [*mah-tehr-yel*] material, equipment
maternel, -elle [*mah-ter-nel*] maternal
  ècole *f.* **maternelle** [*eh-kol mah-ter-nel*] nursery school
mathématiques *f. pl.* [*mah-teh-mah-teek*] mathematics
matière *f.* [*mah-tyer*] matter, material
  matières premières [*mah-tyer pruh-myer*] raw materials
matin *m.* [*mah-tē*] morning
matinée *f.* [*mah-tee-neh*] morning; matinee [theater]
mauvais *adj.* [*mo-ve(z)*] bad
me [*muh*] me
mécanicien *m.* [*meh-kah-nee-syē*] mechanic; engineer
  [of train]
mécanique [*meh-kah-neek*] mechanical
mécanisme *m.* [*meh-kah-neesm*] mecanism
méchant [*meh-shã(t)*] bad, michievous, naughty
mécontent [*meh-kõ-tã(t)*] unhappy
médecin *m.* [*med-sē*] doctor
médecine *f.* [*med-seen*] medicine [profession]

médical, -aux [*meh-dee-kahl, meh-dee-koh*] medical
médicament *m*. [*meh-dee-kah-mã*] medication
Méditerranée *f*. [*meh-dee-te-rah-neh*] Mediterranean (Sea)
méfiance *f*. [*meh-fyãs*] distrust
meilleur, le meilleur [*meh-yuhr, luh meh-yuhr*] better, best
mélange *m*. [*meh-lãzh*] mixture
mélanger *v*. [*meh-lã-zheh*] mix
melon *m*. [*m(uh)-lõ*] melon
membre *m*. [*mãbr*] member; limb [of body]
même *adj*. [*mem*] same, very, self
même *adv*. [*mem*] even
  à meme de [*ah mem d(uh)*] able to
  de même [*duh mem*] likewise
  de même que [*duh mem kuh*] just as
  tout de même [*tood mem*] all the same
memoire *f*. [*mem-wahr*] memory
menace *f*. [*muh-nahs*] threat
menacer *v*. [*muh-nah-seh*] threaten
ménage *m*. [*meh-nahzh*] housework, household
ménagère *f*. [*meh-nah-zher*] housekeeper, housewife
mendiant, -te [*mã-dyã(t)*] beggar
mendier *v*. [*mã-dyeh*] beg
mener *v*. [*muh-neh*] lead, conduct
mensonge *m*. [*mã-sõzh*] lie
mensuel, -elle [*mã-swel*] monthly
menteur, -euse [*mã-tuhr, mã-tuhz*] liar
menthe *f*. [*mãt*] mint
mentionner *v*. [*mã-syo-neh*] mention
mentir *v. irreg*. [*mã-teer*] lie
menton *m*. [*mã-tõ*] chin
menu *m*. [*muh-nii*] menu
menuisier *m*. [*muh-nwee-zyeh*] carpenter
mépris *m*. [*meh-pree*] contempt
mépriser *v*. [*meh-pree-zeh*] scorn
mer *f*. [*mer*] sea
mercerie *f*. [*mer-suh-ree*] notions, dry goods
Merci [*mer-see*] Thank you
mercredi *m*. [*mer-kruh-dee*] Wednesday

mère *f.* [*mer*] mother
mérite *m.* [*meh-reet*] merit
mériter *v.* [*meh-ree-teh*] deserve
merveilleux, -euse [*mer-ve-yuh, mer-ve-yuhz*] wonderful
mes [*meh*] my
mesdames, mesdemoiselles [*meh-dahm, med-mwah-zel*]
    ladies, young ladies
message *m.* [*meh-sahzh*] message
messager *m.* [*meh-sah-zheh*] messenger
messe *f.* [*mes*] mass [eccl.]
mesure *f.* [*muh-zür*] measure
  fait sur mesure [*fe sür muh-zür*] custom made
mesurer *v.* [*muh-zü-reh*] measure
métal, -aux *m.* [*meh-tahl, meh-toh*] metal
méthode *f.* [*meh-tod*] method
métier *m.* [*meh-tyeh*] trade
mètre *m.* [*metr*] meter [39.4 inches]
métro *m.* [*meh-troh*] subway
metteur en scène *m.* [*me-tuhr ã sen*] director [films]
mettre *v. irreg.* [*metr*] put, set; put on [clothing]
meuble *m.* [*muhbl*] a piece of furniture, furniture
meubler *v.* [*muh-bleh*] furnish
  chambre *f.* **meublée** [*shã-bruh muh-bleh*] furnished room
meurtre *m.* [*muhrtr*] murder
meurtrier *m.* [*muhr-tree-yeh*] murderer
microbe *m.* [*mee-krob*] germ
midi *m.* [*mee-dee*] noon
miel *m.* [*myel*] honey
le mien, la mienne [*luh myē, la myen*] mine
miette *f.* [*myet*] crumb
mieux, le mieux [*myuh, luh myuh*] better, best
mignon, -nne [*mee-nyõ, mee-nyon*] cute
milieu, -x *m.* [*meel-yuh*] middle; social circle, surroundings
militaire [*mee-lee-ter*] military
mille *m. inv.* [*meel*] thousand
milliard *m.* [*meel-yahr*] billion
million *m.* [*meel-yõ*] million
mince [*mēs*] thin

mine _f._ [_meen_] looks, appearance
  Elle a bonne mine [_el ah bon meen_] She looks well
minéral, -aux [_mee-neh-rahl, mee-neh-roh_] mineral
mineur _m._ [_mee-nuhr_] miner
mineur, -eure [_mee-nuhr_] minor, infant
minimum _m._ [_mee-nee-mom_] minimum
ministère _f._ [_mee-nees-ter_] ministry
ministre _m._ [_mee-neestr_] minister
minorité _f._ [_mee-no-ree-teh_] minority
minuit _m._ [_mee-nwee_] midnight
minuscule [_mee-nüs-kül_] tiny
minute _f._ [_mee-nüt_] minute
miroir _m._ [_meer-wahr_] mirror
misérable [_mee-zeh-rahbl_] miserable
mode _f._ [_mod_] fashion, style
  à la mode [_ah lah mod_] fashionable
modèle _m._ [_mo-del_] model
moderne [_mo-dern_] modern
modeste [_mo-dest_] modest
modifier _v._ [_mo-dee-fyeh_] modify, change
modiste _f._ [_mo-deest_] milliner
moi [_mwah_] me; I
  moi-même [_mwah-mem_] myself
moi _m._ [_mwah_] self, ego
moindre [_mwēdr_] less
  le moindre [_luh mwēdr_] the least
moins [_mwē_] less, fewer, minus
  au moins [_oh mwē_] at least
  à moins de, à moins que [_ah mwē d(uh), ah mwē kuh_]
    unless
  de moins en moins [_duh mwē-zã mwē_] less and less
mois _m._ [_mwah_] month
moisson _f._ [_mwah-sõ_] harvest
moitié _f._ [_mwah-tyeh_] half
moment _m._ [_mo-mã_] moment
mon [_mõ_] my
monarchie _f._ [_mo-nahr-shee_] monarchy
monastère _m._ [_mo-nah-ster_] monastery

monde *m.* [*mōd*] world
mondial, -aux [*mō-dyahl, mō-dyoh*] world, world-wide
monétaire [*mo-neh-ter*] monetary
monnaie *f.* [*mo-ne*] money, currency
   de la monnaie [*dlah mo-ne*] change
monotone [*mo-no-ton*] monotonous
monsieur, messieurs [*muh-syuh, meh-syuh*] gentleman, gentlemen
   Monsieur [*muh-syuh*] Mister, Sir
montagne *f.* [*mō-tahñ*] mountain
montant [*mō-tã(t)*] uphill
montant *m.* [*mō-tã*] amount, post
monter *v.* [*mō-teh*] go up; carry up
montre *f.* [*mōtr*] watch
montrer *v.* [*mō-treh*] show
monument *m.* [*mo-nü-mã*] monument
moral, -aux [*mo-rahl, mo-roh*] moral
moral *m.* [*mo-rahl*] morale, spirit
morale *f.* [*mo-rahl*] moral
morceau, -eaux *m.* [*mor-soh*] piece
mordre *v.* [*mordr*] bite
mort *f.* [*mor*] death
mort *adj.* [*mor(t)*] dead
mortel, -elle [*mor-tel*] deadly
mot *m.* [*moh*] word
moteur *m.* [*mo-tuhr*] motor, engine
motif *m.* [*mo-teef*] motive
motocyclette *f.* [*mo-to-see-klet*] motorcycle
mou, molle [*moo, mol*] soft
mouche *f.* [*moosh*] fly
se moucher *v.* [*smoo-sheh*] blow one's nose
mouchoir *m.* [*moo-shwahr*] handkerchief
moudre *v. irreg.* [*moodr*] grind
mouillé [*moo-yeh*] wet
moule *f.* [*mool*] mussel
moule *m.* [*mool*] mold
moulin *m.* [*moo-lē*] mill
   moulin à vent [*moo-lē ah vã*] windmill

moulu [*moo-lü*] ground
mourir *v. irreg.* [*moo-reer*] die
mousse *f.* [*moos*] moss; foam [of a beverage]
moustache *f.* [*moos-tahsh*] mustache
moustique *m.* [*moos-teek*] mosquito
moutarde *f.* [*moo-tahrd*] mustard
mouvement *m.* [*moov-mā*] movement, motion
moyen, -enne [*mwah-ĕ, mwah-en*] average, medium
   au moyen de [*oh mwah-ēd(uh)*] by means of
moyens *m. pl.* [*mwah-ē*] means
moyenne *f.* [*mwah-yen*] average
muet, muette [*mweh, mwet*] dumb
munitions *f. pl.* [*mü-nee-syō*] munitions, ammunition
mur *m.* [*mür*] wall
mûr [*mür*] mature, ripe
mûrir *v.* [*mü-reer*] ripen
muscle *m.* [*müskl*] muscle
musée *m.* [*mü-zeh*] museum
musical, -aux [*mü-zee-kahl, mü-zee-koh*] musical
musicien, -enne [*mü-zee-syĕ, mü-zee-syen*] musician
musique *f.* [*mü-zeek*] music
mutilé [*mü-tee-leh*] mutilated, disabled
mutuel, -elle [*mü-twel*] mutual
myope [*myop*] near-sighted
mystère *m.* [*mees-ter*] mystery
mystérieux, -euse [*mees-teh-ryuh, mees-teh-ryuhz*] mysterious

N

nager *v.* [*nah-zheh*] swim
naïf, naïve [*nah-eef, nah-eev*] naive
naissance *f.* [*ne-sãs*] birth
naître *v. irreg.* [*netr*] be born
   Je suis né en France [*zhuh swee neh ã frãs*] I was born
     in France

nappe *f.* [*nahp*] tablecloth
nation *f.* [*nah-syõ*] nation
national, -aux [*nah-syo-nahl, nah-syo-noh*] national
nationalité *f.* [*nah-syo-nah-lee-teh*] nationality, citizenship
natte *f.* [*naht*] braid
nature *f.* [*nah-tür*] nature
naturel, -elle [*nah-tü-rel*] natural
naturellement [*nah-tü-rel-mã*] naturally
naufrage *m.* [*noh-frahzh*] shipwreck
naval, navals *adj.* [*nah-vahl*] naval
navet *m.* [*nah-ve*] turnip
navire *m.* [*nah-veer*] ship
ne, n' [*nuh*] not
  ne ... pas [*nuh ... pah*] not
  ne ... guère [*nuh ... gher*] hardly
  ne ... plus [*nuh ... plü*] no more, no longer
  ne ... que [*nuh ... kuh*] only
néanmoins [*neh-ã-mwẽ*] nevertheless
nécessaire [*neh-seh-ser*] necessary
nef *f.* [*nef*] nave
négatif, -ive [*neh-gah-teef, neh-gah-teev*] negative
négatif *m.* [*neh-gah-teef*] negative
négliger *v.* [*neh-glee-zheh*] neglect
négociant *m.* [*neh-go-syã*] dealer
neige *f.* [*nezh*] snow
  flocon *m.* **de neige** [*flo-kõd nezh*] snowflake
  tempête *f.* **de neige** [*tã-pet duh nezh*] snow storm, blizzard
neiger *v.* [*ne-zheh*] snow
  Il neige [*eel nezh*] It's snowing
nerf *m.* [*ner*] nerve
nerveux, -euse [*ner-vuh, ner-vuhz*] nervous
n'est-ce pas [*nes pah*] isn't that so
  Il est allé, n'est-ce pas? [*ee-le-tah-leh, nes pah*] He went, didn't he?
net, nette [*net*] neat, clear
nettoyage *m.* [*ne-twah-yahzh*] cleaning
nettoyer *v.* [*ne-twah-yeh*] clean
  nettoyer à sec [*ne-twah-yeh ah sek*] dry-clean

neuf [*nuhf*] nine
neuf, neuve [*nuhf, nuhv*] new
neutre [*nuhtr*] neutral
neveu, -eux *m.* [*nuh-vuh*] nephew
nez *m.* [*neh*] nose
ni . . . ni [*nee . . . nee*] neither . . . nor
nid *m.* [*nee*] nest
nièce *f.* [*nyes*[niece
nier *v.* [*nee-eh*] deny
niveau, -aux *m.* [*nee-voh*] level
noble [*nobl*] noble
Noël *m.* [*no-el*] Christmas
  Joyeux Noël! [*zhwah-yuh no-el*] Merry Christmas!
noeud *m.* [*nuh*] knot, bow
noir *adj.* [*nwahr*] black
noir, noire *n.* [*nwahr*] Negro
noix *f.* [*nwah*] nut, walnut
  noix de muscade [*nwahd müs-kahd*] nutmeg
nom *m.* [*nõ*] name; noun
  nom de famille [*nõd fah-meey*] last name
nombre *m.* [*nõbr*] number
nombreux, -euse [*nõ-bruh, nõ-bruhz*] numerous
  famille *f.* **nombreuse** [*fah-meey nõ-bruhz*] large family
nommer *v.* [*no-meh*] name, appoint
non [*nõ*] no
nord *m.* [*nor*] north
  nord-est *m.* [*nor-est*] northeast
  nord-ouest *m.* [*nor-west*] northwest
normal, -aux [*nor-mahl, nor-moh*] normal
Norvége *f.* [*nor-vezh*] Norway
norvègien, -ienne [*nor-veh-zhyẽ, nor-veh-zhyen*] Norwegian
nos *pl.* [*noh*] our
notamment [*no-tah-mã*] notably
note *f.* [*not*] note, memo; grade, mark; bill, invoice
noter *v.* [*no-teh*] note
notion *f.* [*noh-syõ*] notion
notre [*notr*] our
le nôtre [*luh nohtr*] ours

nouer *v.* [*nweh*] tie
nouilles *f. pl.* [*nooy*] noodles
nourrir *v.* [*noo-reer*] feed
nous [*noo*] we, us
   nous trois [*noo trwah*] the three of us
nouveau, -vel, -velle [*noo-voh, noo-vel*] new
nouveauté *f.* [*noo-voh-teh*] novelty
nouvelle *f.* [*noo-vel*] a piece of news
novembre *m.* [*no-vãbr*] November
noyer, se noyer *v.* [*nwah-yeh, s(uh) nwah-yeh*] drown
nu [*nü*] bare, nude
nuage *m.* [*nwahzh*] cloud
nuageux, -euse [*nwah-zhuh, nwah-zhuhz*] cloudy
nuisible [*nwee-zeebl*] harmful
nuit *f.* [*nwee*] night
   Bonne nuit [*bon nwee*] Good night
nul, nulle [*nül*] null, worthless; no
   nulle part [*nül pahr*] nowhere
numéro *m.* [*nü-meh-roh*] number
   numéro de téléphone [*nü-meh-rohd teh-leh-fon*]
     telephone number
nylon *m.* [*nee-lõ*] nylon

O

obéir (à) *v.* [*o-beh-eer (ah)*] obey
obéissant [*o-beh-ee-sã(t)*] obedient
objectif *m.* [*ob-zhek-teef*] objective; lens
objection *f.* [*ob-zhek-syõ*] objection
   faire *v.* **objection** [*fer ob-zhek-syõ*] object
objet *m.* [*ob-zhe*] object
obligation *f.* [*o-blee-gah-syõ*] obligation, bond
obligatoire [*o-blee-gah-twahr*] obligatory, compulsory
obliger *v.* [*o-blee-zheh*] oblige
obscurité *f.* [*op-skü-ree-teh*] obscurity, darkness

observation *f.* [*op-ser-vah-syõ*] observation
observer *v.* [*op-ser-veh*] observe
obstacle *m.* [*op-stahkl*] obstacle
obtenir *v. irreg.* [*op-tuh-neer*] obtain, get
occasion *f.* [*o-kah-syõ*] occasion, opportunity; bargain
   d'occasion [*do-kah-syõ*] second-hand, used
occidental, -aux [*ok-see-dã-tahl, ok-see-dã-toh*] western
occupé [*o-kü-peh*] busy, occupied
occuper *v.* [*o-kü-peh*] occupy
   s'occuper (de) [*so-kü-peh (duh)*] take care of, handle
océan *m.* [*o-seh-ã*] ocean
octobre *m.* [*ok-tobr*] October
oculiste *m.* [*o-kü-leest*] eye doctor
odeur *f.* [*o-duhr*] odor, smell
ouvre-boîte *m.* [*oo-vruh-bwaht*] can opener
oeil *m.* **yeux** *pl.* [*uhy, yuh*] eye
   coup *m.* **d'oeil** [*koo-duhy*] glance
   jeter *v.* **un coup d'oeil** [*zh(uh)-teh ē koo duhy*] glance
oeuf, oeufs *m.* [*uhf, uh*] egg
   oeuf à la coque [*uh-fah lah kok*] soft boiled egg
   oeufs brouillés [*uh broo-yeh*] scrambled eggs
   oeuf dur [*uhf düür*] hard boiled egg
   oeuf au plat [*uh-foh plah*] fried egg
oeuvre *f.* [*uhvr*] work
   oeuvre d'art *f.* [*uh-vruh dahr*] work of art
offenser *v.* [*o-fã-seh*] offend
offensif, -ive [*o-fã-seef, o-fã-seev*] offensive
office *m.* [*o-fees*] service
officiel, -elle [*o-fee-syel*] official
officier *m.* [*o-fee-syeh*] officer
offre *f.* [*ofr*] offer, supply, bid
offrir *v.* [*o-freer*] offer
oignon *m.* [*o-nyõ*] onion
oiseau, -eaux *m.* [*wah-zoh*] bird
olive *f.* [*o-leev*] olive
   huile *f.* **d'olive** [*weel do-leev*] olive oil
ombragé [*õ-brah-zheh*] shady
ombre *f.* [*õbr*] shade, shadow

omelette *f.* [*om-let*] omelet
omettre *v. irreg.* [*o-metr*] omit
omission *f.* [*o-mee-syõ*] omission
omnibus *m.* [*om-nee-büs*] local bus
on *impers. pron.* [*õ*] one, they, people
oncle *m.* [*õkl*] uncle
ondes courtes *f. pl.* [*õd koort*] short wave
ongle *m.* [*õgl*] nail
ont *3d pers. pl. pres. tense of* AVOIR [*õ*] have
onze [*õz*] eleven
opéra *m.* [*o-peh-rah*] opera
opération *f.* [*o-peh-rah-syõ*] operation
opérer *v.* [*o-peh-reh*] operate
opinion *f.* [*o-pee-nyõ*] opinion
opposé [*o-poh-zeh*] opposite
s'opposer à *v.* [*so-poh-zeh ah*] oppose, be opposed to
opposition *f.* [*o-poh-zee-syõ*] opposition
or *conj.* [*or*] now
or *m.* [*or*] gold
   d'or [*dor*] golden
orage *m.* [*o-rahzh*] storm
oral, -aux [*o-rahl, o-roh*] oral
orange *f.* [*o-rãzh*] orange
orchestre *m.* [*or-kestr*] orchestra, band
orchidée *f.* [*or-kee-deh*] orchid
ordinaire [*or-dee-ner*] ordinary, common
ordonnance *f.* [*or-do-nãs*] prescription
ordonné [*or-do-neh*] orderly
ordre *m.* [*ordr*] order, command
ordures *f. pl.* [*or-dür*] garbage
oreille *f.* [*o-rey*] ear
oreiller *m.* [*o-reh-yeh*] pillow
organe *m.* [*or-gahn*] organ
organisation *f.* [*or-gah-nee-zah-syõ*] organization
organiser *v.* [*or-gah-nee-zeh*] organize
orgue *m.*, **orgues** *f. pl.* [*org*] organ [music]
orgueil *m.* [*or-guhy*] pride
orgueilleux, -euse [*or-guh-yuh, or-guh-yuhz*] proud

Orient *m.* [*or-yã*] East
  Extrême Orient [*ek-strem or-yã*] Far East
  Moyen Orient [*mwah-yē-nor-yã*] Middle East
  Proche Orient [*pro-shor-yã*] Near East
oriental, -aux [*or-yã-tahl, or-yã-toh*] oriental, eastern
original, -aux [*o-ree-zhee-nahl, o-ree-zhee-noh*] original
origine *f.* [*o-ree-zheen*] origin
  à l'origine [*ah lo-ree-zheen*] originally
originel, -elle [*o-ree-zhee-nel*] original
ornement *m.* [*or-nuh-mã*] ornament
ornière *f.* [*or-nyer*] rut
orphelin *m., f.* [*or-fe-lē*] orphan
orteil *m.* [*or-tey*] toe
orthographe *f.* [*or-to-grahf*] spelling
os *m.* [*os;* pl.: *o*] bone
oser *v.* [*oh-zeh*] dare
otage *m.* [*o-tahzh*] hostage
ôter *v.* [*oh-teh*] remove
ou [*oo*] or
  ou . . . ou [*oo . . . oo*] either . . . or
  où [*oo*] where
oublier *v.* [*oo-blee-eh*] forget
ouest *m.* [*west*] west
oui [*wee*] yes
ours *m.* [*oors*] bear
outil *m.* [*oo-tee*] tool, implement
outre-mer [*oo-truh-mer*] overseas
ouvert [*oo-ver(t)*] open
ouverture *f.* [*oo-ver-tür*] opening
ouvrage *m.* [*oo-vrahzh*] work
ouvreuse *f.* [*oo-vruhz*] usher
ouvrier, -ière [*oo-vree-eh, oo-vree-er*] worker
ouvrir *v. irreg.* [*oo-vreer*] open; turn on [water]
oxygène *m.* [*ok-see-zhen*] oxygen

P

page *f.* [*pahzh*] page
paiement *m.* [*pe-mã*] payment
paille *f.* [*pahy*] straw
pain *m.* [*pẽ*] bread
   pain grillé [*pẽ gree-yeh*] toast
pair *adj.* [*per*] even
paire *f.* [*per*] pair
paisible [*peh-zeebl*] peaceful
paix *f.* [*pe*] peace
palais *m.* [*pah-le*] palace
pâle [*pahl*] pale
pâlir *v.* [*pah-leer*] grow pale
palmier *m.* [*pahl-myeh*] palm
palourde *f.* [*pah-loord*] clam
pamplemousse *f.* [*pã-pluh-moos*] grapefruit
pancarte *f.* [*pã-kahrt*] sign
panier *m.* [*pah-nyeh*] basket
panique *f.* [*pah-neek*] panic
panne *f.* [*pahn*] breakdown
  en panne [*ã pahn*] having [car] trouble
  en panne d'essence [*ã pahn deh-sãs*] out of gas
pansement *m.* [*pãs-mã*] bandage
pantalon *m.* [*pã-tah-lõ*] trousers, pants, slacks
pantoufle *f.* [*pã-toofl*] slipper
pape *m.* [*pahp*] Pope
papeterie *f.* [*pah-peh-tree*] stationer's
papier *m.* [*pah-pyeh*] paper
  papier hygénique [*pah-pyeh-ee-zheh-neek*] toilet paper
  papier peint [*pah-pyeh pẽ*] wallpaper
  papier à lettres [*pah-pyeh ah letr*] writing paper, stationery
papillon *m.* [*pah-pee-yõ*] butterfly
paquebot *m.* [*pahk-boh*] steamship

Pâques *m. pl.* [*pahk*] Easter
paquet *m.* [*pah-ke*] package, pack
par [*pahr*] through, by
  par-ci par-là [*pahr-see pahr-lah*] here and there
  par hasard [*pahr ah-zahr*] by chance
paradis *m.* [*pah-rah-dee*] paradise
paragraphe *m.* [*pah-rah-grahf*] paragraph
paraître *v. irreg.* [*pah-retr*] appear, seem
  il paraît [*eel pah-re*] it seems
parallèle [*pah-rah-lel*] parallel
paralyser *v.* [*pah-rah-lee-zeh*] paralyze
parapluie *m.* [*pah-rah-plwee*] umbrella
parc *m.* [*pahrk*] park
parce que [*pahrs kuh*] because
parcourir *v. irreg.* [*pahr-koo-reer*] travel through; look
  through
parcours *m.* [*pahr-koor*] distance covered; route
pardessus *m.* [*pahr-duh-sü*] overcoat
par-dessus [*pahrd-sü*] over
pardon *m.* [*pahr-dō*] pardon
pardonner *v.* [*pahr-do-neh*] forgive, pardon
  Pardon! [*pahr-dō*] Excuse me!
pare-brise *m.* [*pahr-breez*] windshield
pare-choc *m.* [*pahr-shok*] bumper
pareil, -eille [*pah-rey*] alike, like
parent *m.* [*pah-rã*] relative
parenté *f.* [*pah-rã-teh*] relationship, kindred
paresse *f.* [*pah-res*] laziness
paresseux, -euse [*pah-re-suh, pah-re-suhz*] lazy
parfait [*pahr-fe(t)*] perfect
parfois [*pahr-fwah*] sometimes
parfum *m.* [*pahr-fẽ*] perfume; flavor
pari *m.* [*pah-ree*] bet
parier *v.* [*pahr-yeh*] bet
parlement *m.* [*pahr-luh-mã*] parliament
parler *v.* [*pahr-leh*] talk, speak
  Parlez-vous français? [*pahr-leh-voo frã-se*] Do you speak
  French?

parmi [*pahr-mee*] among
paroisse *f.* [*pahr-wahs*] parish
parole *f.* [*pah-rol*] (spoken) word, remark, promise
parrain *m.* [*pah-rē*] godfather
part *f.* [*pahr*] part, share
  à part [*ah pahr*] apart, except for, aside
  nulle part [*nül pahr*] nowhere
  quelque part [*kel-kuh pahr*] somewhere
  d'autre part [*doh-truh pahr*] moreover
  d'une part . . . d'autre part [*dün pahr . . . doh-truh pahr*]
    on the one hand . . . on the other hand
  de la part de [*dlah pahr duh*] on behalf of, from, sent by
  faire *v.* **part** [*fer pahr*] announce
  faire-part *m.* [*fer-pahr*] announcement
partager *v.* [*pahr-tah-zheh*] share, divide
parti *m.* [*pahr-tee*] party
participe *m.* [*pahr-tee-seep*] participle
participer *v.* [*pahr-tee-see-peh*] participate
particulier, -iere [*pahr-tee-kü-lyeh, pahr-tee-kü-lyer*]
    particular, individual
partie *f.* [*pahr-tee*] part
  en partie [*ã pahr-tee*] partly
partir (de) *v. irreg.* [*pahr-teer (duh)*] leave, depart
  à partir de . . . [*ah pahr-teer duh*] from . . . on
  partir en courant [*pahr-teer ã koo-rã*] run away
  Il est temps de partir [*ee-le tãd pahr-teer*] It's time to
    be going
partout [*pahr-too*] everywhere
  partout où [*pahr-too oo*] wherever
parvenir *v. irreg.* [*pahr-vuh-neer*] reach, succeed
pas [*pah*] not
  pas du tout [*pah dü too*] not at all
pas *m.* [*pah*] step, pace
  faire *v.* **un (des) pas** [*fer ē (deh) pah*] step, take a step
passage *m.* [*pah-sahzh*] passage
  passage à niveau [*pah-sah-zhah nee-voh*] railroad crossing
passager, -ère *adj.* [*pah-sah-zheh, pah-sah-zher*] passing,
    fleeting, momentary

passager, -ère n. [*pah-sah-zheh, pah-sah-zher*] passenger
passant, -te [*pah-sã(t)*] passer-by
passé m. [*pah-seh*] past
passeport m. [*pahs-por*] passport
passer v. [*pah-seh*] pass; spend [time]
  se passer de [*spah-seh duh*] do without
passerelle f. [*pahs-rel*] bridge; gangplank
passif, -ive [*pah-seef, pah-seev*] passive
passion f. [*pah-syõ*] passion
passionné [*pah-syo-neh*] passionate
pastèque f. [*pahs-tek*] watermelon
pasteur m. [*pahs-tuhr*] minister
pâte f. [*paht*] dough, pasta
pâté m. [*pah-teh*] pâté
patience f. [*pah-syãs*] patience
patient [*pah-syã(t)*] patient
patin m. [*pah-tẽ*] skate
  patins à glace [*pah-tẽ ah glahs*] ice skates
  patins à roulettes [*pah-tẽ ah roo-let*] roller skates
patiner v. [*pah-tee-neh*] skate
patinoire f. [*pah-tee-nwahr*] skating rink
patisserie f. [*pah-tees-ree*] pastry, pastry shop
patrie f. [*pah-tree*] native country
patriotique [*pah-tree-o-teek*] patriotic
patron m. [*pah-trõ*] pattern [for sewing]; boss, employer
patte f. [*paht*] paw
paupière f. [*poh-pyer*] eyelid
pause f. [*pohz*] pause
pauvre [*pohvr*] poor
pauvreté f. [*poh-vruh-teh*] poverty
payer v. [*peh-yeh*] pay
  C'est moi qui paie [*se mwah kee peh*] It's my treat
pays m. [*peh-ee*] country, nation
paysage m. [*peh-ee-zahzh*] landscape
péage m. [*peh-ahzh*] toll
peau, peaux f. [*poh*] skin
pêche f. [*pesh*] peach; fishing
péché m. [*peh-sheh*] sin

pêcher *v.* [*peh-sheh*] fish
pécher *v.* [*peh-sheh*] sin
pêcheur *m.* [*peh-shuhr*] fisherman
pédale *f.* [*peh-dahl*] pedal
peigne *m.* [*peñ*] comb
peigner *v.* [*pe-nyeh*] comb
peindre *v. irreg.* [*pēdr*] paint
peine *f.* [*pen*] penalty, suffering
  à peine [*ah pen*] hardly
peintre *m.* [*pētr*] painter
peinture *f.* [*pē-tür*] painting, paint
  peinture à l'huile [*pē-tur ah lweel*] oil painting
pelle *f.* [*pel*] shovel
pellicule *f.* [*peh-lee-kül*] film
pelouse *f.* [*p(uh)-looz*] lawn
pelure *f.* [*p(uh)-lür*] peel
pencher *v.* [*pā-sheh*] lean
  se pencher [*spā-sheh*] lean over
pendant [*pā-dā*] during
  pendant que [*pā-dā k(uh)*] while
pendre *v.* [*pādr*] hang
pendule *f.* [*pā-dül*] clock
pénétration *f.* [*peh-neh-trah-syō*] penetration, insight
pénible [*peh-neebl*] hard
péniche *f.* [*peh-neesh*] barge
pensée *f.* [*pā-seh*] thought
penser *v.* [*pā-seh*] think
  penser à [*pā-seh ah*] think of, about; reflect on; remember
  penser de [*pā-seh duh*] think about, have an opinion on
pension *f.* [*pā-syō*] boarding house
pensionnaire *m., f.* [*pā-syo-ner*] boarder
pensionnat *m.* [*pā-syo-nah*] boarding school
pente *f.* [*pāt*] slope
percer *v.* [*per-seh*] break through
perche *f.* [*persh*] pole
perdre *v.* [*perdr*] lose
perdu [*per-dü*] lost
père *m.* [*per*] father

perfection *f.* [*per-fek-syō*] perfection
période *f.* [*pehr-yod*] period
périr *v.* [*peh-reer*] perish
perle *f.* [*perl*] pearl
permanent [*per-mah-nã(t)*] permanent
permanente *f.* [*per-mah-nãt*] permanent (wave)
permettre *v. irreg.* [*per-metr*] allow, let, permit
　permettre à ... de faire ... [*per-me-trah ... duh fer ...*]
　　allow [someone] to do [something]
permis *m.* [*per-mee*] license, permit
　permis de conduire [*per-meed kō-dweer*] driver's license
permission *f.* [*per-mee-syō*] permission; leave
perruque *f.* [*peh-rük*] wig
persil *m.* [*per-see*] parsley
persister *v.* [*per-sees-teh*] persist
personalité *f.* [*per-so-nah-lee-teh*] personality
personnage *m.* [*per-so-nahzh*] person
personne *pron.* [*per-son*] nobody, no one; anybody, anyone
personne *f.* [*per-son*] person
personnel, -elle [*per-so-nel*] personal
personnel *m.* [*per-so-nel*] personnel
personnellement [*per-so-nel-mã*] personally
persuader *v.* [*per-swah-deh*] persuade
perte *f.* [*pert*] loss
pertinent [*per-tee-nã(t)*] relevant
peser *v.* [*puh-zeh*] weigh
pessimiste *adj.* [*peh-see-meest*] pessimistic
pessimiste *m., f.* [*peh-see-meest*] pessimist
petit [*p(uh)-tee(t)*] little, small
　petite fille *f.* [*p(uh)-teet feey*] granddaughter
　petits-enfants *m. pl.* [*p(uh)-tee-zã-fã*] grandchildren
　petit fils *m.* [*p(uh)-tee fees*] grandson
　petit à petit [*ptee-tah ptee*] little by little
pétition *f.* [*peh-tee-syō*] petition
pétrole *m.* [*peh-trol*] oil, petroleum
peu [*puh*] little, few
　un peu [*ē puh*] a little, a few
　peu à peu [*puh ah puh*] little by little

peuple *m.* [*puhpl*] people, nation; lower classes
peur *f.* [*puhr*] fear
   avoir *v.* **peur** [*ah-vwahr puhr*] be afraid
   faire *v.* **peur à** [*fer puhr ah*] frighten
peureux, -euse [*puh-ruh(z)*] fearful
peut-être [*puh-tetr*] maybe, perhaps
phare *m.* [*fahr*] lighthouse; headlight
pharmacie *f.* [*fahr-mah-see*] drugstore, pharmacy
philosophe *m.* [*fee-lo-sof*] philosopher
philosophie *f.* [*fee-lo-so-fee*] philosophy
phoque *m.* [*fok*] seal
photo *f.* [*fo-to*] photo, photograph
photographe *m.* [*fo-to-grahf*] photographer
photographier *v.* [*fo-to-gra-fyeh*] photograph
phrase *f.* [*frahz*] sentence
physique [*fee-zeek*] physical
pianiste *m., f.* [*pyah-neest*] pianist
piano *m.* [*pyah-noh*] piano
pic *m.* [*peek*] peak
pichet *m.* [*pee-she*] pitcher
pièce *f.* [*pyes*] coin; play [theatre]; patch; room
   pièces de rechange [*pyes duhr-shãzh*] spare parts
pied *m.* [*pyeh*] foot
   pieds nus [*pyeh nü*] barefoot
   à pied [*ah pyeh*] on foot
   coup *m.* **de pied** [*kood pyeh*] kick
piège *m.* [*pyezh*] trap
pierre *f.* [*pyer*] stone
piété *f.* [*pyeh-teh*] piety
piéton *m.* [*pyeh-tõ*] pedestrian
pieux, pieuse [*pyuh, pyuhz*] pious
pigeon *m.* [*pee-zhõ*] pigeon
pile *f.* [*peel*] pile, heap; battery
pilier *m.* [*peel-yeh*] pillar
pillule *f.* [*peel-lül*] pill
pilote *m.* [*pee-lot*] pilot
pin *m.* [*pẽ*] pine
pinceau, -aux *m.* [*pẽ-soh*] brush

pincer *v.* [*pē-seh*] pinch
pioche *f.* [*pyosh*] pick
pipe *f.* [*peep*] pipe
piquer *v.* [*pee-keh*] sting; stitch
piqûre *f.* [*pee-kür*] insect bite; injection, shot
pire [*peer*] worse
  le pire [*luh peer*] worst
pis [*pee*] worse
piscine *f.* [*pee-seen*] swimming pool
piste *f.* [*peest*] track
  piste d'atterrissage [*pees-tuh dah-teh-ree-sahzh*] runway
pistolet *m.* [*pees-to-le*] pistol
pitié *f.* [*pee-tyeh*] pity
  avoir *v.* **pitié de** [*ah-vwahr pee-tyeh duh*] pity
pittoresque [*pee-to-resk*] picturesque
placard *m.* [*plah-kahr*] cupboard, closet
place *f.* [*plahs*] place; public square
  à la place [*ah lah plahs*] instead
  de la place [*duh lah plahs*] room
placer *v.* [*plah-seh*] place; invest
plafond *m.* [*plah-fõ*] ceiling
plage *f.* [*plahzh*] beach
plaie *f.* [*ple*] wound, sore
plaindre *v. irreg.* [*plēdr*] pity, be sorry for
  se plaindre (de) *v. irreg.* [*s(uh) plēdr (duh)*] complain
    (of, about)
plaine *f.* [*plen*] plain
plaire à *v. irreg.* [*pler ah*] please
  S'il vous plaît [*seel voo ple*] Please
plaisanter *v.* [*ple-zã-teh*] joke
plaisanterie *f.* [*ple-zã-tree*] joke
plaisir *m.* [*ple-zeer*] pleasure
  avec plaisir [*ah-vek ple-zeer*] with pleasure
plan *m.* [*plã*] plan; city map
planche *f.* [*plãsh*] board
plancher *m.* [*plã-sheh*] floor
planète *f.* [*plah-net*] planet
plante *f.* [*plãt*] plant

planter *v.* [*plã-teh*] plant
plastique [*plahs-teek*] plastic
plat [*plah*] flat
plat *m.* [*plah*] dish
plateau, -eaux *m.* [*plah-toh*] tray
plâtre *m.* [*plahtr*] plaster, plaster cast
plein [*plē, plen*] full
  Le plein normal [*luh plē nor-mahl*] Fill up with regular
pleurer *v.* [*pluh-reh*] cry
pleuvoir *v. irreg.* [*pluh-vwahr*] rain
  Il pleut [*eel pluh*] It's raining
pli *m.* [*plee*] fold, wrinkle
plier *v.* [*plee-yeh*] bend, fold
plomb *m.* [*plõ*] lead
plombage *m.* [*plõ-bahzh*] filling
plombier *m.* [*plõ-byeh*] plumber
plonger *v.* [*plõ-zheh*] dive
pluie *f.* [*plwee*] rain
plume *f.* [*plüm*] feather
plupart [*plü-pahr*] most, majority
  la plupart du temps [*lah plü-pahr dü tã*] most of the time
pluriel *m.* [*plür-yel*] plural
plus [*plü(s)*] more, plus
  le plus [*luh plü(s)*] the most
  au plus [*oh plüs*] at the most
  de plus [*duh plüs*] besides, furthermore
  de plus en plus [*duh plü-zã plü*] more and more
  ne . . . plus [*nuh . . . plü*] no longer, no more, not again
  plus . . . plus [*plü . . . plü*] the more . . . the more
plusieurs [*plü-zyuhr*] several
plutôt (que) [*plü-toh (kuh)*] rather (than)
pneu *m.* [*pnuh*] tire
  pneu crevé [*pnuh kruh-veh*] flat tire
poche *f.* [*posh*] pocket
poêle *f.* [*pwahl*] frying pan
poêle *m.* [*pwahl*] stove
poème *m.* [*po-em*] poem
poète *m.* [*po-et*] poet

poids *m.* [*pwah*] weight

poignée *f.* [*pwah-nyeh*] handful; handle

poignet *m.* [*pwah-nye*] wrist

poil *m.* [*pwahl*] hair

poing *m.* [*pwē*] fist

  coup *m.* **de poing** [*kood pwē*] punch, blow

point *m.* [*pwē*] point; stitch

  point final [*pwē fee-nahl*] period

  point d'interrogation [*pwē dē-teh-ro-gah-syō*] question mark

  point de vue [*pwēd vü*] point of view, viewpoint

  point mort [*pwē mor*] neutral [gear]

pointe *f.* [*pwēt*] point

pointu [*pwē-tü*] pointed, sharp

pointure *f.* [*pwē-tür*] size

poire *f.* [*pwahr*] pear

poireau, -eaux *m.* [*pwah-roh*] leek

pois, petits pois *m.* [*pwah, ptee-pwah*] pea, peas

poison *m.* [*pwah-zō*] poison

poisson *m.* [*pwah-sō*] fish

poitrine *f.* [*pwah-treen*] breast, chest

poivre *m.* [*pwahvr*] pepper

pôle *m.* [*pohl*] pole

poli [*po-lee*] polite, courteous

police *f.* [*po-lees*] police

  commissariat *m.* **de police** [*ko-mee-sahr-yahd po-lees*] police station

policier *m.* [*po-lee-syeh*] policeman

polir *v.* [*po-leer*] polish

politesse *f.* [*po-lee-tes*] courtesy

politique *adj.* [*po-lee-teek*] political

politique *f.* [*pol-lee-teek*] policy; politics

  politique extérieure [*po-lee-teek ek-stehr-yuhr*] foreign policy

Pologne *f.* [*po-loñ*] Poland

polonais [*po-lo-ne(z)*] Polish

pommade *f.* [*po-mahd*] cream

pomme *f.* [*pom*] apple

pomme de terre *f.* [*pom duh ter*] potato

pompe *f.* [*pŏp*] pump
pompier *m.* [*pŏ-pyeh*] fireman
ponctuel, -elle [*pŏk-twel*] punctual
pont *m.* [*pŏ*] bridge; deck [of a ship]
population *f.* [*po-pü-lah-syŏ*] population
porc *m.* [*por*] pork
porcelaine *f.* [*por-suh-len*] porcelain, china
porche *m.* [*porsh*] porch
port *m.* [*por*] port, harbor
portail *m.* [*por-tahy*] gate
portatif, -tive [*por-tah-teef, por-tah-teev*] portable
porte *f.* [*port*] door
portée *f.* [*por-teh*] range
portefeuille *m.* [*por-tuh-fuhy*] wallet
porte-monnaie *m.* [*port-mo-ne*] change-purse
porter *v.* [*por-teh*] carry, bear, wear
porteur *m.* [*por-tuhr*] porter
portier *m.* [*por-tyeh*] doorman
portière *f.* [*por-tyer*] car door
portrait *m.* [*por-tre*] portrait
portugais [*por-tü-ghe(z)*] Portuguese
Portugal *m.* [*por-tü-gahl*] Portugal
pose *f.* [*pohz*] pose
poser *v.* [*poh-zeh*] put, place, lay, pose
  poser une question [*poh-zeh ün kes-tyŏ*] ask a question
position *f.* [*po-zee-syŏ*] position
posséder *v.* [*po-seh-deh*] possess, own
possession *f.* [*po-se-syŏ*] possession
possibilité *f.* [*po-see-bee-lee-teh*] possibility
possible [*po-seebl*] possible
poste *f.* [*post*] post office
  poste restante [*post res-tãt*] general delivery
poste *m.* [*post*] position, post, station; receiver, set
  poste à essence [*post ah eh-sãs*] gas station
poster *v.* [*pos-teh*] mail
pot *m.* [*poh*] pot
potage *m.* [*po-tahzh*] soup
pot d'échappement *m.* [*poh deh-shahp-mã*] muffler

pot-de-vin *m.* [*pohd-vē*] bribe
poteau, -eaux *m.* [*po-toh*] post
poterie *f.* [*pot-ree*] pottery
potiron *m.* [*po-tee-rõ*] pumpkin
poubelle *f.* [*poo-bel*] garbage can
pouce *m.* [*poos*] thumb; inch
poudre *f.* [*poodr*] powder
poule *f.* [*pool*] hen
poulet *m.* [*poo-le*] chicken
pouls *m.* [*poo*] pulse
poumon *m.* [*poo-mõ*] lung
poupée *f.* [*poo-peh*] doll
pour [*poor*] for
pourboire *m.* [*poor-bwahr*] tip
pour cent [*poor sã*] percent
pourcentage *m.* [*poor-sã-tahzh*] percentage
pourquoi [*poor-kwah*] why
   pourquoi pas? [*poor-kwah pah*] why not?
pourri [*poo-ree*] rotten
poursuivre *v. irreg.* [*poor-sweevr*] pursue
pourtant [*poor-tã*] however
pourvu que [*poor-vü k(uh)*] provided that
pousser *v.* [*poo-seh*] push; grow
poussière *f.* [*poo-syer*] dust
poussiéreux, -euse [*poo-syeh-ruh, poo-syeh-ruhz*] dusty
poutre *f.* [*pootr*] beam, girder
pouvoir *m.* [*poo-vwahr*] power
pouvoir *v. irreg.* [*poo-vwahr*] be able, can, may
   Il se peut . . . [*eel suh puh*] It may be . . .
   Puis-je partir? [*pweezh pahr-teer*] May I go?
   Je n'y peux rien [*zhnee puh ryē*] I can't do anything
      about it
pratique [*prah-teek*] practical
pratiquement [*prah-teek-mã*] practically
pratiquer *v.* [*prah-tee-keh*] practice
pré *m.* [*preh*] meadow
précaution *f.* [*preh-koh-syõ*] precaution, caution
précédemment [*preh-seh-dah-mã*] formerly

précédent [*preh-seh-dā(t)*] previous
précéder *v.* [*preh-seh-deh*] precede
précieux, -euse [*preh-syuh, preh-syuhz*] precious
précis [*preh-see(z)*] precise
précisément [*preh-see-zeh-mā*] precisely
préciser *v.* [*preh-see-zeh*] specify
préférable [*preh-feh-rahbl*] preferable
préféré [*preh-feh-reh*] favorite, preferred
préférence *f.* [*preh-feh-rãs*] preference
préférer *v.* [*preh-feh-reh*] prefer
préfet *m.* [*preh-fe*] perfect
préjugé *m.* [*preh-zhü-zheh*] prejudice
préliminaire [*preh-lee-mee-ner*] preliminary
prématuré [*preh-mah-tü-reh*] premature
premier, -ière [*pruh-myeh, pruh-myer*] first
   premiers secours *m.* [*pruh-myehs-koor*] first aid
prendre *v. irreg.* [*prãdr*] take, pick up
   prendre part à [*prãdr pahr ah*] participate in
prénom *m.* [*preh-nõ*] first name
préparation *f.* [*preh-pah-rah-syõ*] preparation
préparer *v.* [*preh-pah-reh*] prepare
près (de) [*pre d(uh)*] near; close (to)
présence *f.* [*preh-zãs*] presence
présent *adj.* [*preh-zã(t)*] present
présentation *f.* [*preh-zã-tah-syõ*] introduction, presentation
présenter *v.* [*preh-zã-teh*] introduce, present
préserver *v.* [*preh-zer-veh*] preserve
président *m.* [*preh-zee-dã*] president
presque [*presk*] almost, nearly
presqu'île *f.* [*pres-keel*] peninsula
presse *f.* [*pres*] press
pressé [*preh-seh*] in a hurry
presser *v.* [*preh-seh*] press
pressing *m.* [*preh-seeng*] dry-cleaners
pression *f.* [*pre-syõ*] pressure
prestige *m.* [*pres-teezh*] prestige
présumer *v.* [*preh-zü-meh*] presume
prêt *m.* [*pre*] loan

prêt [*pre(t)*] ready
prêt-à-porter *m.* [*pre-tah-por-teh*] ready-to-wear
prétendre *v.* [*preh-tãdr*] pretend
prétentieux, -euse [*preh-tã-syuh, preh-tã-syuhz*] pretentious
prêter *v.* [*pre-teh*] lend
prêtre *m.* [*pretr*] priest
preuve *f.* [*pruhv*] proof, evidence
prévenir *v. irreg.* [*prev-neer*] warn, notify [in advance]
prévoir *v. irreg.* [*preh-vwahr*] forsee
prier *v.* [*pree-yeh*] pray
prière *f.* [*pree-yer*] prayer
primitif, -tive [*pree-mee-teef, pree-mee-teev*] primitive
principal, -aux [*prẽ-see-pahl, prẽ-see-poh*] principal, main
principalement [*prẽ-see-pahl-mã*] principally, mainly
principe *m.* [*prẽ-seep*] principle
printemps *m.* [*prẽ-tã*] spring
prise *f.* [*preez*] plug; outlet
prison *f.* [*pree-zõ*] prison, jail
prisonnier, -ière [*pree-zo-nyeh, pree-zo-nyer*] prisoner
privé [*pree-veh*] private
priver *v.* [*pree-veh*] deprive
privilège *m.* [*pree-vee-lezh*] privilege
prix *m.* [*pree*] price, prize
probable [*pro-bahbl*] probable, likely
probablement [*pro-bah-bluh-mã*] probably
problème *m.* [*pro-blem*] problem
procédé *m.* [*pro-seh-deh*] method
procédure *f.* [*pro-seh-dür*] procedure
procès *m.* [*pro-se*] case, suit
prochain [*pro-shẽ, pro-shen*] next
proche [*prosh*] close
procuration *f.* [*pro-kü-rah-syõ*] proxy
procurer *v.* [*pro-kü-reh*] obtain
production *f.* [*pro-dük-syõ*] production
produire *v. irreg.* [*pro-dweer*] produce
produit *m.* [*pro-dwee*] product
professeur *m.*, **femme professeur** *f.* [*pro-fe-suhr, fahm pro-fe-suhr*] professor, teacher

profession *f.* [*pro-fe-syõ*] profession
professionnel, -elle [*pro-fe-syo-nel*] professional, vocational
profit *m.* [*pro-fee*] profit
profiter *v.* [*pro-fee-teh*] profit
  profiter de [*pro-fee-teh duh*] take advantage of
profond [*pro-fõ(d)*] deep
  peu profond [*puh pro-fõ(d)*] shallow
profondeur *f.* [*pro-fõ-duhr*] depth
programme *m.* [*pro-grahm*] program
progrès *m.* [*pro-gre*] progress
progresser *v.* [*pro-gre-seh*] progress
progressif, -ive [*pro-gre-seef, pro-gre-seev*] progressive
projet *m.* [*pro-zhe*] project
prolonger *v.* [*pro-lõ-zheh*] prolong
promenade *f.* [*prom-nahd*] outing
  promenade à pied [*prom-nahd ah pyeh*] walk
  promenade à bicyclette [*prom-nahd ah bee-see-klet*]
    bike ride
  promenade à cheval [*prom-nahd ah shvahl*] horseback ride
  promenade en voiture [*prom-nahd ã vwah-tür*] ride, drive
se promener *v.* [*sprom-neh*] go for a walk, ride
promesse *f.* [*pro-mes*] promise
promettre *v. irreg.* [*pro-metr*] promise
promotion *f.* [*pro-moh-syõ*] promotion
prompt [*prõ(t)*] prompt
pronom *m.* [*pro-nõ*] pronoun
prononcer *v.* [*pro-nõ-seh*] pronounce
prononciation *f.* [*pro-nõ-syah-syõ*] pronunciation
propagande *f.* [*pro-pah-gãd*] propaganda
proportion *f.* [*pro-por-syõ*] proportion
à propos [*ah pro-poh*] by the way
proposer *v.* [*pro-poh-zeh*] propose
proposition *f.* [*pro-poh-zee-syõ*] proposal, proposition
propre [*propr*] clean; one's own
propreté *f.* [*pro-pruh-teh*] cleanliness
propriétaire *m., f.* [*pro-pree-yeh-ter*] landlord, landlady,
  owner
propriété *f.* [*pro-pree-yeh-teh*] property, estate

prospère [*pros-per*] prosperous
prospérité *f.* [*pros-peh-ree-teh*] prosperity
protection *f.* [*pro-tek-syõ*] protection
protéger *v.* [*pro-teh-zheh*] protect, guard
protestant [*pro-tes-tã(t)*] Protestant
protester *v.* [*pro-tes-teh*] protest
prouver *v.* [*proo-veh*] prove
provenir *v. irreg.* [*prov-neer*] come from
proverbe *m.* [*pro-verb*] proverb
province *f.* [*pro-vẽs*] province
provincial, -aux [*pro-vẽ-syahl, pro-vẽ-syoh*] provincial
provisions *f. pl.* [*pro-vee-zyõ*] provisions
provoquer *v.* [*pro-vo-keh*] provoke
prudence *f.* [*prü-dãs*] prudence
prune *f.* [*prün*] plum
pruneau, -eaux *m.* [*prü-noh*] prune
psychanalyse *f.* [*psee-kah-nah-leez*] psychoanalysis
psychiatre *m.* [*psee-kyahtr*] psychiatrist
psychologique [*psee-ko-lo-zheek*] psychological
public *m.* [*püb-leek*] public, audience
public, -lique [*püb-leek*] public
publication *f.* [*püb-lee-kah-syõ*] publication
publicité *f.* [*püb-lee-see-teh*] publicity, advertising
publier *v.* [*püb-lee-yeh*] publish
puce *f.* [*püs*] flea
puis [*pwee*] then
puisque [*pweesk*] since
puissant [*pwee-sã(t)*] powerful
puits *m.* [*pwee*] well
pull-over *m.* [*pül-o-vuhr*] pullover
punaise *f.* [*pü-nez*] bedbug; thumb tack
punir *v.* [*pü-neer*] punish
punition *f.* [*pü-nee-syõ*] punishment
pur [*pür*] pure
purée *f.* **de pommes de terre** [*pü-rehd pom duh ter*] mashed
   potatoes
pyjama *m.* [*pee-zhah-mah*] pajamas
pyramide *f.* [*pee-rah-meed*] pyramid

Q

qu': que [*k(uh)*] that
quai *m.* [*keh*] dock, pier
qualité *f.* [*kah-lee-teh*] quality
quand [*kã*] when
    quand même [*kã mem*] all the same
quant à [*kã-tah*] as for
quantité *f.* [*kã-tee-teh*] quantity, amount
quarante [*kah-rãt*] forty
quart *m.* [*kahr*] quarter
    quart d'heure [*kahr duhr*] quarter hour
quartier *m.* [*kar-tyeh*] neighborhood
    quartier général [*kar-tyeh zheh-neh-rahl*] headquarters
quatorze [*kah-torz*] fourteen
quatre [*kahtr*] four
quatre-vingt-dix [*kah-truh-vē-dees*] ninety
quatre-vingts [*kah-truh-vē*] eighty
que *conj.* [*k(uh)*] that; than
    J'espère que vous viendrez [*zhes-per kuh voo vyē-dreh*]
        I hope (that) you will come
    Il est plus grand que son frère [*ee-le plü grãk sõ frer*]
        He is taller than his brother
que *interr. pron.* [*k(uh)*] what
que *rel. pron.* [*k(uh)*] whom, which, that
    l'arbre que j'ai vu [*lahrbr kuh zheh vü*] the tree (which,
        that) I saw
    l'homme que j'ai vu [*lom kuh zheh vü*] the man (whom,
        that) I saw
quel, quelle *interr. adj.* [*kel*] which, what
    Quelle auto prenez-vous? [*ke-loh-toh pruh-neh voo*]
        Which car are you taking?
    Quelle est la date de . . . [*ke-le lah daht duh*] What is the
        date of . . .

Quel âge a-t-il? [*ke-lahzh ah-teel*] How old is he?

quelconque [*kel-kõk*] whatever

quelque, quelques [*kel-k(uh)*] some, any

  quelque peu [*kel-kuh puh*] somewhat

quelque chose [*kel-kuh shohz*] something, anything

quelquefois [*kel-kuh fwah*] sometimes

quelque part [*kel-kuh pahr*] somewhere

  quelque part ailleurs [*kel-kuh pahr ah-yuhr*] somewhere else

quelqu'un [*kel-kẽ*] someone, anyone

querelle f. [*kuh-rel*] quarrel

qu'est-ce que *interr. pron.* [*kes-k(uh)*] what [as object of verb]

  Qu'est-ce que c'est? [*kes kuh se*] What is this?, What is it?

  Qu'est-ce que c'est que cela? [*kes kuh sek slah*] What's that?

qu'est-ce qui *interr. pron.* [*kes kee*] what [as subject]

question f. [*kes-tyõ*] question

questionnaire m. [*kes-tyo-ner*] questionnaire

questionner v. [*kes-tyo-neh*] question

quête f. [*ket*] search; collection

queue f. [*kuh*] tail; line, file, queue

  faire v. **la queue** [*fer lah kuh*] stand in line

qui *interr. pron.* [*kee*] who, whom

  qui est-ce qui [*kee es kee*] who

  qui est-ce que [*kee es k(uh)*] whom

qui *rel. pron.* [*kee*] who, that, whom, which

quiconque [*kee-kõk*] whoever

quinine f. [*kee-neen*] quinine

quinze [*kẽz*] fifteen

quittance f. [*kee-tãs*] receipt

quitter v. [*kee-teh*] leave

  Ne quittez pas [*nuh kee-teh pah*] Hold the line

quoi [*kwah*] what

  A quoi pensez-vous? [*ah kwah pã-seh voo*] What are you thinking about?

  Il n'y a pas de quoi [*eel nee yah pahd kwah*] Don't mention it

quoi qui, quoi que [*kwah kee, kwah k(uh)*] whatever

  quoi qu'on dise [*kwah kõ deez*] whatever they say

quoique [*kwahk*] although
quotidien, -enne [*ko-tee-dyē, ko-tee-dyen*] daily

R

rabbin *m.* [*rah-bē*] rabbi
raccomoder *v.* [*rah-ko-mo-deh*] mend, darn
raccourcir *v.* [*rah-koor-seer*] shorten
raccrocher *v.* [*rah-kro-sheh*] hang up
race *f.* [*rahs*] race
racheter *v.* [*rahsh-teh*] redeem
racine *f.* [*rah-seen*] root
raconter *v.* [*rah-kõ-teh*] tell
radiateur *m.* [*rah-dyah-tuhr*] radiator
radical, -aux [*rah-dee-kahl, rah-dee-koh*] radical
radio *f.* [*rah-dyoh*] radio
radio(graphie) *f.* [*rah-dyoh-(grah-fee)*] x-ray
radis *m.* [*rah-dee*] radish
rafraîchir *v.* [*rah-freh-sheer*] cool, refresh
rafraîchissant [*rah-freh-shee-sã(t)*] refreshing
rafraîchissement *m.* [*rah-freh-shees-mã*] refreshment
rage *f.* [*rahzh*] rage; rabies
ragoût *m.* [*rah-goo*] stew
raide [*red*] steep; stiff
raie *f.* [*re*] part
raisin *m.* [*re-zē*] grapes
  raisin sec [*re-zē sek*] raisin
raison *f.* [*re-zõ*] reason
  avoir *v.* **raison** [*ah-vwahr re-zõ*] be right
raisonnable [*re-zo-nahbl*] reasonable, sensible
ralentir, se ralentir *v.* [*rah-lã-teer, s(uh) rah-lã-teer*] slow
    down
  Ralentissez! [*rah-lã-tee-seh*] Slow down!
ramasser *v.* [*rah-mah-seh*] gather (up, together)
rame *f.* [*rahm*] oar

ramener v. [*rahm-neh*] bring back
rancune f. [*rã-kün*] grudge, bitterness
rang m. [*rã*] row
ranger v. [*rã-zheh*] put in order, clean up
rapide [*rah-peed*] fast, rapid, quick
rapide m. [*rah-peed*] express (train)
rapidement [*rah-peed-mã*] rapidly
rappeler v. [*rah-pleh*] remind, recall
  se rappeler v. [*srah-pleh*] remember
rapport m. [*rah-por*] profit; relation; report
rapprochement m. [*rah-prosh-mã*] bringing together
rapprocher v. [*rah-pro-sheh*] bring closer
raquette f. [*rah-ket*] racket
rare [*rahr*] rare, scarce
rarement [*rahr-mã*] rarely, seldom
se raser v. [*srah-zeh*] shave
rasoir m. [*rah-zwahr*] razor
rassembler v. [*rah-sã-bleh*] assemble
rassurer v. [*rah-sü-reh*] reassure
rat m. [*rah*] rat
raté m. [*rah-teh*] failure
rateau, -eaux m. [*rah-toh*] rake
rater v. [*rah-teh*] miss
rattraper v. [*rah-trah-peh*] catch up with
ravi [*rah-vee*] overjoyed
rayon m. [*re-yõ*] ray; spoke; shelf; department (store)
rayonne f. [*re-yon*] rayon
réaction f. [*reh-ahk-syõ*] reaction
réaliser v. [*reh-ah-lee-zeh*] carry out
réalité f. [*reh-ah-lee-teh*] reality
récemment [*reh-sah-mã*] recently
récent [*reh-sã(t)*] recent
réception f. [*reh-sep-syõ*] party, reception
récession f. [*reh-se-syõ*] recession
recette f. [*ruh-set*] recipe
recevoir v. *irreg.* [*ruh-suh-vwahr*] receive, get; entertain
réchaud m. [*reh-shoh*] hot plate
recherche f. [*r(uh)-shersh*] search, research

rechercher *v.* [*r(uh)-sher-sheh*] look for

récif *m.* [*reh-seef*] reef

récipient *m.* [*reh-see-pyā*] container

réciproque [*reh-see-prok*] mutual

   C'est réciproque [*se reh-see-prok*] It's mutual

récit *m.* [*reh-see*] account

réciter *v.* [*reh-see-teh*] recite

réclamation *f.* [*reh-klah-mah-syō*] complaint, claim

réclame *f.* [*reh-klahm*] advertisement, special offer

réclamer *v.* [*reh-klah-meh*] complain, protest

récolte *f.* [*reh-kolt*] crop, harvest

recommandation *f.* [*r(uh)-ko-mā-dah-syō*] recommendation

recommander *v.* [*r(uh)-ko-mā-deh*] recommend

   lettre *f.* **recommandée** [*letr ruh-ko-mā-deh*] registered letter

recommencer *v.* [*r(uh)-ko-mā-seh*] begin again

récompense *f.* [*reh-kō-pās*] reward

récompenser *v.* [*reh-kō-pā-seh*] reward

reconnaissance *f.* [*r(uh)-ko-ne-sās*] gratitude

reconnaissant [*r(uh)-ko-ne-sā(t)*] grateful, thankful

   Je vous suis très reconnaissant [*zhvoo swee trer-ko-ne-sā*]
     I am much obliged to you

reconnaître *v. irreg.* [*r(uh)-ko-netr*] recognize

record *m.* [*r(uh)-kor*] record

récréation *f.* [*reh-kreh-ah-syō*] recreation; recess [school]

rectangle *m.* [*rek-tāgl*] rectangle

reçu *m.* [*r(uh)-sü*] receipt

recueillir *v. irreg.* [*r(uh)-kuh-yeer*] gather, take in

reculer *v.* [*r(uh)-kü-leh*] move back

rédacteur *m.* [*reh-dahk-tuhr*] editor

redouter *v.* [*r(uh)-doo-teh*] fear

réduction *f.* [*reh-dük-syō*] reduction

réduire *v. irreg.* [*reh-dweer*] reduce

réel, réelle [*reh-el*] real, actual

réellement [*reh-el-mā*] really, actually

référence *f.* [*reh-feh-rās*] reference

réfléchir *v.* [*reh-fleh-sheer*] reflect

refléter *v.* [*r(uh)-fleh-teh*] reflect

réflexe *m.* [*reh-fleks*] reflex

réflexion f. [*reh-flek-syõ*] reflection
réforme f. [*reh-form*] reform
réformer v. [*reh-for-meh*] reform
réfrigérateur m. [*reh-free-zheh-rah-tuhr*] refrigerator
refroidir v. [*r(uh)-frwah-deer*] cool
refuge m. [*r(uh)-füzh*] refuge
réfugié, -ée [*reh-fü-zhyeh*] refugee
refus m. [*r(uh)-fü*] refusal
refuser (de) v. [*r(uh)-fü-zeh (duh)*] refuse, decline (to)
regagner v. [*r(uh)-gah-nyeh*] regain
regard m. [*r(uh)-gahr*] look
regarder v. [*r(uh)-gahr-deh*] look at, watch
régime m. [*reh-zheem*] diet
  suivre v. irreg. **un régime** [*sweev-rē reh-zheem*] be on a diet
régiment m. [*reh-zhee-mã*] regiment
région f. [*reh-zhyõ*] region, area, district
registre m. [*r(uh)-zheestr*] register
règle f. [*regl*] rule; ruler, measure
règlement m. [*re-gluh-mã*] regulation
régler v. [*reh-gleh*] regulate, settle, set
règles f. pl. [*regl*] menstrual period
règne m. [*reñ*] reign
régner v. [*reh-nyeh*] reign
regret m. [*r(uh)-gre*] regret
regretter v. [*r(uh)-greh-teh*] regret
régulier, -ière [*reh-gü-lyeh, reh-gü-lyer*] regular
rein m. [*rē*] kidney [anat.]
  reins m. pl. [*rē*] lower back
reine f. [*ren*] queen
rejeter v. [*ruhzh-teh*] reject
rejoindre v. irreg. [*r(uh)-zhwēdr*] rejoin
relatif à [*r(uh)-lah-teef ah*] pertaining to
relation f. [*r(uh)-lah-syõ*] relation, connection
relativement [*r(uh)-lah-teev-mã*] relatively
relever v. [*ruhl-veh*] pick up; note
religieuse f. [*r(uh)-lee-zhyuhz*] nun, sister
religieux, -euse [*r(uh)-lee-zhyuh, r(uh)-lee-zhyuhz*] religious
religion f. [*r(uh)-lee-zhyõ*] religion

remarquable [r(uh)-mahr-kahbl] remarkable, outstanding

remarque f. [r(uh)-mahrk] remark

remarquer v. [r(uh)-mahr-keh] notice, remark

remboursement m. [rã-boors-mã] refund

rembourser v. [rã-boor-seh] repay

remède m. [r(uh)-med] remedy

remerciements m. pl. [r(uh)-mer-see-mã] thanks

remercier v. [r(uh)-mer-syeh] thank

remettre v. irreg. [r(uh)-metr] put on again; remit; postpone
  se remettre [s(uh) r(uh)-metr] recover

remise f. [r(uh)-meez] reduction, discount

remonter v. [r(uh)-mõ-teh] wind [a watch]; climb back up
  [a hill]

remords m. [r(uh)-mor] remorse

remorquer v. [r(uh)-mor-keh] tow

remorqueur m. [r(uh)-mor-kuhr] tugboat

remplacer v. [rã-plah-seh] replace

remplir v. [rã-pleer] fill

rencontre f. [rã-kõtr] encounter, meeting

rencontrer v. [rã-kõ-treh] meet, encounter

rendement m. [rãd-mã] yield

rendez-vous m. [rã-deh-voo] appointment, date

rendre v. [rãdr] return, give back
  rendre compte de [rãdr kõt duh] report
  se rendre [s(uh) rãdr] surrender
  se rendre compte (de) [s(uh) rãdr kõt (duh)] realize

renforcer v. [rã-for-seh] strengthen

renommée f. [r(uh)-no-meh] fame

renoncer (à) v. [r(uh)-nõ-seh (ah)] renounce

renouveler v. [r(uh)-noo-vleh] renew

renseignement m. [rã-se-nyuh-mã] piece of information

renseigner v. [rã-se-nyeh] inform

rentrée f. [rã-treh] reopening; first day of classes

rentrer v. [rã-treh] return

renverser v. [rã-ver-seh] spill; turn over

renvoyer v. irreg. [rã-vwah-yeh] send back; expel, dismiss
  renvoyer à plus tard [rã-vwah-yeh ah plü tahr] postpone

répandu [reh-pã-dü] widespread

réparation *f.* [*reh-pah-rah-syõ*] repair

réparer *v.* [*reh-pah-reh*] repair, fix

répartition *f.* [*reh-pahr-tee-syõ*] distribution

repas *m.* [*r(uh)-pah*] meal

repasser *v.* [*r(uh)-pah-seh*] iron

répéter *v.* [*reh-peh-teh*] repeat; rehearse

répétition *f.* [*reh-peh-tee-syõ*] repetition; rehearsal
  répétition générale [*reh-peh-tee-syõ zheh-neh-rahl*]
    dress rehearsal

répondre (à) *v.* [*reh-põdr (ah)*] reply, answer

réponse *f.* [*reh-põs*] answer, reply

reporter *v.* [*r(uh)-por-teh*] take back; carry forward

repos *m.* [*r(uh)-poh*] rest

se reposer *v.* [*s(uh) r(uh)-poh-zeh*] rest

reprendre *v. irreg.* [*r(uh)-prãdr*] resume, take back

représentant *m.* [*r(uh)-preh-zã-tã*] representative,
    congressman
  représentant de commerce [*r(uh)-preh-zã-tãd ko-mers*]
    traveling salesman

représentation *f.* [*r(uh)-preh-zã-tah-syõ*] performance
    [theatre]

représenter *v.* [*r(uh)-preh-zã-teh*] represent

repriser *v.* [*r(uh)-pree-zeh*] mend

reproche *f.* [*r(uh)-prosh*] reproach

reprocher *v.* [*r(uh)-pro-sheh*] reproach

reproduction *f.* [*r(uh)-pro-dük-syõ*] reproduction

reproduire *v. irreg.* [*r(uh)-pro-dweer*] reproduce; copy

république *f.* [*reh-püb-leek*] republic

réputation *f.* [*reh-pü-tah-syõ*] reputation

réseau, -eaux *m.* [*reh-zoh*] network

réserve *f.* [*reh-zerv*] reserve, restriction

réservoir *m.* **à essence** [*reh-zer-vwah-rah eh-sãs*] gas tank

résidence *f.* [*reh-zee-dãs*] residence
  résidence universitaire [*reh-zee-dã-sü-nee-ver-see-ter*]
    dormitory

résident, -te [*reh-zee-dã(t)*] resident

résister *v.* [*reh-zees-teh*] resist

résolution *f.* [*reh-zo-lü-syõ*] resolution

résoudre v. irreg. [reh-zoodr] solve
respect m. [res-pe] respect
respectable [res-pek-tahbl] respectable
respecter v. [res-pek-teh] respect
respirer v. [res-pee-reh] breathe
responsabilité f. [res-põ-sah-bee-lee-teh] responsibility, liability
responsable adj. [res-põ-sahbl] responsible
responsable m., f. [res-põ-sahbl] officer; person in charge
ressemblance f. [r(uh)-sã-blãs] resemblance
ressembler v. [r(uh)-sã-bleh] resemble
resserrer v. [r(uh)-seh-reh] tighten
ressort m. [r(uh)-sor] spring
ressource f. [r(uh)-soors] resource
restaurant m. [res-to-rã] restaurant
restaurer v. [res-to-reh] restore
reste m. [rest] remainder; leftover (food)
rester v. [res-teh] remain, stay
résultat m. [reh-zül-tah] result
résumé m. [reh-zü-meh] summary
résumer v. [reh-zü-meh] sum up
retard m. [r(uh)-tahr] delay
  en retard [ãr-tahr] late
retenir v. irreg. [r(uh)-t(uh)-neer] keep, detain; reserve
retirer v. [r(uh)-tee-reh] withdraw
  se retirer [sruh-tee-reh] retire, withdraw
retouche f. [r(uh)-toosh] alteration
retour m. [r(uh)-toor] return
retourner v. [r(uh)-toor-neh] return, go back, turn around, turn over
  se retourner [s(uh) r(uh)-toor-neh] turn around, over
retraite f. [r(uh)-tret] retreat; retirement
  prendre v. **sa retraite** [prãdr sahr-tret] retire
rétrécir v. [reh-treh-seer] shrink
retrouver v. [r(uh)-troo-veh] recover
réunion f. [reh-ü-nyõ] meeting
réunir v. [reh-ü-neer] bring together
réussir v. [reh-ü-seer] succeed

revanche *f.* [*r(uh)-vãsh*] revenge
rêve *m.* [*rev*] dream
réveil *m.* [*reh-vey*] awakening
réveil *m.* [*reh-vey*] alarm clock
réveiller *v.* [*reh-veh-yeh*] wake
  se réveiller [*sreh-veh-yeh*] wake up
révéler *v.* [*reh-veh-leh*] disclose, reveal
revendication *f.* [*r(uh)-vã-dee-kah-syõ*] claim, demand
revenir *v. irreg.* [*ruhv-neer*] come back, come again, return
revenu *m.* [*ruhv-nü*] income
rêver *v.* [*reh-veh*] dream
rêverie *f.* [*rev-ree*] daydream
réviser *v.* [*reh-vee-zeh*] revise
revoir *v. irreg.* [*r(uh)-vwahr*] see again
  au revoir [*ohr-vwahr*] good-bye
révolution *f* [*reh-vo-lü-syõ*] revolution
revolver *m.* [*reh-vol-ver*] revolver
revue *f.* [*r(uh)-vü*] magazine, review
rez-de-chaussée *m.* [*rehd-shoh-seh*] ground floor
rhum *m.* [*rom*] rum
rhumatisme *m.* [*rii-mah-teesm*] rheumatism
rhume *m.* [*rüm*] cold
riche [*reesh*] rich
richesse *f.* [*ree-shes*] wealth
ride *f.* [*reed*] wrinkle
rideau, -eaux *m.* [*ree-doh*] curtain
ridicule [*ree-dee-kül*] ridiculous
ridiculiser *v.* [*ree-dee-kü-lee-zeh*] ridicule
rien [*ryẽ*] nothing, anything
  Ça ne fait rien [*sahn fe ryẽ*] Never mind
rime *f.* [*reem*] rhyme
rinçage *m.* [*rẽ-sahzh*] rinse
rincer *v.* [*rẽ-seh*] rinse
rire *m.* [*reer*] laugh, laughter
rire *v. irreg.* [*reer*] laugh
risque *m.* [*reesk*] risk
rite *m.* [*reet*] rite
rivage *m.* [*ree-vahzh*] shore

rive *f.* [*reev*] bank, shore
rivière *f.* [*ree-vyer*] river
riz *m.* [*ree*] rice
robe *f.* [*rob*] dress
   robe du soir [*rob dü swahr*] evening dress
robinet *m.* [*ro-bee-ne*] faucet
rocher *m.* [*ro-she*] rock
rognon *m.* [*ro-nyō*] kidney [food]
roi *m.* [*rwah*] king
rôle *m* [*rohl*] role
romain [*ro-mē, ro-men*] Roman
roman [*ro-mã, ro-mahn*] Romanesque
roman *m.* [*ro-mã*] novel
romancier, -ière [*ro-mã-syeh, ro-mã-syer*] novelist
romantique [*ro-mã-teek*] romantic
rompre *v. irreg.* [*rōpr*] sever, break (off)
rond [*rō(d)*] round
ronfler *v.* [*rō-fleh*] snore
rose *adj.* [*rohz*] pink
rose *f.* [*rohz*] rose
rosée *f.* [*roh-zeh*] dew
rôti [*roh-tee*] roasted
rôti *m.* [*roh-tee*] roast
rôtir *v.* [*roh-teer*] roast
roue *f.* [*roo*] wheel
   roue de secours [*rood suh-koor*] spare tire
rouge [*roozh*] red
rouge *m.* [*roozh*] rouge
   rouge à levres [*roo-zhah levr*] lipstick
rougeole *f.* [*roo-zhol*] measles
rouille *f.* [*rooy*] rust
rouiller *v.* [*roo-yeh*] rust
rouleau, -eaux *m.* [*roo-loh*] roll, roller
rouler *v.* [*roo-leh*] roll
roulette *f.* [*rou-let*] little wheel, castor
roussir *v.* [*rou-seer*] scorch
route *f.* [*root*] road, highway
routine *f.* [*roo-teen*] routine

roux, rousse [*roo(s)*] red-headed
royal, -aux [*rwah-yahl, rwah-yoh*] royal
royaume *m.* [*rwah-yom*] kingdom
ruban *m.* [*rü-bã*] ribbon
rubéole *f.* [*rü-beh-ol*] rubella, German measles
rubis *m.* [*rü-bee*] ruby
rude [*rüd*] rough
rue *f.* [*rü*] street
ruée *f.* [*rweh*] rush
rugir *v.* [*rü-zheer*] roar
ruine *f.* [*rween*] ruin
ruisseau, -eaux *m.* [*rwee-soh*] stream; gutter
rumeur *f.* [*rü-muhr*] rumor
rural, -aux [*rü-rahl, rü-roh*] rural
russe [*rüs*] Russian
rythme *m.* [*reetm*] rhythm

S

s': **se, si** See SE, SI
sa [*sah*] his, her, its
sable *m.* [*sahbl*] sand
sablonneux, -euse [*sah-blo-nuh, sah-blo-nuhz*] sandy
sabot *m.* [*sah-boh*] wooden shoe
sac *m.* [*sahk*] bag, sack
   sac à main [*sah-kah mē*] purse, handbag
sacré [*sah-kreh*] sacred
sacrifice *m.* [*sah-kree-fees*] sacrifice
sage [*sahzh*] wise
sagesse *f.* [*sah-zhes*] wisdom
saignant [*se-nyã(t)*] bloody; rare [meat]
saigner *v.* [*se-nyeh*] bleed
sain [*sē, sen*] healthy
   sain et sauf [*sē eh sohf*] safe and sound
   sain d'esprit [*sē des-pree*] sane

saint [*sĕ(t)*] holy; Saint
saint, -te [*sĕ(t)*] saint
saisir *v.* [*seh-zeer*] seize
saison *f.* [*se-zõ*] season
salade *f.* [*sah-lahd*] salad
salaire *m.* [*sah-ler*] wages
salarié, -ée [*sah-lahr-yeh*] wage earner
sale [*sahl*] dirty
salé [*sah-leh*] salty
saleté *f.* [*sahl-teh*] dirt, dirtiness
sali [*sah-lee*] soiled
salière *f.* [*sahl-yer*] salt shaker
salle *f.* [*sahl*] room, hall
   salle d'attente [*sahl dah-tãt*] waiting room
   salle de bains [*sahl duh bẽ*] bathroom
   salle de classe [*sahl duh klahs*] classroom
   salle à manger [*sahl ah mã-zheh*] dining room
salon *m.* [*sah-lõ*] living room
   salon de coiffure [*sah-lõd kwah-für*] beauty parlor
saluer *v.* [*sah-lweh*] greet; bow
salut *m.* [*sah-lü*] safety; salute
salutations *f. pl.* [*sah-lü-tah-syõ*] greetings
samedi *m.* [*sahm-dee*] Saturday
sandale *f.* [*sã-dahl*] sandal
sandwich *m.* [*sã-dweetsh*] sandwich
sang *m.* [*sã*] blood
sang-froid *m.* [*sã-frwah*] composure
sanitaire [*sah-nee-ter*] sanitary
sans [*sã*] without
   sans que [*sã k(uh)*] without
  Il est parti sans que je le voie [*ee-le pahr-tee sãk zhuhl vwah*] He left without my seeing him
santé *f.* [*sã-teh*] health
  A votre santé! [*ah votr sã-teh*] Here's to you!, To your health!
sapin *m.* [*sah-pẽ*] fir tree, Christmas tree
sarcastique [*sahr-kahs-teek*] sarcastic
satin *m.* [*sah-tẽ*] satin

satire *f.* [*sah-teer*] satire
satirique [*sah-tee-reek*] satirical
satisfaction *f.* [*sah-tees-fahk-syõ*] satisfaction
satisfaire *v. irreg.* [*sah-tees-fer*] satisfy
satisfaisant [*sah-tees-fuh-zã(t)*] satisfactory
satisfait [*sah-tees-fe(t)*] satisfied
sauce *f.* [*sohs*] sauce, gravy
saucisse *f.* [*soh-sees*] sausage
sauf *prep.* [*sohf*] except
saumon *m.* [*soh-mõ*] salmon
saut *m.* [*soh*] jump
sauter *v.* [*soh-teh*] jump
sauvage [*soh-vahzh*] wild
sauver *v.* [*soh-veh*] save, rescue
sauvetage *m.* [*sohv-tahzh*] rescue
savant *m.* [*sah-vã*] scholar
saveur *f.* [*sah-vuhr*] flavor, taste
savoir *v. irreg.* [*sah-vwahr*] know [something], know of, know how to
   à savoir [*ah sah-vwahr*] namely
savon *m.* [*sah-võ*] soap
scandale *m.* [*skã-dahl*] scandal
scarlatine *f.* [*skahr-lah-teen*] scarlet fever
sceau *f.* [*soh*] seal
scène *f.* [*sen*] scene; stage
schéma *m.* [*sheh-mah*] diagram, outline
scie *f.* [*see*] saw
science *f.* [*syãs*] science
scientifique *adj.* [*syã-tee-feek*] scientific
scientiste *m., f.* [*syã-teest*] scientist
scier *v.* [*see-eh*] saw
scierie *f.* [*see-ree*] sawmill
scolaire [*sko-ler*] school
sculpture *f.* [*skül-tür*] sculpture
se *refl. pron.* [*suh*] him-, her-, itself; themselves, oneself
séance *f.* [*seh-ãs*] session
seau *m.* [*soh*] bucket, pail
sec, sèche [*sek, sesh*] dry

sécher v. [*seh-sheh*] dry
second adj. [*s(uh)-gõ(d)*] second
secondaire [*s(uh)-gõ-der*] secondary
seconde f. [*s(uh)-gõd*] second
secouer v. [*s(uh)-kweh*] shake
secours m. [*s(uh)-koor*] help
  Au secours! [*ohs-koor*] Help!
secret m. [*s(uh)-kre*] secret
secrétaire m., f. [*s(uh)-kreh-ter*] secretary
section f. [*sek-syõ*] section
sécurité f. [*seh-kü-ree-teh*] security
séduire v. irreg. [*seh-dweer*] seduce
seigle m. [*segl*] rye
seigneur m. [*se-nyuhr*] lord
sein m. [*sẽ*] breast
  au sein de [*oh sẽ duh*] in the bosom of, within
seize [*sez*] sixteen
séjour m. [*seh-zhoor*] stay
sel m. [*sel*] salt
selle f. [*sel*] saddle
selon [*s(uh)-lõ*] according to
semaine f. [*s(uh)-men*] week
  la semaine prochaine [*lahs-men pro-shen*] next week
  la semaine dernière [*lahs-men der-nyer*] last week
semblable [*sã-blahbl*] similar
sembler v. [*sã-bleh*] seem
  faire v. **semblant** [*fer sã-blã*] pretend
semelle f. [*s(uh)-mel*] sole [of shoe]
semer v. [*s(uh)-meh*] sow
sénat m. [*seh-nah*] senate
sénateur m. [*seh-nah-tuhr*] senator
sens m. [*sãs*] sense
  bon sens [*bõ sãs*] common sense
  sens unique [*sã-sü-neek*] one way
sensible [*sã-seebl*] sensitive
sentence f. [*sã-tãs*] sentence
sentier m. [*sã-tyeh*] path
sentiment m. [*sã-tee-mã*] feeling

sentimental, -aux [sã-tee-mã-tahl, sã-tee-mã-toh]
  sentimental
sentir v. irreg. [sã-teer] feel; smell
  se sentir [suh sã-teer] feel
séparation f. [seh-pah-rah-syõ] separation
séparé [seh-pah-reh] separate
séparément [seh-pah-reh-mã] separately
séparer v. [seh-pah-reh] separate
sept [set] seven
septembre m. [sep-tãbr] September
septième [set-yem] seventh
sergent m. [ser-zhã] sergeant
série f. [seh-ree] series
sérieusement [sehr-yuhz-mã] seriously
sérieux, -euse [sehr-yuh, sehr-yuhz] serious
serment m. [ser-mã] oath
  prêter v. **serment** [pre-teh ser-mã] take an oath
sermon m. [ser-mõ] sermon
serpent m. [ser-pã] snake
serpillière f. [ser-pee-yer] rag [to wash the floor]
serré [seh-reh] tight
serrer v. [seh-reh] tighten, squeeze
  serrer la main [seh-reh lah mẽ] shake hands
serrure f. [seh-rür] lock
serrurier m. [seh-rür-yeh] locksmith
serveuse f. [ser-vuhz] waitress
service m. [ser-vees] service
  de service [duh ser-vees] on duty
serviette f. [ser-vyet] napkin; towel; briefcase
  serviettes hygiéniques [ser-vyet ee-zhyeh-neek] sanitary
    napkins
servir v. irreg. [ser-veer] serve
  se servir de [suh ser-veer duh] use
ses [seh] his, her, its
seuil m. [suhy] threshold
seul [suhl] alone, only
  tout seul, toute seule [too suhl, toot suhl] all alone
seulement [suhl-mã] only

sévère [*seh-ver*] severe
sevrer *v.* [*suh-vreh*] wean
sexe *m.* [*seks*] sex
shampooing *m.* [*shã-pwē*] shampoo
short *m.* [*short*] shorts
si *conj.* [*see*] if, whether
  même si [*mem see*] even if
  si, oui ou non [*see wee oo nõ*] whether or not
si *adv.* [*see*] so, such a, such
siècle *m.* [*syekl*] century
  au quinzième siècle [*oh kēz-yem syekl*] in the fifteenth
    century
siège *m.* [*syezh*] seat; headquarters
sien, sienne *poss. pron.* [*luh syē*] hers, his, its
sieste *f.* [*syest*] nap
siffler *v.* [*see-fleh*] whistle
sifflet *m.* [*see-fle*] whistle
signal, -aux *m.* [*see-nyahl, see-nyoh*] signal
signaler *v.* [*see-nyah-leh*] signal
signature *f.* [*see-nyah-tür*] signature
signe *m.* [*seeñ*] sign
  faire *v.* **signe** [*fer seeñ*] wave
signer *v.* [*see-nyeh*] sign
signifier *v.* [*see-nyee-fyeh*] mean
silence *m.* [*see-lãs*] silence
silencieusement [*see-lã-syuhz-mã*] silently
silencieux, -euse [*see-lã-syuh, see-lã-syuhz*] silent
simple [*sēpl*] simple, mere, casual
simplement [*sē-pluh-mã*] merely
sincère [*sē-ser*] sincere
sinon [*see-nõ*] otherwise
situation *f.* [*see-twah-syõ*] situation
situé [*see-tweh*] situated
six [*sees*] six
sixième [*see-zyem*] sixth
ski *m.* [*skee*] skiing
  faire *v.* **du ski** [*fer dü skee*] ski
slip *m.* [*sleep*] underpants

smoking *m.* [*smo-keeng*] tuxedo, dinner jacket
sobre [*sobr*] sober
S.N.C.F. *f.* [*es-en-seh-ef*] French National Railways
social, -aux [*so-syahl, so-syoh*] social
socialisme *m.* [*so-syah-leesm*] socialism
socialiste *m., f.* [*so-syah-leest*] socialist
société *f.* [*so-syeh-teh*] society
  société anonyme [*so-syeh-teh ah-no-neem*] corporation
soda *m.* [*so-dah*] soda water
soeur *f.* [*suhr*] sister
sofa *m.* [*so-fah*] sofa
soi [*swah*] oneself, himself, herself; it
  soi-même [*swah-mem*] oneself
  chez soi [*sheh swah*] at one's home, home
soie *f.* [*swah*] silk
soif *f.* [*swahf*] thirst
  avoir *v.* **soif** [*ah-vwahr swahf*] be thirsty
soigner *v.* [*swah-nyeh*] take care of, heal
soigneusement [*swah-nyuhz-mā*] carefully
soigneux, -euse [*swah-nyuh, swah-nyuhz*] careful
soin *m.* [*swē*] care
  premiers soins [*pruh-myeh swē*] first aid
soir *m.* [*swahr*] evening
  le soir [*luh swahr*] in the evening
  ce soir [*suh swahr*] tonight
soirée *f.* [*swah-reh*] evening, evening party
soit *3d pers. pres. subj. of* ÊTRE [*swah*] so be it
  soit . . . soit [*swah . . . swah*] either . . . or
soixante [*swah-sãt*] sixty
soixante-dix [*swah-sãt-dees*] seventy
sol *m.* [*sol*] ground
soldat *m.* [*sol-dah*] soldier
solde *m.* [*sold*] balance; clearance (sale)
sole *f.* [*sol*] sole [fish]
soleil *m.* [*so-ley*] sun
  coup *m.* **de soleil** [*kood so-ley*] sunburn
solide [*so-leed*] solid
solitaire [*so-lee-ter*] solitary

solitude *f.* [*so-lee-tüd*] solitude
solliciter *v.* [*so-lee-see-teh*] solicit, apply for
solution *f.* [*so-lü-syõ*] solution
sombre [*sõbr*] dark, dismal
sombrer *v.* [*sõ-breh*] sink
somme *f.* [*som*] sum
   en somme [*ã som*] all told
sommeil *m.* [*so-mey*] sleep
   avoir *v.* **sommeil** [*ah-vwahr so-mey*] be sleepy
sommet *m.* [*so-me*] summit, top
somnoler *v.* [*som-no-leh*] doze
son *poss. pron.* [*sõ*] his, her, its
son *m.* [*sõ*] sound
songer (à) *v.* [*sõ-zheh (ah)*] think about
sonner *v.* [*so-neh*] ring, sound
sonnerie *f.* [*son-ree*] ringing
sont *3d pers. pl. pres. tense of* ÊTRE [*sõ*] are
sorcière *f.* [*sor-syer*] witch
sort *m.* [*sor*] lot
sorte *f.* [*sort*] sort, kind
sortie *f.* [*sor-tee*] evening out; exit
sortir (de) *v. irreg.* [*sor-teer (duh)*] leave, go out (of); take
   out
souci *m.* [*soo-see*] worry, care
se soucier (de) *v.* [*suh soo-syeh (duh)*] care (for, about)
soucoupe *f.* [*soo-koop*] saucer
soudain [*soo-dẽ, soo-den*] sudden
souffle *m.* [*soofl*] breath, wind
souffler *v.* [*soo-fleh*] blow, blow out
souffrir *v. irreg.* [*soo-freer*] suffer
souhait *m.* [*swe*] wish
souhaiter *v.* [*swe-teh*] wish
soulagement *m.* [*soo-lahzh-mã*] relief
soulager *v.* [*soo-lah-zheh*] relieve
soulever *v.* [*sool-veh*] lift, raise
   se soulever [*suh sool-veh*] rise; revolt
soulier *m.* [*sool-yeh*] shoe
souligner *v.* [*soo-lee-nyeh*] underline; stress

soumettre *v. irreg.* [*soo-metr*] submit
soupape *f.* [*soo-pahp*] valve
soupçon *m.* [*soop-sõ*] suspicion
soupçonner *v.* [*soop-so-neh*] suspect
soupe *f.* [*soop*] soup
soupière *f.* [*soo-pyer*] soup tureen
soupir *m.* [*soo-peer*] sigh
souple [*soopl*] flexible
source *f.* [*soors*] source; spring, well
sourcil *m.* [*soor-see*] eyebrow
sourd [*soor(d)*] deaf
sourire *m.* [*soo-reer*] smile
sourire *v. irreg.* [*soo-reer*] smile
souris *f.* [*soo-ree*] mouse
sous [*soo*] under
sous-marin *m.* [*soo-mah-rē*] submarine
sous-sol *m.* [*soo-sol*] basement, cellar
soustraction *f.* [*soos-trahk-syõ*] subtraction
sous-vêtement *m.* [*soo-vet-mã*] underwear
soutenir *v. irreg.* [*soot-neer*] support
souterrain [*soo-te-rē, soo-te-ren*] underground
soutien *m.* [*soo-tyē*] support
soutien-gorge *m.* [*soo-tyē-gorzh*] brassiere
souvenir *m.* [*soov-neer*] memory, souvenir
se souvenir (de) *v.* [*suh soov-neer (duh)*] remember
souvent [*soo-vã*] frequently, often
spacieux, -euse [*spah-syuh, spah-syuhz*] spacious
sparadrap *m.* [*spah-rah-drah*] adhesive tape
speaker, speakerine [*spee-kuhr, speek-reen*] announcer
spécial, -aux [*speh-syahl, speh-syoh*] special
spécialement [*speh-syahl-mã*] especially
spécialité *f.* [*speh-syah-lee-teh*] specialty
spectacle *m.* [*spek-tahkl*] show, spectacle
spectateur, -trice [*spek-tah-tuhr, spek-tah-trees*] spectator, bystander
spirituel, -elle [*spee-ree-twel*] spiritual; witty
splendide [*splã-deed*] splendid
sport *m.* [*spor*] sport, athletics

sportif, -ive [*spor-teef, spor-teev*] athletic
squelette *m.* [*skuh-let*] skeleton
stade *m.* [*stahd*] stadium, athletic field; stage
stage *m.* [*stahzh*] training period
starter *m.* [*stahr-ter*] choke
station *f.* [*stah-syõ*] station
   station service [*stah-syõ ser-vees*] service station,
     gas station
stationnaire [*stah-syo-ner*] stationary
stationnement *m.* [*stah-syon-mã*] parking
   stationnement interdit [*stah-syon-mã ẽ-ter-dee*] no parking
statue *f.* [*stah-tü*] statue
sténo *m., f.* [*steh-noh*] stenographer
strict [*streekt*] strict
strictement [*streek-tuh-mã*] strictly
structure *f.* [*strük-tür*] structure
stupide [*stü-peed*] stupid
style *m.* [*steel*] style
stylo *m.* [*stee-loh*] pen
   stylo-bille [*stee-loh-beey*] ballpoint pen
substance *f.* [*süb-stãs*] substance
substituer *v.* [*süb-stee-tweh*] substitute
substitution *f.* [*süb-stee-tü-syõ*] substitution
subtil [*süb-teel*] subtle
subvention *f.* [*süb-vã-syõ*] subsidy
subventionner *v.* [*sub-vã-syo-neh*] subsidize
succès *m.* [*sük-se*] success
succession *f.* [*sük-seh-syõ*] succession; estate [of deceased]
succursale *f.* [*sü-kür-sahl*] branch
sucre *m.* [*sükr*] sugar
sucré [*sü-kreh*] sweet
sucrier *m.* [*sü-kree-yeh*] sugar bowl
sud *m.* [*süd*] south
Suède *f.* [*swed*] Sweden
suédois [*sweh-dwah(z)*] Swede, Swedish
suffire *v. irreg.* [*sü-feer*] suffice, be enough
   Ça suffit! [*sah sü-fee*] That's enough!
suffisant [*sü-fee-zã(t)*] sufficient

suggérer v. [*süg-zheh-reh*] suggest
suggestion f. [*süg-zhes-tyõ*] suggestion
suicide m. [*swee-seed*] suicide
se suicider v. [*suh swee-see-deh*] commit suicide
suis *1st pers. sing. pres. tense of* ÊTRE [*swee*] I am
Suisse f. [*swees*] Switzerland
suisse n & adj. [*swees*] Swiss
suite f. [*sweet*] succession, what follows
  de suite [*duh sweet*] in succession, without stopping
  tout de suite [*tood sweet*] at once
  par la suite [*pahr lah sweet*] later on
  à la suite de [*ah lah sweet duh*] following, as a result of
suivant [*swee-vã(t)*] following, next
suivre v. *irreg.* [*sweevr*] follow
  suivre un cours [*swee-vrẽ koor*] take a course
sujet m. [*sü-zhe*] subject
  au sujet de [*oh sü-zhe d(uh)*] about, concerning
superbe [*sü-perb*] superb
superficiel, -elle [*sü-per-fee-syel*] superficial
supérieur [*sü-pehr-yuhr*] superior
superstitieux, -euse [*sü-per-stee-syuh, sü-per-stee-syuhz*] superstitious
supplément m. [*sü-pleh-mã*] supplement; extra serving; additional charge
supplémentaire [*sü-pleh-mã-ter*] additional, extra
supplier v. [*sü-plee-yeh*] implore
supporter v. [*sü-por-teh*] endure, bear
supposer v. [*sü-po-zeh*] suppose, assume
supposition f. [*sü-po-zee-syõ*] assumption
supprimer v. [*sü-pree-meh*] suppress, destroy
sur prep. [*sür*] on, over, upon
sûr [*sür*] sure, safe
sûrement [*sür-mã*] surely
sûreté f. [*sür-teh*] safety
surface f. [*sür-fahs*] surface
surmonter v. [*sür-mõ-teh*] overcome
surnom m. [*sür-nõ*] nickname
surprenant [*sür-pruh-nã(t)*] surprising

surprendre *v. irreg.* [*sür-prãdr*] surprise
  surprendre . . . à faire . . . [*sür-prãdr . . . ah fer . . .*]
    catch [someone] doing [something]
surprise *f.* [*sür-preez*] surprise
surtout [*sür-too*] mainly, especially
surveiller *v.* [*sür-ve-yeh*] supervise, watch
survie *f.* [*sür-vee*] survival
survivant, -te *n. & adj.* [*sür-vee-vã(t)*] survivor, surviving
survivre *v. irreg.* [*sür-veevr*] survive
susceptible [*sü-sep-teebl*] touchy
suspect *adj.* [*süs-pe(kt)*] suspicious
suspendre *v.* [*süs-pãdr*] suspend, hang up
syllabe *f.* [*see-lahb*] syllable
sympathique [*sẽ-pah-teek*] likeable
symphonie *f.* [*sẽ-fo-nee*] symphony
symptôme *m.* [*sẽp-tohm*] symptom
syndical, -aux [*sẽ-dee-kahl, sẽ-dee-koh*] labor
syndicat *m.* [*sẽ-dee-kah*] labor union
synthétique [*sẽ-teh-teek*] synthetic
systématique [*sees-teh-mah-teek*] systematic
système *m.* [*sees-tem*] system
  système métrique [*sees-tem meh-treek*] metric system

T

t': te [*tuh*] to you, yourself
ta [*tah*] your
tabac *m.* [*tah-bah*] tobacco
table *f.* [*tahbl*] table
tableau, -eaux *m.* [*tah-bloh*] picture
  tableau d'affichage [*tah-bloh dah-fee-shahzh*] bulletin board
  tableau noir [*tah-bloh nwahr*] blackboard
tablier *m.* [*tah-blee-yeh*] apron
tache *f.* [*tahsh*] spot, stain
tâche *f.* [*tahsh*] task

tacher *v.* [*tah-sheh*] stain
tâcher *v.* [*tah-sheh*] try
tact *m.* [*tahkt*] tact
taille *f.* [*tahy*] height; waist; size [of clothing]
tailleur *m.* [*tah-yuhr*] suit; tailor
se taire *v. irreg.* [*suh ter*] keep silent
  Taisez-vous! [*te-zeh-voo*] Be quiet!
talent *m.* [*tah-lã*] talent
talon *m.* [*tah-lõ*] heel
tambour *m.* [*tã-boor*] drum
tandis que [*tã-dee k(uh)*] while, whereas
tant de [*tã duh*] so much, so many
  tant que [*tã kuh*] as long as
tante *f.* [*tãt*] aunt
tantôt [*tã-toh*] soon
taper *v.* [*tah-peh*] strike, knock; type [write]
tapis *m.* [*tah-pee*] carpet, rug
tapisserie *f.* [*tah-pees-ree*] tapestry
tard *adv.* [*tahr*] late
  Il est tard [*ee-le-tahr*] It's late
tarder à *v.* [*tahr-deh ah*] be slow to
  tarder de [*tahr-deh duh*] long to
tarif *m.* [*tah-reef*] price, price list
tarte *f.* [*tahrt*] pie
tas *m.* [*tah*] pile
tasse *f.* [*tahs*] cup
tâter *v.* [*tah-teh*] feel
taureau, -eaux *m.* [*toh-roh*] bull
taux *m.* [*toh*] rate
taxi *m.* [*tahk-see*] taxi, cab
te [*tuh*] you
technique [*tek-neek*] technical
teindre *v. irreg.* [*tẽdr*] dye
teinture *f.* [*tẽ-tür*] dye
teinturerie *f.* [*tẽ-tur-ree*] cleaner's shop
tel, telle [*tel*] such
  tel que, telle que [*tel kuh*] such as
télégramme *m.* [*teh-leh-grahm*] telegram

télégramme international [*teh-leh-gram ē-ter-nah-syo-nahl*] cable

téléphone *m.* [*teh-leh-fon*] telephone

  coup *m.* **de téléphone** [*kood teh-leh-fon*] telephone call

téléphoner *v.* [*teh-leh-fo-neh*] telephone

téléphoniste *m.*, *f.* [*teh-leh-fo-neest*] telephone operator

télévision *f.* [*teh-leh-vee-zyō*] television

  poste *m.* **de télévision** [*post duh teh-leh-vee-zyō*] television set

téméraire [*teh-meh-rer*] daring, rash

témoignage *m.* [*teh-mwah-nyahzh*] testimony

témoigner *v.* [*teh-mwah-nyeh*] testify

témoin *m.* [*teh-mwē*] witness

  être *v.* **témoin** [*e-truh teh-mwē*] witness

température *f.* [*tã-peh-rah-tür*] temperature

tempête *f.* [*tã-pet*] storm

temple *m.* [*tãpl*] temple, church [of Protestants]

temporaire [*tã-po-rer*] temporary

temps *m.* [*tã*] time, weather

  de temps en temps [*duh tã-zã tã*] from time to time

  en même temps [*ã mem tã*] at the same time

  passer *v.* **du temps** [*pah-seh dü tã*] spend time

  Quel temps fait-il? [*kel tã fe-teel*] What's the weather like?

  Combien de temps faut-il pour . . . ? [*kō-byēd tã foh-teel poor*] How long does it take to . . . ?

tendance *f.* [*tã-dãs*] tendency, inclination

tendre [*tãdr*] tender

tendre *v.* [*tãdr*] tend

tendresse *f.* [*tã-dres*] affection

tenir *v. irreg.* [*t(uh)-neer*] hold

  se tenir [*stuh-neer*] stand, behave

  tenir compte de [*t(uh)-neer kōt duh*] take into account

  tenir à [*t(uh)-neer ah*] insist on

  Tiens! [*tyē*] Well!

tension *f.* [*tã-syō*] strain, tension

tentation *f.* [*tã-tah-syō*] temptation

tente *f.* [*tãt*] tent

tenter *v.* [*tã-teh*] try

terme *m.* [*term*] term
terminus *m.* [*ter-mee-nüs*] terminus
terrain *m.* [*te-rē*] land, lot
   terrain de jeu [*te-rēd zhuh*] playground
terrasse *f.* [*te-rahs*] terrace
   terrasse du café [*te-rahs dü kah-feh*] sidewalk café
terre *f.* [*ter*] earth, land, ground
   par terre [*pahr ter*] on the ground, on the floor
   à terre [*ah ter*] ashore
terreur *f.* [*te-ruhr*] terror
terrible [*te-reebl*] terrible, awful
territoire *m.* [*te-ree-twahr*] territory
tes [*teh*] your
testament *m.* [*tes-tah-mā*] will
tête *f.* [*tet*] head
   mal *m.* **à la tete** [*mahl ah lah tet*] headache
tétine *f.* [*teh-teen*] nipple
têtu [*teh-tü*] stubborn
texte *m.* [*tekst*] text
thé *m.* [*teh*] tea
théâtre *m.* [*teh-ahtr*] theatre
théière *f.* [*teh-yer*] teapot
théorie *f.* [*teh-o-ree*] theory
thermomètre *m.* [*ter-mo-metr*] thermometer
ticket *m.* [*tee-ke*] ticket
tiède [*tyed*] lukewarm
le tien, la tienne [*luh tyē, lah tyen*] yours
tiers *m.* [*tyer*] third
tige *f.* [*teezh*] stem
timbre(-poste) *m.* [*tēbr (post)*] postage stamp
timide [*tee-meed*] shy, timid
tirer *v.* [*tee-reh*] draw (out), pull; shoot, fire
   tirer la chasse [*tee-reh lah shahs*] flush the toilet
tiroir *m.* [*teer-wahr*] drawer
tissage *m.* [*tee-sahzh*] weaving
tisser *v.* [*tee-seh*] weave
tissu *m.* [*tee-sü*] cloth
titre [*teetr*] title; diploma

toi [*twah*] you
toi-même [*twah-mem*] yourself
toile *f.* [*twahl*] cloth; painting
  toile cirée [*twahl see-reh*] oilcloth
  toile d'araignée [*twahl dah-reh-nyeh*] spiderweb
toilette *f.* [*twah-let*] toilet, grooming
  faire *v.* **sa toilette** [*fer sah twah-let*] get dressed
toit *m.* [*twah*] roof
tomate *f.* [*to-maht*] tomato
tombe *f.* [*tõb*] tomb
tomber *v.* [*tõ-beh*] fall
  laisser *v.* **tomber** [*leh-seh tõ-beh*] drop
ton [*tõ*] your
ton *m.* [*tõ*] tone
tonne *f.* [*ton*] ton
tonneau, -eaux *m.* [*to-noh*] barrel
tonnerre *m.* [*to-ner*] thunder
torchon *m.* [*tor-shõ*] dishtowel
tordre *v.* [*tordr*] twist
tordu [*tor-dü*] crooked, twisted
tornade *f.* [*tor-nahd*] tornado
torrent *m.* [*to-rã*] mountain stream
tort *m.* [*tor*] wrong
  avoir *v.* **tort** [*ah-vwahr tor*] be wrong
  faire *v.* **tort à** [*fer tor ah*] wrong
  à tort [*ah tor*] wrongly
  à tort et à travers [*ah tor eh ah trah-ver*] in a haphazard
    way
torture *f.* [*tor-tür*] torture
torturer *v.* [*tor-tü-reh*] torture
tôt [*toh*] early
  plus tôt [*plü toh*] sooner
tôt ou tard [*toh oo tahr*] sooner or later
total, -aux [*to-tahl, to-toh*] total
touchant [*too-shã(t)*] touching
toucher *v.* [*too-sheh*] touch; cash [a check]
toujours [*too-zhoor*] always, forever
tour *f.* [*toor*] tower

tour *m.* [*toor*] turn, tour, trick
   chacun à son tour [*shah-kē ah sõ toor*] each one in turn
   À qui le tour? [*ah keel toor*] Whose turn is it?
   jouer *v.* **un tour à** [*zhweh ē toor ah*] play a trick on
     [someone]
touriste *m., f.* [*too-reest*] tourist
tourne-disques *m.* [*toor-nuh-deesk*] phonograph, record-
   player
tourner *v.* [*toor-neh*] turn, revolve; stir [cooking]
tournevis *m.* [*toor-nuh-vees*] screwdriver
tousser *v.* [*too-seh*] cough
tout, toute [*too(t)*] the whole, all
   tout le monde [*tool mõd*] everybody
tout *pron.* [*too*] everything
   C'est tout! [*se too*] That's all!
tout *adv.* [*too*] altogether, quite
   tout en faisant . . . [*too-tã fuh-zã*] while doing . . .
   tout à coup [*too-tah koo*] suddenly
   Pas du tout [*pah dü too*] Not at all
   tout à fait [*too-tah fe*] altogether, quite
   tout à l'heure [*too-tah luhr*] a while ago; in a little while
   tout de même [*toot mem*] all the same
   tout de suite [*toot sweet*] at once
toutefois [*toot-fwah*] however
toux *f.* [*too*] cough
trac *m.* [*trahk*] stage-fright
trace *f.* [*trahs*] trace
tracteur *m.* [*trahk-tuhr*] tractor
tradition *f.* [*trah-dee-syõ*] tradition
traditionnel, -elle [*trah-dee-syo-nel*] traditional
traducteur, -trice [*trah-dük-tuhr, trah-dük-trees*] translator
traduction *f.* [*trah-dük-syõ*] translation
traduire *v. irreg.* [*trah-dweer*] translate
tragédie *f.* [*trah-zheh-dee*] tragedy
tragique [*trah-zheek*] tragic
trahir *v.* [*trah-eer*] betray
trahison *f.* [*trah-ee-zõ*] treason
train *m.* [*trẽ*] train

train transatlantique [*trē trā-zaht-lā-teek*] boat train
en train de [*ā trē d(uh)*] in the act of
  Il est en train de s'habiller [*ee-le-tā trēd sah-bee-yeh*]
    He is getting dressed
traîner v. [*treh-neh*] drag, drag out
trait m. [*tre*] characteristic; facial feature
traite f. [*tret*] bank draft; milking [of a cow]
traité m. [*treh-teh*] treaty
traitement m. [*tret-mā*] treatment; salary
traiter v. [*treh-teh*] treat, deal with
traître m. [*tretr*] traitor
tramway m. [*trahm-we*] streetcar
tranche f. [*trāsh*] slice
tranquille [*trā-keel*] quiet, calm
  Laissez-moi tranquille [*leh-seh-mwah trā-keel*] Don't
    bother me
transat m. [*trā-zaht*] deck chair, lawn chair
transformer v. [*trās-for-meh*] transform
transmettre v. irreg. [*trās-metr*] transmit
transmission f. [*trās-mee-syō*] transmission
transpiration f. [*trās-pee-rah-syō*] perspiration
transpirer v. [*trās-pee-reh*] perspire
transport m. [*trās-por*] transportation
transporter v. [*trās-por-teh*] transport, carry
travail, -aux m. [*trah-vahy, trah-voh*] work, job, labor
travailler v. [*trah-vah-yeh*] work
travailleur m. [*trah-vah-yuhr*] worker, laborer
travers m. [*trah-ver*] defect
  à travers [*ah trah-ver*] across, through
  de travers [*duh trah-ver*] crooked
traversée f. [*trah-ver-seh*] crossing
traverser v. [*trah-ver-seh*] cross
trébucher v. [*treh-bü-sheh*] stumble
treize [*trez*] thirteen
tremblement de terre m. [*trā-bluh-mād ter*] earthquake
trembler v. [*trā-bleh*] tremble
  trembler de froid [*trā-blehd frwah*] shiver
trempé [*trā-peh*] soaking wet

tremper v. [trã-peh] soak
trente [trãt] thirty
très [tre] very
  très bien [tre byẽ] very well
trésor m. [treh-zor] treasure
  trésor public [treh-zor püb-leek] treasury
trésorerie f. [treh-zor-ree] treasury
trésorier, -ière [treh-zor-yeh, treh-zor-yer] treasurer
triangle m. [tree-yãgl] triangle
tribord m. [tree-bor] starboard
tribunal, -aux m. [tree-bü-nal, tree-bü-noh] court
tricher v. [tree-sheh] cheat
tricostéril m. [tree-ko-steh-reel] bandaid
tricot m. [tree-koh] knitting; knitted garment
tricoter v. [tree-ko-teh] knit
trier v. [tree-yeh] sort
trompette f. [trõ-pet] trumpet
triomphant [tree-õ-fã(t)] triumphant
troubler v. [troo-bleh] disturb
troupeau, -eaux m. [troo-poh] flock
triste [treest] sad, dismal
tristesse f. [trees-tes] sadness
trois [trwah] three
troisième [trwah-zyem] third
trolley m. [tro-le] trolley (car)
tromper v. [trõ-peh] deceive, mislead
  se tromper [strõ-peh] make a mistake
tromperie f. [trõp-ree] deceit, cheating
tronc m. [trõ] trunk
trône m. [trohn] throne
trop [troh] too
  trop de [troh d(uh)] too much, too many
trottoir m. [tro-twahr] sidewalk
trou m. [troo] hole
trouble m. [troobl] disturbance
troupe f. [troop] troop
trouver v. [troo-veh] find
  se trouver [stroo-veh] be, happen; be located

bureau *m.* **des objets trouvés** [*bü-roh deh-zob-zhe troo-veh*]
    lost and found
truc *m.* [*trük*] device, gadget
truite *f.* [*trweet*] trout
T.S.F. *f.* [*teh-es-ef*] radio
tu [*tü*] you
tube *m.* [*tüb*] tube
tuberculose *f.* [*tü-ber-kü-lohz*] tuberculosis
tuer *v.* [*tü-eh*] kill
tuile *f.* [*tweel*] tile; bad break
tunnel *m.* [*tü-nel*] tunnel
turc, turque *n. & adj.* [*türk*] Turk, Turkish
Turquie *f.* [*tür-kee*] Turkey
tuyau, -aux *m.* [*twee-yoh*] pipe
    tuyau de vidange [*twee-yohd vee-dãzh*] drain
type *m.* [*teep*] type
typique [*tee-peek*] typical
tyran *m.* [*tee-rã*] tyrant
tyrannie *f.* [*tee-rah-nee*] tyranny

U

ultérieur [*ül-tehr-yuhr*] further
un, une [*ẽ, ün*] a, an; one
unanime [*ü-nah-neem*] unanimous
uniforme *adj. & n.* [*ü-nee-form*] uniform
union *f.* [*ü-nyõ*] union
unique [*ü-neek*] sole
uniquement [*ü-neek-mã*] only
unir, s'unir *v.* [*ü-neer, sü-neer*] unite
uni [*ü-nee*] united
unité *f.* [*ü-nee-teh*] unity, unit
univers *m.* [*ü-nee-ver*] universe
universel, -elle [*ü-nee-ver-sel*] universal
université *f.* [*ü-nee-ver-see-teh*] university, college

urbain [*ür-bē, ür-ben*] urban
urgent [*ür-zhā(t)*] urgent
  cas *m.* **urgent** [*kah ür-zhā*] emergency
usage *m.* [*ü-zahzh*] use, custom
  usage personnel [*ü-zahzh per-so-nel*] personal use
usé [*ü-zeh*] worn, worn out
user *v.* [*ü-zeh*] wear out
usine *f.* [*ü-zeen*] factory
ustensile *m.* [*üs-tā-seel*] utensil
utile [*ü-teel*] helpful, useful
utilisé [*ü-tee-lee-zeh*] used
utilité *f.* [*ü-tee-lee-teh*] utility

V

va *3d pers. sing. pres. tense of* ALLER [*vah*] goes
vacances *f. pl.* [*vah-kās*] vacation
vacarme *m.* [*vah-kahrm*] uproar
vaccination *f.* [*vahk-see-nah-syō*] vaccination
vache *f.* [*vahsh*] cow
vague [*vahg*] vague
vague *f.* [*vahg*] wave
vain [*vē, ven*] vain
vaincre *v. irreg.* [*vēkr*] conquer
vaisselle *f.* [*ve-sel*] dishes
valable [*vah-lahbl*] valid
valeur *f.* [*vah-luhr*] value
valise *f.* [*vah-leez*] suitcase
vallée *f.* [*vah-leh*] valley
valoir *v. irreg.* [*vahl-wahr*] be worth
  Cela vaut dix dollars [*slah voh dee do-lahr*] It's worth
    ten dollars
  valoir la peine [*vahl-wahr lah pen*] be worthwhile
  valoir mieux [*vahl-wahr myuh*] be better
vanille *f.* [*vah-neey*] vanilla

vanité f. [vah-nee-teh] vanity
vaniteux, -euse [vah-nee-tuh, vah-nee-tuhz] vain
se vanter v. [suh vã-teh] brag
vapeur f. [vah-puhr] steam
varicelle f. [vah-ree-sel] chicken pox
varier v. [vahr-yeh] vary
variété f. [vahr-yeh-teh] variety
variole f. [vahr-yol] smallpox
vase m. [vahz] vase
vaste [vahst] vast
Vatican m. [vah-tee-kã] Vatican
veau, -eaux m. [voh] calf; veal
véhicule m. [veh-ee-kül] vehicle
veille f. [vey] eve
veiller v. [ve-yeh] stay wake, watch over
veilleur (de nuit) m. [ve-yuhr (duh nwee)] (night) watchman
veine f. [ven] vein; luck (fam.)
velours m. [v(uh)-loor] velvet
vendanges f. pl. [vã-dãzh] grape harvest
vendeur, -euse [vã-duhr, vã-duhz] sales clerk, seller
vendre v. [vãdr] sell
  à vendre [ah vãdr] for sale
vendredi m. [vã-druh-dee] Friday
venez 2d pers. pl. pres. tense of VENIR [v(uh)-neh] come
vengeance f. [vã-zhãs] vengeance
venir v. irreg. [v(uh)-neer] come
  venir de faire [v(uh)-neer duh fer] have just done
  faire v. **venir** [fer vuh-neer] send for
vent m. [vã] wind
vente f. [vãt] sale
  vente aux enchères [vã-toh-zã-sher] auction
ventilateur m. [vã-tee-lah-tuhr] fan
ventre m. [vãtr] stomach
ver m. [ver] worm
verbe m. [verb] verb
verdict m. [ver-deekt] verdict
verger m. [ver-zheh] orchard
vérifier v. [veh-ree-fyeh] verify

véritable [*veh-ree-tahbl*] genuine
vérité *f.* [*veh-ree-teh*] truth
verre *m.* [*ver*] glass
verrou, -ous *m.* [*ve-roo*] lock, bolt
vers [*ver*] toward
vers *m.* [*ver*] verse
verser *v.* [*ver-seh*] pour
vert [*ver(t)*] green
vertical, -aux [*ver-tee-kahl, ver-tee-koh*] vertical
vertige *m.* [*ver-teezh*] dizziness
   avoir *v.* **le vertige** [*ah-vwahr luh ver-teezh*] feel dizzy
vertu *f.* [*ver-tü*] virtue
vertueux, -euse [*ver-twuh, ver-ıwuhz*] virtuous
veste *f.* [*vest*] jacket, suit-coat
vestiaire *m.* [*ves-tyer*] cloak-room
veston *m.* [*ves-tõ*] coat, sport jacket
vêtement *m.* [*vet-mã*] garment, clothes
vétérinaire *m.* [*veh-teh-ree-ner*] veterinarian
veuf *m.* [*vuhf*] widower
veuillez *impers. form of* VOULOIR [*vuh-yeh*] please
   Veuillez agréer, etc. [*vuh-yeh-zah-greh-eh* . . .] Sincerely
     yours, Yours truly
veuve *f.* [*vuhv*] widow
vexer *v.* [*vek-seh*] vex
viande *f.* [*vyãd*] meat
vice *m.* [*vees*] vice
victime *f.* [*veek-teem*] victim
victoire *f.* [*veek-twahr*] victory
vidange *m.* [*vee-dãzh*] oil change
vide [*veed*] empty
vider *v.* [*vee-deh*] empty
vie *f.* [*vee*] life
vieil *m.* **vieille** *f.* [*vyey*] old
vieillard *m.* [*vye-yahr*] old man
vieillesse *f.* [*vye-yes*] old age
viens *2d pers. sing. pres. tense of* VENIR [*vyẽ*] come
vierge *f.* [*vyerzh*] virgin
vieux, vieil *m.,* **vieille** *f.* [*vyuh, vyey*] old

vif, vive [*veef, veev*] lively

vigilant [*vee-zhee-lã(t)*] watchful

vigne *f.* [*veeñ*] grapevine

vignoble *m.* [*vee-nyobl*] vineyard

vigoureux, -euse [*vee-goo-ruh, vee-goo-ruhz*] vigorous

vilain [*vee-lẽ, vee-len*] nasty, naughty

village *m.* [*vee-lahzh*] village

ville *f.* [*veel*] city, town

vin *m.* [*vẽ*] wine

vinaigre *m.* [*vee-negr*] vinegar

vingt [*vẽ*] twenty

violence *f.* [*vyo-lãs*] violence

violent [*vyo-lã(t)*] violent

violer *v.* [*vyo-leh*] violate; rape

violet, -ette [*vyo-le(t)*] purple

violette *f.* [*vyo-let*] violet [flower]

violon *m.* [*vyo-lõ*] violin

virage *m.* [*vee-rahzh*] curve, turn

virgule *f.* [*veer-gül*] comma

vis *f.* [*vees*] screw

visa *m.* [*vee-zah*] visa

visage *m.* [*vee-zahzh*] face

viser *v.* [*vee-zeh*] aim at

visible [*vee-zeebl*] visible

vision *f.* [*vee-zyõ*] vision

visite *f.* [*vee-zeet*] visit

   rendre *v.* **visite à** [*rãdr vee-zeet ah*] visit, call on

visiter *v.* [*vee-zee-teh*] visit

visiteur, -euse [*vee-zee-tuhr, vee-zee-tuhz*] visitor

vital, -aux [*vee-tahl, vee-toh*] vital

vitamine *f.* [*vee-tah-meen*] vitamin

vite [*veet*] fast, quickly

vitesse *f.* [*vee-tes*] speed; gear [of auto]

   changer *v.* **de vitesse** [*shã-zhehd vee-tes*] change gear

   à toute vitesse [*ah toot vee-tes*] at full speed

   en seconde (vitesse) [*ã suh-gõd (vee-tes)*] in second gear

vitrail, -aux *m.* [*vee-trahy, vee-troh*] stained glass window

vitre *f.* [*veetr*] window pane

vitrine *f.* [*vee-treen*] shop windowpane
vivant [*vee-vã(t)*] alive, lively
vivre *v. irreg.* [*veevr*] live
vocabulaire *m.* [*vo-kah-bü-ler*] vocabulary
vocation *f.* [*vo-kah-syõ*] vocation
voeu, -eux *m.* [*vuh*] vow
voici [*vwah-see*] here is, here are
voilà [*vwah-lah*] there is, there are
　Le voilà, Les voilà [*luh vwah-lah, leh vwah-lah*] There it is,
　　There they are
voile *m.* [*vwahl*] veil
voile *f.* [*vwahl*] sail
voir *v. irreg.* [*vwahr*] see
voisin, -ine [*vwah-zẽ, vwah-zeen*] neighbor
voiture *f.* [*vwah-tür*] car
　En voiture [*ã vwah-tür*] All aboard
voix *f.* [*vwah*] voice
　à haute voix [*ah oht vwah*] aloud
vol *m.* [*vol*] flight; theft
volant *m.* [*vo-lã*] steering wheel
volcan *m.* [*vol-kã*] volcano
voler *v.* [*vo-leh*] fly; steal, rob
volet *m.* [*vo-le*] shutter
voleur, -euse [*vo-luhr, vo-luhz*] robber, thief
volontaire *n. & adj.* [*vo-lõ-ter*] volunteer, voluntary
volonté *f.* [*vo-lõ-teh*] will (power)
volontiers [*vo-lõ-tyeh*] willingly
volume *m.* [*vo-lüm*] volume
volumineux, -euse [*vo-lü-mee-nuh, vo-lü-mee-nuhz*] bulky
vomir *v.* [*vo-meer*] vomit
vont *3d pers. pl. pres. tense of* ALLER [*võ*] go
vos [*voh*] your
vote *m.* [*vot*] vote
voter *v.* [*vo-teh*] vote
votre [*votr*] your
le vôtre, la vôtre [*luh vohtr, lah vohtr*] yours
vouloir *v. irreg.* [*vool-wahr*] want
　Voudriez-vous . . . ? [*voo-dree-yeh voo*] Would you like . . . ?

Je voudrais bien [*zhvoo-dre byẽ*] I'd like (to)
en vouloir à [*ã vool-wahr ah*] have a grudge against
vouloir dire [*vool-wahr deer*] mean
Veuillez agréer, etc. [*vuh-yeh-zah-greh-eh . . .*] Sincerely yours, Yours truly
vous [*voo*] you
vous même, vous-mêmes [*voo-mem*] yourself, yourselves
voûte *f.* [*voot*] arch
voyage *m.* [*vwah-yahzh*] journey, trip
voyage d'agrément [*vwah-yahzh dah-greh-mã*] pleasure trip
  Bon voyage? [*bõ vwah-yahzh*] Have a good trip!
  agence *f.* **de voyages** [*ah-zhãs duh vwah-yahzh*] travel agency
  chèque *m.* **de voyage** [*shek duh vwah-yahzh*] traveler's check
voyager *v.* [*vwah-yah-zheh*] travel
voyageur, -euse [*vwah-yah-zhuhr, vwah-yah-zhuhz*] traveler
voyelle *f.* [*vwah-yel*] vowel
voyons *1st pers. pl. pres. tense of* VOIR [*vwah-yõ*] let's see
vrai [*vre*] true
vraiment [*vre-mã*] really
vraisemblable [*vre-sã-blahbl*] likely
vue *f.* [*vü*] sight, view
vulgaire [*vül-gher*] vulgar
vulnerable [*vül-neh-rahbl*] vulnerable

W — Z

wagon *m.* [*vah-gõ*] railroad car
  wagon-lit *m.* [*vah-gõ-lee*] sleeping car
  wagon-restaurant *m.* [*vah-gõ-res-to-rã*] dining car
W.C. *m. pl.* [*veh-seh*] toilets
y *adv. & pron.* [*ee*] there; to it, at it
  il y a [*eel yah*] there is, there are
  y a-t-il . . . ? [*yah-teel*] is there . . . ?, are there . . . ?

  J'y suis! [*zhee swee*] I've got it!
  Ca y est [*sah ye*] That's it
  Je n'y suis pour rien [*zhnee swee poor ryē*] I had nothing
     to do with it
  tout y est [*too-tee e*] it's all there
zéro *m.* [*zeh-roh*] zero
zone *f.* [*zohn*] zone
zoo *m.* [*zoh-oh*] zoo

Phrases for Use Abroad

Helpful Expressions

Good morning/afternoon/evening.
Bonjour/Bonjour/Bonsoir.
Bõ-zhoor/Bõ-swahr.

Hello. How do you do?
Bonjour. Comment allez-vous?
Bõ-zhoor. ko-mã-tah-leh voo?

Goodbye. See you later.
Au revoir. A tout à l'heure.
Ohr-vwahr. Ah too-tah luhr.

Please.	**Excuse me.**
S'il vous plaît.	Pardon.
Seel voo ple.	*Pahr-dõ.*

Thank you.	**You're welcome.**
Merci.	De rien.
Mer-see.	*Duh ryẽ.*

This is Mr./Mrs./Miss . . . .
Je vous présente Monsieur/Madame/Mademoiselle . . . .
Zhvoo preh-zãt muh-syuh/mah-dahm/mahd-mwah-zel . . . .

My name is . . . .
Je m'appelle . . . .
Zhuh mah-pel . . . .

What is your name?
Comment vous appelez-vous?
Ko-mã voo-zah-pleh-voo?

311

I am pleased to meet you.
Je suis enchanté de faire votre connaissance.
Zhuh swee-zã-shã-tehd fer votr ko-ne-sãs.

I don't understand.
Je ne comprends pas.
Zhuhn kõ-prã pah.

I don't know.
Je ne sais pas.
Zhuhn seh pah.

Could you speak more slowly, please?
Pourriez-vous parler plus lentement, s'il vous plaît?
Poor-yeh-voo pahr-leh plü lãt-ma, seel voo ple?

Could you repeat, please?
Pourriez-vous répéter, s'il vous plaît?
Poor-yeh-voo reh-peh-teh, seel voo ple?

Do you speak English?
Parlez-vous anglais?
Pahr-leh-voo ã-gle?

Where?	**When?**
Où?	Quand?
Oo?	*Kã?*

Can you help me, please?
Pardon, pourriez-vous m'aider?
Pahr-dõ, poor-yeh-voo meh-deh?

How do you say . . . in French?
Comment dit-on . . . en français?
Ko-mã dee-tõ . . . ã frã-se?

What does . . . mean?
Que veut dire . . .?
Kuh vuh deer . . . ?

Time and Weather

What time is it?
Quelle heure est-il?
Kel uhr e-teel?

(At) what time . . . ?
A quelle heure . . . ?
Ah kel uhr . . . ?

How is the weather today?
Quel temps fait-il aujourd'hui?
Kel tã fe-teel oh-zhoor-dwee?

It's a beautiful day. There will be rain tomorrow.
Il fait beau. Il va pleuvoir demain.
Eel fe boh. Eel vah pluh-vwahr duh-mē.

Customs

May I see your passport/visa/papers, please?
Votre passeport/votre visa/vos papiers, s'il vous plaît?
Vo-truh pahs-por/vo-truh vee-zah/voh pah-pyeh, seel voo ple?

Do you have anything to declare?
Avez-vous quelque chose à déclarer?
Ah-veh-voo kel-kuh shohz ah deh-klah-reh?

It's for my personal use.
C'est pour mon usage personnel.
Se poor mõ-nü-zahzh per-so-nel.

How long are you staying?
Combien de temps allez-vous rester?
Kõ-byē duh tã ah-leh-voo res-teh?

I will be here for . . . days/weeks/months.
Je compte rester . . . jours/semaines/mois.
Zhuh kõt res-teh . . . zhoor/smen/mwah.

Money

How much?
C'est combien, s'il vous plaît?
Se kõ-byẽ, seel voo ple?

Where can I cash this traveler's check?
Où est-ce que je peux toucher ce chèque de voyage?
Oo es kuhzh puh too-sheh suh shek duh vwah-yahzh?

When does the bank open/close?
Quand ouvre/ferme la banque?
Kã oovr/ferm lah bãk?

Please give me some small change.
Je voudrais de la petite monnaie, s'il vous plaît.
Zhvoo-dre dlah pteet mo-ne, seel voo ple.

What is the rate of exchange for dollars?
Quel est le cours du dollar?
Kel el koor dü do-lahr?

At the Hotel

I reserved a single/double room by mail/telephone.
J'ai retenu par lettre/téléphone une chambre à un lit/à deux
    lits.
Zhehr-tuh-nü pahr letr/teh-leh-fon ün shã-brah ẽ lee/ah duh lee.

I want a room with/without bath.
Je voudrais une chambre avec/sans salle de bain.
Zhvoo-dre ün shãbr ah-vek/sã sahl duh bẽ.

How much is this room?
Quel est le prix de la chambre?
Kel el preed lah shãbr?

Are meals included?
Est-ce que les repas sont compris?
Es kuh lehr-pah sõ kõ-pree?

Is there a special rate by the week?
Est-ce qu'il y a des prix spéciaux pour une semaine?
Es keel yah deh pree speh-syoh poor ün smen?

I would like something cheaper.
Je voudrais quelque chose de moins cher.
Zhvoo-dre kel-kuh shohz duh mwẽ sher.

Where is the manager?
Je voudrais voir le directeur, s'il vous plaît.
Zhvoo-dre vwahr luh dee-rek-tuhr, seel voo ple.

I want to check my valuables in your safe.
Est-ce que vous avez un coffre pour les objets de valeur?
Es kuh voo-zah-veh ẽ kofr poor leh-zob-zhed vah-luhr?

Please give me the key to my room.
S'il vous plaît, je voudrais la clé de ma chambre.
Seel voo ple, zhvoo-dre lah klehd mah shãbr.

Send a boy for my luggage.
Pouvez-vous m'envoyer quelqu'un pour mes bagages?
Poo-veh-voo mã-vwah-yeh kel-kẽ poor meh bah-gahzh?

Communications

Where is the post office/telegraph office?
Où est la poste?
Oo e lah post?

When does it open/close?
Quelle est l'heure d'ouverture/de fermeture?
Kel e luhr doo-ver-tür/duh fer-muh-tür?

Where can I buy some stamps?
Où est-ce que je peux acheter des timbres?
Oo es kuhzh puh ahsh-teh deh tẽbr?

Where is the nearest mail box?
Où est la boîte aux lettres la plus proche?
Oo e lah bwaht oh letr lah plü prosh?

I want to send this letter/package via airmail/special delivery.
Je voudrais envoyer cette lettre/ce paquet par avion/en
    exprès.
*Zhvoo-dre ã-vwah-yeh set letr/suh pah-keh pahr ah-vyõ/ã-
    nek-spres.*

How much postage do I need on this letter/package?
C'est combien pour affranchir cette lettre/ce paquet?
Se kõ-byẽ poor ah-frã-sheer set letr/spah-keh?

I want to insure this package.
Je veux assurer ce paquet.
Zhvuh ah-sii-reh spah-keh.

Please forward my mail to . . . .
Pouvez-vous faire suivre mon courrier à . . . ?
Poo-veh-voo fer sweevr mõ koor-yeh ah . . . ?

Where is the nearest telephone?
Où est le téléphone le plus proche?
Oo el teh-leh-fon luh plii prosh?

Do you have a telephone directory?
Avez-vous un annuaire?
Ah-veh-voo ẽ-nah-nii-er?

I want to make a long-distance call.
Je voudrais l'inter.
Zhvoo-dre lẽ-ter.

I want to call . . . .
S'il vous plaît, donnez-moi . . . .
Seel voo ple, do-neh mwah . . . .

Please call station-to-station/collect/person-to-person.
Je voudrais faire un appel normal/une communication en
  P.C.V./un appel avec préavis.
*Zhvoo-dre fer ē-nah-pel nor-mahl/ün ko-mü-nee-kah-syō ã
  peh-seh-veh/ē-nah-pel ah-vek preh-ah-vee.*

The line is busy.
La ligne est occupée.
Lah leeñ e-to-kü-peh.

This is . . . . May I speak to . . . .
Ici . . . . Puis-je parler à . . . ?
Ee-see . . . . Pweezh pahr-leh ah . . . ?

Please hold the line.
Ne quittez pas, s'il vous plaît.
Nuh kee-teh pah, seel voo ple.

Hang up please.
Raccrochez, s'il vous plaît.
Rah-kro-sheh, seel voo ple.

Laundry/Dry Cleaning

Where is a laundry/dry cleaner/laundromat?
Où y a-t-il une blanchisserie/une teinturerie/une laverie
  automatique?
*Oo yah-teel ün blã-shee-sree/ün tē-tür-ree/ün lah-vree o-toh-
  mah-teek?*

Please wash these clothes.
Voici du linge à laver, s'il vous plaît.
Vwah-see dü lēzh ah lah-veh, seel voo ple.

I don't want any starch, please.
Je ne veux pas d'amidon, s'il vous plaît.
Zhuhn vuh pah dah-mee-dō, seel voo ple.

When will my clothes be ready?
Quand est-ce que mon linge sera prêt?
Kã-tes kuh mõ lēzh srah pre?

I want these clothes dry cleaned.
Je voudrais faire nettoyer ces vêtements.
Zhvoo-dre fer ne-twah-yeh seh vetmã.

Please press these trousers.
Je voudrais faire repasser ces pantalons.
Zhvoo-dre fer ruh-pah-seh seh pã-tah-lõ.

Hairdresser/Barber

I would like a haircut/trim.
Pouvez-vous me couper les cheveux/rafraîchir ma coupe, s'il
  vous plaît?
*Poo-veh-voom koo-peh leh shvuh/rah-fre-sheer mah koop, seel
  voo ple?*

Make it shorter, please.
Plus court, s'il vous plaît.
Plii koor, seel voo ple.

I would like a shampoo and set.
Je voudrais un shampooing et une mise en plis.
Zhvoo-dre ẽ shã-pwẽ eh iin mee-zã plee.

Getting Around

When is the next flight to . . . ?
Quand part le prochain vol pour . . . ?
Kã pahr luh pro-shẽ vol poor . . . ?

I want a ticket to . . . , please.
Pardon, je voudrais un billet pour . . . .
Pahr-dõ, zhvoo-dre ẽ bee-ye poor . . . .

Is lunch/dinner served on this flight?
Est-ce qu'il y a un déjeuner/dîner à bord?
Es keel yah ē deh-zhuh-neh/dee-neh ah bor?

I want to reconfirm my flight.
Je voudrais reconfirmer mon vol.
Zhvoo-dre ruh-kõ-feer-meh mõ vol.

Take my bags to my cabin, please.
S'il vous plaît, pouvez-vous apporter mes affaires à ma
    cabine?
*Seel voo ple, poo-veh-voo ah-por-teh me-zah-fer ah mah kah-
    been?*

What time is lunch/dinner/breakfast?
A quelle heure est le déjeuner/dîner/petit déjeuner?
Ah kel uhr el deh-zhuh-neh/dee-neh/ptee deh-zhuh-neh?

At what time does the boat dock?
A quelle heure est-ce que le bateau arrive à quai?
Ah kel uhr es kuhl bah-toh ah-reev ah keh?

Where is the ticket window?
Où est le guichet des billets?
Oo el ghee-sheh deh bee-ye?

May I have a timetable?
Je voudrais un horaire.
Zhvoo-dre ē-no-rer.

**How much is a one-way/round trip first-class/second class
    ticket to . . . ?**
Combien coûte un aller simple/un aller-retour en première/
    en seconde pour . . . ?
*Kõ-byē koot ē-nah-leh sēpl/ē-nah-lehr-toor ã pruh-myer/ã
    suh-gõd poor . . . ?*

I want to reserve a seat/a berth.
Je voudrais louer une place/une couchette.
Zhvoo-dre lweh ün plahs/ün koo-shet.

From which track does the train for . . . leave?
De quel quai part le train pour . . . ?
Duh kel keh pahr luh trĕ poor . . . ?

What time does this train leave?
A quelle heure part ce train?
Ah kel uhr pahr strĕ?

Is this train an express or a local?
Est-ce que c'est un rapide ou un omnibus?
Es kuh se-tĕ rah-peed oo ĕ-nom-nee-büs?

Is this seat taken?
Est-ce que cette place est occupée?
Es kuh set plahs e-to-kü-peh?

When is the dining car open?
A quelle heure ouvre le wagon-restaurant?
Ah kel uhr oovr luh vah-gõ-res-to-rã?

Which way to the lavatory, please?
Pourriez-vous m'indiquer les toilettes, s'il vous plaît?
Poor-yeh-voo mĕ-dee-keh leh twah-let, seel voo ple?

I want to check this baggage.
Je voudrais enregistrer ces bagages.
Zhvoo-dre ãr-zhees-treh seh bah-gahzh.

Where is the bus station?
Où est l'arrêt des cars?
Oo e lah-re deh kahr?

When is the next bus to . . . ?
Quand part le prochain car pour . . . ?
Kã pahr luh pro-shĕ kahr poor . . . ?

How long is the trip?
Combien de temps dure le trajet?
Kõ-byĕd tã dür luh trah-zhe?

Where do I get off to go to . . . ?
Où dois-je descendre pour aller à . . . ?
Oo dwahzh deh-sãdr poor ah-leh ah . . . ?

Take me to . . . .
Je veux aller à/au/à la . . . .
Zhvuh ah-leh ah/oh/ah lah . . . .

I am in a hurry to catch a bus/train/plane.
C'est pressé. Je dois prendre un car/un train/un avion.
Se pre-seh. Zhdwah prãd-rē kahr/trē/nah-vyõ.

Where can I rent a car?
Où est-ce que je peux louer une auto?
Oo es kuhzh puh lweh ü-noh-toh?

Do you charge by the day only, or by the mile as well?
Est-ce qu'on paie à la journée seulement ou aussi au
    kilomètre?
Es kõ pe ah lah zhoor-neh suhl-mã oo oh-see oh kee-lo-metr?

Where is the nearest gas station?
Où se trouve le poste d'essence le plus proche?
Oos troov luh post de-sãs luh plü prosh?

Fill it up with regular/premium, please.
Je voudrais le plein normal/super, s'il vous plaît.
Zhvoo-dre luh plē nor-mahl/sü-per, seel voo ple.

Please check the oil/tires/water/battery.
Pouvez-vous vérifier l'huile/les pneus/l'eau/les accus?
Poo-veh-voo veh-ree-fyeh lweel/leh pnuh/loh/leh-zah-kü?

My car doesn't work.	**I have a flat tire.**
Je suis en panne.	J'ai un pneu crevé.
Zhuh swee-zã pahn.	*Zheh ē pnuh kruh-veh.*

I am having trouble with the . . . .
J'ai des ennuis de . . . .
Zheh deh-zã-nwee duh . . . .

Is there a mechanic here?
Est-ce qu'il y a un mécanicien ici?
Es keel yah ē meh-kah-nee-syē ee-see?

When will my car be ready?
Quand est-ce que l'auto sera prête?
Kã-tes kuh loh-toh srah pret?

Shopping

Where is there a bookstore?
Où y a-t-il une librairie?
Oo yah-teel ün lee-bre-ree?

. . . a department store?
. . . un grand magasin?
. . . ē grã mah-gah-zē?

. . . a pharmacy?
. . . une pharmacie?
. . . ün fahr-mah-see?

. . . a grocery?
. . . une épicerie?
. . . ün eh-pees-ree?

. . . a photo shop?
. . . un magasin de photo?
. . . ē mah-gah-zēd foh-toh?

On what floor are the clothes/leather goods?
A quel étage sont les vêtements/la maroquinerie?
Ah kel eh-tahzh sõ leh vet-mã/lah mah-ro-keen-ree?

How much does this cost?
Combien est-ce que ça coûte?
Kõ-byē es kuh sah koot?

Have you anything better/cheaper?
Avez-vous quelque chose de mieux/de meilleur marché?
Ah-veh-voo kel-kuh shohz duh myuh/duh me-yuhr mahr-sheh?

Is this handmade?
Est-ce que c'est fait-main?
Es kuh se fe-mē?

Does this come in any other color?
Avez-vous la même chose en d'autres couleurs?
Ah-vee-voo lah mem shohz ã doh-truh koo-luhr?

This is too large/small.
C'est trop grand/petit.
Se troh grã/ptee.

Please give me a sales slip for this purchase.
Je voudrais un reçu pour cet achat, s'il vous plaît.
Zhvoo-dre ēr-sü poor se-tah-shah, seel voo ple.

Do you accept checks/traveler's checks?
Est-ce que vous acceptez des chèques/des chèques de voyage?
Es kuh voo-zahk-sep-teh deh shek/deh shek duh vwah-yahzh?

I would like a roll of color/black and white film.
Je voudrais une pellicule photo en couleurs/en noir et blanc.
Zhvoo-dre ün peh-lee-kül foh-toh ã koo-luhr/ã nwahr eh blã.

I would like a Super-8/8 mm. movie film.
Je voudrais un film Super-8/de 8 millimètres.
Zhvoo-dre ē feelm sü-per-weet/duh weet mee-lee-metr.

Here are some films to develop.
Voici des pellicules à développer.
Vwah-see deh peh-lee-kül ah deh-vlo-peh.

I'm just looking.
Je veux seulement regarder ce que vous avez.
Zhvuh suhl-mã ruh-gahr-deh skuh voo-zah-veh.

Sightseeing

How long will the tour last? What will I see?
Combien de temps dure la visite? Qu'est-ce qu'on y voit?
Kõ-byēd tã dür lah vee-zeet? Kes kõ-nee vwah?

Where is the museum/cathedral?
Où est le musée/la cathédrale?
Oo el mü-zeh/lah kah-teh-drahl?

What hours are the museums open?
Quelles sont les heures d'ouverture des musées?
Kel sõ leh-zuhr doo-ver-tür deh mü-zeh?

Do we have to pay to go in?
Est-ce qu'il faut payer pour entrer?
Es keel foht peh-yeh poor ã-treh?

What is the name of that building/monument?
Comment s'appelle ce bâtiment/ce monument?
Ko-mã sah-pel sbah-tee-mã/smo-nü-mã?

Entertainment

I would like to see an opera/a game.
Je voudrais assister à un opéra/à un match.
Zhvoo-dre ah-sees-teh ah ẽ-no-peh-rah/ah ẽ mahtsh.

Please let me have two orchestra/balcony seats/a box.
Je voudrais deux fauteuils d'orchestre/deux places au
balcon/une loge.
*Zhvoo-dre duh foh-tuhy dor-kestr/duh plahs oh bahl-kõ/ün
lozh.*

I want to eat breakfast/lunch/dinner.
Je voudrais un petit déjeuner/un déjeuner/un dîner.
Zhvoo-dre ẽ ptee deh-zhuh-neh/ẽ deh-zhuh-neh/ẽ dee-neh.

We would like a table for two, please.
Nous voudrions une table pour deux, s'il vous plaît.
Noo voo-dree-yõ ün tahbl poor duh, seel voo ple.

May we have a menu/wine list, please?
Je voudrais un menu/la carte des vins, s'il vous plaît.
Zhvoo-dre ẽ muh-nü/lah kahrt deh vẽ, seel voo ple.

What do you recommend?
Qu'est-ce que vous nous conseillez?
Kes kuh voo noo kõ-seh-yeh?

Please bring the check.
S'il vous plaît, l'addition.
Seel voo ple, lah-dee-syõ.

Is the tip included?
Est-ce que le service est compris?
Es kuhl ser-vees e kõ-pree?

Where do I pay?
Où faut-il payer?
Oo foh-teel peh-yeh?

There is a mistake in the bill.
Il y a une erreur dans l'addition.
Eel yah ün e-ruhr dã lah-dee-syõ.

Health

I don't feel well.
Je ne me sens pas bien.
Zhuhn muh sã pah byẽ.

I need a doctor/dentist.
Je veux voir un docteur/un dentiste.
Zhvuh vwahr ẽ dok-tuhr/ẽ dã-teest.

I have a headache/stomach ache/toothache.
J'ai mal à la tête/mal au ventre/mal aux dents.
Zheh mahl ah lah tet/mahl oh vātr/mahl oh dã.

I have a bad cold/fever.
J'ai un gros rhume/de la fièvre.
Zheh ē groh rüm/dlah fyevr.

My . . . is burned/hurt/bleeding.
Mon/ma . . . s'est brûlé/blessé/perd du sang.
Mõ/mah . . . se brü-leh/bleh-seh/per dü sã.

Please make up this prescription.
Pouvez-vous me préparer cette ordonnance, s'il vous plaît.
Poo-veh-voom preh-pah-reh set or-do-nãs, seel voo ple.

Emergencies

Help!
Au secours!
Ohs-koor!

Police!
Police!
Po-lees!

Please call a policeman/an ambulance.
S'il vous plaît, appelez la police/une ambulance.
Seel voo ple, ah-pleh lah po-lees/üin ã-bü-lãs.

I need a lawyer.
Je veux un avocat.
Zhvuh ē-nah-vo-kah.

I want to call the American Embassy.
Je veux téléphoner à l'ambassade américaine.
Zhvuh teh-leh-fo-neh ah lã-bah-sahd ah-meh-ree-ken.

I've been robbed.
On m'a volé.
Õ mah vo-leh.

Is there anyone here who speaks English?
Est-ce que quelqu'un parle anglais?
Es kuh kel-kē pahrl ã-gle?

I am lost.
Je me suis perdu.
Zhuhm swee per-dü.

I don't know where my hotel/car is.
Je ne sais pas où se trouve mon hôtel/mon auto.
Zhuhn seh pah oos troov mõ-noh-tel/mõ-noh-toh.

I have lost a suitcase/an umbrella/my purse.
J'ai perdu une valise/un parapluie/mon sac.
Zheh per-dü ün vah-leez/ē pah-rah-plwee/mõ sahk.

I missed the train/bus/plane.
J'ai manqué le train/le car/l'avion.
Zheh mã-keh luh trē/luh kahr/lah-vyō.

Someone is injured.
Il y a un blessé.
Eel yah ē bleh-seh.

Menu Reader

Beverages

apéritif [*ah-peh-ree-teef*] wine or other drink before meals
bière [*byer*] beer
   bière à la pression [*byer ah lah pre-syō*] draught beer
   un demi de bière [*ē duh-meed byer*] a glass of draught beer
café [*kah-feh*] coffee
   café au lait [*kah-feh oh le*] coffee with hot milk
   café-crème [*kah-feh krem*] coffee with cream
chocolat chaud [*shoh-koh-lah shoh*] hot chocolate
cidre [*seedr*] cider
citron pressé [*see-trō pre-seh*] lemonade
eau [*oh*] water
   eau minérale [*oh mee-neh-rahl*] mineral water
glaçon [*glah-sō*] ice cube
jus de fruit [*zhüd frwee*] fruit juice
lait [*le*] milk
   lait grenadine [*le gruh-nah-deen*] grenadine syrup mixed
      with milk
limonade [*lee-mo-nahd*] soda
martini [*mahr-tee-nee*] sweet vermouth
menthe à l'eau [*mã-tah loh*] mint-flavored syrup with water
pastis [*pahs-tees*] anis-flavored aperitif
porto [*por-toh*] port
soda orange (citron, etc.) [*so-dah o-rãzh (see-trō)*] orange
   (lemon, etc.) flavored soft drink
thé [*teh*] tea
   thé au citron [*teh oh see-trō*] tea with lemon
vin [*vē*] wine
   vin blanc [*vē blã*] white wine
   vin ordinaire [*vē or-dee-ner*] ordinary wine
   vin rosé [*vē roh-zeh*] rosé wine
   vin rouge [*vē roozh*] red wine

The Menu

à la, à l' (with adjective of country, province, etc.) [*ah lah*]
   prepared in the style of (the country mentioned)
   à la Française [*ah lah frã-sez*] in the French style (often
      cooked in butter)
   à la Provençale [*ah lah pro-vã-sahl*] Provençal style (often
      with tomatoes, olives and olive oil)
abricot [*ah-bree-koh*] apricot
agneau [*ah-nyoh*] lamb
ail [*ahy*] garlic
ananas [*ah-nah-nah*] pineapple
anchois [*ã-shwah*] anchovy
artichaut [*ahr-tee-shoh*] artichoke
   fonds d'artichaut [*fõ dahr-tee-shoh*] artichoke hearts
asperges [*ah-sperzh*] asparagus
aubergine [*oh-ber-zheen*] eggplant
avocat [*ah-vo-kah*] avocado

baba au rhum [*bah-bah oh rom*] sponge cake soaked in rum
      sauce
baguette [*bah-ghet*] long thin loaf of bread
banane [*bah-nahn*] banana
béchamel [*beh-shah-mel*] cream sauce
beignets [*be-nye*] fritters
betterave [*be-trahv*] beet
beurre [*buhr*] butter
bifteck [*beef-tek*] steak (small)
   bien cuit [*byẽ kwee*] well done
   à point [*ah pwẽ*] medium
   saignant [*se-nyã*] rare
biscuits [*bees-kwee*] cookies, crackers
boeuf [*buhf*] beef
   boeuf bourguignon [*buhf boor-ghee-nyõ*] beef stew cooked
      in wine
bonbons [*bõ-bõ*] candy
bouilli [*boo-yee*] boiled
boudin [*boo-dẽ*] blood sausage

bouillabaisse [*boo-yah-bes*] thick fish soup, specialty of
    Marseille
brioche [*bree-osh*] light roll, for breakfast or snack
brochet [*bro-she*] pike
brochette [*bro-shet*] skewer, kebabs

cacahuètes [*kah-kah-wet*] peanuts
canard [*kah-nahr*] duck
    canard à l'orange [*kah-nahr ah lo-rãzh*] duck with orange
    sauce
carottes [*kah-rot*] carrots
carte [*kahrt*] menu
céleri [*sel-ree*] celery
cerises [*sreez*] cherries
cervelle [*ser-vel*] brains
champignons [*shã-pee-nyõ*] mushrooms
charcuterie [*shahr-kü-tree*] pork products, salami, etc.
Châteaubriand [*shah-toh-bree-yã*] thick fillet steak
chou [*shoo*] cabbage
chou à la crème [*shoo ah lah krem*] cream puff
choucroute garnie [*shoo-kroot gahr-nee*] sauerkraut with
    different kinds of sausages
chou-fleur [*shoo-fluhr*] cauliflower
choux de Bruxelles [*shood brü-sel*] Brussels sprouts
citron [*see-trõ*] lemon
civet de lièvre [*see-ved lyevr*] hare stewed in wine sauce
compote de fruits [*kõ-pot duh frwee*] stewed fruit
    compote de pommes [*kõ-pot duh pom*] applesauce
concombres [*kõ-kõbr*] cucumbers
confiture [*kõ-fee-tür*] jam
coq au vin [*kok oh vẽ*] chicken cooked in wine
coquille Saint Jacques [*ko-keey sẽ zhahk*] scallops served in
    shell, with cream sauce
cornichons [*kor-nee-shõ*] small pickles
côtelette, côte [*koht-let, koht*] chop
courgettes [*koor-zhet*] zucchini
couscous [*koos-koos*] steamed semolina, with chicken, mutton,
    etc., vegetables and sauce; specialty of North Africa

couvert [*koo-ver*] place setting, cover charge
crème [*krem*] cream, pudding
   crème anglaise [*krem ã-glez*] boiled custard
   crème Chantilly [*krem shã-tee-yee*] sweetened whipped
      cream
crêpes [*krep*] thin pancakes, rolled with jelly or other filling
   crêpes Suzette [*krep sü-zet*] crepes with orange sauce,
      flamed
cresson [*kre-sõ*] watercress
crevettes [*kruh-vet*] shrimp
croissant [*krwah-sã*] crescent-shaped roll
crudités [*krü-dee-teh*] raw vegetables sometimes marinated
cuisses de grenouille [*kwees duh gruh-nooy*] frogs' legs
cuit [*kwee*] cooked

dattes [*daht*] dates
dinde [*dẽd*] turkey

écrevisses [*eh-kruh-vees*] crayfish
endives [*ã-deev*] Belgian endive
entrecôte [*ã-truh-koht*] steak
épinards [*éh-pee-nahr*] spinach
escalope de veau [*es-kah-lop duh voh*] veal steak
escargots [*es-kahr-goh*] snails
faisan [*fuh-zã*] pheasant
fait maison [*fe me-zõ*] homemade
farci [*fahr-see*] stuffed
fèves [*fev*] lima beans (dried)
figues [*feeg*] figs
flan [*flã*] baked custard
foie [*fwah*] liver
au four [*oh foor*] baked
fraises [*frez*] strawberries
framboises [*frã-bwahz*] raspberries
frit [*free*] fried
fromage [*fro-mahzh*] cheese
   fromage de chèvre [*fro-mahzh duh shevr*] goat cheese
fruit [*frwee*] fruit

    fruits confits [*frwee kŏ-fee*] candied fruit
    fruits de mer [*frweed mer*] seafood
fumé [*fü-meh*] smoked
gâteau [*gah-toh*] cake
gauffres [*gohfr*] waffles
gigot [*zhee-goh*] leg of lamb
glace [*glahs*] ice cream
gratiné, au gratin [*grah-tee-neh, oh grah-tē*] prepared with
    cream sauce, topped with crumbs and/or cheese
grillade [*gree-yahd*] broiled meat
grillé [*gree-yeh*] broiled, grilled

hareng [*ah-rã*] herring
haricots [*ah-ree-koh*] beans
    haricots blancs [*ah-ree-koh blã*] Navy beans
    haricots verts [*ah-ree-koh ver*] green beans
homard [*oh-mahr*] lobster
huile [*weel*] oil
huîtres [*weetr*] oysters

jambon [*zhã-bõ*] ham

laitue [*leh-tü*] lettuce
langouste [*lã-goost*] small lobster
lapin [*lah-pē*] rabbit
lièvre [*lyevr*] hare

macédoine [*mah-seh-dwahn*] mixed diced vegetables
maïs [*mah-ees*] corn
maquereau [*mahk-roh*] mackerel
mariné [*mah-ree-neh*] marinated
melon [*muh-lõ*} melon
menu [*muh-nü*] menu
    menu du jour [*muh-nü dü zhoor*] today's menu
miel [*myel*] honey
morue [*mo-rü*] cod
moules [*mool*] mussels
moutarde [*moo-tahrd*] mustard
mouton [*moo-tõ*] mutton

nature [*nah-tür*] plain
navet [*nah-ve*] turnip

oeuf [*uhf*] egg
  oeuf à la coque [*uh-fah lah kok*] soft-boiled egg
  oeuf au plat [*uh-foh plah*] fried egg
  oeufs brouillés [*uh brooh-yeh*] scrambled eggs
  oeuf dur [*uhf dür*] hard-boiled egg
oie [*wah*] goose
oignon [*o-nyõ*] onion
olives [*o-leev*] olives
omelette [*om-let*] omelet

pain [*pẽ*] bread
pamplemousse [*pã-pluh-moos*] grapefruit
pané [*pah-neh*] breaded
pâté de fois gras [*pah-tehd fwah grah*] paste made from goose livers
pâtes alimentaires [*paht ah-lee-mã-ter*] pasta: noodles, etc.
pâtisserie [*pah-tees-ree*] pastry
paupiettes [*poh-pyet*] thin slices of meat, stuffed, braised
pêche [*pesh*] peach
petits pois [*ptee pwah*] green peas
petits fours [*ptee foor*] small frosted cakes
plat de résistance [*plahd reh-zees-tãs*] main course
plat du chef [*plah dü shef*] specialty of the chef
poché [*po-sheh*] poached
poivre [*pwahvr*] pepper
poivron [*pwah-vrõ*] green pepper
pomme [*pom*] apple
pomme de terre [*pom duh ter*] potato
  pommes de terre au gratin [*pom duh ter oh grah-tẽ*] scalloped potatoes
  pommes de terre en robe des champs [*pom duh ter ã rob deh shã*] baked potatoes
  pommes (de terre) frites [*pom (duh ter) freet*] French fried potatoes

   purée de pommes de terre [*pü-rehd pom duh ter*] mashed
      potatoes
porc [*por*] pork
potage [*po-tahzh*] soup
pot-au-feu [*po-toh-fuh*] beef and vegetables in broth
poule [*pool*] hen
poulet [*poo-le*] chicken
pruneaux [*prü-noh*] prunes
prunes [*prün*] plums

quenelle [*kuh-nel*] ground fish or veal, molded and prepared in
      sauce; specialty of Lyon

ragoût [*rah-goo*] stew
raisin [*re-zē*] grape
   raisins secs [*re-zē sek*] raisins
ratatouille [*rah-tah-tooy*] tomatoes, zucchini, eggplant,
      peppers, cooked with herbs and olive oil; specialty of
      Nice
ris de veau [*reed voh*] sweetbreads
rissolé [*ree-so-leh*] browned
riz [*ree*] rice
rognons [*ro-nyō*] kidneys
rosbif [*roz-beef*] roast beef
rôti [*roh-tee*] roast

salade [*sah-lahd*] salad
   salade de fruits [*sah-lahd duh frwee*] fruit cup
   salade de riz [*sah-lahd duh ree*] rice salad (with tomatoes,
      olives, anchovies, peppers)
   salade Niçoise [*sah-lahd nee-swahz*] tomatoes, hard-boiled
      eggs, anchovies, olives, etc.
   salade verte [*sah-lahd vert*] tossed salad
saucisse [*soh-sees*] hot, cooked sausage, or sausage to cook
saucisson [*soh-see-sō*] hard sausage: to slice and serve cold
saumon [*soh-mō*] salmon
sauté [*soh-teh*] sauteed

sel [*sel*] salt
sole [*sol*] sole
soupe [*soop*] soup
   soupe à l'ail [*soop ah lahy*] garlic soup
   soupe à l'oignon [*soop ah lo-nyõ*] onion soup
   soupe de légumes [*soop duh leh-güm*] vegetable soup
spécialité de la maison [*speh-syah-lee-tehd lah me-zõ*] specialty
   of the house
sucre [*sükr*] sugar

tarte [*tahrt*] pie
thon [*tõ*] tuna
tomate [*to-maht*] tomato
tournedos [*toor-nuh-doh*] steak from fillet
truite [*trweet*] trout

veau [*voh*] veal
   blanquette de veau [*blã-ket duh voh*] veal stewed in cream
    sauce
viande [*vyãd*] meat
   viande froide [*vyãd frwahd*] cold meat (roast)
   viande hachée [*vyãd ah-sheh*] ground beef
vinaigrette [*vee-ne-gret*] vinegar and oil sauce
volaille [*vo-lahy*] poultry
vol-au-vent [*vol-oh-vã*] patty shell filled with some creamed
   food

yaourt [*yah-oor*] yogurt

A Concise French Grammar

Nouns

French nouns have grammatical gender: every one is masculine or feminine, and every noun in this dictionary is marked *m.* or *f.* Remembering gender is easier if you learn a new noun with its article or an adjective. For various reasons which you will understand later, it is harder to remember the gender of words beginning with vowel sounds. Make a special effort here, since the gender of the nouns determines much of the grammar of the rest of the sentence.

Nouns usually add *-s* to form the plural, unless the noun ends in *-s*, *-x*, or *-z*, in which case there is no change. All other plural forms are marked in the dictionary. The most common irregular plural is *-aux*.

Articles

An article agrees with the noun it precedes, and in context is often the best clue to the gender and number of the noun.

● The definite article, the, is *le*, m., or *la*, f. Both become *l'* before vowel sounds (one reason why the gender of these nouns is harder to distinguish). The plural article for both genders is *les*. In spoken French, adding an *-s* to a noun normally does not change its pronunciation, and the article is often the only sign that a word is plural:

le livre [*luh leevr*] the book
les livres [*leh leevr*] the books
la table [*lah tahbl*] the table
les tables [*leh tahbl*] the tables
l'arbre [*lahrbr*] the tree
les arbres [*leh-zahrbr*] the trees

The masculine and the plural forms of the definite article, *le*, *les*, always contract with the prepositions *à* and *de*:

à le becomes **au** [*oh*]   **à les** becomes **aux** [*oh*]
de le becomes **du** [*dü*]   **de les** becomes **des** [*deh*]

• The indefinite article, a, an, is *un*, m., or *une*, f. French also has a plural indefinite article, *des*, m. and f.:

un livre a book   **des livres** books
une table a table   **des tables** tables

French tends to use articles more than English does. One exception is with nouns indicating profession, nationality, or religion, if they are not modified in any way, and not preceded by *c'est*, it is:

> **Il est professeur.** He is a teacher.
> **Elle est Américaine.** She is an American.

BUT **C'est un bon professeur.** He is a good teacher.

• The partitive article is used when speaking of an indefinite quantity. The best English equivalent would be "some" or "any," but often English does not express the idea at all. The partitive article has four forms: *du* (m.), *de la* (f.), *de l'* (m. and f. before vowel sounds), and *des* (all plural nouns). It is used particularly with words like *have*, *want*, *order*, etc. Examples:

> **Avez-vous des journaux?** Do you have (any) newspapers?
> **Je voudrais du café, de l'eau, et de la salade.**
> I would like (some) coffee, water, and salad.

If you can put *some* or *any* in your English sentence, even if you would not ordinarily use either word, you probably need the partitive in your French sentence.

In negative sentences and after expressions of quantity, both the partitive and the indefinite article are replaced by *de*:

> **J'ai des frères.** I have brothers.
> **Je n'ai pas de frères.** I have no brothers.

> **Il a des livres.** He has books.
> **Il a beaucoup de livres.** He has many books.
> **Il a un livre.** He has a book.
> **Il n'a pas de livres.** He has no books.

Qualifying Adjectives

Adjectives agree with the nouns they modify in gender and number. To make the feminine form of the adjective you add -*e* to the masculine singular, unless it ends in -*e*. To make the plural you add -*s* to the correct (masculine or feminine) singular form, unless it ends in -*s* or -*x*. Examples:

m. sing.	m. pl.	f. sing.	f. pl.	
vert	verts	verte	vertes	green
parfait	parfaits	parfaite	parfaites	perfect
jeune	jeunes	jeune	jeunes	young
mauvais	mauvais	mauvaise	mauvaises	bad

Adding -*e* or -*es* often means that you will pronounce a consonant in the feminine form that is silent in the masculine form. In the dictionary the pronunciation of the masculine singular is always given, and the added consonant pronounced in the feminine is included in parentheses.

green vert [*ver(t)*]
bad mauvais [*moh-ve(z)*]

Adjectives that do not follow this pattern are considered irregular, and the feminine singular or masculine plural forms are given in the dictionary. Examples:

marvellous merveilleux, -euse [*mer-ve-yuh, mer-ve-yuhz*]
rural rural, -aux (m, pl) [*rü-rahl, rü-roh*]

Be sure to use the feminine singular of these irregular adjectives, not the masculine plural, to form the feminine plural.

Most adjectives follow the noun they modify. Some very common ones precede it: *grand*, big, tall; *petit*, small; *bon*, good; *mauvais*, bad; *joli*, pretty; *gros*, fat, big; *long*, long; *court*, short; *jeune*, young; *beau*, beautiful, handsome; *nouveau*, new; and *vieux*, old. The last three, all irregular, have a special form used before masculine singular words beginning with a vowel sound: *bel*, *nouvel*, *vieil*. Examples:

un beau chapeau a beautiful hat
un bel enfant a beautiful child

un nouveau livre a new book
un nouvel habit a new suit of clothes

un vieux monsieur an old man
un vieil hôtel an old hotel

In English we put one noun before another and use the first as an adjective: bed-room, lawn-mower, night-stand. Not so in French. If the word isn't an adjective, it cannot be used as one, and a phrase must be used:

chambre à coucher room for sleeping
tondeuse à gazon cutter for lawn
table de nuit table for night

With one exception, adjectives are compared regularly:

COMPARATIVE:

more than (-er than) **plus . . . que**
      Louise est plus grande que Françoise.
        Louise is taller than Frances.

as . . . as **aussi . . . que**
      Jean est aussi grand que Pierre.
        John is as tall as Peter.

less . . . than **moins . . . que**
      Louise est moins grande que Sophie.
        Louise is less tall than Sophie.

SUPERLATIVE:

the most (the -est) **le (la, les) plus**
      Louise est la plus grande fille de la classe.
        Louise is the tallest girl in the class.
      Anne et Marie sont les plus petites filles de la classe.
        Anne and Mary are the smallest girls in the class.

the least **le (la, les) moins**
      Henri est le garçon le moins intelligent de la classe.
        Henry is the least intelligent boy in the class.

NOTE: French uses *de* after a superlative; English uses *in*.

The position of the adjective remains the same as for the positive form. If the adjective follows the noun, the definite article is used twice:

le garçon le moins intelligent the least intelligent boy

The one adjective that has irregular comparative and superlative forms is *bon*, good. They are: *meilleur(e)*, better, and *le (la, les) meilleur(e)*, best.

Personal Pronouns

French has subject and object pronouns like English I, me;
he, him, plus indirect object pronouns, and a special category of pronouns used in a stressed position.

Subject	Direct Object	Indirect Object	Stressed*
je I	**me** me	**me** to me	**moi**
tu you	**te** you	**te** to you	**toi**
il he, it	**le** him, it	**lui** to him	**lui**
elle she, it	**la** her, it	**lui** to her	**elle**
on (indefinite)	**se** himself, herself, itself	**se** to himself, herself, itself	**soi**
nous we	**nous** us	**nous** to us	**nous**
vous you	**vous** you	**vous** to you	**vous**
ils they, *m.*	**les** them, *m.*	**leur** to them, *m.*	**eux**
elles they, *f.*	**les** them, *f.*	**leur** to them, *f.*	**elles**
	se themselves	**se** to themselves	**soi**

*The translation of the stressed pronouns varies with
their use.

The second person singular pronouns, *tu*, etc., need some
explanation. The same is true of the corresponding verb
forms that we will see later. In English we say *you* to everyone. In French there are two possibilities when speaking to
one person: the second person singular, *tu*, called the familiar
form, or the second person plural, *vous*, used as a polite
singular. In the plural, *vous* is used for everyone. As a foreigner you will say *vous* to almost everyone, except to very
young children.

● Subject pronouns are used only as the subject of a verb,
never alone or after a comparison (taller than *I*, etc.). In these
latter cases, use the stressed pronouns:

Qui parle français? Lui.
   Who speaks French? He does.
Elle est plus grande que moi.
   She is taller than I.
The stressed forms are also used after prepositions:
J'ai parlé avec elle.   I spoke with her.

● The third person direct object pronouns, *le, la, les*, can refer to persons or things. The indirect object pronouns, *lui, leur*, refer only to persons. (*Y* is used for things, as we will see later.) All object pronouns normally precede the verb, where they can be used with *en* and *y*, important French pronouns for which there are no direct English equivalents.

En replaces *de* plus a noun or pronoun referring to things or to a situation, not a person. It also is used instead of a partitive expression or with an expression of quantity. In these latter cases it can refer to persons. Examples:

Voulez-vous des poires? Oui, j'en voudrais.
 Do you want some pears? Yes, I would like some.
Combien de frères avez-vous? J'en ai trois.
 How many brothers do you have? I have three.
Je suis content de cela. J'en suis content.
 I am pleased with that. I am pleased with it.

BUT:

Je suis content de Jean. Je suis content de lui.
 I am pleased with John. I am pleased with him.

Y replaces *à* (and, of course, *au* and *aux*) plus a noun or pronoun signifying a thing, or any expression indicating a place. Examples:

Marie est-elle en ville? Oui, elle y est.
 Is Marie in town? Yes, she is.
Je pense à cela. J'y pense.
 I am thinking about that. I am thinking about it.
Je réponds aux lettres. J'y réponds.
 I am answering the letters. I am answering them.

BUT:

Je réponds à mon père. Je lui réponds.
 I am answering my father. I am answering him.

If more than one pronoun precedes the verb (three is the maximum), their order is as follows:

Y and *en* are closest to the verb, and *y* precedes *en*:

Je m'en souviens.   I remember.
Il l'y a mis.   He put it there.
Il y en a.   There is/are some.

When used together, *le*, *la*, or *les* always precedes *lui* or *leur*:

Elle la lui donne.   She gives it to him/her.
Il les leur donne.   He gives them to them.

The other pronouns come first, farthest from the verb:

Il me le donne.   He gives it to me.
Je vous les apporte.   I bring them to you.
Je t'en remercie.   I thank you (for it).
Elle nous y a amenés.   She brought us there.

After an affirmative imperative all pronouns follow the verb. They keep the same order, except for *nous*, *vous*, *me*, and *te*, which follow everything except *y* and *en*. When *me* and *te* are final, they are replaced by their stressed forms, *moi* and *toi*. Examples:

Donnez-les-leur.   Give them to them.
Donnez-le-moi.   Give it to me.
Donnez m'en.   Give some to me.

You will frequently find French verbs that are translated into English by a verb plus a preposition: *attendre* is translated *wait for*, for example. The reverse is also true: *to obey someone* is translated into French by a verb plus a prepositional phrase: *obéir à quelqu'un*. Pay attention to this difference: if the French expression uses a prepositional phrase, you must use an indirect object pronoun if you want to replace it. Examples:

J'attends Jean. Je l'attends.
   I am waiting for John. I am waiting for him.
J'obéis à mon père. Je lui obéis.
   I obey my father. I obey him.

● The reflexive pronoun *se*, direct or indirect object, singular or plural, can show that the subject acts upon itself, or simply may give a different meaning to the verb.

● *On* is an indefinite third person pronoun used only as subject. It is translated in different ways: "people," "they," "one," "you" (in the impersonal sense — "you go three blocks . . ."), or simply by the passive voice.

on pense que it is thought that
on dit que they say that
on dirait que you'd say that
on vous demande au téléphone you are wanted on the
telephone

Other Pronouns and Adjectives

An adjective is used with a noun, a pronoun instead of a
noun. But since the words are sometimes the same or similar,
we will discuss pronouns and adjectives together.

• Demonstrative adjectives and pronouns: this, that,
these, those. The demonstrative adjective has four forms:

m. sing. **ce** (**cet** before vowel sounds)
f. sing. **cette**
pl. **ces** (for both genders)

(Note that expressions like *cet ami*, this friend, m., and *cette
amie*, this friend, f., sound exactly alike.)

These demonstrative adjectives generally mean *this* or
these:

ce matin this morning   **ces livres** these books

If you want to say *that* or *those*, add *-là* to the noun the
demonstrative adjective modifies:

ce matin-là that morning   **ces livres-là** those books

To distinguish between *this* or *these* and *that* or *those*, add
-ci for this, these, and *-là* for that, those:

Ce livre-ci est rouge; ce livre-là est vert.
This book is red; that book is green.

The demonstrative pronoun has a neuter form *ceci*, this (in
general), and *cela*, that (in general), in addition to the masculine and feminine forms *celui, ceux; celle, celles*. These
latter forms are never used alone. You can add *-ci* or *-là*:

celui-ci, *m.*	this one	**celle-ci,** *f.*	this one
celui-là, *m.*	that one	**celle-là,** *f.*	that one
ceux-ci, *m.*	these	**celles-ci,** *f.*	these
ceux-là, *m.*	those	**celles-là,** *f.*	those

These forms can also be followed by *de*:

celle de Jean the one of John's *or* John's

or by a subordinate clause:

celui que j'ai trouvé the one I found

● Possessive adjectives and pronouns: In French these forms agree in gender and number *with the object possessed.*

First the adjectives:

English	*If the object possessed is*		
	m. sing.	*f. sing.*	*m. or f. pl.*
my	**mon**	**ma (mon)**	**mes**
your	**ton**	**ta (ton)**	**tes**
his, her, its	**son**	**sa (son)**	**ses**
our		**notre**	**nos**
your		**votre**	**vos**
their		**leur**	**leurs**

(Before all nouns beginning with a vowel sound, use *mon, ton, son*.)

The French sentence will not tell you the sex of the possessor. *Son livre* can be "his book" or "her book." If you really need to distinguish (you will be surprised at how often it is clear from the context) add *à lui* or *à elle*:

son livre à lui his book **son livre à elle** her book

Be careful not to confuse *ses* and *leurs*. *Ses* refers to several objects belonging to one person, *leurs* to several objects belong to several persons.

The possessive pronouns resemble the adjectives:

English	*If the object possessed is:*			
	m. sing.	*f. sing.*	*m. pl.*	*f. pl.*
mine	**le mien**	**la mienne**	**les miens**	**les miennes**
yours	**le tien**	**la tienne**	**les tiens**	**les tiennes**
his, hers, its	**le sien**	**la sienne**	**les siens**	**les siennes**
ours	**le nôtre**	**la nôtre**	**les nôtres**	
yours	**le vôtre**	**la vôtre**	**les vôtres**	
theirs	**le leur**	**la leur**	**les leurs**	

● Interrogative adjectives and pronouns: what, which, who, whom, whose. The interrogative adjective, *quel, quels*, *quelle*, *quelles*, agrees with the noun it modifies.

Quel jour sommes-nous?
   What day is it? *Literally,* What day are we?
Quelle est la date de . . . ?
   What is the date of . . . ?
A quel livre pensez-vous?
   What book are you thinking about?

There are several interrogative pronouns: *Lequel*, m. sing., *laquelle*, f. sing., *lesquels*, m. pl., and *lesquelles*, f. pl., translate "Which one(s)?" Examples:

Voilà deux livres. Lequel voulez-vous?
   Here are two books. Which one do you want?

But you would use the adjective to say:

Quel livre voulez-vous?
   Which book do you want?

(*A* and *de* contract with these pronouns the same way they do with the definite articles: *auquel, auxquels, auxquelles; duquel, desquels, desquelles.*)

Qui, who, whom, refers to persons and can be used as subject or object. Very often, particularly in spoken French, *qui* is replaced by a longer form, *Qui est-ce qui* for the subject, *qui est-ce que* for the object. Both forms are correct:

Qui vient?/Qui est-ce qui vient?
   Who comes? Who is coming?
Qui voyez-vous?/Qui est-ce que vous voyez?
   Whom do you see?

Note that when you use *qui est-ce que* you keep the normal word order (subject before verb), but when you use *qui* referring to the object of the verb, the subject follows the verb (*voyez-vous*).

Qui can follow a preposition:

A qui écrivez-vous?   To whom are you writing?

It is used to translate *whose*? (the question, not the relative pronoun):

A qui est ce livre?   Whose book is this?

Que (*Qu'*) refers to things. In speech *que*, like *qui*, is usually replaced by a longer form: *Qu'est-ce qui* (subject) or *Qu'est-ce que* (object), but both are correct:

Qu'arrive-t-il?/Qu'est-ce qui arrive?
What is happening
Que fait-il?/Qu'est-ce qu'il fait?
What is he doing?

Again you must invert subject and verb if you use the short form. For more detail, see the section on questions.

Quoi, what, is used after prepositions:

A quoi pensez-vous?   What are you thinking about?
De quoi parlez vous?   What are you talking about?

● Relative pronouns vary according to their roles in the subordinate clause:
The subject, who, which, that, is *qui*:

la fille qui est venue   the girl who came
l'auto qui est en bas   the car which is down below

The direct object, whom, which, that, is *que*:

la fille que j'ai vue   the girl (whom) I saw
l'auto que j'ai achetée   the car (which) I bought

(Note that when it is the object, the relative can often be omitted in English, but never in French.)
The preposition *de* and its object, whose, of whom, of which, is *dont*:

la fille dont j'ai le livre   the girl whose book I have
(Note the word order: French says, "of whom I have the book.")
l'homme dont je parle   the man of whom I am speaking

The object of other prepositions: *qui* for persons (*à qui, pour qui, etc.*), *lequel* for things (*auquel, pour laquelle*, etc.).

l'homme à qui j'ai parlé   the man to whom I spoke
la table sur laquelle j'ai mis mon livre
the table on which I put my book

When using relative pronouns, remember that some verbs are followed by a preposition in English and not in French, and vice versa. If your French verb needs a preposition, choose your relative pronoun accordingly:

l'instrument dont il joue   the instrument he plays
   to play = **jouer de**
l'homme qu'il attend   the man he is waiting for
   to wait for = **attendre**
la lettre à laquelle il répond   the letter he is answering
   to answer = **répondre à**

Adverbs

Regular adverbs are formed by adding -*ment* to the adjective. The comparison of adverbs is regular: *plus* (*moins*) for the comparative form, *le plus* (*le moins*) for the superlative. There are a few irregular forms:

bien well	**mieux** better	**le mieux** best
	aussi bien as well	
	moins bien less well	**le moins bien** least well
beaucoup much, very much, many	**plus** more	**le plus** most
peu little	**moins** less	**le moins** least

Note that *beaucoup* and *peu* by themselves are adverbs, linked to the verb. *Beaucoup de* and *peu de* are expressions of quantity, referring to the following noun:

Je l'aime beaucoup (peu).   I like him very much (little).
J'ai beaucoup (peu) de livres.   I have many (few) books.

This difference exists for many expressions. A word without *de* is an adverb; the same word with *de* refers to the following noun, usually as an expression of quantity or a preposition:

Il habite très près.   He lives very near.
Il habite près de l'église.   He lives near the church.

Many adverbs have a negative meaning. We will talk about them in the section on sentence structure.

Prepositions

Prepositions in different languages never correspond exactly. Here we'll mention just a few points:

- In French you cannot end a sentence with a preposition.
- Remember that a preposition may follow a verb in one language but not in the other.
- In English the real action of a verb is often expressed by a preposition which follows it: go in, come in. French will use a verb to translate the preposition rather than the English verb:

go in, come in   **entrer**
go out, come out   **sortir**
run in, run out   **entrer, sortir (en courant)**
go across, walk across   **traverser**
run across   **traverser en courant** (NOT: **courir à travers**)

Many common examples of this are given in the dictionary. If you don't find the one you want, try to translate the idea contained in the preposition.

Verbs

French verbs have different forms for the different persons and numbers, as well as for the different tenses.

French also has a separate category of verbs, reflexive verbs, in which the subject and object of the verb are the same. They are shown in the dictionary with the reflexive pronoun *se* (or *s'*). When these verbs are conjugated, they take the reflexive pronoun (*me, te, se, nous, vous, se*) that agrees in person and number with the subject (see tables).

The infinitive of the verb is given in the dictionary. The conjugation tables at the end of this grammar show how to form four simple and four compound tenses, plus the subjunctive and the imperative. Note that French has no progressive form. Generally you should translate the progressive form of an English tense as you would the simple form — *I am sleeping* like *I sleep*, for example. There is one exception, as we will see.

The *present* tense translates the English present. *Je parle*, I talk.

The *imperfect* corresponds to the past progressive: *Je parlais*, I was talking; or to expressions showing habitual action: I used to talk, I would talk for hours every day. The imperfect does not translate the ordinary English past (I talked), except for verbs which express a state rather than an action:

I knew it. **Je le savais.**

He was sick. **Il était malade.**

The *past indefinite* (*J'ai parlé*, I talked, I have talked) looks like the present perfect in English, but it also translates the ordinary past tense. It is the past tense you will use most often. Often the past indefinite and the imperfect are used together, the past indefinite to note a fact that happened, and the imperfect to describe the surrounding circumstances:

Je lisais quand il a parlé. I was reading when he spoke.

The *past perfect* (*J'avais parlé*, I had talked) is used as it is in English.

The *future* (*Je parlerai*, I will talk) is used as it is in English. It is also used after *when*, where in English we use the present.

The *future perfect* (*J'aurai parlé*, I will have talked) is used as it is in English, and after *when*.

The *conditional* (*Je parlerais*, I would talk) expresses what you would do *if*. It is not used in the if-clause, but in the other part of the sentence:

Si j'étais riche, j'irais en Floride.

If I were rich, I would go to Florida.

The conditional can also be used in indirect statements, in which case it can follow *si*, if.

Je me demandais s'il serait là.

I wondered if he would be there.

The *conditional perfect* (*J'aurais parlé*, I would have talked) expresses what would have happened if something else had or had not happened.

The *subjunctive* (. . . *que je parle*, . . . that I may, should, etc.,talk) is used almost exclusively in the subordinate clauses. It is used to indicate doubt, wish, joy, sorrow, etc. Some verbs are always followed by the subjunctive: *désirer*, desire;

préférer, prefer; *souhaiter*, wish; *regretter*, regret; *vouloir*, want; and the impersonal expression *il faut*, it is necessary. Note that these verbs can also take an infinitive. This is possible only if both verbs have the same subject. Say:

Je regrette d'être ici.   I am sorry to be here.
NOT **Je regrette que je sois ici.**

But you must say:

Je regrette qu'il soit ici.
    I am sorry that he is here.

Avoid *il . . . que . . . il, je . . . que . . . je*, and so on.

Some other verbs are followed by the indicative when they are affirmative, but by the subjunctive when negative or interrogative: *penser*, think; *croire*, believe; *espérer*, hope. Certain conjunctions must always be followed by the subjunctive: *avant que*, before; *jusqu'à ce que*, until; *en attendant que*, until; *bien que*, although; *quoique*, although; *à moins que*, unless; *pourvu que*, provided that; *afin que*, in order that; *de sorte que*, in order that; *sans que*, without. Again, if the subjects of both clauses are the same, you *may* be able to use a preposition which takes an infinitive: *avant de* instead of *avant que*, for example:

Il est venu avant de partir.
NOT **Il est venu avant qu'il parte.**
    He came before he left/leaving.

Compound tenses (past indefinite, past perfect, future perfect and conditional perfect) are formed as in English with an auxiliary and the past participle of the verb. *Avoir*, to have, is the auxiliary most commonly used, for all transitive verbs and for most others. *Être*, to be, is the auxiliary used for *all reflexive verbs* and for certain other verbs which express movement or change of state. Non-reflexive verbs conjugated with *être* are marked in the dictionary (*Aux:* ÊTRE).

In verbs conjugated with *être* the past participle agrees in number and gender with the *subject* of the verb. If the auxiliary is *avoir*, the participle agrees only with a *preceding direct object* (object pronoun, but not *en*, or relative pronoun). Otherwise the participle keeps the masculine singular form.

Jean est allé en ville. John went to town. (Subject is m. sing.)
Marie est allée en ville. Mary went to town. (Subject is f. sing.)
Jean a pris des chemises. John took some shirts. (Object follows)
Il les a prises. He took them. (Object precedes)
les chemises qu'il a prises. the shirts he took. (Object precedes)

The passive voice is formed as in English, but it is used much less frequently.

Sentence Structure

An affirmative sentence generally follows the same pattern as in English, except that most adjectives follow the noun. Adverbs usually follow the verb, and in a compound tense a short adverb is usually found between the auxiliary and the participle: *Elle a bien lu,* She read well. Pronoun objects precede the verb (or the auxiliary, which is the main verb grammatically speaking — the conjugated verb). Prepositional phrases go where they do in English.

● To form a *question* you have a choice:

1. You can begin the sentence with *Est-ce que,* Is it that . . . , and use normal word order:

Vous avez des pommes. You have apples.
Est-ce que vous avez des pommes? Do you have apples?

2. You can invert the pronoun subject and verb (auxiliary in compound tenses) and join them with a hyphen:

Vous avez des pommes. Avez-vous des pommes?

If the sentence has a noun subject, it remains where it is, and the corresponding subject pronoun is added after the verb:

Votre frère est venu. Your brother came.
Votre frère est-il venu? Did your brother come?

In the third person singular a *t* sound is needed between verb and subject. If the verb doesn't already end in *d* or *t*, add a *t*: *parle-t-il?* — just because it sounds better.

Est-ce que is easier; inversion is more elegant. You might use inversion for verbs you know well, *Est-ce que* for anything complex.

● French *negations* have two parts: *ne* before the verb and another negative word after it. *Ne . . . pas* (not) is most frequent. Others are:

ne . . . **plus**	no longer	ne . . . **rien**	nothing
ne . . . **que**	only	ne . . . **aucun**	no
ne . . . **personne**	nobody	ne . . . **ni . . . ni**	neither . . .
ne . . . **jamais**	never	ni . . . ni . . . **ne**	nor
ne . . . **guère**	hardly		

Examples:

Je vais en ville. Je ne vais pas en ville. I am (not) going to town.

Il a lu ce livre. Il n'a pas lu ce livre. He read/did not read this book.

Il a de l'argent. Il n'a plus d'argent. He has (no more) money.

(Remember that indefinite articles and partitives become *de* in a negation.) *Ne* precedes any pronouns that come before the verb:

Je ne les lui ai pas donnés. I didn't give them to him.

Il ne m'en a pas donné. He didn't give me any.

In compound tenses the second part of the negation usually follows the auxiliary. *Personne*, *que*, *ni . . . ni*, and *aucun* follow the participle. If *rien*, *personne*, or *aucun* is the subject of the sentence, it is in the normal subject position:

Personne n'est venu. Nobody came.

To make a negative imperative, form the negative sentence and omit the subject.

(vous) Ne faites pas ça! Don't do that.

● Remember that no auxiliary is used in French questions or negations, no equivalent of *do*. This can cause problems. Take for example, "*I want a beer. Do you?*" The first part is easy: *Je voudrais une bière.* But you can't say *Faites-vous? Faire* is never used this way. You can say *Et vous?*, And you?, or *En voulez-vous une?*, Do you want one? This principle is quite general: you cannot use an auxiliary, even in a compound tense, to avoid repeating the main verb: you cannot say "He had come." "Had he?" Either repeat the verb or find another expression. Often *Oui* or *Non* may be enough.

Conjugating Verbs

A French verb has two parts — the stem, which changes from verb to verb, and the ending, which changes according to person, number and tense. Conjugating a verb is a matter of finding the right stem and adding the proper ending: *chant-e*, *chant-ions*, etc. A regular verb keeps the same stem, while an irregular verb may have several. The endings remain basically the same.

There are three groups of regular verbs which you will recognize by the ending of the infinitive:

1. Verbs in *-er* (*chanter*, to sing). Nine tenths of all verbs.
2. Verbs in *-ir* (*finir*, to finish). About 300 verbs.
3. Verbs in *-re* (*vendre*, to sell). Only 20–30 verbs.

In addition to a verb from each group, the table shows the conjugation of a reflexive verb, *se laver*, to get washed. Not all reflexive verbs are from the first group!

We give three basic forms for each verb: infinitive, present participle, and past participle. The way to find the stem for each tense is explained just before the conjugation of that tense for -er verbs. The stem precedes the hyphen. The endings which follow it must be added to the stem of the verb you are using. The pronunciation of some endings is given.

-ER VERBS

INF.   chant-er

PRES. PART.   chant-ant

PAST PART.   chant-é(e)

PRESENT: For the singular, use the stem of the infinitive; for the plural, the stem of the present participle. This is the only tense where different groups have different endings.

je	chant-e	nous	chant-ons
tu	chant-es	vous	chant-ez
il, elle	chant-e	ils, elles	chant-ent

IMPERFECT: Use the stem of the present participle.

je	chant-ais	nous	chant-ions
tu	chant-ais	vous	chant-iez
il	chant-ait	ils	chant-aient

FUTURE: Use the infinitive without -r (-re for -re verbs).

je	chante-rai	nous	chante-rons
tu	chante-ras	vous	chante-rez
il	chante-ra	ils	chante-rent

CONDITIONAL: The conditional stem is *always* the same as the future stem.

je	chante-rais	nous	chante-rions
tu	chante-rais	vous	chante-riez
il	chante-rait	ils	chante-raient

SUBJUNCTIVE: For *nous* and *vous*, use the *nous* and *vous* forms of the *imperfect* tense. For the other forms, use the stem of the third person plural of the *present* tense (chantent, finissent, vendent, lavent). Here the two stems are the same, but this rule will help for irregular verbs.

que je	chant-e	que nous	chant-ions
que tu	chant-es	que vous	chant-iez
qu'il	chant-e	qu'ils	chant-ent

For the compound tenses, use the proper form of *avoir* and *être* with the past participle. See page 358 for the conjugation of *avoir* and *être*. The (e) is to remind you that the participle can change to agree with its subject or object. See page 350.

PAST INDEFINITE: Use the present tense form of the auxiliary verb with the past participle.

j'ai	chanté(e)	nous avons	chanté(e)
tu as	chanté(e)	vous avez	chanté(e)
il a	chanté(e)	ils ont	chanté(e)

PAST PERFECT: Use the imperfect tense form of the auxiliary verb with the past participle.

j'avais   chanté(e), etc.

FUTURE PERFECT: Use the future tense form of the auxiliary
                  verb with the past participle.
                  j'aurais chanté(e), etc.

CONDITIONAL PERFECT: Use the conditional tense form of
                       the auxiliary verb with the past
                       participle.
                       j'aurais chanté(e), etc.

IMPERATIVE: Use the second person singular, without -*s*,
              first and second person plural of present tense.
              First person plural translates: Let's sing!
              Chante!
              Chantons!
              Chantez!

-IR VERBS

TENSE FORMATION: See under -ER VERBS.

INF.   fin-ir
PRES. PART.   finiss-ant
PAST PART.   fini(e)

PRESENT:	je	fin-is	nous	finiss-ons
	tu	fin-is	vous	finiss-ez
	il, elle	fin-it	ils, elles	finiss-ent

IMPERFECT:	je	finiss-ais	nous	finiss-ions
	tu	finiss-ais	vous	finiss-iez
	il	finiss-ait	ils	finiss-aient

FUTURE:	je	fini-rai	nous	fini-rons
	tu	fini-ras	vous	fini-rez
	il	fini-ra	ils	fini-ront

CONDITIONAL:	je	fini-rais	nous	fini-rions
	tu	fini-rais	vous	fini-riez
	il	fini-rait	ils	fini-raient

SUBJUNCTIVE:	que je	finiss-e	que nous	finiss-ions
	que tu	finiss-es	que vous	finiss-iez
	qu'il	finiss-e	qu'ils	finiss-ent

PAST INDEFINITE:	j'ai	fini(e)	nous avons	fini(e)
	tu as	fini(e)	vous avez	fini(e)
	il a	fini(e)	ils ont	fini(e)

PAST PERFECT: j'avais fini(e), etc.
FUTURE PERFECT: j'aurai fini(e), etc.
CONDITIONAL PERFECT: j'aurais fini(e), etc.
IMPERATIVE: Finis!
              Finissons!
              Finissez!

-RE VERBS

TENSE FORMATION: See under -ER VERBS.

INF.   ven-dre
PRES. PART.   ven-dant
PAST PART.   vend-u(e)

PRESENT: je   vend-s   nous   vend-ons
              tu   vend-s   vous   vend-ez
              il, elle vend (add *t* if   ils, elles vend-ent
              ending not *d* or *t*)

IMPERFECT: je   vend-ais   nous   vend-ions
              tu   vend-ais   vous   vend-iez
              il   vend-ait   ils   vend-aient

FUTURE: je   vend-rai   nous   vend-rons
              tu   vend-ras   vous   vend-rez
              il   vend-ra   ils   vend-ront

CONDITIONAL: je   vend-rais   nous   vend-rions
              tu   vend-rais   vous   vend-riez
              il   vend-rait   ils   vend-raient

SUBJUNCTIVE: que je vend-e   que nous vend-ions
              que tu vend-es   que vous vend-iez
              qu'il   vend-e   qu'ils   vend-ent

PAST INDEFINITE: j'ai   vendu(e)   nous avons   vendu(e)
                  tu as vendu(e)   vous avez   vendu(e)
                  il a   vendu(e)   ils ont   vendu(e)

PAST PERFECT: j'avais vendu(e), etc.
FUTURE PERFECT: j'aurai vendu(e), etc.
CONDITIONAL PERFECT: j'aurais vendu(e), etc.
IMPERATIVE: Vends!
              Vendons!
              Vendez!

REFLEXIVE VERBS

INF.	se lav-er
PRES. PART.	lav-ant
PAST PART.	lav-é(e)

PRESENT

je me	lav-e		nous nous	lav-ons
tu te	lav-es		vous vous	lav-ez
il se	lav-e		ils se	lav-ent

IMPERFECT:

je me	lav-ais		nous nous	lav-ions
tu te	lav-ais		vous vous	lav-iez
il se	lav-ait		ils se	lav-aient

FUTURE:

je me	lave-rai		nous nous	lave-rons
tu te	lave-ras		vous vous	lave-rez
il se	lave-ra		ils se	lave-ront

CONDITIONAL:

je me	lave-rais		nous nous	lave-rions
tu te	lave-rais		vous vous	lave-riez
il se	lave-rait		ils se	lave-raient

SUBJUNCTIVE:

que je me	lav-e		que nous nous	lav-ions
que tu te	lav-es		que vous vous	lav-iez
qu'il se	lav-e		qu'ils se	lav-ent

PAST INDEFINITE:

je me suis	lavé(e)	nous nous sommes	lavés (lavées)
tu t'es	lavé(e)	vous vous êtes	lavés (lavées)
il s'est	lavé(e)	ils se sont	lavés (lavées)

PAST PERFECT:
je m'étais lavé(e), etc.

FUTURE PERFECT:
je me serai lavé(e), etc.

CONDITIONAL PERFECT:
je me serais lavé(e), etc.

IMPERATIVE:
   Lave-toi! Lavons-nous! Lavez-vous!

Irregular Verbs

Most important are *avoir* and *être*.

                    AVOIR, to have

INF.   avoir
PRES. PART.   ayant
PAST PART.   eu(e) [*ii*]
PRESENT:

j'ai	nous avons
tu as	vous avez
il a	ils ont

IMPERFECT:

j'avais	nous avions
tu avais	vous aviez
il avait	ils avaient

FUTURE:

j'aurai	nous aurons
tu auras	vous aurez
il aura	ils auront

CONDITIONAL:

j'aurais	nous aurions
tu aurais	vous auriez
il aurait	ils auraient

The auxiliary for the compound tenses is *avoir* itself.

PAST INDEFINITE:

j'ai	eu(e)	nous avons	eu(e)
tu as	eu(e)	vous avez	eu(e)
il a	eu(e)	ils ont	eu(e)

PAST PERFECT:
   j'avais   eu(e), etc.

FUTURE PERFECT:
   j'aurai   eu(e), etc.

CONDITIONAL PERFECT:
  j'aurais eu(e), etc.

SUBJUNCTIVE:

que j'aie [*eh*]	que nous ayons
que tu aies	que vous ayez
qu'il ait	qu'ils aient

IMPERATIVE:
  Aie.
  Ayons.
  Ayez.

ÊTRE, to be

INF.   être

PRES. PART. étant

PAST PART.   été

PRESENT:

je suis	nous sommes
tu es	vous êtes
il est	ils sont

IMPERFECT:

j'étais	nous étions
tu étais	vous étiez
il était	ils étaient

FUTURE:

je serai	nous serons
tu seras	vous serez
il sera	ils seront

CONDITIONAL:

je serais	nous serions
tu serais	vous seriez
il serait	ils seraient

The auxiliary for the compound tenses is *avoir*.

PAST INDEFINITE:

j'ai été	nous avons été
tu as été	vous avez été
il a été	ils ont été

PAST PERFECT:
  j'avais été, etc.

FUTURE PERFECT:
  j'aurai été, etc.

CONDITIONAL PERFECT:
  j'aurais été, etc.

SUBJUNCTIVE:

que je	sois [*swah*]	que nous	soyons
que tu	sois	que vous	soyez
qu'il	soit	qu'ils	soient

IMPERATIVE:
  Sois.
  Soyons.
  Soyez.

For all other irregular verbs, we give here the three basic forms: infinitive, present participle, and past participle. For some verbs this is enough to derive all tenses (the derivation of each tense is explained above before the regular conjugation of that tense). We list only forms you cannot find in this way. Most verbs are irregular in the present. (Remember that the imperative is always the same as the present, and that the third person plural of the present is used to form most of the subjunctive. If the present is irregular, these forms follow the same irregularities, and we won't mention them.) The stem of the future, too, is often irregular. (Remember that the conditional always has the same stem as the future.) Many verbs refer you to another that is conjugated in the same way. For compound verbs, see the basic verb, *venir* for *prévenir*, for example.

s'abstenir abstain *See* VENIR
acheter buy

  present participle achetant
  past participle acheté
  present achète, achètes, achète, achetons, achetez,
    achètent
  future achèterai

accueillir welcome *See* CUEILLIR
acquérir acquire

  present participle acquérant
  past participle acquis
  present acquiers, acquiers, acquiert, acquérons,
    acquérez, acquièrent
  future acquerrai

aller go

  present participle allant
  past participle allé
  present vais, vas, va, allons, allez, vont
  future irai
  subjunctive aille, ailles, aille, allions, alliez, aillent

apercevoir see *See* DEVOIR
apparaître appear *See* CONNAÎTRE
appartenir belong *See* VENIR
apprendre learn *See* PRENDRE
appeler call

  present participle appelant
  past participle appelé
  present appelle, appelles, appelle, appelons, appelez,
    appellent
  future appellerai

s'asseoir sit down

  present participle asseyant
  past participle assis
  present assieds, assieds, assied, asseyons, asseyez,
    asseyent
  future assoirai

atteindre attain *See* CRAINDRE
battre beat

  present participle battant
  past participle battu
  present bats, bats, bat, battons, battez, battent

boire drink

  present participle buvant

past participle bu
present bois, bois, boit, buvons, buvez, boivent

bouillir boil

present participle bouillant
past participle bouilli
present bous, bous, bout, bouillons, bouillez, bouillent

céder yield *See* PRÉFÉRER
comprendre understand *See* PRENDRE
concevoir conceive *See* DEVOIR
conclure conclude

present participle concluant
past participle conclu

conduire lead

present participle conduisant
past participle conduit
present conduis, conduis, conduit, conduisons,
   conduisez, conduisent

connaître know

present participle connaissant
past participle connu
present connais, connais, connaît, connaissons,
   connaissez, connaissent

conquérir conquer *See* ACQUÉRIR
consentir consent *See* SORTIR
construire build *See* CONDUIRE
coudre sew

present participle cousant
past participle cousu
present couds, couds, coud, cousons, cousez, cousent

courir run

present participle courant
past participle couru
future courrai

couvrir cover *See* OUVRIR
craindre fear

present participle craignant

past participle craint
present crains, crains, craint, craignons, craignez, craignent

croire believe

present participle croyant
past participle cru
present crois, crois, croit, croyons, croyez, croient

croître grow

present participle croissant
past participle crû
present croîs, croîs, croît, croissons, croissez, croissent

cueillir pick

present participle cueillant
past participle cueilli
present cueille, cueilles, cueille, cueillons, cueillez, cueillent
future cueillerai

cuire cook *See* CONDUIRE
décevoir deceive *See* DEVOIR
découvrir discover *See* OUVRIR
décrire describe *See* ÉCRIRE
défaire undo *See* FAIRE
démentir deny *See* SORTIR
déteindre fade *See* CRAINDRE
détruire destroy *See* CONDUIRE
devoir owe, be obliged to

present participle devant
past participle dû
present dois, dois, doit, devons, devez, doivent
future devrai

dire say

present participle disant
past participle dit
present dis, dis, dit, disons, dites, disent

dissoudre dissolve

present participle dissolvant

past participle dissout
present dissous, dissous, dissout, dissolvons, dissolvez, dissolvent

dormir sleep

present participle dormant
past participle dormi
present dors, dors, dort, dormons, dormez, dorment

écrire write

present participle écrivant
past participle écrit
present écris, écris, écrit, écrivons, écrivez, écrivent

élire elect *See* LIRE

émouvoir move (feelings)

present participle émouvant
past participle ému
present émeus, émeus, émeut, émouvons, émouvez, émeuvent
future None

envoyer send

present participle envoyant
past participle envoyé
present envoie, envoies, envoie, envoyons, envoyez, envoient
future enverrai

espérer hope *See* PRÉFÉRER
éteindre extinguish *See* CRAINDRE
extraire extract *See* CROIRE

faire do, make

present participle faisant
past participle fait
present fais, fais, fait, faisons, faites, font
future ferai
present subjunctive fasse, fasses, fasse, fassions, fassiez, fassent

falloir be necessary *See* VALOIR

[Only third person singular forms are used.]

fuir flee

present participle fuyant
past participle fui
present fuis, fuis, fuit, fuyons, fuyez, fuient

haïr hate

present participle haïssant
past participle haï
present hais, hais, hait, haïssons, haïssez, haïssent

inclure include *See* CONCLURE
inscrire register *See* ÉCRIRE
instruire instruct *See* CONDUIRE
introduire introduce *See* CONDUIRE
jeter throw *See* APPELER
joindre join *See* CRAINDRE
lire read

present participle lisant
past participle lu
present lis, lis, lit, lisons, lisez, lisent

mentir lie, tell an untruth *See* SORTIR
mettre put

present participle mettant
past participle mis
present mets, mets, met, mettons, mettez, mettent

moudre grind *See* RÉSOUDRE
mourir die

present participle mourant
past participle mort
present meurs, meurs, meurt, mourons, mourez, meurent
future mourrai

naître be born

present participle naissant
past participle né
present nais, nais, naît, naissons, naissez, naissent

offrir offer *See* OUVRIR
ouvrir open

present participle ouvrant

past participle ouvert
present ouvre, ouvres, ouvre, ouvrons, ouvrez, ouvrent

paraître appear *See* CONNAÎTRE

partir leave *See* SORTIR

peindre paint *See* CRAINDRE

plaindre complain *See* CRAINDRE

plaire please

present participle plaisant
past participle plu
present plais, plais, plaît, plaisons, plaisez, plaisent

pleuvoir rain

present participle pleuvant
past participle plu
present pleut [Third person singular only.]
future pleuvra [Third person singular only.]
subjunctive pleuve [Third person singular only.]

pouvoir be able

present participle pouvant
past participle pu
present peux, peux, peut, pouvons, pouvez, peuvent
future pourrai
subjunctive puisse, puisses, puisse, puissions, puissiez,
   puissent

prendre take

present participle prenant
past participle pris
present prends, prends, prend, prenons, prenez,
   prennent

produire produce *See* CONDUIRE

recevoir receive *See* DEVOIR

réduire reduce *See* CONDUIRE

renvoyer send back *See* ENVOYER

résoudre resolve

present participle résolvant
past participle résolu
present résous, résous, résout, résolvons, résolvez,
   résolvent

rire laugh
  present participle riant
  past participle ri

savoir know
  present participle sachant
  past participle su
  present sais, sais, sait, savons, savez, savent
  imperfect savais, savais, savait, savions, saviez, savaient
  future saurai
  subjunctive sache, saches, sache, sachions, sachiez,
    sachent
  imperative sache, sachons, sachez

séduire seduce *See* CONDUIRE
sentir feel *See* SORTIR
servir serve
  present participle servant
  past participle servi
  present sers, sers, sert, servons, servez, servent

sortir leave
  present participle sortant
  past participle sorti
  present sors, sors, sort, sortons, sortez, sortent

souffrir suffer *See* OUVRIR
sourire smile *See* RIRE
suffire suffice
  present participle suffisant
  past participle suffit
  present suffis, suffis, suffit, suffisons, suffisez, suffisent

suivre follow
  present participle suivant
  past participle suivi
  present suis, suis, suit, suivons, suivez, suivent

taire be silent *See* PLAIRE
teindre dye *See* CRAINDRE
tenir hold *See* VENIR

traduire translate *See* CONDUIRE
vaincre conquer

present participle vainquant
past participle vaincu
present vaincs, vaincs, vainc, vainquons, vainquez,
  vainquent

valoir be worth

present participle valant
past participle valu
present vaux, vaux, vaut, valons, valez, valent
future vaudrai
subjunctive vaille, vailles, vaille, valions, valiez, vaillent

venir come

present participle venant
past participle venu
present viens, viens, vient, venons, venez, viennent
future viendrai

vivre live

present participle vivant
past participle vécu
present vis, vis, vit, vivons, vivez, vivent

voir see

present participle voyant
past participle vu
present vois, vois, voit, voyons, voyez, voient
future verrai

vouloir want

present participle voulant
past participle voulu
present veux, veux, veut, voulons, voulez, veulent
future voudrai
subjunctive veuille, veuilles, veuille, voulions, vouliez,
  veuillent
imperative veuille, veuillions, veuillez

Charming Blue

by Kristine Grayson

―⁓―

He's lived through ages with the curse of attracting women… who end up dead…

Once upon a time, he was the most handsome of princes, destined for great things. But now he's a lonely legend, hobbled by a dark history. With too many dead in his wake, Bluebeard escapes the only way he knows how—through the evil spell of alcohol. But it's a far different kind of spell that's been ruining his life for centuries.

How will she survive this killer Prince Charming?

Jodi Walters is a fixer, someone who can put magic back in order. She's the best in Hollywood at her game. But Blue has a problem she's never encountered before—and worse, she finds herself perilously attracted to him.

―⁓―

"A beguiling mystery is matched in power by the palpable and forbidden attraction… one of the best series installments to date." —*Publishers Weekly*

For more Kristine Grayson, visit:

www.sourcebooks.com

About the Author

Kris DeLake is one of writer Kristine Kathryn Rusch's many pen names. In addition to writing as Kris DeLake in romance, Rusch also writes romance as Kristine Grayson (who specializes in paranormals) and Kristine Dexter (who prefers romantic suspense). In mystery, Rusch writes as the Edgar- and Shamus-nominated Kris Nelscott. In science fiction and fantasy, Rusch is known by her real name. She's a bestselling double Hugo winner in science fiction. To find out more about her work, including her popular nonfiction blog, go to www.kristinekathrynrusch.com.